The Citizen's Last Stand:
Are YOU Ready?

Jeff L. Wright

If you believe the message of this book is important for others to have, please share your copy and/or direct others to purchase copies by going directly to Amazon.com and typing in the search box: "The Citizen's Last Stand." Kindle and paperback copies are available on Amazon. I have no PR or Publicist, just me and those involved Citizens who share the message. It is only through YOUR action that the message spreads through FB, email and other social media and personal means.

Published by JOT Creative
jotcreative.net

This book is dedicated to Mom and Dad, Colette and sons Travis and Alex.

It is also dedicated to all our Ancestors who allowed us to be here and to our Descendants yet to see the true America.

It is certainly dedicated to Larry and Nancy.

Table of Contents

Acknowledgements

I wish to extend my grateful appreciation to the folks who assisted and advised me throughout the process of producing this work.

Bob Adelmann finally convinced me that the time was right to get going. By agreeing to collaborate on the book, Bob gave me the impetus to proceed, after all this time, with the task of sharing my accumulation of observations and conclusions reached after a lifetime spent in military intelligence, in high technology systems engineering and in political activism. His constant, steady hand during the initial Draft development, and editing additions to the book, proved invaluable in 'getting through the weeds' while writing the main text. His ability to bring out more clearly the ideas, and be the check on my exposition, proved to be of tremendous assistance. Bob's advice and counsel are so greatly appreciated.

Jonathan Horner picked up from where Bob had moved me along, bravely volunteering to collaborate in *"taking it to the next level."* Jonathan unreservedly invested his skills as a generalist, and his insights as a broad and deep thinker, to flesh-out and clarify many of the ideas, concepts and terms used throughout the book. Our extensive conversations, on the genesis and nature of events, proved to be very helpful during the long and arduous 'last stretch' to complete the manuscript, as we revised, rewrote, rephrased, reworded, edited, proofed, corrected and (more or less) 'smoothed' out my writing. My hat is off to you, old friend!

With vast room for my own improvement, the final product is more a reflection of my own stubbornness than Bob and Jonathan's continued attempts to 'fix it.'

With the benefit of their differing areas of expertise, Paul Prentice and Chuck Corry provided me with the various reality checks and sober reviews required to stay on the right track. (Or at least to help eliminate the worst of my wandering around.)

Paul was highly appreciated through some of the more difficult technical aspects of the economic and monetary ideas. As the principal founder, and a co-founder, of the Pikes Peak Economics Club back in

2004, we have years of long exchanges on how economics have evolved (and devolved).

Chuck's old-school approach, using the 'red pen' review method, made his revisions to the manuscript look very much like the paper towels used in emergency rooms to clean up. His contribution of the **Foreword** confirmed that the essence of the book is true to my original intent.

Carl Bruning did much the same for me with his review. I first met Carl while working on Congressman Ron Paul's Presidential campaign in 2007-08 in Wyoming, Colorado and New Mexico. That campaign gave us both a lot of sleepless nights and tortuous days. Carl is a thoughtful, truly patriotic American, and a former Air Force officer and pilot with a deep concern for our Country. His check on my view of the evolution of the Military Industrial Complex, and its current state of being, was another important marker for me in writing and developing this book.

Mary Zennett's review and approval check-off of the early chapters, and particularly the ones associated with the WARBI Paradox and Conspiracy, was of great help. It helped validate that those concepts and ideas represent a direct and objective look at human behavior, one that is more readily understandable than several academic texts on similar subjects.

Charlie Aligaen provided the emblematic cover art that gives the book its final wrapper. It is both thought-provoking and very appropriate to our theme. Charlie is a good friend and campaigner who was always there during the Ron Paul 2008 campaign. He is a very gifted graphic artist with many other talents. His soft-spoken way and easy manner have been a pleasure from the very beginning.

Teddy Otero provided the publication formatting, and the set-up, to enable all the web-related follow-on activity, that may result from the manuscript's production and release. If the book is favorably received, Teddy is the reason that it will have the infrastructure to grow across the Web.

Thank you one and all.

JW

Foreword

For as long as the history of mankind is known individuals, families, cities, and governments have been attempting to ignore and evade the iron dictates of the first law of economics: You cannot consume more than you produce.

That law is often more familiarly expressed as: *"Ain't no such thing as a free lunch;"* or *"Don't eat the seed corn."*

There have been innumerable attempts throughout human history to evade this cruel reality. All of them have eventually failed, as the United States is in the midst of doing today.

Individuals, families, cities, and nations grow wealthy for a variety of reasons usually involving luck, hard work, water, navigable waterways, fortunate climate and soil, discovery of previously untapped resources, and human inventiveness and ingenuity. But that wealth always invites predators, typically in the form of lawyers and governments.

Like witch doctors, American legislators have long believed that if they simply passed another law they could sidestep the essential need to actually produce the means of survival. And if one law is necessary and good, e.g., *"Thou shall not kill,"* then ten thousand more must be even better.

By passing innumerable laws they have handed their voodoo on to multitudinous bureaucracies who have imposed ever heavier burdens of taxation and regulation on to the backs of the citizenry. Eventually the populace cannot produce enough to sustain the load.

Through chicanery the government has used the inventiveness of individuals to produce an illusion of wealth by printing 'money' as a medium of exchange. Ultimately it has no more value than the paper it is embossed upon as there is no wealth in the form of commodities to sustain their fiat currency.

Governments compensate by printing more.

To distract the multitude from its dire straits, governments throughout history have waged imperial wars, as Washington D.C. does today. Such wars are supposed to bring riches to the conquering heroes.

Instead, they inevitably debase the aggressor's currency and drain its wealth.

As the wars and government deplete the wealth of the once prosperous society, the restless citizenry is kept quiet with what was once referred to as *"bread and circuses"* during the decline of the Roman Empire. In the United States today, the government quells the masses with food stamps and football. That aids the growth of government to the delight of lawyers, bureaucrats, and war profiteers, but hastens the destruction of the nation's riches.

Based on his extensive experience with national security, working in the bowels of financial institutions, contracting with technological leaders in Silicon Valley, and testifying in numerous legislative hearings, Jeff Wright takes us on both a personal and intellectual tour through the maze America has lost itself in. He offers some insights on how we might come out the other side but presents no magic elixir that might painlessly cure our ills.

Anyone who thinks America is somehow above the iron rules of nature should read this book. Those who know we are involved in an economic and political train wreck will find this an insightful review of the tragedy from one who has so long warned against it.

Charles E. Corry, Ph.D.
President, Equal Justice Foundation
Fellow, Geological Society of America

Preface

In my estimation, we are living through the final death rattle of the '2nd American Republic' and the initial stages of the screaming, tortuous birth of the '3rd American Republic.' Very few of the left-right political stripe will yet admit that all the 20th Century attempts at economic and political nationalism were an epic failure, and are now collapsing around us.

The '1st American Republic' expired in the ashes of the Civil War, after a relatively short run of 75 years. It died on the pretext of ending slavery, and in the reality of the world's first 'total war.' It was buried unceremoniously during 35 years of Reconstruction, the Indian Wars, and the Closing of the West. The rise of a select corporate and governmental fusion, into nascent corporatist-fascism during the 20th Century, helped ensure its end. The opening gambit of *"New Nationalism"* by Theodore (Teddy) Roosevelt tamped down the dirt on its grave.

At the dawn of the 20th Century, the Teddy Roosevelt Progressives put the 2nd American Republic payload on track to the launch pad. Woodrow Wilson and later, Franklin Delano Roosevelt (FDR), launched it as the new 'Superstate,' fueled by a spectacular spending spree of economic nationalism.

The 2nd American Republic orbited all over the map for another 75 years on the various pretexts of the Progressive era. Those were generated during WWI, the Great Depression and WWII, and by the Bretton Woods Monetary Accord and the Cold War. After Teddy Roosevelt's *"Square Deal"* and New Nationalism, and Wilson's *"Making the world safe for Democracy,"* the pretexts morphed into FDR's *"New Deal"* and proceeded apace with the defeat of the Axis powers, the Korean War, the Cold War, the Viet Nam War and the Great Society. The first Progressives reached their apogee in 1967. Almost that entire trajectory was fueled by the Federal Reserve Corporation (FRC), along with deficit spending and *"petrodollar re-cycling."* It was enabled and facilitated by the central-banking cartel created for its usefulness in such endeavors.

When its orbit began to seriously decay, the 2nd American Republic received an even larger refueling boost to higher orbit in August of 1971. That required huge transfusions of 'fiat' money (literally producing money by decree from the FRC) to keep it aloft. The existing international monetary regime of Bretton Woods, negotiated coming out of WWII, was ripped up and tossed in the waste can by Arthur Burns, Richard Nixon and Congress.

The U.S. Space Ship 'Superstate' began its final orbital decay in the last quarter of the 20th Century. The de-orbiting process was caused by the inertial drag of the Cold War, the various 'Wars' on Poverty, Drugs and Crime, the Desert Storm and Enduring Freedom conflicts, and the ever increasing Neo-Conservative warfare state adding its bulk to the still growing Neo-Liberal Progressive welfare state. It re-entered the atmosphere at the dawn of the 21st Century, smashing in a fiery heap in the smoldering, toxic pile of the World Trade Center's Twin Towers on 9/11.

The G.W. Bush and Obama Global War on Terror (GWOT), with its accompanying background of fiscal-financial irresponsibility and crises, will someday be seen as the 'bouncing of the rubble' of this empire's disassembly and dissolution.

We are now inexorably and inevitably transitioning into the "*Grand Correction.*" The hoped for New American Century/Progressive Empire is now, early in the 21st Century, finally expiring amid Mt. Everest-sized mountains of debt, amassed since the early 1970s by printing vast amounts of phony money. That counterfeiting spree will prove to have been a relatively short-lived phenomenon. It is the last desperate stand of the Progressive Century and the 2nd American Republic. As this is being written, the final break-up is already underway.

We now stand on the cusp of the '3rd American Republic' and "*the Citizen's Last Stand.*" This book is about enabling the emergence of the 3rd American Republic.

America's restoration can only begin with each individual **Citizen** taking personal action. There is no other alternative scenario in which any true republic can exist.

The 2nd American Republic was always doomed. It began as a mish-mash of a 'reconstructed' 1st American Republic, combined with the artifice of New Nationalism, as initially envisioned by Teddy Roosevelt, and further invigorated by Woodrow Wilson. FDR took that initial re-design much further along, sending the new 2nd American Republic into a steep climb towards the Progressives' dream of achieving orbital velocity. He was aided and abetted by the severe tests and pressures put on The People by the Great Depression and WWII.

FDR succeeded in constructing an initial, and apparently functional, top-down nationalist, welfare/warfare state where none was ever intended, or even imagined, by the Founders.

During the Cold War, each in their own way, Truman, Eisenhower, Kennedy and Lyndon Johnson, with the latter's wholly unrealistic Great Society promising to deliver "*Guns and Butter*," continued building up the composite warfare and welfare state with the active connivance of successive Congresses. The citizens, whose political discipline and will-power had been sapped during the previous 30 years, permitted it to proceed without any check or accountability.

Ronald Reagan then put the warfare portion of the equation on steroids, inadvertently enabling the Neo-Conservative's hand-in-hand philosophies of "*deficits don't matter*" and "*nation-building*" (more correctly—'state-building') that followed.

On virtual cruise control, Presidents Geo. H.W. Bush and W.J. Clinton continued ramping up the warfare/welfare state that was now firmly established and accepted, as both normal and desirable, by most of the citizenry.

The two most recent Presidents, George W. Bush and B.H. Obama, arrived in office just in time to preside over the beginning of the unplanned take-down and disassembly of the warfare/welfare state, the wholly inescapable consequence of 'blowback' and mountains of debt. Their two administrations more clearly than ever reveal the institutionalized incompetency and the 'tag-team' nature, of the NeoCon/Progressive political duopoly.

President G.W. Bush threw the No Child Left Behind and the Medicare Prescription Drug Benefit into the welfare state portion of the mix. President Obama adopted and accelerated the Global War on Terror and the War on Drugs, along with his own contribution to the undeclared war on civil liberties with his *"ObamaCare."* However, the next phase of Obama's, or his potential successor's, plans will never attain the hyperbolic trajectory of a total nationalist state. That is impossible. There will be a fiscal collapse, the inevitable result of the veritable Himalaya of debt that has been accrued.

It is easy to predict that this book may not 'sit well' with Americans who grew comfortable and complacent, reliant on the payload of easy conveniences that the 2nd American Republic delivered during the latter half of the 20th Century.

The 'house of cards' 2nd American Republic's fundamental problem is that it could not possibly be sustained indefinitely. It was built on a consumptive model of wealth, based on Keynesian economics and fiat money, accompanied by the hugely counter-productive, hyper-regulatory psychosis inherent in a warfare/welfare state.

Most Americans are apparently unwilling to admit the guy (and team) that they elected as 'their man' could ever screw up so badly. Denial and avoidance of the truth is the norm. The real truth reflects back, all too clearly, on their own poor choices in not living up to the inherent responsibilities of being an engaged citizen. They have not recognized how badly the government can and will behave when firm control and management by *"We the People"* is absent.

I suspect that about half of the potential readers of this book will immediately condemn it outright, regardless of the evidence, the logic or the reasoning presented in my analysis. They will not accept any objective conclusions that run counter to their belief in the goodness of the welfare/warfare state that they have been co-opted into, and trained from childhood to support. Over the decades that behavior became an embedded feature of the 2nd American Republic. It has gone from bad to worse as 'counter-factual' mythical histories and beliefs have taken further hold throughout the population.

Denial is one of the strongest innate human behaviors, followed by the fear response. The two behaviors are inextricably linked. The denial of otherwise obvious and self-evident reality is thus facilitated by the fear of making any change to one's system of beliefs. Therefore, many citizens are currently 'lost' to the cause of restoring a functioning Republic. This book is addressed to the "*Remnant*" who still remain.

Younger Americans are emerging from the murk of disinformation ready to gain a truer understanding of how a viable political-economic system should operate. A significant proportion of them did once believe in the power elite's counter-factual view of history, due to an exceedingly poor education system, and generations of media propaganda and myth-making. However, enough of them can still analyze and think critically despite all those attempts to brainwash them. They are beginning to flex their political muscle, and seeking ways to make positive contributions to our future.

It is very encouraging to me how many younger Americans seem to innately sense that there is something deeply wrong in our Country's conduct, both domestically and overseas. During the past decade, that mostly unconscious inner knowledge has doubtless driven the cultural and commercial success of popular movies and books such as "*The Matrix*" series, "*V for Vendetta*" and recently, "*The Hunger Games.*" But these younger citizens have a hard time acting effectively without understanding how we got here, and why the general population behaves as it does.

As of this writing, there is a small but growing number of citizens who will recognize and understand several of the topics covered in the book. I estimate that this group, which I will hereafter refer to as the 'American Remnant,' is somewhere between 3 and 5% of our population, or about 10 to 15 million people out of 310 million! This book can serve to further enlighten them in certain areas that they have never examined about themselves, or in other people's behavior. Additionally, it should help in furthering their understanding of this Country's 'clear and present danger' and what will be useful in devising an 'action plan' to save it. Since this book is intended primarily for the American Remnant, some other readers may find it to be slow and hard going, due to the number and density of ideas covered. That is a good thing. Some of the topics require a significant amount of thought and revisiting to fully grasp.

There is a second group, comprising another 40 to 50 million people, who will most likely discern the truth when they see it, especially when actively demonstrated by the actions of the American Remnant. For both groups, I intend this book to illuminate additional ideas not yet broadly considered, or understood, by most of them. Perhaps these ideas and concepts will persuade them to think, and act, in ways that they have never considered, or tried before.

Once the American Remnant begins to act consistently and cooperatively, on the same page and across the board, necessary changes will come quickly in the form of a true 'paradigm shift' in this Country's conduct of its economic and political affairs. The majority of the population, now largely bereft of understanding or interest, will eventually follow along since that is in their nature. This time they will find it very much to their benefit to closely follow the lead, even more so than they did after the first Revolution, the Civil War, or the wars of the 20th and early 21st Century.

The American Remnant must act now! There is only a short 'window of opportunity' remaining to restore our foundational principles and ideals to their rightful preeminence. Almost a century has elapsed with dangerous political and economic policies increasingly damaging our true interests as a People, and our long-term survival as a free Republic. We must reverse, and then completely abolish, the bad behaviors now rooted in the governmental structure, and do so quickly.

It is not too late, if we act with the same conviction and commitment as our ancestors did when creating this Country.

The Revolution to restore the Republic will only be violent if the current crop of unprincipled leaders, the looters in both major ideological parties, make it so.

Failing to act will automatically guarantee the worst of all fates, throwing this once great Country straight onto the midden heap of history.

The 3rd Republic may very well be the *"Last Stand"* of freedom and liberty for the next century, and in centuries to come. Are you ready?

Jeff L. Wright—September, 2012

Introduction

*One cannot claim knowledge until expressed
and passed on to others who see its legitimacy.*
- Anonymous

Dring ... dring ... dring ...

My eyes shot open as the phone rang insistently. The clock on the nightstand read 6:52 AM, Mountain Daylight Time. Beside me, Colette, my wife, groaned, half-asleep and half-frustrated. "Who on earth is that?" she said, passing over the phone. As I had done so many times before, when abruptly awakened at night and early morning to deal with work emergencies, I grabbed the phone and automatically mumbled:

"This is Jeff ..."

"Jeff! Turn on your TV; something is happening at the World Trade Center!"

It was my neighbor Ilene, who seemed very excited. She knew that I had spent much of the 1990's working in the Financial District of Lower Manhattan in New York City.

"What is it?" I responded, still half dazed from being dragged out of a deep sleep.

"I don't know. They think a small plane or something ran into one of the Towers just a few minutes ago."

I picked the remote from the nightstand, turned on the TV, and began scanning through the channels.

Colette stirred, sighed, and got out of bed, knowing only too well that our sleep time was over. To her everlasting credit, she had been very patient throughout all the years of our marriage, realizing that such calls were an unfortunate but unavoidable consequence of my work.

"OK, I'll watch and see what's going on. Thanks, Ilene," I said before hanging up.

By then, I had found the first channel, soon to be nearly every station, broadcasting images of smoke pouring out of the north and east sides of the North Tower of the World Trade Center (WTC). From the volume of smoke, I knew instantly that it had not been caused by the collision of a small plane. In fact, it would be something much more sinister for the future of America, in ways that most citizens have yet to comprehend and understand.

I heard water running in the bathroom sink behind me and then Colette called out: "So what is going on?"

"I am not sure," I replied, as I continued pressing the channel selection buttons.

I surfed through station after station listening to, and watching, different reports to find out if anyone had a handle on it. Nobody seemed to know much of anything except that smoke was pouring out of 1 WTC Building.

Old memories rekindled in my mind of events at the WTC on February 26, 1993. That day a truck bomb detonated in the parking garage, several levels below the ground floor of the North Tower, during an earlier unsuccessful terrorist attack.

On that particular day, I was in Bridgewater, New Jersey, working as a Senior Consulting Engineer for AT&T as part of a Systems Integration group building large 'enterprise' networks for their clients. The people in the office scrambled to make sure that all employees and contractors working on various projects at the WTC Complex were safe. They were. For the remainder of the 1990's, those of us that worked there had often wondered aloud what would happen if terrorists tried again.

"What if those towers ever came down?" we would ask each other during lunches on the patio of the World Financial Center across the West Side Highway, while staring up at the enormous Twin Towers looming above.

The phone rang several times in the next few minutes. It was friends and family asking if I was watching the unfolding event, and expressing relief that I was not in NYC, as I had been for much of the previous decade. After sharing assurances and speculations, we would hang up, and I returned to flipping through the channels to watch the latest reports.

I had just turned around to say something to Colette when her voice suddenly rose, "Look at that!" I turned back just in time to watch Flight

175 smash into the South Tower at 590 miles per hour, exploding in a ball of flame. It was 7:03 AM, Mountain Standard Time.

At that exact moment, I truly understood, saying quietly under my breath, "We're under attack!"

Then I suddenly realized with mounting apprehension and dread that one of my contract System Engineers, and good friend, Nancy Yuen-Ngo, was likely to be in the North Tower. She was probably on the 97th floor above where the first plane impacted. Nancy was a quietly brilliant engineer, working at Marsh & McLennan (MMC), one of the earliest and largest derivative-trading firms. She was probably at her desk that morning, along with 357 other MMC employees and contractors who died on 9/11.

It seemed imperative then to find out where my friends and colleagues were located throughout the WTC complex. I started dialing cell phones and office numbers. Every connection was either a 'fast busy' signal or an immediate switch to voice mail. I finally reached another friend and contract engineer, Mario.

Mario is from Brooklyn, and had been working for the previous 4 years in Manhattan on a Merrill Lynch Information Technology (IT) corporate-wide network. Mario said that everyone he had reached so far was fine but that phone and cell switches were overloaded. Most of the time he was also getting 'fast busy' signals or voice mail connects. He had discovered that his brother, who worked for the Bank of New York in Building 7, was all right.

Mario then quietly said "You know where Nancy is ..." not completing the sentence. Before hanging up, we agreed to stay in touch, and share our results, as we sought to account for everyone we knew who might be in the Twin Towers.

Colette was crying as she listened to Mario and me talking. Stupidly, I asked her what was wrong.

"I am so glad you're not there. If this was just a few months ago, you'd probably be working there right now, somewhere in those buildings," she said in a shaky voice.

We hugged, and I tried to comfort her by saying almost everything in life involves such 'luck' but that I was very fortunate to be safe, while others were not.

She was, of course, correct. Up until late 2000, I had first been a Consulting Systems Engineer, and later a Consulting Chief Engineer, with AT&T Business Solutions. I worked with AT&T personnel and my own contract engineers throughout the WTC. My firm had many different projects in various parts of the Downtown Financial District, all over Manhattan, and in three of the five boroughs. Between 1995 and 2000, I had spent nearly 300 nights at the WTC Marriott, right at the base of the Twin Towers. Much of that time, I had a permanent room assigned to me by the Marriott staff, since I was constantly coming and going.

Except on sold-out weeks, since I spent so much time there, my firm and our contract engineers were only charged $99 a night. Anyone who has spent any time in New York City knows that one normally cannot get a downscale hotel (read "dump") in Manhattan for $99, especially the Marriott. I am still using up Marriott Points that I accrued from that time, over a decade ago.

Sitting on the bed in my home, on the eastern plains of Colorado, I was far away from the helter-skelter of New York. When the Towers collapsed, image after image flashed through my brain of all the places, and all the rooms, throughout that gigantic complex where I worked so many years. In my mind's eye, I could see the equipment, desks and furniture being crushed, and windows blowing out as the building pancaked in on itself. Everything, that I had so taken for granted, was suddenly crashing down into the ground in billowing clouds of dust, and it was all being transmitted in real time on the TV, seared into my mind like a red hot branding iron.

As I watched the unfolding horror on the screen, I did not know that in a little more than 3 weeks, I would be walking the perimeter of the smoldering WTC site. I could never have imagined becoming nauseous from the odors of burning rubble and chemicals. This was mixed in with the unmistakable smell of death. I could not avoid breathing in the stench as I circled around that horrendous and heartbreaking pile of twisted debris, where so many perished and whose remains were never found.

Running in all directions around the smoldering pit, where the Twin Towers had once stood so proudly, were strung every kind of communications and power cables. Some were exposed. Others were partially protected by hastily constructed plywood plenums. Every 50 feet or so, private security, or NYPD officers were stationed on guard duty.

The WTC pit was not only a physical hole but a 'virtual' one. Beneath the WTC complex, was a major fiber optic and communications-switching center for the WTC offices, and surrounding market exchanges, commercial offices and financial firms in downtown Manhattan. The collapse of the Twin Towers had created a gaping void in that massive and extended fiber and power infrastructure.

To get the market exchanges back up and running, to reassure both citizens and the World that *"America (was) still in business,"* temporary connecting cables were laid haphazardly all over the downtown area. These 'jury-rigged' lines were essential to reconnect and keep the various systems and associated sub-systems in operation, during the weeks immediately following the attack.

It took months to finally reroute and repair the underground connections. During that entire period, most Americans never realized that major stock market and financial firms in New York were literally running on exposed cables snaking through the streets.

Posted everywhere around the site were hastily erected plywood walls, and chain link fences, all pasted with family photographs of missing persons. Accompanying most of them were frantic messages pleading for help in finding them.

It was important to me as a person, and as an American, to walk the complete perimeter to come to terms with, and somehow assimilate, what occurred on 9/11. I had returned to NYC in early October for Nancy Yuen-Ngo's memorial service. She had indeed died on that awful day. In common with so many others, none of her remains were ever found. All the other people that I knew personally, working in and around the Complex, escaped before the Twin Towers, or Building 7, collapsed. Thousands of others were not so fortunate.

Nancy's name is now inscribed on the Memorial with all the other dead. Someday soon, I will visit the Memorial to read her name with my own eyes. I was moved to tears when I read my friend Mario's email describing his visit, and his reactions when he read Nancy's name. She was a dutiful daughter, loving wife and a dedicated mother, who took great delight in her two young daughters, in addition to being a brilliant and hard-working engineer.

Ten years later, in her memory, and for all those others who died there, I undertook writing this book to document my experiences and my observations. The event, facts and myths of 9/11 eerily parallel, and explain on many different levels, what happened, and what continues to happen, in America to this very day. What I hope to convey, and explain, in this book will differ significantly from conventional wisdom, as expressed by the mainstream media, and promulgated by those in power.

As I thought ever more deeply on the events of 9/11, my feelings of sorrow turned into anger and then into disgust. My anger was first directed at the so-called 'terrorists' and their controllers, who had conceived and executed the plan to bring down the Twin Towers. My disgust arose from understanding the broader context and origin of this, and many other events that have and continue to adversely affect this once great Country.

I am not a 'conspiracy theorist.' In fact, my personal experience leads to very different conclusions about what actually happens in the real world. In many respects, the truth of what occurred on 9/11, and why it did, is much simpler than I would have originally thought. The root causes are subtle manifestations of typical human behavior. Human nature is generally consistent, as observed for many thousands of years, and recorded throughout History. The machinations of those involved in historical events may give the appearance of great complexity. That only masks their underlying simplicity.

That does not make the explanations any less sinister, or less detrimental, in their implications or outcomes. Human beings, even the super-rich and the power elites, are generally and specifically much less competent than many in the conspiracy ranks believe. This may not satisfy many readers of this book who may consider themselves to be 'conspiracy theorists.' I will cover this subject in much greater detail in later chapters.

The purpose of this book is to lay out the larger framework of how we arrived at our present situation, at home and abroad, and then propose a barely used method to restore the Republic. The correct choice of methodology will determine whether we are at the "*beginning of the end*" or at the "*end of the beginning*" of a viable republican form of government with democratic features.

The attacks of September 11, 2001, that murdered my friend and colleague, and so many others, will soon be understood as being a pivotal point for our Country, and for the World.

There are always consequences to any behavior and actions. It should be obvious to all Americans that the decisions made by our so-called 'leaders' since 9/11, seem to be deliberately ensuring the demise of the Republic. One **could say** that our leaders are intentionally destroying this Country. But that conclusion ignores typical human behavior. The tragic results of decisions made by those in power are mostly unintentional, arising largely from sheer incompetence on a massive scale.

In fact, the responsibility for the damage to this Country has more to do with an apathetic and uninformed citizenry that permits our elected and appointed leaders to behave badly. Americans have chosen them and let them run amuck, only to re-elect or re-appoint them, no matter how badly they perform. Unless drastic steps are taken by better informed citizens, the future of the Republic appears to be bleak. However, there is some reason for optimism **if** the correct intentional decisions are made from this point forward.

My contention is that Americans have allowed themselves to be duped, dumbed-down and misdirected by their elected, and un-elected, leaders for decades, because they choose to be. Allowing oneself to be misled is more convenient than taking a hard, objective, systematic and disciplined look at one's own system of beliefs and our system of governance. It is easier than getting involved in doing something meaningful about it.

The "*comfort in ignorance*" is exactly the opposite of the original idea of "*American Exceptionalism*," first explained 160 years ago by Alexis de

Tocqueville. It has been perverted and turned upside down. Its original meaning, as described by historian Gordon Wood, was:

> *Our beliefs in liberty, equality, constitutionalism, and the well-being of ordinary people came out of the Revolutionary era. So too did our idea that we Americans are a special people with a special destiny to lead the world toward liberty and democracy.*

That is the way it was for nearly 120 years. The population was always on the path towards increased wealth, greater enlightenment, better relations with our neighbors and enhanced personal liberty and freedom. In other words, we were a **Nation of Principles** setting a better example for the World. Yes, there were mistakes and stumbles along the way. However, Americans seemed to be learning from their lapses and succeeding.

Today, American Exceptionalism has been perverted to mean that "*We can do anything we want and we can do no wrong simply because we are Americans ... and damn the cost.*" That imperialist attitude is totally at odds with the foundational principles of our Republic.

The events of September 11, 2001 brought matters to a crisis point. Most Americans are unaware of the connecting links that are essential in understanding why 9/11 occurred. As a consequence, virtually every citizen is unaware that subsequent decisions and policies have made the overall situation far worse, rather than improving it.

My purpose in writing this book is to illustrate a number of those 'connection points' resulting from direct observations. My conclusions, made from a variety of vantage points, are the direct consequence of a career in military intelligence, network technology, process and organizational consulting, and political activism.

If the reader decides that my ideas and conclusions are incorrect, then so be it. I only hope that critics can offer better explanations, instead of simply resorting to 'ad hominem' attacks, which is the path that they usually take.

In the following chapters, drawing both from personal experience, and decades of research, I will set forth why a more accurate and complete understanding of what lies behind the attacks of September 11, 2001, is so critically important. It is important not only for my fellow citizens, our children and grandchildren, but also for this Republic as a Union of Sovereign States, and set a good example for the World. In so doing, I hope that my explanations and conclusions will also serve to shed some light on why so much seems to be going awry in the American Republic of the 21st Century.

Someday, we may know the specifics of what actually happened on that terrible day. For now, it is important to have a better understanding of the events that led up to it. Learning from what happened will hopefully make crystal clear the dangers of not altering our course. Extolling our present leadership for having a steady hand on the wheel, when the Ship of States is headed straight for the rocks, and certain destruction, is supreme folly.

We can and must alter our direction by learning from, rather than ignoring our mistakes. To put it in the simplest and bluntest terms possible, we are guilty of madness by continuing as we are.

Insanity is doing the same thing over and over again but expecting different results.

Interestingly, that quote originated from the *"Basic Text of Narcotics Anonymous,"* published in 1982.

We must all awake from our shared state of social, economic and political narcosis.

1

The Making of One American

An ant on the move does more than a dozing ox.
–Lao Tzu

*The notion that a radical is one who hates his country is naïve and usually
idiotic. He is, more likely, one who likes his country more than the rest
of us, and is thus more disturbed than the rest of us when he sees it
debauched. He is not a bad citizen turning to crime; he is a good
citizen driven to despair.*
–H.L. Mencken

This book is not intended to be about me. It is about all of us, about who
we are and how we behave as citizens in taking charge of our own
destinies. No matter our backgrounds, each of us must come to
understand and behave by a common set of principles that respect
immutable natural law. Then we can get along and advance our Country,
governance, and civilization. This book is also about what we hope that
our children and grandchildren can have for themselves, everything that
we have not attained ourselves, but want them to have the opportunity to
achieve.

Although I have been told many times that my background is not that
of a typical American, I disagree. It has been in many ways very typical
while being, at the same time, unique in a variety of aspects. That could
describe almost anyone. When we compare ourselves to others, there are
many similarities that hold true across a wide range of cultures and
economic circumstances. Sometimes there are subtle, even profound,
differences. I found that to be true no matter which state or country that I
visited, or lived in.

11

Of course, everyone is influenced by the culture in which they live. Changes in the population's norms are also inevitable as time passes. That influences one's perspective. However, some principles are so common that there are few who could fail to understand them.

I have known many people who have accomplished as much as I ever did, and others much more, in making their own way through life. My upbringing and subsequent adult journey is my own 'American Experience.' It carried me along to the point that I felt compelled to write this book.

Life began for me as a Californian, born in Los Angeles. California was arguably one of the most cutting-edge cultures in the world in the 1950s and 1960s. At that time, my Dad was an aerospace worker at North American Aviation (NAA). He started working there in the early 1950s. He was assigned to various manufacturing, hangar and test facilities around the Los Angeles Basin, and in the Mojave Desert. He worked on several fighter, bomber and experimental aircraft programs. That work later led him into the Manned Space Flight Program.

One of my most precious mementos is an autographed color photograph of test pilot Scott Crossfield, standing in front of 'his' X-15. Dad brought the photo home and gave it to me after we visited the hangar, where I met Mr. Crossfield in 1962. That same X-15 experimental 'spaceplane' now hangs in the Smithsonian's National Air and Space Museum. Later on, Dad worked on the XB-70 bomber program and the Apollo Command and Service Module Spacecraft, among others, with Mr. Crossfield. Dad retired after working on the Space Shuttle Program at Rockwell International, which had acquired NAA. That merger took place during a time when he was laid-off work.

In marked contrast to his later occupation, Dad started out as a country boy, growing up on a farm in central North Carolina during the Great Depression. His mother died when he was two years old. Dad was sent to live with relatives along with his younger brother. Doing basic farm work, such as plowing the cotton and tobacco fields with mules, was routinely expected of him by the age of 7 or 8. He was ardent about our family's history and, over three decades, documented it with his cousin, James Cooper, in great detail.

Our (6x) Great-grandfather, Adam Wright, served in the 4th (Col. Thackston's) Regiment from North Carolina during the American Revolutionary War. The Wrights and the Coopers have served in this Country's military through subsequent generations, from the very beginning of the Republic. So we have a deep and long-standing stake in the American Republic.

Mom was a Los Angeles native and very much a woman of her time. She was a city girl, being born, raised and continuing to live in Inglewood, California, her entire life, before marrying my father. Her parents had moved from New Jersey with her brother before she was born. Her family lineage was largely Scots who had immigrated to America in the mid-1800s. She met Dad in 1953 while working as an account and billing clerk for the Bell System. She was well read and loved to learn something about many fields of science. While I was growing up, our house was always full of magazines and books of all types. Mom was a person possessed of great natural curiosity.

When she was a young girl, her father had given her a photo of the first experimental particle cyclotron. The picture was taken for the 1939 World's Fair in New York, which she attended with her family. She pulled it out of her saved news clippings and showed it to me when I was a boy. Later on, I developed an interest in particle physics and, on several occasions, visited the giant Fermilab synchrotron outside of Batavia, Illinois.

My father's work, and my mother's interests, constantly stimulated my curiosity for everything scientific and technological. Growing up as I did, it was easy to become intensely interested in aerospace and science. Wanting to be some sort of technologist or scientist later in life seemed completely natural. Like many kids at that time, I was also entranced with the idea of becoming an astronaut.

Dad had successfully made the transition, from a rural farm upbringing, to a modern techno-industrial lifestyle, but he was determined that my sister and I also had some rural experiences of our own.

He was also an avid outdoorsman along with many of his friends. Among them were a number of World War I & II veterans, aerospace workers, machinists, tradesmen and other skilled workers who had come to California from all over the Country. There were also a lot more career women already in the workforce in California. Many of the women that I lived around did not fit the "*Leave it to Beaver*" stereotype of a stay-at-home mom.

I grew up around families and people who were shooters. They went camping, hunting and fishing all over California and the American West. It seemed that everyone belonged to one of the many "*Rod and Gun clubs*" that proliferated at the time. Many of them were "*Taft-Goldwater Republicans*" but there were some "*Roosevelt Democrats*," too. However, in our house, Roosevelt was known as "*That man!*," for many good reasons.

Republican or Democrat, growing up during the Great Depression and wartime, and veterans of military service and various industries, many were knowledgeable ammo-reloaders, competitive trap and skeet shooters, pistol and rifle shooters and collectors of all kinds of firearms. That included women as well as men. They talked frequently about the politics of the day and the Constitution. It was just part of everyday life, as commonplace as breathing in that environment. Dad began taking me to the gun range with his friends when I was six years old. He liked to shoot a couple times a week. Some of his friends went to the gun range even more often than he did.

I grew up to love the American West and the Rocky Mountains. I inherited Dad's wanderlust and enjoyment of all things natural. He was a dedicated rock hound and prospector. He once dragged back to a dirt road, over a distance of more than a mile, a 100-lb+ chunk of petrified wood that he found out in the Nevada desert. Today, he would probably be arrested by the BLM, or some other government agency, for doing so.

I have hiked, back-packed, horse-packed, hunted and fished about half of the mountain ranges of the American Rockies, and in the Cascades and the Sierra Nevada. I have also been to the Chugach Mountains, and fished north of the Yukon River and the Arctic Circle in Alaska. I have walked across the Wai'anae Range, up Moana Kea/Loa, around Waialeale and through Haleakala while living in Hawaii. I have hiked and gone caving in the Maya Mountains in Belize and into

14

Guatemala, and stood on top of Mt. Fujiyama in Japan. No matter where I traveled around the world, the north-central Rocky Mountains remain, for me, the Center of the Universe.

Mom and Dad's friends, whether Democrat or Republican, and no matter their race or ethnicity, were very conservative people by nature. Some were churchgoers, some were not. They believed in family and America. They believed in real Capitalism, the rule of law, the peaceful ordering of society and a strict defense of the Country from enemies both external and home-grown. They appreciated alcoholic beverages but seldom to excess (but it was the 1950s and 1960s—and it was California!). For all their differences, they respected each other while working to build a better America.

Nearly everyone seemed to smoke cigarettes, cigars or pipes, and the old-timers chewed tobacco. They exemplified the multiple variations of the God-fearing, patriotic, hard-working, and rock-solid American. They were beginning to appreciate the benefits of tolerance for other points of view. This all made California, and the West, an interesting and intriguing place for me, growing up during the 1950s and 1960s.

Recently, President Obama stated that such people are the ones who *"cling to their guns and religion."* However, his statement that they have *"... antipathy to people who aren't like them or anti-immigrant sentiment or anti-trade sentiment as a way to explain their frustrations,"* was not much in evidence. My parents' friends were very 'diverse' by the standards of today's lexicon, both ethnically and culturally. Mom taught me there is only one race—the human race.

When I was 8 years old, we moved from the south-central Los Angeles area to Diamond Bar, California. At that time, it was a small suburb of less than 2,000 people in the Chino Hills. Today, the population numbers about 55,000. Back then, it was still considered to be 'in the country.' Due to the civil rights movement, tensions were rising in urban areas. Shortly after we moved, the Watts riots broke out just a few miles from where we had lived in El Segundo.

Dad quickly became acquainted with a local rancher in Diamond Bar. We acquired horses that grazed on his place for free. In exchange, we would fix miles of fence and helped run his cattle on thousands of acres of southern California hill country. The old Diamond Bar Ranch had been carved out of the still older Spanish land grant of Rancho Los Nogales. There were miles and miles of walnut and oak studded hills with creeks, and abundant wildlife of every description.

My sister, Gigi, and I went in together, with $102 saved from doing chores, or yard work for our neighbors, and bought our first horse, Chico. He was a decent, if sometimes skittish, Palomino purchased at the Chino Horse Auction. Unfortunately, a high-strung filly kicked him and broke his leg in three places, so we had to put Chico down during the summer when I turned 11 years old.

My favorite horse was my Dad's Buck who was half Morgan and half Quarter Horse. I roamed all over those hills with Buck, Chico and our other horse, Red. I learned how to ride, rope, tend livestock, mend fences and sleep out under the stars on my own. I collected and kept all kinds of critters that we found out there in the back country, including snakes and reptiles of all descriptions, tarantulas, bees, turtles, even an injured raptor or two. My Mom was not very happy with that hobby, especially when one of our big rattlesnakes escaped and gave birth under the A/C unit!

At 12, I went to work in my first real job for a livestock provider and event producer's outfit. Les Jones had moved his operation from Carbon Canyon to Diamond Bar. Then and there, I learned the meaning of hard work, something that stayed with me for my entire life. Les was tough but fair. I learned that when he yelled, always at the top of his lungs: "*DAMMIT, MOVE THEM CATTLE, BOY!,*" that he was not actually mad at me. He was trying to 'incentivize' me.

I had convinced him, and his operation manager, Richard, that I really wanted the job. I did so by hanging around all the time that I could, and working for free, to prove my willingness and ability to do the work. Les started me at 75 cents an hour. I worked every weekend, and often after school. After 6 months, I got a raise to a $1 an hour. Ten dollars, even for a long day, was a virtual fortune for a boy in the 1960s. Some days, we worked 10-12 hours in the spring and summer. Les and Richard would be arrested by the child labor authorities today.

During the summers, I made really good money working 5-6 days a week. I learned how to harness and hitch mules and horses to wagons, to quickly saddle, unsaddle and put away a rental string of horses, and to conduct seasonal day and night rides taking dozens of "*dudes*" into the hills. I learned how to 'doctor' injured or sick animals, breed stallions at stud to mares, and help break horses and mules. In addition, I learned how to load stacked hay high on the wagon, feed several hundred head twice a day, clean and re-bed stalls, pens and arenas, and work rodeo and stock events.

One could rightly say that, as a kid, I was constantly floating between two very different worlds. Dad's workplace was filled with astronauts, test pilots, engineers, spacecraft, rockets, jets, computers and all sorts of space technology. My alternate "*Old West*" lifestyle was filled with cowboys and cowgirls, ranching, livestock, rodeo, hunting, fishing, shooting, trapping and collecting 'critters.' I never once thought there was anything unusual about any part of my life.

Growing up, in a Taft-Goldwater Republican household, inevitably meant that politics, current events, and the Constitution were regular topics of discussion. We watched Walter Cronkite or "*The Huntley-Brinkley Report*" on the nightly news around the dinner table and discussed what was happening in America, and around the world. Both of my parents encouraged my interests in science, technology and politics. I remember watching my first Republican and Democratic National Conventions on TV in 1964.

I was fairly good at math and science, having been placed in a program for Mentally-Gifted Minors (MGM) in the California school system by 5th grade. I also developed skill as a speed reader. The MGM program was begun in the 1960s because of the Space Program. It was intended to develop future scientists, engineers and technicians for the endless possibilities that seemed to be dawning for space exploration, and because of the Cold War underway against the Soviets. The MGM program was for those that tested out in the top percentile of the students in the State.

So I also wound up being an early 'nerd.' My high school freshmen ID card (no one will ever see it again but me!) shows me with a pocket protector stuffed with pens and pencils! The picture did not show the cowboy boots that I also wore nearly every day. In Elementary and Junior

High School, taking an advanced curriculum meant that I would likely receive a full-ride scholarship in the California college and university system, if I kept progressing and passing tests.

By 7th and 8th grade, MGM students were already completing high school requirements (known as "AP" today) in math and science. I socialized, studied and took courses with some very gifted kids, many of whom went on to have interesting careers in science, technology, and the arts. It was pretty interesting stuff!

However, all that came to an abrupt end in 1970, when my Dad was laid off by Rockwell International, due to cutbacks in the Apollo program. Tens of thousands of highly-skilled scientists, engineers, technicians, assemblers, managers and the like were sent out the door. The very considerable strains on the Federal Budget were glaringly obvious due to President Johnson's War on Poverty, and the Viet Nam War, with the unrealistic promise that his policies could successfully deliver both "*Guns and Butter*" for America.

The Country could not afford Johnson's policies, and Nixon's subsequent "Peacemaker" agenda, along with funding the exploration and future development of the Moon. Something had to give. Politics being politics, it was the Space Program that went first.

The moon-bound spacecraft, scheduled to end with the Apollo 20 mission, had either already been completely assembled, or had all their parts ready for final assembly. By the time that Apollo 14 lifted off the launch pad, there was no longer any need to keep more than mission-critical personnel on board. Tens of thousands of highly skilled technical personnel, including senior executives, went out the door, and into a bad economy without suitable new job openings.

The Program was formally canceled after the flight of Apollo 17. Parts of the last unused spacecraft can still be seen at the Johnson Space Flight Center in Houston, Texas. I took my youngest son, Alex, there when he was in 7th Grade to show him the vehicles that his Grandpa had helped build.

It was a devastating blow to Dad and his friends, who had been the scientists, engineers, managers and technicians who had created the Space Program from scratch. At that time, Dad was a Spacecraft Quality

Assurance Specialist for several components on the Apollo Command and Service modules. Many of those involved in the Program expected it to be privatized after Apollo 20. Then it all simply fell apart.

It would be years of delays before the Space Shuttle, originally proposed as part of a complete system along with the Space Station, would get underway. That was too late for most of the workers in the Manned Space Flight Program. The Shuttle became the *"Space Truck to Nowhere"* without the existence of the corresponding Space Station.

It was nearly three decades later, at a price 10 times the original amount projected (and achieving perhaps 1/10 of the original goals), before the final configuration of the International Space Station (ISS) was completed. It was finished just as the Shuttle reached the end of its useful life. The maintenance of the ISS, and its future, are a big question mark at this time. NASA's follow-on Moon/Mars Constellation program has recently been effectively canceled due to the same dawning reality of budget math. It will be private companies, such as Space X, Virgin Galactic, XCOR and other ventures that finally begin the **sustainable** privatization of space flight.

As costs skyrocketed, each Shuttle launch averaged $1.5 billion over the life of the program! That did not make for very good payload economics. Losing two of the Shuttles during the life time of the Program did not help either. However, that eventuality had been predicted in the engineering reliability calculations made during its design. The economics of government contracting are stark and can sometimes be brutally apparent.

Meanwhile, the laid off Apollo workers had to find something else to do. Bureaucratic self-preservation, and turf battles within NASA, had ensured that there were no private, commercial manned spaceflight competitors. That was accomplished by controlling the remaining government space and science programs. In concert with the Department of Defense (DoD), NASA effectively kept the aerospace companies, and any potential start-ups, out of manned space flight until the monopolistic status of the Shuttle Program was authorized and guaranteed.

None of the aerospace defense contractors were going to jeopardize their billions in defense contracts with private space ventures. Of course,

NASA denies any of this. However, I listened to those who had worked in the Program and heard their disappointment at first hand. I also witnessed similar policies in action when I worked as an engineering manager on the Consolidated Space Operations Center (CSOC) in the early 1980s. CSOC was an Air Force program to build military Mission Control and Operations centers for various space-based defense programs in Colorado Springs.

The Shuttle Operations Complex (SOC) portion of that program was canceled in 1986 after the Challenger explosion. Other space projects continued to dwindle. Meanwhile, the costs for the Shuttle and ISS soared. We were also preoccupied with the potential scaling up of President Reagan's Strategic Defense Initiative (SDI), also called the "*Star Wars*" programs. SDI turned into a huge government boondoggle of its own that has persisted, in various forms, to this very day.

Dad, along with many of his friends and colleagues, remained very unhappy about NASA's rigid control of manned space flight. As long as NASA and the DoD controlled it, their monopoly of the Shuttle Program set back commercial advances by decades. Not until the first decade of the 21st Century, have private sector companies, with few ties to NASA or the DoD, finally entered into substantial private space ventures to (horror of horrors!) actually make a profit. Only private enterprise will enable and ensure a **profitable** and **sustainable** presence in space, free of the vagaries of federal budgeting, bureaucratic turf wars and careerist maneuvering, and lack of vision by professional politicians, who are selfishly obsessed with being re-elected, no matter the cost to this Country's technological leadership.

After several months in a fruitless job search in 1970, my parents decided there was little choice. We had to leave California for my Dad to find employment somewhere else. We had vacationed several times in the North Central Rockies and the Idaho-Montana mountains throughout the 1960s. "*The place to go is Idaho,*" was that state's marketing phrase. So, off we went. My parents sold our home in Diamond Bar and packed everything up. We left California in July of 1971, moving to Star, Idaho, a farm community with a population of 350.

Dad had been in California for nearly 25 years. He figured that it was simply time to move on. Mom had never lived anywhere else. It was much more difficult for her. I thought that it was one of the best things to ever happen to me. My sister was of a different opinion. Much later on, I think that she came to see it as a plus.

I love the mountains and the wide open spaces of Idaho. For Dad and me, it was 'Heaven on Earth.' Idaho had very few people, a small fraction of the population of California, with beautiful country and an economic base of farming, ranching, logging and extraction industries. Admittedly, for my Mom and sister, it was more like being marooned on a distant planet compared to Southern California.

My folks acquired some acreage outside of Star and then built a house with the help of a local contractor. Dad and I built a garage and a barn. We fenced in the sage brush and the dry-land crop fields that remained from the original farm. With our new neighbors, we installed irrigation pipes and planted alfalfa and grass. My folks served on the water co-op board. We acquired a couple more horses, some bees, chickens and a few cattle to raise while Dad looked for work.

As quickly as I could, I 'settled' into High School in Meridian, Idaho, looking to make friends. That was not easy. The cultural divide between southern California and southern Idaho was fairly wide in those days. Even though I had spent just as much time as any of the other kids my age doing ranch work, my sister and I were still referred to as "*California Hippies.*" Few were interested in hearing about science and space technology. It was simply not part of the culture in Idaho. It was understandable but frustrating. Most of my friends in California, just like me, lived and breathed the early Space Program.

Meridian High had no advanced curriculum. I had no choice but retake classes that I had already completed in California. Otherwise, I could not graduate. Needless to say, that did not help hold my interest in schoolwork. As my interest in school waned, my grades also dropped. I could sleep through most of the classes. I was able to just take tests to maintain a B- or high C average. That prevented too much parental wrath at home.

Thankfully, my parents understood what was happening. In hindsight, even though I disliked most of my teachers, it was a bad situation for all concerned. By the time graduation arrived, I was ranked about 235 in a class of 323. I had so little enthusiasm that I did not even attend the graduation ceremony. The school had demanded that I rent a graduation suit just to get the tassel. So I did not bother.

To keep from being bored, I decided to make as much money as possible by working all the time during the remainder of High School. I bought a 1965 Ford Falcon with the money that I had saved from working for Les Jones in Diamond Bar back in California. I purchased it before I took the driver's license test at age 15. I was already bored to tears riding the bus 42 miles round-trip, bouncing on the back roads to the high school every day.

The 'deal' that I made with my parents was very straightforward. I was expected to maintain a 'B' average (give or take), buy my own car, pay for my own insurance and gas, and do the work around the Star place that was expected of me. If I did all that satisfactorily, then they figured that I was responsible enough to pretty much come and go as I pleased throughout the remainder of High School. They even allowed me to drive my car alone back and forth across Nevada, from Idaho to Los Angeles, to visit my friends in California—at the ripe old age of 16. How many parents would let their sons do that today, I wonder?

I tried to keep 3 part-time jobs going at once. That allowed me to party, ski, fish and hunt with my friends anytime that I was able to get away, and had the money. In the fall, quite a few students used to show up at school with shotguns, handguns and rifles in the car, and go hunting or target shooting after school. Imagine that happening today! There is now a state law in Idaho that would have put us in jail.

I worked in a pawn shop, delivered used furniture and appliances, bussed tables, washed pots and dishes, bucked hay and cut wood. I did just about anything to make money. I had many absences and tardy slips. The only thing that probably kept me from being expelled during my Junior and Senior years was Mr. Leon Fairbanks, the electricity and electronics teacher.

Against all the odds, and despite a great deal of resistance, Mr. Fairbanks was a visionary in the Meridian School System. In a 600-square mile rural district, consisting mainly of farming or ranching, he managed to persuade the school 'authorities' to start a 2-year electronics curriculum. There was no space, and little money, but Mr. Fairbanks was not deterred. He took over the basement of the old Cloverdale Elementary School (circa 1910s) between the corn, onion and potato fields out on Fairview Avenue in the east part of Meridian. To get there, we had to drive ourselves, since there was no money for a bus.

It was drafty and cold in the basement, except when the boiler ran full blast to heat the upper floors during the winter. Then it was too hot. Mr. Fairbanks collected a bunch of old electronic gear and basic test equipment, along with some rudimentary work benches. With my buddies, Dave and Mark, I decided to try it out. We constructed our own lab benches for test work. Mr. Fairbanks loaned us slide rules, and other supplies, until we could purchase our own. We worked assigned theory problems and formulae everyday on paper.

Mr. Fairbanks probably saved me from having a much less interesting life. In learning electronics, I found something that really set my mind buzzing again. It was math, science and technology! We attended a two and a half hour class, three days a week, for two years. The math went far beyond what Meridian High taught in the regular courses. Furthermore, these were real-life applications! We went on field trips to power stations and places that actually used the latest electrical and electronic technology of the day.

Most days, I looked forward to his class, except when I was dog-tired from work the night before. All my absences occurred in my other classes, but not in Electricity and Electronics. During my junior year, I was a janitor at the High School from four to seven AM. I held other jobs after school up until midnight. It is hardly surprising that I slept in so many classes.

Mr. Fairbanks and Mr. North, the English instructor, were the two teachers who saved public school for me. Mr. North would pound on my work in class: "*Mr. Wright, are you ever going to learn what 'dangling participle' means?*" (Uh-maybe). I found out later that he had written my parents a long note during my senior year, when I was in his English II (or was it English III?) class, praising my promise as a writer if I would just keep working at it. I hope that he would not be too disappointed with my efforts here.

When the military recruiters showed up at Meridian High, during the second half of my Junior Year, I was more than ready to try something new. I selected the Navy because my Dad had served in it.

He had related how he enjoyed his time in the Navy, even though it was during wartime. A few years later, I received the only letter that he ever wrote to me when I was overseas. I was stationed on the island of Okinawa during the 35th Anniversary of the invasion. He had been on a Destroyer Escort offshore during the bombardment in April, 1945. He was proud, and somewhat amazed, that his son was serving there 35 years later.

I had usually been fairly successful at taking tests. When the Navy recruiter showed up at the High School for qualification tests, I dove right in. And I kept taking them. After the first round of testing, I took another 'weird' math and puzzle test series in a locked room, down at the recruiting station in Boise. Then a recruiter came out to Star, and talked to my parents and me about career choices in something that he called the Naval Security Group. He did not offer any other training track. At first, I thought it was some kind of military police group. As it turned out, I would not have wanted anything else. He said he could not talk too much about it in detail because it was *"highly classified"* work.

He did bring a short booklet for me to read with a rather vague description of the field. He explained that it could involve both shipboard and land-based service all over the World, potentially working at U.S. Embassies, in *"intelligence collection stations"* and being sort of an *"electronic spy."* Those words got my full attention, believe me.

A spy? You want me to be a spy? At that time, I was washing dishes, bussing tables, cutting wood, bucking hay, moving irrigation pipe, in other words, doing whatever I could find. And he was telling me that '*I could travel the world and be a spy?*'

He said, in a matter-of-fact way: "*Well, yes, but only if you complete the schools and training. The drop-out rate in this training, once you've qualified, after a few more tests and completing boot camp, is about 94%.*"

It sounded like a challenge to me. (Yeah, right! "*... a few more tests ...*")

This development was not a problem, since I had expected that I would wind up in the draft for Viet Nam anyhow. We were supposed to be pulling out, but it seemed to me that matters were uncertain from day to day. I wanted to join the Navy and also to pick what I would do there. However, I had never given much thought about the potentially more interesting things that I could do as part of the Military—like being a spy! Only later, would I learn it was not exactly what I had envisioned. I received an education that neither my parents nor I could ever have expected!

"*You also have to be able to complete a special security review,*" the recruiter said. Great! Count me in! I did not think much at the time about what that all meant. So I signed up for delayed entry and reported for induction in August, 1974.

About 22 months later, in May of 1976, I had come through that particular training pipeline successfully. I had beaten the odds and reported to my first duty station in Wahiawa, Hawaii. That site was the master station for the Pacific BULLSEYE HFDF network of the Naval Security Group (NSG), and the main routing/switching site for all Pacific/Fleet communications. Not an embassy yet, but it was Hawaii!

NSG was more an arm of the super-secret National Security Agency (NSA), also known in Washington, DC, as "*No Such Agency,*" rather than a naval service intelligence organization. NSG and its cousins, the Army Security Agency (ASA) and the Air Force Security Service (AFSS), operated together, and shared personnel and systems as extensions of the NSA. The Marine component was attached to NSG. At the time, almost no one in the government knew who, or what these organizations included, not even members of the U.S. Congress. NSG was one of the more technically advanced of such organizations in the Military.

To arrive in Hawaii, I had successfully completed basic and advanced electronics, three phases of Electronic Tech school, two phases of NSG

Cryptologic Tech school, and two ASA Cryptographic Equipment and Tech Control 'C' schools. Then there were final qualifications, and an advanced signal communications security (COMSEC) systems school. Attendance and classwork was eight to ten hours a day for six days a week, plus regular military training and duties.

If one failed any of these, one wound up either in fleet duty, the nuclear power program, or possibly in submarine service. I was not really interested in spending my time below the waves on patrol, so I stuck to it and became a "Cryptotech." I also did not want to return to Idaho (for obvious reasons) for "*nuke school*" at the Idaho National Engineering Lab (INEL). I knew that Arco, Idaho, the first nuclear-powered town in the USA, was in the middle of nowhere. It was not that far away from where I had hunted antelope with my Dad!

I was granted a Top Secret Security Clearance, but only after passing an extensive background FBI/NIS investigation, and signing what seemed like endless documents essentially stating that my genetic line (or something like that) would end immediately, should I ever reveal anything that I knew. Or, if I ever disclosed anything for the next 20 years or so, my life would be forfeit (or so it seemed!).

Additional special security (SI, SCI) compartmented clearances would be added to the Top Secret one, as I proceeded to work through operational platform sites. Such sites are the ones seen in pictures and videos with giant satellite dishes and other specialized antennae, and the "*golf ball*" radomes. The conspiracy nets identify them as *Echelon Sites.* I was exposed to all the different aspects of SIGINT (Signals Intelligence) and COMINT (Communications Intelligence) collection and analysis systems.

It turned out that the work of the NSG/NSA was very much what I wanted to do from a technical perspective. I could not have asked for more of a challenge in technological terms. With my general systems inclination, I had a natural intellectual interest and affinity for system engineering, and test work, in the sort of new technologies that were coming on line. A mere three years removed from bucking hay, I was installing and synchronizing atomic clocks, cryptologic gear and working on some of the most advanced computer, SIGINT and COMINT collection systems ever designed up to that time.

The extent of these programs was known to few people until very recently. My eyes were opened wide at what was going on across the globe, and 'under the sheets.' Things quickly changed in the late 1970s after the war in Viet Nam ended. A shift in emphasis from true national security needs to what I came to view as *"dirt collection"* on enemies, adversaries and even our own allies, in order to affect political solutions, became the order of the day. This has created a huge moral dilemma for this Country that must be remedied.

At the end of my service hitch, somewhat surprisingly, both the Navy and the Agency offered me multiple financial and career incentives to stay on with one or the other. I decided not to pursue any of those offers because of what I had witnessed. I was convinced, from my firsthand experience, as later chapters will affirm, that the path we were (and are) taking was (and is) not the proper way to conduct foreign policy, or ensure a high degree of safety and security for our Country.

My attitude had already caused several clashes with senior officers, and enlisted personnel, regarding what I viewed as constitutionally, morally, and ethically questionable activities in theater. A few agreed with me. Most did not. The apparatus of the intelligence services was encroaching into political areas with no valid or justifiable cause for involvement. In fact, the only reason it was happening was because the intelligence services had the capability and, an important point to note, because they could get away with it. They had the funding. Furthermore, they were accountable to virtually no one. There was no real oversight. All eyes had been averted or distracted.

My on-job performance was always highly rated throughout my service. I had received several awards and commendations, along with regular and early rank advancements. However, my previous clashes with higher authority did not bode well for a long-term career in the Navy, or in the Agency. I therefore decided that it was time to learn more on the 'outside' in order to better comprehend and understand what I had seen in *"the hall of mirrors."*

I returned to the States, after six years in the service, to start a new civilian career.

As I prepared to move into the next phase of my life, I had already encountered two radically different experiences in my life's journey. One was similar in many respects to most lives in the America of the mid-20th Century, with a few interesting twists and turns between my upbringing in California and Idaho.

The other was a unique and rare opportunity, afforded by working in the developing high-tech surveillance apparatus field, and in large-scale networking technology. This early exposure equipped me to see what was coming, in far greater detail and more objectively than most citizens. My early education in the *"intel and defense biz"* undoubtedly had a significant effect in shaping my philosophy during the next 30 years of my life.

My life was also personally shaped by many of the people I met, and served with, in the Military. Most importantly, I met and married Colette, my wife of thirty years, while she was serving six years in the Navy as a Radioman. Interestingly, her family also has a history of service to this Country. All three sisters served in the Military. Her older sister was in the Navy, too. Her younger sister and her husband met in the Army, from which he retired after 20 years of service. Colette was also a national disaster volunteer with the Red Cross for 14 years. I would respectfully submit that one would be hard pressed to find any American family that is more in tune with the nature of volunteer service, and love of Country, than ours.

It seemed that the America for which my (6x) Great-granddaddy Adam Wright fought over two hundred years ago, and the soon-to-be-written U.S. Constitution that the American victory facilitated, were not turning out the way that I had been taught to expect. Despite the benefit of hindsight, it is still surprising to me how my time in the military service/intelligence complex inexorably set me on a course that took me directly to the WTC, and the subsequent fall of the Twin Towers on 9/11.

2

The Rise and Fall of the 2nd Republic

Only powerful people have liberty.
—Sun Yat-sen

Decades of experience, ranging from assignments in military intelligence and defense systems on through to my work in high-level, high-stake government and commercial telecommunications systems, provided me with a rather unique vantage point from which to observe how various converging effects of our overseas involvements led directly to the events of 9/11. This was of great benefit in developing a comprehensive understanding of the dysfunctional state of today's gigantic U.S. global empire. As we shall explain further, this highly delusional dysfunction was aided and abetted by the Federal Reserve during the past four decades. For those with eyes to see, and the willingness to think things through once presented with the connecting facts, I will expose one of the major constructs of the late 2nd Republic, namely the Security-Surveillance Superstate.

Before leaving the Naval Security Group/National Security Agency at the end of 1980, my assigned work involved building and maintaining systems platforms that collected, analyzed and communicated full-spectrum SIGINT and COMINT intelligence data throughout the Pacific Region. In turn, this data was consumed by various agencies in Washington D.C. Those operations focused primarily on the Soviet Union, Central Asia and China, as well as North Korea, and other regional governments, both friendly and unfriendly, throughout Asia and the Far East.

Like vast vacuum pumps, the platforms sucked in, analyzed and then spewed out endless streams of information to feed the voracious appetites of the NSA, the CIA, the Pentagon and the National Command Authority (NCA), along with the National Security Council (NSC) at the White House. All these organizations consume enormous volumes of intelligence data of every sort across the full spectrum of sources that can be tapped and accessed. Working in each of those areas, it was easy for me to see what all sides were doing, both overtly and covertly. I was trained to piece large puzzles together. Author James Bamford popularized the NSA nickname, "*The Puzzle Palace*," to describe that environment.

The NSA of those days was jokingly referred to as the "*No Such Agency*," but it hardly compares to today's "*Never Say Anything*" colossus.

The Conversion of the MIC into the MIISSC

The average American is completely unaware of the size and the influence of the "*Military Industrial Complex*" (MIC), the existence of which President Eisenhower had implicitly warned us to beware in his farewell speech in 1960. Since then, over half a century later, it has engorged to such a degree, and has become so complex, that the term "MIC" is an inadequate description. It is now far more accurate to refer to it as the *Military Industrial Intelligence Security State Complex* (MIISSC). It is a pervasive presence, especially in its Intelligence and Security manifestations.

The MIISSC is truly gigantic. The most visible military components are seen in videos and photos of multi-billion dollar carrier battle groups cruising the high seas, various high-tech fighters and bombers flying overhead, and pictures of the Pentagon and the Service Academies. In reality, whatever is shown publicly is just a tiny fraction of the infrastructure. Barely the tip of the iceberg is visible.

According to various official and non-governmental estimates, the U.S. government has between 900 and 1,100 significant overseas military bases, installations and units positioned around the World. Add to that number Embassies in 190 countries and a wide range of other 'agency-in-the-field' offices in more than 135 countries. If all the currently deployed and supplied 'bases, installations and units' in every category are also counted as part of the current global deployment infrastructure, then the true number may be double that amount, as high as 2,000 or more.

The only way to be certain is to have a complete list of facilities. Excepting the fact that there is a problem in the reckoning. The Pentagon could not account for, and identify in its records, over $1 trillion in spending during the 1990s! America expends a staggering amount of money on its MIISSC, more than the next 23 nations combined, and about half of what all other countries spend on their military forces and associated agencies.

When adding up the expenditures required to maintain all the MIISSC components now in full operation, the sum easily exceeds the defense spending of 2/3 of the rest of the World! Most citizens are in the dark about these expenditures because so much is hidden from view by the blur of agencies, budget trickery and the excuse of *"national security."* The government classifies hundreds of millions of *"Top Secret"* documents but it declassifies very few of them.

Amazingly, even the previous pace of enlargement ramped up in the past decade. The NSA is currently on an enormous building binge. It is adding millions of square feet of new computer and analysis space, with capabilities so vast that even those formerly in the intelligence community struggle to come up with appropriate descriptions of their scope.

Just one data warehouse site in Bluffdale, UT, will cost $2 billion. As part of the STELLAR WIND program, that one individual site will be able to store virtually anything desired that is sucked in off the Internet and fed into the TURBULENCE system for analysis. (These are the published, but perhaps not the actual code name used within the NSA). The Bluffdale site will tie into five other centers already completed, or yet to be constructed, in Hawaii and elsewhere. It gives new meaning to the term 'deep-net data mining.' The 'deep net' is anything that is occurring in the digital infrastructure lying below the 'user level' of the Web.

In one way or another, the NSA is tapped into virtually every part of the domestic telecommunication infrastructure with various *"national technical* (data collection) *means."* There are physical and virtual tap points in TelCo (telephone company) Central Office switch complexes that have been in place since the 1970s. The NSA is a hydra-headed electronic octopus. It can 'link in,' from the fiber level and up, with its own or Allied computing complexes, onshore and offshore, to collect and analyze all tapped communications systems with technology that transcends any current definition of 'ultrafast.'

How many readers know what an *exabyte*, a *zettaflop*, or a *yottaflop* is, and how many zeros there are in a *septillion*? These words are now in common usage at the NSA. Such number-crunching capabilities are the Orwellian realization of Admiral Poindexter's "*Total Information Awareness*" program, amplified by unimaginable orders of magnitude from the time when he proposed it, more than a decade ago.

Some parts of the apparatus are hidden in nearly plain sight inside other agencies, such as the Homeland Security Agency (HSA), the Drug Enforcement Agency (DEA), the Bureau of Alcohol, Tobacco and Firearms Enforcement (BATFE), the Internal Revenue Service (IRS), the Federal Bureau of Investigation (FBI) and even the Coast Guard. That does not include some 2000 private contractor companies which are also involved. The latter have become almost as large and numerous as the government's own agencies. The Feds expend yet more billions on them. HSA alone has 230,000 employees and has built 17 million square feet of new office space since its establishment, immediately after 9/11.

The trillions upon trillions of dollars that we have spent since the end of the Cold War have not provided true security for America but instead have worsened it. What those trillions have actually purchased is a hugely misaligned and aggressively **militaristic** system, not a defensive one. Those misspent trillions **have made for a very well-fed MIISSC** and created a security and surveillance superstate. Ironically, as our capability and interventionism overseas grows, so has our **insecurity.**

Ever wonder why our leaders keep telling us that, despite all those trillions spent, there are even more threats? Wonder why they tell us there are more terrorists and more hobgoblins than ever before, in all corners of the World, who are out to get us, endangering our 'National Security?' It would seem, according to them, that we are more insecure than when the Soviets were pointing 25,000 nukes at the USA! The real reason is very simple. We are literally manufacturing many of our own demons, imagined and real.

We waste most of that money, for the wrong reasons, on 'solutions' that are actually counter-productive. Endless issues and problems are being created by our government, acting like a child that pokes a stick in a hornet's nest and then gets stung. It is hard to escape the conclusion that we are also poking sticks in the eyes of our global neighbors because we can.

We also do so because we have to maintain the flow of oil imports, prop-up our currency and cater to the duplicitous interests of the corporatist MIISSC. That is the unsavory part of the security and surveillance superstate, the American Empire, that no one cares to confront or discuss. It is something that the political class does not speak about, or want the public to know anything about.

Of course, there **are** visible humanitarian and relief efforts broadcast by the media on TV. That puts a pleasant PR face on our global presence. To a limited degree, those efforts provide some positive counterbalancing effect.

Interestingly, when even a single video, featuring a misguided attack on innocent civilians in Iraq, was released via Wikileaks, the whole security surveillance infrastructure went nuts. Yet literally thousands of routine and covert missions have taken place. They are still occurring almost daily. Most of what actually happened in the last decade will never see the light of day. We have no idea what they actually accomplished, or how many went awry.

What about the 'missions' that produced a minimum of 200,000+ Iraqi and other civilian casualties in Iraq, Afghanistan and "*elsewhere*"? Americans do not want to know how many negative incidents occurred. Worst of all, when young Americans die on secret missions gone wrong, it is rarely reported on the evening news. For most of the time since 1950, such incidents were never reported.

We have little idea what the invisible Intelligence, Security and State apparatus truly looks like. According to the Washington Post, in its series "*Top Secret America*," there are now more than 850,000 active "*Top Secret*" security clearances. That is an absurdly large number, far beyond any rational 'defense' needs. During the height of the Cold War, the total was less than one-fifth that number.

Far fewer personnel were actually required to guard America against our prior adversaries who were, by any objective and realistic criteria, far more dangerous than those currently threatening us. Millions died or were wounded, with approximately 500,000 Americans killed, wounded or missing-in-action, during our struggles with communists, socialists and various dictators since 1950.

All the identified terrorist groups combined have killed about 40,000, and wounded another 60,000 people, in attacks during the past 60 years around the globe. A few thousand of those casualties were Americans. With a correctly provisioned and deployed defense force, it would be highly unlikely that they could do any worse to us in the next 60 years. But we do not have a correctly provisioned and deployed force to meet **real threats.** So what is really going on? It is very simple. Our security surveillance state is running amuck, like a rogue elephant on steroids. The MIISSC remains focused on contracts, toys, politics, and control of the population, not on the true security of our Country or its citizens.

It was not NASA that was the originator of most modern Information Technology (IT), and other similar developments, as portrayed in the media. It was the NSA and its surrogates. They were either the prime instigator, or hugely influential, in the development of the super-computing industry, of advanced data communications networks, of many critical aspects of satellite communications and monitoring capabilities, of earth imaging, infrared mapping, spread-spectrum radio frequency communications, and much more. It is not that hard for them to be at the forefront of such advancements. The NSA is the world's largest employer of mathematicians, among other technical fields of scientific expertise.

For example, the first time that I worked on a system utilizing plasma displays, and advanced spread spectrum technology, was in 1978. Such technology had already been around for some time at NSA's HQ in Ft Meade. Most civilian tech types, with an interest in technological advancements, would probably be quite surprised by that date. That is just two examples of many technologies developed and deployed by the NSA, long before they saw widespread adoption anywhere else.

The intelligence gathering agencies continue to push the state-of-the-art in all related technologies. Unfortunately, many of those will be misapplied, actually used to the detriment, rather than the benefit, of American citizens. Many will backfire through the Law of Unintended Consequences, or far exceed any rational limitations on their capabilities that are appropriate in a constitutional republic.

Shortly after the creation of the Universities Research Network, which then grew into ARPANET, the experimental foundation of much of the early Internet, such enabling technologies had already been appropriated and advanced by the intelligence apparatus throughout the 1970s. They spread through various secure communications systems, vastly increasing their reliability, power and performance. Encrypted voice communication was another key technology that had been employed on an operational basis ever since the 1960s. Such technologies are now at a highly advanced level, in use throughout the entire intelligence gathering infrastructure.

A perfect example is the Hubble telescope, NASA's most powerful such instrument. For more than two decades, it has been used for deep space imaging. As everyone should know by now, the Hubble is little more than a civilian variant of the "Keyhole" (KH) spy satellite. The Hubble telescope is pointed outwards into Space rather than being focused down onto the planetary surface. And there is only one Hubble telescope. Dozens of Keyhole satellites, and other such super-secret space systems, have been deployed in programs managed by the National Reconnaissance Office (NRO) over the past decades. The scale of the 'black' programs, with expenditures carefully hidden in Defense budgets, so that no officials need ever publicly explain them, is simply unimaginable to the average American.

The NRO just gave the last of their KH 'birds' to NASA as a gift.

Due to the highly sophisticated high-technology 'toys' that intelligence agencies have at their disposal, they were (and still are) incredibly attractive to anyone interested in advanced technology, especially at the 'bleeding edge' of the 'state-of-the-art,' whether in research and development, or during initial deployment and implementation. As a consequence, many brilliant scientists and technologists are attracted to, and absorbed into, the intelligence-security-state portions of the MIISSC. That is where many opportunities and jobs are sequestered.

A small portion of the technology was shared and developed with our allies, or became 'leakage' when Agency engineers and techs went into private industry. However, forward planning has been to stay more than 10 to 15 years ahead of our enemies, more than 3 to 5 years ahead of our allies, and at least 10 years ahead of commercial industry. Look at the stir that weaponized computer viruses, such as Stuxnet and Flame, have created. So far, those are the only visible ones. It is fairly certain that more such viruses are out there, with even more to come, ever since NSA/DNI opened that Pandora's box.

What Are the Implications for You and Me?

None of that technology is necessarily bad, in and of itself. However, one must look at all the implications, and the uses to which the technology is applied, instead of what is being most visibly touted.

Arthur C. Clarke, the great science fiction writer, wrote in his book *"Profiles of the Future,"* published in 1961, that:

Any sufficiently advanced technology is indistinguishable from magic.

Most of what the NSA, and its associated agencies, accomplished during the 1970s, 1980s and through the middle of the 1990s, would have been considered *"magic"* by the rest of the World. Some of that technological lead has since been eroded but, in most areas, the U.S. agencies are still well ahead of whatever is available anywhere else.

When as a young, eager enlistee in the summer of 1974, I left Idaho and started down the training pipeline, I had no idea about any of this. Neither did 99.8% of America's citizens. Today, it is likely that 97% still have no real clue, except for what they see in the movies, and on police and investigative shows on TV. Most depictions are largely fictitious, consisting of superficial and flashy drivel for mass consumption.

It was mildly amusing to watch a recent National Geographic special that claimed to have gained *"unprecedented access"* to a very small number of NSA Operation centers. To the average viewer, it probably seemed as though they were seeing previously closely-guarded *"Top Secret"* information. However, at the end of the show, the narrator admitted that access had actually been very tightly monitored and controlled. Every single recorded image in the video, showing the installations and interviews, was reviewed and edited. Nothing left the premises without intense scrutiny. A great deal was deleted. What remained was intended to show the Agency in a favorable light, actually revealing little, or nothing, of importance. Of course, the censorship was justified in the name of *"National Security."*

Although the acronym, NSA, has entered into the common vernacular, even fewer citizens understand the scope and depth of the capabilities, now under the control of the recently created office of Director of National Intelligence (DNI). It is an organization of 16 agencies created by the Intelligence Reform and Terrorism Prevention (IRTP) Act, signed into law in December, 2004. The Naval Security Group, and several other agencies where I began my career, have been completely subsumed into the massive intelligence gathering apparatus reporting to the DNI.

James Bamford, a New York Times bestselling author, has detailed some of the NSA's and the DNI's capabilities, beginning with the *"Puzzle Palace"* (1982), and then more recently in *"Body of Secrets"* (2002) and *"The Shadow Factory"* (2008). Bamford actually began his career, during the Viet Nam War, as an administrative tech in the same place that I did, the Naval Security Group. His first book freaked-out the core leadership at the Agency. In actuality, it barely scratched the surface.

Bamford's books exposed, and continue to expose, a view of the nature, and some detail, of the intelligence community's superstructure. Nevertheless, it needs to be clearly recognized that it is still only a limited portrayal of the true nature of the beast. The actual surveillance superstate, that the government is continually expanding, is almost completely hidden out-of-sight from the average U.S. citizen.

There is a frightening downside. The unprecedented capabilities of this superstate are now being unleashed on citizens as well as enemies. There is the hugely expensive TRAILBLAZER, which has been canceled, and the ongoing TURBULENCE programs at NSA. They are emplaced with minimal public exposure or input. Such programs are increasingly and inexorably disregarding our rights and liberties as Americans.

Even as this was being written, Congress authorized the FAA to allow the operation of drone surveillance aircraft all over the U.S., not just along the borders. It is estimated that there will be tens of thousands of drones in the skies, around the clock, across North America and the whole western hemisphere, by 2020. Nothing has been released publicly, even after a year of inquiries, as to who will use them, and for what purposes.

I have no quarrel whatsoever with advanced intelligence capabilities being employed to safeguard us against our actual enemies and adversaries. What is extremely dangerous about this capability and power is its increasingly unfettered and routine utilization anywhere and everywhere. That is something that the profoundly uninformed public does not realize. There is a dual agenda at work. The true debate should be about the difference between appropriate use of these capabilities versus actual and potential abuse. Because so much remains hidden out of sight and notice, there has never been a real public debate regarding either side of the issue. The abuse of these powers will increase every day while the People continue to be distracted.

In late 1986, I finally left the defense contracting business to work in the commercial sector. Even then, it was quite evident to me that the technologies of the surveillance superstate were far too attractive to remain sequestered within the boundaries of legitimate National Security and Defense concerns. It was obvious that they would be increasingly—**primarily because they could be**—used by the government against the citizens of this Country. Even before the passage of the PATRIOT Act, and the Intelligence Reform and Terrorism Prevention (IRTP) Act, those fears were all too real. Since then, the growth of the government's surveillance machinery has increased exponentially.

There are very obvious dangers of putting such powers under the control of anyone, even with proper oversight and accountability, and then naively expecting that they will not be misused, and then abused. History has demonstrated, time and time again, the truth of Lord Acton's famous observation that:

Power tends to corrupt; absolute power corrupts absolutely.

The chilling conclusions of *"The Stockholm Syndrome"* experiment, the psychological phenomenon also known as capture-bonding, must be taken very seriously. It certainly applies to the present relationship between the government and a large proportion of the citizenry. There are always rationalizations advanced by the abuser for abuse. Fixing the barn door, after the horse has bolted, is not the way to proceed in a Constitutional Republic, with its enshrined system of checks and balances. Orwellian Big Brother powers must be prevented from taking root in advance, instead of after-the-fact attempts to remedy them, when the damage has already occurred.

Even during the 1970s and the early 1980s, this dangerous shift to ever increasing abuses of surveillance capabilities had begun. We used our technological *"magic"* to monitor our allies, no longer focusing just on enemies and adversaries. And if we could get away with it, then why not do so? The self-justification was "what they didn't know couldn't hurt us, and that was all to the better, right?" Succumbing to the temptation to spy inevitably escalated into covert manipulations of allied governments. The consequences have already been seen, and they will continue. No officials of the U.S. government wish to discuss, or even acknowledge, such problems. Most of them have never been publicly disclosed. There are now very few whistle blowers willing to go public after the attacks on Thomas Andrews Drake, and a few other former NSA employees.

During the Cold War, certain training operations, such as *"Able Archer,"* nearly precipitated a Third Word War, because the inherent paranoia of the Soviet Union's leadership was being further exacerbated by U.S. manipulations. There is inherent risk in meddling in the affairs of others, instead of just holding them at bay as one's enemy or adversary.

Able Archer is the only reported incident but it was not unique. Even more dangerous is the ease of accomplishing palace intrigues in smaller and less powerful countries. Most people have little or no understanding of 'blowback,' a word used to describe the consequences of a covert or overt operation gone wrong, and the resultant damage, whether at home or abroad. If the activities by secretive and unaccountable branches of government are allowed to persist, it is a clear and present danger to us in this Country, and to the rest of the World.

The Causes and Effects of Blowback

The causes and the effects of blowback form a tiny part of public discourse. Since the 1970's, the U.S. Government's use of its real and perceived advantages in monitoring, archiving and analysis capabilities has increased our overseas interventionism. It was simply too tempting to resist engaging in covert manipulation of events in other countries, usually without any of it becoming common knowledge. That will prove to be a long-term detriment to our Country.

Zbigniew Brzezinski, National Security Advisor under President Carter, provided a few clues regarding the covert interventions by the U.S. in Afghanistan, Iran and Central Asia, between 1978 and 1985. Those tidbits were revealed in highly edited, semi-opaque interviews in Le Monde and CounterPunch magazines, and in TV talk shows after 1998. There is much more to those stories than anything yet disclosed anywhere in the media. The covert interventions had a large contributing effect on the events of 9/11. Only a few Americans have any clue as to the wide range and scope of U.S. interventionism overseas. The few cases, ever mentioned in the media, provide no more than the barest outline of what actually went on.

As a more visible example, there are criminal gangs that we now fight, inside and outside the United States, known as the Mara Salvatrucha (also called MS, Mara, MS-13 or M-18). They are scattered across Central America, Mexico and into the United States. They are the lineal descendants of the Nicaraguan Contras, the very ones that we armed and equipped during the Reagan administration to fight the Sandinistas. Remember the Iran-Contra scandal?

The Sandinistas owe their name to Augusto Ce′sar Sandino. During the first part of the 20th Century, Sandino witnessed the maltreatment of Nicaraguans, including his own family, by U.S. Marines invading and occupying his country on behalf of Standard Oil and the United Fruit Co. Those interventions began in 1912. The U.S. installed the puppet Somoza regime which oppressed the populace for 40 years, until it was finally overthrown by the Sandinistas.

Sandino began the resistance movement during the early stages of the invasion. Other U.S. military invasions took place between 1898-1934 in The Philippines, Mexico, Cuba, Haiti, Puerto Rico, Panama, Honduras and the Dominican Republic. Those actions by the U.S. led to the descriptive term *"Banana Republic,"* coined by the writer O. Henry in 1904. Ever since, the negative repercussions have persisted throughout the Western Hemisphere. Remember Noriega in Panama, the Duvalier family in Haiti and the Grenada incident in *"Operation Urgent Fury?"* Is anyone aware of our covert activities in Peru, Argentina, Ecuador and Chile?

Smedley D. Butler (1881-1940) rose to the rank of Major General and, at the time of his death, was the Marine Corps' most highly-decorated soldier. Butler was involved in, and even commanded, some of those interventions in Central America, the Caribbean, Europe, Asia and The Philippines. He grew very disenchanted with his role as a tool of imperialists. After retiring, Butler wrote *"War is a Racket,"* a booklet published in 1935. It detailed the manipulation of this Country's military forces by commercial interests in order to exploit those regions. This discreditable part of our history is largely unknown. Very little has been written about it. Interventionism, and its consequent blowback, has long and dishonorable precedent in our Country's foreign policy, just as General Butler documented, based on his own first hand experiences.

Another example of blowback was supporting and aiding the Mujehaddin, some of whom morphed into Al Qaeda and the Taliban. As part of their baggage, they brought along the Afghan poppy crops that provide the basic feedstock for the worldwide heroin trade. In the 1980s, they were 'freedom fighters.' By the 1990s and 2000s, the very same people had transitioned into *"terrorists."* The U.S. invasion in

41

Afghanistan has quickly returned that country to its premier status in the global heroin trade.

In light of these outrages, how could anyone be surprised by the blowback and hatred directed at the U.S.? It is the direct consequence of our spying, meddling, interdictions, interventionisms and invasions. There is a profound difference between defending our Country against our real enemies as opposed to harvesting the bad fruit of our own reckless foreign adventurism.

As will be further discussed in Chapters 3 and 4, similar involvement in 60 or more countries by the U.S. during the 20th Century, has created blowback coming out of the Middle East, Central Asia, Africa and South America. It is actually a miracle that we have escaped this long without suffering several additional major terrorist attacks.

Considering the revitalized, emergent modern version of "*Islamo-fascism*," and in light of the fertility rate of the Islamic culture, we have to do some deep thinking with regard to how true defense works, and how real security can be achieved. The current model is not working at all. Furthermore, it is exponentially more costly than it needs to be. That would seem to indicate that a very different form of "*Constructive Strategic Engagement*" and disengagement is required, rather than continuing to follow the Cold War tactics and strategy we used against The Soviet Union and its satellite countries.

Only those willing to be truly objective, can discern how U.S. interventionism itself is the underlying cause of so many instances of blowback directed at this Country. Despite the cover stories, and government justifications, interventionism overseas is nothing less than naked imperialism, whenever it suits our supposed 'interests.' That is not true American Exceptionalism at work. It has little to do with "*dealing with the realities of terrorism or evil*," as certain people in power would have the citizens believe. It is the U.S. Government's policies and actions that are having such an ill effect on our Country. Very few citizens, and virtually no politicians, appear to have the ability, desire or honesty to recognize the truth of the matter.

How Did This Happen?

To some, it might seem quaint to recall the Founding Father's views on self-defense, and their injunctions to refrain from overseas entanglements. How many American leaders or citizens, up until 1910, could have ever believed that the United States would devolve into the world's policeman and so-called *"nation-builder?"* Probably not a single one of them could have so imagined, even in their worst nightmares.

The Founders specifically and emphatically warned their descendants not to repeat the mistakes of History, the very ones that they had so carefully studied and considered. They hoped to ensure against those 'errors of intent' being repeated in the future by creating a strictly limited, constitutional form of government. They put their—apparently misplaced—trust in the citizens to continue to be informed, and to pro-actively participate in the political process.

Our current malaise has not happened because the World has suddenly become a more dangerous place. That is simply untrue. It is because we have wandered far off the course that the Founding Fathers charted for us. That wise and well-reasoned course was based on their profound understanding of human nature, something that has not changed since their days.

The World has always been a dangerous place. But today's actual risks do not require us to adopt the deeply flawed policies that we are currently employing. Not even the threat of Mutual Assured Destruction (MAD) during the Cold War caused the compromising of our foundational ideals and principles, now being routinely made in the name of the so-called Global War on Terror. Such compromises are emphatically not required to face the comparatively less dangerous threats of non-governmental entities, such as terrorists and gangsters.

The new threats to our Union should instead generate a much smarter, tougher and multi-disciplinary response. It should be based on careful and impartial examination of the root causes of actual, not imaginary, threats. Why are we allowing political and corporate opportunists the opportunity to exploit any real, or imagined, dangers to tighten their grip on us, and a large part of the globe, simply to satisfy their narrow and short-term interests at our moral and fiscal expense?

It is not the 'new' dangers that would have surprised the Founders. It would be our current methods of responding to them, both at home and overseas. The unrecognized negative implications for Our Country, by following such deeply flawed policies, are growing far too explicit to ignore any longer. Due to the reckless behavior of our leaders, enabled by the apathy and ignorance of the citizenry, those policies pose a massive threat to the future success of the American Experiment.

What Has Been Achieved?

Have all of our costly wars, interventions and manipulations made us happier and more prosperous? Well, perhaps happier, if one is on anti-depressants, which many citizens are! Or if it means achieving momentary prosperity, at the cost of piling up an enormous long-term debt, one that can never actually be paid off! The sad reality is that all our wars, interventions and manipulations have vastly increased our external threats, and our own internal social and economic danger.

How many people are aware that there are 45 U.S. military bases and installations surrounding Iran? In addition, there are aircraft carrier battle groups, submarines and numerous other warships, deployed throughout the Mediterranean, the Indian Ocean and the Persian Gulf. Think about the implications, especially as the calls continue for yet another intervention, yet another 'police action,' yet another potential war, this time in Iran, or Syria, or Yemen, or in the latest country to suddenly become our 'worst enemy.'

Americans are not actually paying ~$3.50 a gallon for gas and diesel fuel. There is actually a surcharge of $1-2 on every gallon pumped out of wells throughout the Middle East. The surcharge is being levied indirectly through taxes. It funds our overseas military presence in order to ensure that 30% of our oil continues to be available from the Middle East. Americans have in actuality been paying $4-6 a gallon gas for quite some time now.

It speaks volumes about the failure of our policies, and the attitude of those in power, that maintaining oil production, and our security, can supposedly only be ensured by military domination. Despite our desire to throw it all in a good light, we are the neighbor bully, and the neighborhood is the World.

Not only is such behavior contrary to our foundational ideals and principles, it is obviously contributing greatly to the impending insolvency and bankruptcy of this Country. Our government is acting in irresponsible ways that no individual citizen is permitted. Is this continuation of our ruinous path down to ethical, moral, financial and fiscal bankruptcy, the only way now open to us Americans to learn a very hard lesson?

There is also blowback right in our midst. It is damaging our society, in ways that no one could have previously believed possible. The Justice Department currently has a training program in place to 'deal with' mentally-ill combat veterans, who have become violently anti-social due to the post-traumatic effects of their tours of duty in our undeclared wars and interventions overseas. Local police, and SWAT teams, are ill-trained, inadequately equipped and unable to effectively 'negotiate' solutions for such 'out-of-control' veterans. Arrests of those veterans for violent crimes are increasing in communities across the Country.

Those charged with 'keeping the peace' are just as unprepared as we were for the returning Viet Nam combat veterans. In many cases, the only response is to shoot or incarcerate them, or go to the morgue where the Vets, and their victims, end up when they kill themselves and others. Our young veterans have the highest rates of suicide, domestic violence, drug abuse, alcoholism and homeless rates seen since Viet Nam, the previous time when we so dramatically ignored the real cost of overseas entanglements in undeclared wars. (Slate: "*Are Veterans More Suicidal Than Ever?*" September, 2011 and IAVA Report: "*Invisible Wounds,*" January, 2009)

Americans seem blind to the side effects on our military personnel. Citizens are easily manipulated to look the other way since most of them lack any military experience. They believe that the troops are being put in harm's way because "*they are protecting our freedoms.*" They go to ball games and attend parades where they cheer and wave small American flags to 'support our troops.' It is all utterly nonsensical.

45

Meanwhile, the Vets with Post Traumatic Stress Syndrome (PTSD), Traumatic Brain Injury (TBI), along with those physically maimed, unemployed, homeless and in trouble with the courts, continue to exist in our midst, without the real support that they need. They are mostly out-of-sight and out-of-mind. The comprehensive support systems needed for Vets are little better than any we have had before, during any of our undeclared wars in the past 100 years. The Veterans Administration admits that it has a backlog of 900,000 disability claims from Vets, with an error rate of nearly 1 in 5 while processing those claims! It often takes **two years** to process a vet's basic claim, and 6 months for a **mental health claim!**

Six-thousand-five-hundred Vets are committing suicide every year. That is almost **six times the average suicide rate** (per 100,000 in the population). This is utterly shameful. But the propaganda machine keeps the pseudo-patriots prattling on with their nonsense. A systematic evaluation of the true results of the last 60 years of U.S. Foreign and Defense policies is long overdue. It must be made. Too much has been swept under the rug for too long. A better approach would be to place the bar far higher with regard to any military involvements, overt or covert, just as mandated in the U.S. Constitution.

We Have to Fix the Mess We Have Allowed our Leaders to Make

To start the process, we should perhaps begin with an in-depth and comprehensive review of embassy traffic in and out of Kabul, Tehran, Islamabad, Ankara and other regional embassies (and intelligence sites). This might reveal where we went wrong in that region over the past 40 years. It alone might open the eyes of naive and ignorant citizens. Such an investigation should include our interaction with nearby allied and adversary military forces, and other intelligence operations inside Iran, Turkey, Iraq and other Middle East (ME) countries.

It would also require public testimony, under oath, from retired military intelligence personnel, State Department, NSA and CIA officers and agents, who worked in those countries and regions. It would require asking the right questions instead of the usual public whitewash. It would require extensively revising the Special Access Caveats and Exemptions

46

classification system. Otherwise, there can be no realistic 'lessons learned' conclusions drawn about the true nature of our activities and, especially, their consequences.

Records and testimony should be obtained from the Russians and former Soviets. Whatever could be found in the surviving Soviet archives about their Afghanistan invasion that contributed in taking down their "*evil empire*" would be very useful. Those records would be provided if it was made clear how badly the Russians would also look, if only one side of the story is presented.

Why is it vital for the American (and perhaps the Russian?) public to finally know what happened 30, 40 and even 50 or more years ago? It should be obvious. Until that happens, the American and Russian public is left only with the skewed 'official' versions. while attempting to make informed conclusion about current events still cloaked in 'official secrecy.' Obviously, nothing can be learned or gained from mistakes that are never revealed. Continued cover-ups, in the hope that time will keep all those events hidden and forgotten, is the epitome of stupidity! How can the People make the correct political judgments about how to govern our Country, if they do not have access to the facts, in order to discern the truth?

Vanishingly few elected officials, or people in the media, have made any serious attempts to sort out what really happens in our foreign relations. To do so would be political and positional suicide. I understand that sort of behavior coming from the Russians and ex-Soviets. I do not understand why we also behave that way. Perhaps it would reveal an unsavory picture of America, as an imperial power, that most seem unwilling to confront? The choice that most are making is to either aggressively deny, or passively ignore, the real implications of our policies.

Unfortunately, even Wikileaks has not revealed much of real substance. All the embassy traffic that Wikileaks has released so far contains no truly interesting station traffic at the "*Top Secret*" level and above. The vast majority of what was released is of the "*Secret NOFORN*" (meaning: no foreign dissemination) classification. Despite the predictions of political Armageddon by the pundits, the Wikileaks 'revelations' were more like a molehill than a mountain.

What actually happened? Independent reviews have already determined that very few of the documents obtained by Wikileaks did any real damage to anything. It was all information that had either been made public before, was known throughout diplomatic and government circles, or was of minor importance. The leaked documents did provide a superficial view of some bad behaviors that merited exposure, and did reveal the deaths of thousands of non-combatants in Iraq and Afghanistan.

I was fortunate to have developed a very early skill as a speed reader. The NSG training and associated work helped hone that skill even further. Keeping up and remembering masses of classified technical and analysis information, at a high level of comprehension, was required to do my job effectively. It also helped me to digest masses of other reports and technical data. That was a net positive advantage in my later commercial career.

While stationed in Japan, I took several International Law, Foreign Policy and Constitutional Law courses through the University of Maryland, via their extension campus in Tokyo. I wanted to have a way to gauge the distance between the academic world of foreign and defense policy being taught, and the reality that I was observing at first hand.

Those courses provided me with many interesting insights. Obviously, there had to be **some** distance between policy and fact. That only made sense. However, the gap between perception and reality, in how our foreign and defense affairs were actually being conducted, was a real eye opener. As for geo-political events of the past few years, it is easy to reach the conclusion that the gap has become much wider as our capabilities have grown, and officialdom has become even more insulated from reality and corrupted by the power at their disposal.

Answer the following questions for yourself:

How can a population of nearly completely uninformed citizens have any hope of making the right governance decisions? On what foundation of facts do they rely when voting and supporting the foreign and defense policies of a government that the People are supposed to control? How can they make informed decisions when they see so little of the reality of our foreign presence, past and present? How could they possibly know who to support in elections, and why they should, in guiding the policies of a free Republic?

At present, we are permitting and enabling a duplicitous and unaccountable *"just trust me"* government to prosecute both our foreign and domestic policies. That is definitely not how a free Republic should function.

During the Ford, and then the Carter Administrations, I watched what was going on at work every day, and then compared it to what my political science and law professors were saying at night. I read all the most current publications and journals covering Far Eastern and Asian foreign policy and international law that I could find. The disconnects between what I knew had actually happened, versus what I read in the academic texts and what was being taught in upper-level courses, were immediately and glaringly obvious. The public back home was being comprehensively and deliberately misled.

Those gaps between perceived and actual reality grew even larger in the 1980s and 1990s, as I watched the Reagan, and then the Bush 41, administrations continue in the same vein. The larger those gaps grew, the less informed were the corresponding decisions made by the citizens. Today, the gap is enormous. The consequences are also increasingly obvious. Just look, objectively, at the state of the Country.

A thorough review by Congress of that 30+ years ago period is mandatory. Revealing the government's internal decision-making process that led to the policies and actions taken in that region, that still remain completely classified, would greatly enlighten the American public. Any continued justification for keeping those activities classified needs to be questioned in detail. Those activities, and others made during the Carter, Reagan, Bush 41 and Clinton administrations, were largely responsible for the blowback that **led directly** to the destruction of the Twin Towers in New York, and the death of my friend and colleague Nancy Yuen-Ngo, and thousands of others. Yet, officialdom continues the denials and cover-ups.

It is a sad fact that is hard for me to forget.

It is not relevant whether or not the government had any foreknowledge of, or even a direct hand in, the 9/11 event, as many conspiracy theorists believe. The obvious fact is that the embedded government culture was already culpable. Its bad behavior has been manifested, time and time again, throughout the course of nearly a century. If not the destruction of the WTC, another attack would have occurred somewhere else, sooner or later. In fact, many attacks already had occurred in Lebanon, Africa, Lockerbie, Berlin, Indonesia, Cambodia, Iran and many other locations. It will occur again and again if this governmental behavior persists.

Throughout the World, we have created or supported monsters, Tin Pot dictators and Mad Hatters, to run countries at our behest, either as our surrogates or simply for convenience. Eventually, the regimes come apart at the seams and are replaced by our new adversaries, as for example, the Shah of Iran by the Ayatollah Khomeini. It is how South Viet Nam ended up with Nguyen Van Thieu and Nguyen Cao Ky. It is a very long list. To expect different outcomes while continuing such flawed and immoral behavior is to be either completely ignorant, or an outright denier, of the truth. Apologists are part of the looting class. We, our kids and grandkids foot the bill. The looters take the money and move on to the next opportunity.

Continuing to keep such occurrences classified, while denying that Islamic, or any other, terrorism is directed at America as part of blowback, actually proves that it is indeed blowback. *"Absence of evidence is not evidence of absence."* I personally have many reasons to know why that is true. The big fight that will ensue, if any real effort is made to release the information deliberately withheld for decades, involving thousands of events, will be just another indicator that certain powerful interests have no interest whatsoever in having their misdeeds and mistakes publicized.

However, that process of uncovering the truth must be accomplished soon if the 3rd stage of this Republic is to take hold and survive. It can be accomplished in ways that do not further jeopardize the present. Citizens just have to step-up, stop looking the other way, and cease believing the propaganda and misinformation produced **every day** by the government, and its kept media.

For the past three decades, it has been my contention that the longer the reality of our foreign and defense policies remains obscured or completely hidden, the worse the final outcome will be for this Country. It should be obvious that if the American public had any real idea about what their government (at the behest of Corporatists and Militarists) has actually been doing over the past century around much of the World, there would be a revolution starting tomorrow morning.

Well, perhaps not, since the population has, so far, been successfully kept in the dark. I ask the reader to simply connect together the events presented throughout this book, and then begin to understand that I am merely exposing the tip of the iceberg. There are massive systemic dysfunctions throughout our Republic requiring urgent attention and remedy!

Continuing to do the wrong things, simply because we can, is no justification whatsoever to continue doing so. That is the ugly truth hidden behind supposed 'national security considerations,' a cloak of hypocritical secrecy constantly invoked to keep such matters out of public view. To disclose the real truth endangers the established power and political status quo. Yet it would definitely benefit the People, whose actual safety and security would greatly improve.

Is This the Way America is Supposed to Work?

Do not mistake my critique as letting the worst enemies of freedom and liberty off the hook. We know who most of them are, despite the confusion in the public mind. There are clear and present dangers. Many of our real enemies are in the Russian Federation, the People's Republic of China, the rising Islamo-fascist movement, and among the other purveyors of totalitarianism, socialism and communism around the World, and within America.

They represent different levels of threat. But they are only part of the problem. We must resist being the pot calling the other kettles around the world "*black*." We need to take an honest and unflinching look at ourselves in order to focus on the real dangers, not on the perceived or imaginary external threats concocted to deflect the citizens' attention away from problems at home. Actually, the most dangerous of our threats are transitioning from external to internal ones, the consequences of our own flawed policies and actions, both at home and abroad.

We shoot ourselves in the foot by dismissing all the acts done in our name as being acceptable mistakes, simple errors, or regrettable necessities, simply because politicians point to external threats. Even if they are real, it is no excuse to abandon our own ideals and principles. The more we continue to do so, the more we become indistinguishable from those whom our leaders claim are *"enemies of freedom"* and *"evil doers."*

To continue to cover-up the secret, centralized control of our political agenda, here and abroad, is obviously a 'national security threat' all of its own. Those who want to continue doing so now represent a greater danger than most external ones.

Here are some thoughts on the subject by previous American leaders:

I know no safe depository of the ultimate powers of the society but the people themselves, [A]nd if we think them not enlightened enough to exercise their control with a wholesome discretion, the remedy is not to take it from them, but to inform their discretion by education. This is the true corrective of abuses of constitutional power.—Thomas Jefferson

America will never be destroyed from the outside. If we falter and lose our freedoms, it will be because we destroyed ourselves.—Abraham Lincoln

And even more directly to the point:

Shall we expect some transatlantic military giant, to step over the ocean, and crush us at a blow? Never! All the armies of Europe, Asia and Africa combined, with all the treasure of the earth (our own excepted) in their military chest; with a Bonaparte for a commander, could not by force, take a drink from the Ohio, or make a track on the Blue Ridge, in a trial of a Thousand years. At what point, then, is the approach of danger to be expected? I answer, if it ever reach us, it must spring up amongst us. It cannot come from abroad. If destruction be our lot, we must ourselves be its author and finisher. As a nation of freemen, we must live through all time, or die by suicide.—Abraham Lincoln

Do you think Jefferson and Lincoln were 'just kidding?'

Does any sort of nuclear capability in the hands of our enemies, change how we need to make it crystal clear to our enemies that we intend to always maintain a powerful and effective defense of this Country? No, it does not. Think it through. The same applies to Islamo-fascism. The events of 9/11 have been used to justify another huge increase in military spending, as opposed to maintaining a realistic strategic and tactical defense.

Remember the hope once expressed that we had reached "*the end of history*" after the conclusion of the Cold War? At that point, we supposedly could finally ramp down the Military Industrial Complex (MIC). That was an opportunity to more effectively adapt to a real and positive change in the past world order, not to create another one to dominate others.

Instead, everything went in exactly the opposite direction, driven by a threat that holds no comparison to the one that preceded it. Nothing we face in the World today can justify the American and other lives lost, and the tens of billions misspent every year. Nor can it justify the loss of individual freedoms and liberties at home. The MIC has morphed into the even more-bloated MIISSC. The instigators had to find, or create, even more hobgoblins, more external threats, to maintain the fiction that they are indispensable and 'protecting' us.

The central fact is that this huge expansion is one of the principal reasons why we are effectively bankrupt. That is a far greater risk to our long-term security than any current adversaries or enemies.

The control games of the insiders in politics, and Big Business, are not just bad for our moral and ethical health as a Country. Funding every cockamamie idea or weapon system for 'national security reasons' is not in our strategic interest. It accelerates the erosion of our civil liberties, resulting in routine intrusions into our private lives with no practical benefits. Our foolish descent into bankruptcy vastly decreases our 'national security' and endangers the personal safety of Americans traveling around the World, too.

The Global War on Terror (GWOT) is perverting and subverting our own wellbeing as a People, and as a Country. The GWOT is now militarizing other federal and civilian law enforcement agencies. As a result, they are no longer exercising the role of 'peace officer' acting on behalf of the citizens. The growing militarization of our local and state police is also subtly nationalizing them. It is speeding up unwholesome changes in every civilian and government entity charged with the role of being *"gatekeepers."* It is instead transforming them into *"enforcers"* and oppressors.

Deny it if you wish, but American citizens are now treated as part of the enemy who are automatically guilty until proven innocent. ("Global ..." includes the USA). Read the reports coming out of the Homeland Security Administration. Look at the effects of the PATRIOT Act, recent Executive Orders and the National Defense Authorization Act (NDAA). Look at the behavior of far too many police officers as they disrespect citizens rights. The rights of those citizens, encountered on a routine basis, are now considered to be 'optional' or non-existent.

It is undeniable, and absolutely no coincidence, that our government's *"War on Everything,"* and seemingly everyone, is now practically synonymous with the words *"United States"* throughout much of the World. This perception is also becoming Standard Operating Procedure here at home. Is the obvious fallacy and lunacy of *"perpetual war for perpetual peace"* really so hard to see? Is locking up an even larger percentage of the domestic population actually a better solution than providing real freedom and liberty so they can be happier and more productive?

Who Benefits?

It is not hard to prove that the Global War on Terror is nothing more than a handy excuse for more funding of the MIISSC, and the banking-corporatist and prison cartels. Just look at the billions of dollars spent on

54

ludicrous contracts that fund and profit developers of all sorts of useless systems, of little or zero actual value, in this supposed Global War on Terror. Tens of billions have been wasted in this way.

Billions are being spent on contracts for glorified security guards to harass, and thus train people to submit, at every airport, train and bus station, and on the roads and highways. Billions are being spent on useless scanners, software and drones. Tens of billions are being wasted on *"nation-building"* and erecting even more military bases and $700 million embassies. Additional billions are being wasted on projects that are never even completed. An estimated 50 to 60 billion dollars has been wasted in Iraq and Afghanistan alone. Billions more are being wasted in the futile and pointless War on Drugs.

There is another aspect to the problem that was clearly understood by M. Tulius Cicero, over 2000 years ago, during the Roman Republic:

A bureaucrat is the most despicable of men, though he is needed as vultures are needed, but one hardly admires vultures whom bureaucrats so strangely resemble. I have yet to meet a bureaucrat who was not petty, dull, almost witless, crafty or stupid, an oppressor or a thief, a holder of little authority in which he delights, as a boy delights in possessing a vicious dog. Who can trust such creatures?

The huge expansion of uncontrolled bureaucracy is easily seen at our local HSA, DEA, TSA, BATFE, or IRS offices. Not much has changed in human behavior during the past 2000 years. What sort of people seeks such jobs?

It is interesting that the Israelis, who have dealt with survival since the inception of their state, employ none of our idiotic airport or transportation technologies, and support personnel, to make travel safer or maintain border security. So why do we? It is those contracts, baby, those big fat contracts!

The destruction of the Twin Towers in 2001 was exactly the *"new Pearl Harbor event"* required by the authors of the Project for the New American Century (PNAC). In their words, not mine:

... to start the process of transformation, even if it brings revolutionary change (to the United States) ...

"*Transformation?*" That sounds like an Obama line. Strange how President Obama's promise when he took office of "*fundamentally transforming America*" echoes the aims of the Project for the New American Century, and the insiders in the Bush 43 administration, is it not? Neither were talking about transforming the way the U.S. Constitution is followed. Or, perhaps they were! Once co-opted to do the dirty work of their superiors, they are now bound to justify those actions as being somehow honorable and right, so they fall into the trap used by all manipulators.

Lord Acton's warning that "*Power tends to corrupt; absolute power corrupts absolutely*" has literally become the definition for what has happened in "*Amerika.*" It fully explains the rise and fall of the '2nd Republic.'

Without detailing every single incident, even without the benefit of access to secret archives, it is well known that ever since the Spanish-American War, various United States governments have used pretexts, provocation, prevarication and manufactured incidents (known as "*false flag*" events) to enter every war in the 20th Century.

A clear pattern has been consistently maintained from the so-called "*attack*" on the USS Maine in Havana Harbor in 1898 that led to the Spanish-American War, to the sinking of HMS Lusitania that contributed to our entry in WWI, to the provocation of the Japanese that led to Pearl Harbor, to Syngman Rhee's constant threats to invade North Korea that led to the pre-emptive invasion of South Korea by the communists, to the USS Maddox "*Gulf of Tonkin*" incident that expanded our interventionism in Viet Nam into a bloody and futile war, and to the "*yellowcake*" and WMD pretexts that lead to the invasion and war in Iraq.

Franklin D. Roosevelt and the Pearl Harbor Attack is a subject all of its own. "*The Pearl Harbor Myth: Rethinking the Unthinkable*" by George Victor (2008), exhaustively documents who knew what, and when they knew it, from Roosevelt on down throughout his administration. It is important to note that the author is a supporter of Roosevelt, yet he still honestly documents the real truth. It is abundantly clear that FDR's administration manipulated the Japanese into war with the U.S. to facilitate our entrance into the European War. That involvement was adamantly opposed by the American public until the provoked Japanese mounted their 'preemptive' attack.

In each of these wars, imperialists within and outside the U.S. government, **employing the skillful use of propaganda** to mobilize public opinion, sought to acquire territory, and further their own political agendas along with corporate and economic interests. The documentation is available and comprehensive. It is all there for the knowing, if one only makes the effort. It is outright denial, along with both unwitting and purposeful *"dumbing down"* in schools and by the media, that blinds the citizenry from understanding the true scope and nature of our overseas involvements. The manipulators know that the public at large is ignorant and easily duped. They utterly depend on it.

It is truly horrifying to realize that my own ancestors, with countless others at home and abroad, often suffered and died unnecessarily throughout the 20th Century. That was due to domestic and foreign manipulators, corrupted by power and unaccountable for their actions. They were only dedicated to their own very narrow and selfish interests, despite the consequences for others and this Country. Since the past is now gone beyond recall, what is even more horrifying is to imagine the millions yet unborn who will suffer in the wars and economic upheavals that will be unleashed if this madness continues.

This is not a pretty picture. The original ideal of American Exceptionalism has been supplanted and perverted into something that can only be called *"Amerikan Destructionism."* Such behavior is completely and utterly unacceptable in a free Republic. It took me a long time to accept the full truth about the change of course of our governance in the 20th Century. Those that love and profit from war **must be stopped**. There is no denying the record, once one is willing to examine it objectively.

There was no predisposition in my background to be anti-government. In fact, just the opposite. However, wars must only be fought for the absolutely correct reasons. Compromising our Country's ethics from the very beginning is not the way to go to war. Early in life, I believed that the basic goodness of our People translated over into the government. I no longer do. The expansive Warfare/Welfare government continues to attract far too many of the wrong personality types.

Again and again, my own personal experiences, observations and research brought me to the point of accepting the unpalatable truth. The actions of a succession of misguided, perverse and outrightly subversive government control-freaks have brought the Country we love to the brink of disaster, if not catastrophe. The lamentable record of both major ideological parties is far too long and comprehensive to be denied.

The great mass of individuals in the general population of this country still holds true to its fundamental beliefs and good intentions. However, most of them are nearly completely misinformed, or clueless, about the many unprincipled individuals who enter and remain in government service. Unfortunately, it is mostly because **citizens choose to be uninformed**. Politicians, and apologists for the government, label anyone as unpatriotic when they ask awkward questions regarding governance and policy. The Federal Government system has been corrupted to the point that it can no longer be considered benevolent, in any sense of that word.

The Founders repeatedly warned of duplicity by the government. The average American wants to continue to believe that the 'public servants' in Washington, D.C., are there to serve the citizens. Some still do serve with honor and integrity, but they are now all too few in number. The purposeful confusion of government with Country only serves the special interests that have seized control of the political and economic system.

In *Thus Spoke Zarathustra,*" Frederich Nietzche wrote "*I, the State, am the People!*" in his ongoing criticism of the then German Empire. Unfortunately, that same phrase now also seems to be applicable to America.

At the policy level in government service, there remains a small number who still believe in the practice of true American Exceptionalism. Unfortunately, a large proportion of those at the top of the bureaucratic structure do not, having been compromised and seduced by power and avarice. In the ranks, many government employees and military service personnel just do what they are told. They do not think much about either the benevolence or the malevolence of what they perform. They simply want to do their jobs and then, at the end of the day, go home to rest and enjoy their families and neighbors. That is how empires are built and die, by the admixture of the mistakes made by corrupted leadership, and the complacency and weariness of the foot soldiers and the lower echelon workers in the bureaucracies.

Sadly, the top players and controllers within the Federal Government, and in the enabling political structure, have been systemically corrupted by power, greed and the desire to maintain control, over both the home front and our vast global empire. The recent Secret Service, FBI, GSA, DoJ, BATFE and similar scandals are just the surface view of their frequent and highly immoral misbehaviors.

This was not supposed to happen. We must not emulate, and fall into ruin, like every other oppressive regime in history. We are better than that, and were given every advantage by the Founders to be the exception to the rule.

We no longer have a government "*of, by and for the people.*" A nearly $4 trillion annual budget offers far too many opportunities for adventurism in far too many places in the Warfare/Welfare state. A $4 trillion budget might be affordable in an economic system with a GDP growing past $22 to 24 trillion. It is not possible in a GDP of $15 trillion that is effectively stagnant. Virtually unlimited deficit spending facilitates misbehavior in government. Too many of those in leadership roles in the Federal Government are only serving their own private purposes by enabling the MIISSC, and an enormous distributionist state, at the expense of the People.

President Eisenhower's warning 50 years ago, about the Military Industrial Complex, seems almost quaint and naive today. He was right, of course. I have seen it with my own eyes in the government and the MIISSC, and then saw it paralleled in the financial and banking industry in the present monetary system.

These cancers in the Body Politic must soon be excised. Otherwise, our Republic will be lost, perhaps forever.

3

Feeding the Rich, Starving the Poor
and Calling It "Capitalism"

*Corruption is worse than prostitution. The latter might endanger
the morals of an individual, the former invariably endangers
the morals of the entire country.*
–Karl Kraus (1874-1936)

*A government, for protecting business only, is but a carcass,
and soon falls by its own corruption and decay*
–Amos Bronson Alcott (1799-1888)

During the late 1980s through the 1990s, my consulting firm provided technical process consulting, design and engineering services for nearly half of the Fortune Top 50 companies. Many of them had a working presence, or were actually located, in New York.

In addition, we also worked on a significant number of *"infrastructure projects"* for large industrial, financial, technology firms and government entities in the Boston-to-Washington corridor. My work took me into large firms throughout the Midwest and to the West Coast. Those projects implemented a number of large scale networks for a significant portion of the information infrastructure of the United States during that period. Many have since been upgraded, some more than once.

During my career in the large-scale network IT business, I met many brilliant people. That led to an interesting insight about two distinguishing characteristics in them. I realized that such people are rarely both highly intelligent and 'street smart' simultaneously. In those infrequent cases when those two attributes are combined in one person, it can result in great achievement—people who are almost transcendent in both ability and accomplishment—and even genius. I closely observed those people to learn everything that I could from their behavior and conduct.

For 15 years, we provided consulting services at the senior executive level for many national and multi-national companies. In some cases, we worked directly with the Chief Executive Officer (CEO). The initial task of my partners and colleagues was firstly to produce, and secondly to condense, the reams of technical and organizational data required to prepare executive summaries of large-scale projects.

Our job then focused on clearly describing how to successfully implement our recommendations at the technical, functional and business level. In that environment, it is important to be very familiar with the formulation and decision-making process at the very top of large organizations.

We met some quite interesting personalities in different aspects of the business, on both sides of the technical and operational divide. One of the most memorable was Fred Smith, Founder and CEO of Federal Express. It was a distinct pleasure to be interviewed by Mr. Smith when I was hired by FedEx. The company is one of the most innovative, best-organized and better-managed companies in the World. I thoroughly enjoyed my time there.

On the other side of the coin, I also soon discovered that there were a surprising number of corrupt 'leaders' in the corporate system, something that really shocked me. I had gone into the commercial world hoping for something better and different than the unwholesome changes taking place in the MIISSC. Usually, these corrupted men and women in Big Business were much less talented but far more manipulative. Some of them could actually be described as being on the 'dark side.' They were fewer in number during my early experiences in the corporate world but more and more of them appeared throughout the 1990s.

The misbehaviors of such bad players in leadership positions were often viewed as positive attributes by their peer group and many subordinates. Those individuals were called 'aggressive' and 'driven.' However, from my vantage point, the harm that they did, compared to their 'contributions,' seemed to be clearly negative and counter-productive. Subsequent events have proven the truth of my observations.

The System

As I observed the inner workings of *"The System,"* I saw how large corporatist constructs will inherently create more and more corruption, particularly in the banking and financial sector. That was a direct consequence arising from the expansion of their own bureaucracies that were increasingly attuned closely to government regulations and monetary policy. It seems only too obvious in retrospect but, 20 years ago, it was not so easily discerned.

The time that I spent earlier in life, dealing with livestock, proved useful when coping with such a reality. Having had my teeth kicked in and ribs bruised, being crushed against stock fences, eating dirt and being splattered with manure, turned out to be handy experiences! It was especially useful for maintaining my perspective when dealing with the unattractive types who infest the political, government, and business arenas where I worked.

I found that bad players are similar, at certain levels, to farm and ranch animals. Some of them have no inkling about what they are doing and need to be 'prodded' or guided into correct behavior. Others were poorly trained and so required complete retraining. The worst needed to be hit on the head with a 2x4, neutered or even put down. (In the latter case, their human counterparts need to be removed from their positions and sent to jail for their crimes).

We have quite a number of the last type in the socio-political and business systems today. They exist at all organizational levels. Their goal seems to use fear, intimidation and borderline (or over-the-line) psychotic behavior to maintain their positions rather than doing something positive, or making something useful. Every successive scandal, every case of fraud and corruption that comes to light in the corporatist and government structure, only serves to underline that such people are omnipresent, like vermin.

We have yet to penetrate the surface of what has happened and continues to happen. We need a thorough investigation and examination of their misbehavior. At present, most such malefactors are never brought to account.

So few ever seem to go to jail. One might say: "*But we convicted Bernie Madoff, Allen Stanford and Rajat Gupta!*" OK, then name five more. Madoff, Stanford and Gupta are petty crooks compared to the hundreds to thousands of real criminals still running free. Stanford, like our current President, appears to be a pathological narcissist. Many corporatists (and politicians!) seem to suffer from some form of Narcissistic Personality Disorder (NPD).

At this point in time, to be brutally frank, there is very little honor and integrity left in many parts of the "*The System.*" The rot is spreading like mold through many corporations, and the constituent parts of the Federal Government—the Executive, the Legislature and the Judiciary. In each case, there are office buildings full of arrogant and unaccountable individuals in positions of power. A descriptive term for them is "*aggressive looters.*" A friend calls them "*Assholes With Power*" (AWP). As the moral hazards inherent in the unbalanced hyper-regulatory state increase, so do their numbers.

Recently, a new word appeared that can be readily applied equally in the government and corporatist sector:

Ineptocracy: *a system of government (or corporatism) where the least capable to lead are elected (or appointed) by the least capable of producing, and where the members of society least likely to sustain themselves or succeed, are rewarded with goods, services and compensation paid for by the confiscated wealth of a diminishing number of true producers.*

That pretty well sums it up, does it not? My partners and I had a pretty deep stake in the networking and information technology business. We had many promising business ventures in the pipeline up until 2000. However, things had happened along the way that altered my perception of America, the government and the present nature of the so-called 'capitalist' system.

For one thing, there is obviously little true capitalism in the now economically unsound and overbuilt banking and financial sector. More and more, that sector is synonymous with successive looting and pillaging. A friend recently introduced me to another term employed in the study of animal and insect behaviors that seems highly appropriate in describing the behavior of many in the financial sector: **kleptoparasite.**

The large financial and banking sectors have been co-opted and taken over by an increasing number of kleptoparasites.

In 2000, I finally pulled the plug on our business in New York. We unilaterally terminated, or let our remaining contracts naturally expire, as it became ever more obvious that some very negative events were about to transpire in the financial and banking sector. That was evident from the types of financial trading and exchange systems being designed, and for whom they were being built. We decided that we were no longer willing to enable the kleptoparasites with our system engineering skills and intellectual resources.

Others might do so, but we would not. I was called a fool to my face for giving up so much money. In actuality, I would not have managed to do many things in my life if I had been solely motivated by money. Nor for that matter, would I be free to speak, write and act as my conscience dictates.

There is still a productive wealth sector with honest players but their numbers are steadily dwindling. There are still companies and ventures producing real goods and essential services that feed the economy, provide real jobs and enable true wealth creation. The nimblest and most creative will survive the coming massive restructuring, as the fittest usually do. However, the depraved and insatiable hyper-regulatory state will still drive a number of them out of business, no matter how superior their product or services might be.

Our main concern should be focused on the bad players in the central bank, financial and corporatist sector whose primary purpose is making money-on-money, by manipulating and milking the financial and exchange markets. I am also deeply concerned by those that feed off the runaway MIISSC, that voracious cuckoo fledgling that has been deposited in the American Nest. It is a bird whose wings are the two political parties, the Democrats and the Republicans, almost equally culpable for the morass in which this once great Country finds itself.

Since 1971, a growing segment of what used to be a viable capitalist banking and investment system, especially before 1930, was morphing into an artificial, crony-corporatist form hard to classify as 'capitalism' by any objective measure. It has become a corporatist system of patronage via governmental favoritism and central bank interventionism. The Federal Reserve's unholy interactions with the kleptoparasitic banking cartel is clear and unmistakable. That is clearly observed in the massive growth of the 'financial services' sector since the abandonment of the gold standard in August, 1971.

Prior to that, from the beginning of the 20th Century, at no point had anything that could even be loosely described as the *"financial services"* sector (making money-on-money) ever contributed more than 7-8% to the GDP. Yet, at the height of the financial sector's profligate growth by 2006, its portion of GDP was nearly 30%! Only cheap, easy fiat money, a rigged tax system and a hyper-regulatory environment, creating a tempting array of moral hazards for the corrupt to exploit, made that possible.

Making money-on-money, instead of true productive wealth creation, reached its zenith in 2006. In the process, it had sucked (or suckered) almost everyone into its seductive 'easy money' machinery. In accordance with Gresham's Law—that bad money forces out the good—it had long before forced the *"good"* money out. Malinvestment reigned supreme. It had manifested itself in a series of growing financial bubbles ever since 1971, something that only a Fed banker, or a Keynesian economist, could condone and love. The Facebook IPO fiasco of 2012 was a simple case of déjà vu.

When all is said and done, and the Grand Correction is completed, we should expect that the artificially engorged financial sector will correct back to pre-1971 levels. The Federal Reserve's injection of 'air' still has to be released. Lest there be any doubt left, **the source of all this is the Federal Reserve,** created by its counter-cyclic manipulation of interest rates, and the injection of fake money and credit into the economic system and the government. The *"cheap and easy money"* supply is at the root of the issue. Never let the Fed apologists deflect attention away from that key point.

Such behavior is indeed a modern form of *"fascism."* The government and its institutions are ignoring the natural market rules of the private sector, selecting winners and losers, and disregarding the constraints of the Constitution. It is abrogating the letter and spirit of the Law as it guts our Republic. It is therefore a variant form of fascism. Accordingly, I refer to our present day reality as *"living in Amerika."*

Amerika crystallized into recognizable form when President George W. Bush, on December 17, 2008, stated that he had:

… abandoned free market principles in order to save the free market system.

As Bugs Bunny might have retorted:

What a Maroon!

Bush turned out to be just another shill, not a true leader of vision and strong moral character. His pronouncement should go down in history as the second crassest quotation of the last 50 years with regard to a free market economy. It is only surpassed by Richard Nixon's statement, after abandoning the Gold Standard in 1971, that:

We are all Keynesians now!

Americans vs. Amerikans

Those Orwellian, Big Brother statements starkly reveal the usurpation of the original American system and its replacement by the **Amerikan** system. Will the usurpers also abandon the Republic's foundational ideals and principles in order to *'save'* it? The patient died but was cured! The coffin that President Nixon built with fiat currency, and petrodollar recycling, put the corpse of our economy on open display, and the second President Bush closed the lid and nailed it shut.

During the 1970s through the 1990s, my varied experiences allowed me to observe much of this coming. Firstly, by witnessing the dominating and deleterious nature of the MIISSC. Secondly, by witnessing the corrupt corporate, commercial banking and financial practices of the 1990s and early 2000s.

If it is not already clear, let us leave no doubt whatsoever. The banking and financial markets are nothing less than a giant electronic game of chance where the house always wins. There is very little integrity left in computerized financial markets. Front-running *"Flash crashes,"* rigged exchanges and manipulated high-frequency trading are endemic and are now embedded, systemic functions of the global financial markets. The technologists essentially built a gigantic electronic casino for the financial services and large bank sector. It was borrowed from, and built upon, the technologies created for the security-surveillance super-state during the 1970s and 1980s.

Unfortunately, even supposedly sophisticated Americans, those who should know better, many with real capital wealth to invest, went along with the game while it was still 'profitable.' Very few really knew (or cared, it seems) about the real price to be paid, with costs that go far beyond the usual definition of deficits and debts, and enduring a little blowback, now and then. The truth becomes very inconvenient when it goes against conventional wisdom. However, the truth is still the truth. Americans need to embrace the truth. Otherwise, we are left without a fighting chance to return to sound fiscal practices and restore the Republic to its founding ideals and principles.

Many of our fellow citizens have already become *"Amerikans"* in thought and deed. They are the Neo-Conservative Nationalist and the Neo-Liberal Progressive factions of the two major political parties. Both factions believe in the desirability of a security and surveillance state, just as they do in a warfare and welfare state. Despite all the public posturing, there are only minor actual differences between the two constituent parts of the political duopoly. Voting records speak much louder than empty public rhetoric. It is essential for both factions that the vast majority of voters remain confused and ignorant.

The factions pretend to be two parties but ideologically, and in practice, they essentially operate as one party with two outward wings. *"Two wings of the same bird of prey,"* as Butler Shaffer describes it. They exalt Big Government and more control in the hands of the few power elite. This is a familiar pattern seen time and time again in human affairs, always culminating in totalitarianism, humanity's greatest threat to itself, and a clear and present danger to all of us.

The rest of the "*Amerikans*" are the large number of poorly informed Republicans, Democrats and Independents, who are easily duped by cynical political operatives. Just observe how they behave! They are like dumb, but inherently powerful, animals led meekly around on tethers attached to nose rings.

The panoply of artificial 'benefits,' created by the welfare, warfare and security state, inexorably drives the growth of government forever upward. The 'benefits' are actually the nose rings that keep the citizens passive and apathetic. Get a critical mass of the population on the Welfare/Warfare payroll and who is going to criticize it? The central flaw in this scheme is that the Fed-fueled deficit gravy train is running off the tracks, in a slow-motion train wreck.

The technologies developed, and the accompanying morally hazardous opportunities thus created, are supposedly ensuring our national security. But they are far too attractive not to be used by the Narcissistic Personality Disorder (NPD) afflicted and the control-freaks embedded in the security-surveillance state. Those same technologies at their command also gave us cells phones, iPads, iPhones, tablets, Kindles, Blackberries, Facebook, Twitter, etc. They are all tied to the Internet and dependent on it. Inevitably, that dependency has given rise to a myriad of surveillance capabilities and techniques now being exploited by the security state.

Watching the Blowback In Our Faces

The events of 9/11, and ever since, are **evidence of nothing else but blowback.** Even though the vast majority of our leaders, and Amerikans, still want to deny it, blowback is coming from all directions. As per usual, the deniers realize that "*a good defense is a good offense*" so they go on the attack. They attach a label of "*Blame America First*" on those who see, understand and comment on what is really happening. Their fake patriotic zeal cannot disguise that Amerika is only reaping what was sown by corrupt and inept leadership with deeply flawed policies, both at home and abroad.

In March of 2003, I wrote an essay, part of which later became the Foreword to the book *"Petrodollar Warfare,"* by William Clark (published in 2005):

The World changed forever on September 11, 2001. It could have changed America in ways that (could) have assured she remained in the ranks of the truly enlightened, liberated nations of Western Civilization. Instead, it seems that opportunity and promise have largely been squandered with a vengeance.

The world changed again on March 19, 2003, with the U.S.-led invasion of Iraq. It is almost assured, unless quick action is taken, that this century will become one of fear, oppression, and economic decline for our nation. Our leaders, of both the Republican and Democratic parties, have continued the pattern of self-destructive behavior practiced with increasing disregard of our original purpose and promise as a nation.

The 20th Century has often been called "The American Century." To be sure, America has much to be proud of from the last century....Our development of the majority of modern technology and infrastructure driving the world to increasing wealth realization had no equal. Until (relatively) recently, our system of distributing the wealth provided by that infrastructure has been the most advanced model ever provided. We are about to throw it all away.

Our increasing tendency to push our (political) model rigidly into other (countries) of the world is in fact the sign of an authoritarian state. That is coupled with a foreign policy that seeks to protect that state's corporate interests through manipulation and intimidation of other governments, directly or through surrogates, backed with both overt and covert projections of military power and intelligence capability.

This face of the American presence in the world is too little talked about or analyzed by the citizens of the United States and especially [by] the general media. Most of it is shielded from view through the system of government security classification measures.

From the late 1940s to the 1980s, for good or ill, many of those force projections were driven by Cold War politics. Our ongoing shoving match with the Soviet Union protected some countries but trampled many smaller countries underfoot. In addition, the adventurism and empires of some of our closest allies have contributed, part and parcel, to our involvement in attempts to control other parts of the globe where our interests are not vital. These are facts, not judgments.

The al-Qaeda attack of September 11, 2001, finally provided the pretext to fully open Pandora's Box. That enabled the unfettered and routine use of all the malevolent technologies of the security and surveillance apparatus. It coincided with the exact point in this Country's history, when the culmination of long-term fiscal and financial folly may finally plunge us into the economic abyss.

Awakening from Slumber

By now, any sane and impartial observer would have concluded that Amerika, in its present fiscal and financial mess, has neither the resources nor the moral authority to *"export democracy"* and *"nation-build."* The fact we attempt to do so is obviously insane and would only merit being laughed off the world stage if tried by any other country. That such a conclusion has not yet been reached, except by a very small fraction of our citizens, is indeed frightening.

The hegemony of the U.S. Dollar, coupled with the Federal Reserve's continuing efforts to devalue our currency, floated artificially by *"petrodollar recycling,"* actually makes the U.S. the world's largest currency and economic manipulator, not China. Amerikan political and media propagandists constantly misdirect the population into believing that China, and other countries, are the supreme practitioners of currency and economic manipulation. Self-evidently, that is not true. The U.S. supplies the world's reserve currency, not China or any other country.

The ongoing operations of the Federal Reserve and Petrodollar recycling, the escalating funding of the MIISSC, tied to the misdeeds of the financial services and banking sector, clearly indicate that the Country is in thrall to a monopolistic banking and corporate super-cartel. It continues to manipulate our currency, and it has enabled a corporatist system that only benefits a tiny group of insiders.

Americans must soon awake from their collective stupor, and objectively review and understand the history of the past 100 years. Only then will they see the truth of why blowback is coming in from all sides.

If you think it is bad now, *"Baby, you ain't seen nothing yet."*

4

What Are We Doing Wrong?

Every time history repeats itself, the price of the lessons goes up.
–Anonymous

*The whole aim of practical politics is to keep the populace alarmed
(and hence clamorous to be led to safety) by menacing it with
an endless series of hobgoblins, all of them imaginary.*
–H.L. Mencken

So what are we doing wrong? The answers are nowhere near as simplistic as: "*They hate us because we're free,*" or "*They hate us because we're capitalists*" or "*They hate us because we practice freedom of religion*" or any other such nonsense. Such shallow thinking displays a profound ignorance and confusion. The underlying causes of the hatred directed at Amerika require some critical analysis, not thoughtless knee-jerk reactions.

The phrase "*Clash of Civilizations*" is often used by people who have looked somewhat deeper. That theory, first proposed by political scientist Samuel Huntington, is that cultural and religious identities are now the primary source of conflict in the post-Cold War period. There is an obvious element of truth in this theory. After all, Western Civilization and Christianity have been clashing with Islam for many years, ever since the 8th Century. However, it is highly unlikely that notion is uppermost in the minds of most of Amerika's antagonists, other than *fundamentalist Jihadists*. People tend to forget, that there still remain far more serious and dangerous enemies of this Country, than Islamic terrorists inflamed with 'theological' zeal.

In point of fact, much of the enmity is the direct consequence of our overseas meddling, interventions and wars over the past 100 years. That is in turn exacerbated by the fundamentalists own intertwined religio-political thinking, principally in the Middle East and Central Asia. While the applicability of Huntington's theory is hotly debated, it remains in the realm of speculation until we build a strategic and tactical defense that is **not** based on a large and provocative military presence, spread across nearly every corner of the globe.

For example, in Asia, Africa, the Middle, Central and Far East, think of it from the point of view of any of the region's poor with **nothing but their religion to hold onto.** They are the ones trampled under "*the feet of fighting elephants.*" They are the ones who are the "*collateral damage*" in the fighting. They have little to fight back with except in those instances when they acquire arms from one of the "*elephants.*" Many of the region's "*angry young men*" are riled up because of joblessness and lack of any real opportunities. Some are co-opted by the local dictators and become their enforcers. Others, also having nothing (literally and figuratively) better to do, become eager recruits in virtually any resistance movement that comes along. In fact, it is natural for them to do so. From their vantage point, it is no different than it was for those in Occupied Europe, who joined the Resistance against the Nazis during WWII.

The situation is ripe for every sort of tin pot, crackpot and megalomaniac dictator to gain a foothold. Over the past 100 years, even in countries where overt conflict did not occur, millions of people became powerless pawns suffering under the oppression of dictators and tyrants, the proxies and puppets of powerful nations and special interests, primarily Amerikan. The Amerika that they see is very different than the hackneyed media portrayal of a benevolent and philanthropic America that is presented for domestic consumption, and promoted by propaganda outlets such as Radio Free America.

It is a portrayal that many in the U.S. may still innocently cherish, since it cunningly exploits the best and noblest American impulses to support the underdog, and give generously to others in bad times.

A quick read-through of Michael Scheuer's book "*Imperial Hubris: Why the West is Losing the War on Terror,*" published in 2004, will provide proper perspective. To get a view as to why the war in Iraq, and the subsequent reconstruction, went so far off course, including any semblance of fiscal and budgetary sanity, read *"Imperial Life in the Emerald City,"* by Rajiv Chandrasekaran, published in 2007. Observe how the Iraq and Afghanistan situations continue to deteriorate everyday with bombings and killings, resulting in ever greater political instability. All this should be proof enough that our policies are not working.

The result of our many provocations is a no-win situation. We have no choice but to protect ourselves from the very enemies that we so casually created and continue to create. Resistance from the resident citizens is simply a predictable result of our repeated short-sighted interventions, even when our international interests were never at risk. These interventions were, and are, largely unknown to the American public. Be aware that there are two levels of engagement—the visible and the invisible—the overt and the covert.

The many repeated interventions around the globe are responsible for our *"Ugly American"* caricature. Remember the *"Yankee Go Home"* slogans painted on buildings and walls in many countries throughout the past half-century?

There is so much that is unseen and unknown, hidden from the American public.

Again, from the Foreword to *"Petrodollar Warfare"* in 2005:

Why is Iran today run by the Ayatollahs? Because the U.S. and UK covertly overthrew Iran's fledgling democracy in 1953 and installed Mohammed Reza Shah Pahlavi—the Shah—in power. The CIA and other American interests also created and supported Osama bin-Laden and his organization in Afghanistan throughout the 1980s, calling them "freedom fighters."

Our government has manipulated, (and) controlled many governments throughout Central and South America with shocking hypocrisy, in total contradiction to our supposed "American Values." That behavior led to their peoples' ever-increasing distrust because we arrogantly meddled in their internal affairs. Among them are Argentina, Colombia, Chile, Ecuador, Guatemala, Haiti, Nicaragua, Panama, Peru and Venezuela. The current President of Venezuela, Hugo Rafael Cha´vez, would probably never have risen to power if that country had been free of Amerikan interference. That man is yet another example of blowback.

We've needlessly created despots and dictators, and inspired terrorist groups, all over the world. Any in-depth research will reveal the extent of our covert and overt operations through the decades. Is it any surprise that Blowback is coming at us from all directions? The American people need to realize that we're not hated simply because we exist. Do an Internet search on almost any country using criteria such as "Country 'X'" + CIA + weapons + military." You'll be shocked by the result.

The very worst long-term blowback invariably occurs as a consequence of puppets emplaced in power. Consider the last Shah of Iran. He was put in power by the British and Soviets, who forced his father to abdicate because he had announced Iran's neutrality in WWII. The CIA, in concert with Britain's MI5, later orchestrated a coup in 1953 against a neutralist elected Prime Minister, Mohammad Mosaddegh. The CIA then proceeded to support, train and equip the Shah's SAVAK secret police which imprisoned and tortured dissidents, while ruthlessly suppressing any opposition. After 26 years of that tyranny, most Iranians wanted the Shah and the U.S. gone.

What a great move that was, Amerika! We created another committed adversary, one that calls us *"The Great Satan,"* indoctrinating its children in that belief. From the Iranian's historical perspective, it is a well merited and justifiable reaction.

Even in cases where we did not install a puppet ruler, we still pulled the strings in ways detrimental to the populations in many foreign lands. Hosni Mubarak repressed the Egyptians for 30 years, with our active connivance and boatloads of money. That policy was justified and condoned because he was *"a good friend of America."* Is there even a slim chance that the next government of Egypt will be a *"friend?"* Denying that our policies have actively aided oppression is to live a lie.

Consider what will happen in Egypt, Libya, Yemen, Syria and Iran. Think about the fates of other Arab countries such as Saudi Arabia, Kuwait, Bahrain and the United Arab Emirates. All of the latter are propped up by Amerika.

We have the aforementioned 45 military installations in the Middle East surrounding Iran. Seen from the Ayatollahs' point of view, Iran is encircled by a superpower that possesses 8,500 nuclear warheads.

That same superpower unquestionably supports Israel which has 300 or more nuclear devices. Is it any wonder that the Iranian government feels threatened enough to want at least a couple of nukes of their own?

In all honesty, would we act any differently if Canada and Mexico were openly hostile to us, had bases all along our northern and southern borders, and possessed many nuclear weapons? How many bases do our largest adversaries, Russia and China, have outside their former Soviet and Chinese satellites? **One!** Russia has a base in Syria with 150 personnel. Now look up the list of U.S. foreign bases on Wikipedia and realize that the listing is incomplete!

The solutions to the simmering crisis in the Middle East cannot be achieved by continuing to manipulate, crush or override the rights and liberties of the peoples in that region. Warfare waged against sovereign citizens of a foreign country is still warfare, no matter what the politicians and MIISSC call it. Terms bandied about, such as *"asymmetrical"* and *"4th generation,"* cannot disguise the truth that engaging in any overt military action in that region, is an absolute dead end for the United States.

But let us ignore everything written up to this point and suppose that it is completely wrong. Let us pretend that it does not actually matter. The plain and simple truth is that we cannot afford it!

Spending What We Do Not Have To Spend

We cannot continue to budget up to half of the $1 trillion-plus a year, spent on maintaining the MIISSC infrastructure, in continuing this so-called *"Global War On Terror."* The few real enemies that we classify as "*terrorists*," successfully hiding amidst millions of innocents, are spending less than $50 million around the globe, yet they effectively have us at a standstill.

Is a 10,000 to 1 spending ratio working? For how much longer can we maintain that idiocy?

The Global War on Terror is a tragic farce and a short-lived illusion. How does a country wage war on non-governmental entities? Terrorism is a form of large-scale criminal behavior. Bear in mind that police usually act only **after** a criminal event. It has always been so. So how can criminals (i.e. terrorists) be defeated before we know what, and where, their next crime (i.e. terrorism) takes place? The same way, of course, that successful policing works in any population. It is by:

1. Changing the conditions which cause the propensity for criminal behavior to increase.
2. Focusing far more efficiently on actual criminals, and on potential criminal acts.

More directly to the point, can this "*War*" really be accomplished with largely conventional military means and methods, with the relatively few "*enemy*" combatants hidden amidst a large population that is conducting its normal day to day business? That is patently preposterous! Is there a better form of camouflage than what the terrorists are utilizing?

Our adversaries are eating meals costing no more than 50 cents a day. Meanwhile, it costs $150 a day just to keep each U.S. soldier fed in the field. Our antagonists buy used AK-47 assault rifles, and rocket-propelled grenade launchers, on the black market for a few bucks each. They build improvised explosive devices (IEDs) costing $50 to $500 to blow up multi-million dollar armored vehicles. The economics alone are staggeringly disproportionate. Throwing yet more lives and money at the problem (that we largely created in the first place) is complete and utter lunacy.

Another MIISSC fantasy (but a profitable business for the U.S. manufacturers) is the absurd notion that we can "*cut off the head*" of the Afghan insurgency by eliminating the leadership—via remote control, no less! This is to be achieved with highly sophisticated combat drones operated by joysticks thousands of miles away from the killing fields. Right!

Meanwhile, the *"rank and file"* insurgents will supposedly be rooted out by *"sending in the troops,"* at enormous cost, despite the inconvenient fact that those adversaries are hidden amidst, and indistinguishable from, the civilian population. Obviously, that has never worked before, but *"this time"* it somehow will?

During the American Revolution, our own militia 'irregulars' taught the British Redcoats the folly of that approach. Lo and behold, over two hundred years later, unable to learn even from our own historical success, we were ensconced in a country known for centuries as the *"Graveyard of Empires!"* The Soviets tried and failed to conquer Afghanistan between 1979 and 1988. Three years later, the Soviet Union collapsed.

A little more than ten years after the Soviet empire's demise, right after the 9/11 attack, which was engineered by those whom we had supported against the Soviets, the U.S. was engaged militarily in Afghanistan. It was, and still is, unmitigated folly. As President Karzai's government disintegrates into complete corruption, the infrastructure remains non-existent, despite the tens of billions of dollars that we have expended.

Then There is the Real Cost of War

Our military operations in Afghanistan continue to kill and maim numerous non-combatants. The MIISSC refer to them as *"collateral damage."* Inexorably and inevitably, we are actually converting additional thousands into enemies, effectively sending them into the 'theological' terrorist organizations that we have utterly failed to neutralize. The Afghani troops are infiltrated with adherents of the Taliban, who proceed to shoot or bomb our soldiers every chance that they get. *"Winning the hearts and minds"* of the Afghans (and Iraqis) is obviously failing, or has failed. Troop *"surges"* there, and expanded war efforts across more countries, to prosecute the Global War On Terror (GWOT) simply does not work. The next large terrorist incident is likely to originate from a hitherto unknown group, independent of any currently identified as actual and potential threats. It will likely be a target that we have never before considered as vulnerable.

Our fatally flawed tactics are actually assisting our enemies. Our clueless strategy is much like throwing gasoline on a fire in an attempt to put it out, and then throwing money on top of the flames. The *"insurgents"* will be right back when we are finally forced to walk-away, once we have completed bankrupting ourselves. In effect, by **pruning** the insurgents, we will have actually succeeded in making them more vigorous, strengthening their determination to regain control of their country.

As of 2011, we left Iraq after nearly 4,500 American lives were lost, another 35,000 wounded, and causing **at least** 150,000 Iraqi casualties. That last number is what the Department of Defense (DoD) admits. It does not include estimates of Traumatic Brain Injury (TBI) that number in the tens of thousands. Various independent, reliable estimates range up to 800,000 Iraqi casualties and ignore the numbers refugees rendered homeless. This war has cost the U.S. some $800 billion up front, with indirect and long-term costs to our economy approaching $3.5 trillion. Yet, Iraq is still dysfunctional. Afghanistan will not be any different. Whoops, there goes another trillion dollars ... or two ... or even more.

Somewhere between 2.5 to 4 million people died in the Viet Nam War. **That is two and a half to four million!** Who 'won' that conflict? It was a no-win situation from the very beginning. Think about this. Would the outcome of an invasion be any different if roles are reversed? If another country invaded us? The answer is obviously **no way!** Such invasions are entirely futile unless one is willing to kill nearly everyone, while destroying practically everything.

Yet voices continue to call for military intervention in Iran, Syria and elsewhere in the Middle East. The GWOT, along with the nonsensical notion that we can successfully conduct pre-emptive war and *"nation-building,"* is a form of ethical, moral, social, fiscal, tactical and strategic madness. Invariably, it is the innocents overseas, and at home, who suffer the negative consequences.

If our 'evil-twin' Amerika was a human being, then he or she would be diagnosed as suffering from a deep-seated and chronic delusional disorder. Such persons require intense counseling to help them to overcome their aberrant thought patterns, with resultant antisocial behaviors and destructive outcomes.

U.S. citizens need to realize that Amerika's profound detachment from reality is a grave threat to global stability and safety.

Once one has penetrated through the surface layer of normality and *"plausible deniability,"* the evidence of the delusional disorder is obvious. Suddenly, one recognizes the ill effects everywhere that one looks, both in this Country and abroad.

As in a 12-step rehabilitation program to treat alcohol and drug addiction in human beings, a successful recovery can only begin when the underlying problems are **recognized and accepted.** Then, and only then, can an effective course of treatment be initiated that treats the causes, rather than the symptoms, of the addiction.

The Global War on Terror (GWOT)

Amerika's maintenance of the GWOT extends far beyond the massive logistical task of providing our troops with the best possible supplies, equipment and technology to execute the unrealistic, and inherently unachievable, directives of successive administrations. It also encompasses how the military services are structured and deployed, and the *"rules of engagement"* that they are ordered to follow, even before setting foot into a *"conflict zone."* Those *"battlespaces"* and conflict zones are no longer called battlefields because of the ever-changing definitions of what so-called *"4th generation"* (4G) warfare entails.

Even a cursory review of the current overall U.S. global force's structure, deployment, methodology and mission profile makes it very clear that it is fiscally unsound. In fact, it is so financially irresponsible that it alone will soon bankrupt us. How about aircraft carriers that cost a staggering $11 billion to build, and then $1 to 2 billion a year to operate, yet can be blown out of the water by a $2 million *"3M-54 Klub, (Sizzler)"* missile fired from either land or sea? Or what about the *"Fifth Generation"* F-22 fighter aircraft? Those alone cost more than $400

81

million each, inclusive of R&D costs, as noted in a recent a General Accountability Office (GAO) report!

We will have spent trillions of dollars in no-win wars in Iraq and Afghanistan and be left with what, exactly? Will Iran be next? Will Yemen or Nigeria? Where will the next pretext originate, in order to continue keeping the citizens distracted? The fiscal madness extends far beyond the military to every nook and cranny of the Welfare/Warfare state. It is an institutionalized and sanctified insanity that has infected the Body Politic, perverting our Country into becoming Amerika.

Beyond 'pure' military operations are the hundreds of billions of dollars consumed by the Department of Homeland Security (DHS), the Transportation Security Administration (TSA), the Drug Enforcement Administration (DEA) and myriad other agencies with bailiwicks that include 'dealing with' the *"Terrorist threat,"* and prosecuting the *"War on Drugs."* One need only take a moment's reflection to understand where this is all leading. We might as well combine them all and call it the '**War on People.**' The Land of the Free has become the land of continuous war, war and more war.

There is our long-standing military presence in South Korea, Japan, Europe and elsewhere. We have been in those places for well over a half century, spending vast sums every year. Tens of billions of dollars have been spent supporting NATO. We have been actually subsidizing the 'defense' of other countries. The maintenance and upkeep of our huge military installations, and enormous embassies, spread all over the world, is hugely contributing to our pending insolvency. Once we are bankrupt, what sort of security and defense structure can be maintained?

The Day the T-bills Die

I asked that very question of Marine General Peter Pace, former Chairman of the Joint Chiefs of Staff, in the fall of 2008. It was during a Hillsdale College conference that I attended with some friends at the Broadmoor Hotel, in Colorado Springs. He was the keynote speaker, in a room filled with about 600 dinner guests. At the end of his remarks, only two questions were allowed. I was lucky to be picked and asked:

When the dollar is abandoned as the world's reserve currency, and the Treasury Department can't sell a T-bill to anyone but the Federal Reserve, what kind of defense can we afford then?

Remember this was back in 2008.

General Pace's first response was that he did not understand the question. I explained further. Then he admitted that he had *"never thought about it in those terms ..."* Obviously, during his 40-year career, Pace's basic assumptions had been formulated during an era of endless Department of Defense (DoD) budget increases. Those increases were enabled largely by deficit spending, and propped up by the fiat money churned out by the Federal Reserve, ever since the abandonment of the Gold Standard in 1971.

My follow-up question was:

How would you maintain your Oath as an officer in such circumstances?

He replied that he just could not imagine any scenario that conflicted with his Oath. The moderator moved on to the next question. Afterwards, we spoke informally but it was apparent that he could not believe, or envision, that the military gravy train might be affected, or even derailed, by fiscal realities.

Only two years later, General Pace's replacement, Admiral Mike Mullen, seemed to see the issue far more clearly. In June of 2010, at a *"Tribute to the Troops"* breakfast in Washington, DC, he said:

Our national debt is our biggest national security threat.

What is that again? Two years later it is our *"biggest ... threat."* Something that his predecessor was utterly unable to visualize? A threat that had been obvious for **at least** a decade! Why are we even paying these people? Of course, the question about honoring their Oath remains unanswered.

By 2008, the *"Great Recession"* was in full swing but most insiders, such as Federal Reserve Chairman Ben Bernanke, and the Federal Open

Market Committee (FOMC) which sets monetary policy, were either in massive denial or ignorant of the implications. The Fed's own transcripts of that period indicate total blindness to the nature and extent of the financial implosion occurring **in plain sight.** Either there is a systemic cognitive dissonance largely comprised of complacency, apathy and ignorance, or they are lying. Which is it? Neither answer is any comfort.

It should astound and frighten every American that virtually anyone outside of the system, who possesses a moderate dose of common sense, can correctly diagnose our fiscal and financial debacle, years before officialdom. The latter had virtually unlimited access to the *"best minds"* in and out of government, and masses of data, both which proved worthless in forecasting anything.

At this point, mention should be made of the disgraceful behavior of many academics, our supposed 'professional' economists. The latter have effectively become the enablers of the irresponsibility, as they shuffle in and out of government office, collecting large salaries and consultant fees.

So, in spite having huge staffs, enormous budgets, and access to the *"best and the brightest experts"* inside and outside of government, officialdom could not (and still cannot) see the handwriting on the wall! How can they 'protect' us if they are not able to discern the blatantly obvious?

Chickenhawks and the Critics of True and Affordable Defense

Those who deny that blowback is the result of deeply flawed foreign and defense policies, will immediately label anyone, who points out any of the above, as *"Blame America First"* isolationists. Nothing could be further from the truth. Only those taking an honest and objective look at the facts can identify the very real, rather than the imaginary, dangers that we are facing today and solve them.

Many of the leading deniers of our failures are obvious 'Chickenhawks.'

Chickenhawk (Wikipedia): The term is meant to indicate that the person in question is cowardly or hypocritical for personally avoiding combat in the past while advocating that others go to war in the present. Generally, the implication is that 'chickenhawks' lack the experience, judgment, or moral standing to make decisions about going to war. The term is not applied to those who avoided military service without subsequently adopting a hawkish political outlook.

Americans should find it particularly repulsive and offensive that the loudest voices clamoring for war have so often never served in the Military. Does that not seem more than a bit ironic? Many of these right-wingers were of age during the Viet Nam era. Yet they actively sought to avoid military service through deferments, or by arranging for stateside service. Many right-wingers and left-wingers have avoided service during peacetime. Most of their children do not volunteer to serve today. The other group of people espousing interventionism directly benefits, in one way or the other, from the continuation and expansion of the MIISSC.

Some of these hypocrites are elected to public office, some are appointed to important government positions, and some of them become *"talking heads"* at places such as the Fox Network and CNN. In the social-conservative movement, many of them profess to hold to *"the sanctity of life of the unborn."* However, they have not extended that same reverence to the lives of young U.S. soldiers sent to be killed, maimed or traumatized in Amerika's interventionism overseas.

Nor do they seem to spare a thought for the carnage inflicted on the 'faceless' native inhabitants, the *"collateral damage,"* in the countries where Amerika has made its incursions. Reverence for human life is inclusive, not a matter of picking and choosing. That is something those in the liberal Progressive movement should also ponder, as they have a growing clutch of Liberal Chickenhawks in their midst, supporting yet another failed Presidency.

At the highest levels of the MIISSC, the focus is mostly on how many contracts can be generated, and where and who they go to. Many contracts, of dubious necessity and questionable technical merit, cost hundreds of billions of dollars, only to be later abandoned.

If the proper defense of the Homeland was truly the highest priority, then the current force structure, deployments and 'defense' spending would be radically different, vastly more effective, and hugely less expensive. What prevents a systematic review and re-thinking of our priorities in addressing actual security concerns, and then the adoption of realistic and cost-effective solutions? It is very simple. The MIISSC Lobby is unlikely to accept any cuts at all, much less the orders of magnitude that are necessary. As Jack Abramoff, the recently released convicted lobbyist, has observed: *"Why should they?"* The vested interests in the MIISSC will exert whatever leverage they can to maintain their influence, and keep their bloated contracts.

Inevitably, there are corrupt and incompetent individuals, embedded throughout the Government and Congress, who are easily persuaded, manipulated, coerced or bribed via 'the backdoor.' Scandal after scandal after scandal has ensued. To hell with the dire fiscal and financial condition of the United States government and the U.S. economy! To hell with whether it actually serves our true defense and foreign policy needs! To hell with how many of our best young people, and innocents overseas, may die to get *"the bad guys!"* That is neither their problem nor concern.

The Cold War ended in 1991. The list of totally unnecessary weapons systems left over from the Cold War, but still being funded for the benefit of the MIISSC, is mind boggling. We are also still mired in idiotic *"standard and complex"* defense systems procurement processes, within whose constraints I once worked. It is the very same procurement process that creates absurdities such as $700 hammers.

There was a 'joke' floating around in the defense system procurements offices where I once worked. *"When the weight of the documents required equals the weight of the equipment being delivered, then we're done."* It did not seem to matter if the delivered system worked properly or not. What counted most was that every nit-picking detail in the voluminous documentation requirements was complete. Any wonder why we have weapons and systems boondoggle after boondoggle?

We have to re-assess everything and simplify, simplify, simplify. It must start with determining the proper goals and objectives for an effective defense that actually assures, rather than diminishes, the security of this Republic. An objective assessment would lead to dramatic changes in operating philosophy, policies and infrastructure. However, that is not happening due to the raft of embedded interests and deep-seated corruption. Reluctance and resistance to change is how previous empires lost their way, bleeding to death from self-inflicted wounds. We are nearing the end of the road of a similar process right now.

Although it does feature some realignment of our global deployment structure, the recently released "*U.S. Defense Strategic Review 2012*," does far too little, and it is far too late. The Review is still permeated with standard Cold War thinking and laden down with GWOT and MIISSC agendas. Predictably, the Chickenhawks, and their minions beholden to the feeding trough at the MIISSC, along with the usual plethora of pseudo-patriots, immediately attacked the Review. Even its very modest changes in force structure and deployments were unacceptable to them.

There are far too many vested interests involved who want to keep the real behind-the-scenes haggling and deal-making out of sight. The Chickenhawks seem to view the military as a ($700?) hammer. All they apparently see around the World are nails that they think need pounding down. After five minutes of specific questioning, most of them would prove that they have little understanding of the stakes. Whatever they did grasp would be largely theoretical rather than practical.

A Word to the Chickenhawks and Warmongers

Please do not conclude that any part of this critique extends to the vast majority of the members of the U.S. Military. As a Veteran myself, along with my personal background and family history, I find attempts by the Chickenhawks and Warmongers to marginalize such critiques as this one, and characterize them as unpatriotic, to be quite frankly beyond disgusting. I and others are simply focusing a critical eye on the mess that they call 'defense spending.' Furthermore, it is they who daily put our military men and women deeper into harm's way. That is utterly shameful and immoral.

The ranks of those who volunteer for military service comprise the backbone, the heart and soul, of the finest public institutions this

Country has produced. The vast majority of them do not make it a career, either.

The problems that I am outlining in this book are not the creation of the typical citizen-soldiers who were, and are, forced to fight in wars, declared or not. Most of them served with distinction and bravery in their defense of the Republic. It is what they have been ordered to do that is the issue. The proper debate focuses on how they are being used and abused. The bulk of the U.S. Military just follows, and attempts to carry out, the orders of their civilian and general staff command. It is among the civilian leadership, politicized general staff and the segment of careerist senior officers and enlisted, where most of the problems reside. Most orders that the military rank and file are tasked to accomplish have little (or nothing) to do with the actual *"defense of our freedoms."*

A fairly good depiction of military personnel in action is shown in the recent movie *"Act of Valor."* It is an excellent showcase for the highly effective Naval Special Warfare Command, a unit for which I (obviously) have a special affinity. The movie profiles, in fine detail, the professionalism and dedication of that Command. What is not shown are the flawed policies and bad decisions behind their orders into action.

On the surface, all looks somewhat understandable, rational and plausible. The military is skillfully using the finest and most advanced training, weaponry, and associated equipment, ever fielded. But far more important to this discussion are the views of those with the power to order or influence military actions, but they are never in evidence in the film.

Let us take as an example, Henry Kissinger, one of the most ruthless (and consistent) practitioners of 'realpolitik' in recent memory. He was the main architect of the devil's bargain that intertwined the U.S. Dollar and the pricing of petroleum (*"petrodollar recycling"*). Along with the incompetence of the Federal Reserve, petrodollar recycling has served to artificially prop up our fiscal house of cards, and to postpone the inescapable financial reckoning due to profligate deficit spending.

Kissinger once said:

Military men are dumb, stupid animals to be used as pawns for foreign policy.

No further comment on that sort of attitude is necessary, is it?

U.S. foreign policy has been a rolling disaster for decades. Calling it, and our defense policies, *"the defense of freedom,"* is the height of Orwellian doublespeak. Ultimately, it comes down to two main issues, opposite sides of the same coin. One is the Executive Branch, with the entrenched bureaucracy of the Federal Government, along with the elected members of Congress and the Judiciary. The other is the complacent, apathetic, and ignorant citizenry who are ultimately responsible for allowing politicians, whom they elect and re-elect, to misuse the U.S. Military. The latter has become a tool to carry out various agendas with very tenuous connections to the actual defense of this Country.

It is also extremely unfortunate that so many of the top echelons of the U.S. Military leadership have failed to demand clear Declaration(s) of War, and fully Constitutional lawful orders, before fielding the forces under their command. They appear to have been thoroughly co-opted by the military toys at their disposal, the many perks that they enjoy, and succumbed to rampant careerism. They have failed to exercise their own responsibilities as citizens, first and foremost. Where are the Dwight D. Eisenhowers when we need them?

The co-opted military leadership seems completely ensnared by the current political status quo and *"K Street Lobbyists."* They have allowed the armed forces to be used as a blunt instrument of policy, carrying out orders that would have been deplored by the Founders, and most Presidents until T. Roosevelt. Orders that go so far beyond common sense that they are literally lunatic.

High-ranking officers and enlisted personnel exist in a paradoxical situation that controls the way that they act and respond. It revolves around the risk of losing their careers if they speak up. However, they do have a powerful tool, one seldom used these days. Its use could bring all this tragic nonsense to a screeching halt, literally overnight. It would require self-sacrifice, an essential element of the 'warrior's code.'

When was the last time that a General Officer, or Senior Enlisted, resigned in protest over un-Constitutional or unlawful orders? When has one refused to follow orders that actually damage the security of this Republic, and **unnecessarily** puts the troops under their command in harm's way? Have there been any examples, even one, in the past decade? Military officers throughout history have "*resigned the field*" when they failed individually, or would not accept the unlawful orders of their superiors. What has happened at the General Officer level these days?

Could careerism have anything to do with it? Are paychecks, perks and program spending more important than honor and integrity? Resignations are submitted and accepted every day in private enterprise for failure, or for disagreeing on policy or business practices with superiors, such as a Board of Directors.

Recently, a phalanx of general staff officers were lined up beside, and behind, the Secretary of Defense, Leon Panetta, when he matter-of-factly told a Senate Committee that the President and Administration did not require Congressional approval to go to war. He implied that only UN approval was required. Not a single General or Admiral got up and walked out, has resigned or spoken out since, regarding this clearly un-Constitutional position taken by the Executive. What happened to their Oath?

Civilian Control of the Military

Obviously, there is a growing dysfunction in the dynamic between civilian control over the military forces and what the latter can reasonably be expected to execute successfully. At least part of the problem is due to the fact that an average of 85% of our politicians and 95% of the general population have never served in the Military.

Without having any practical experience in that environment, civilians have little understanding of the 'military mind-set.' They do not understand the fine balance required in the warrior culture. Unquestioned obedience to orders is often vital for survival in combat but must be, first and foremost, counter balanced by obedience to the Constitution.

It is always useful to have shared experiences to facilitate the meeting of minds. No other positions of such importance (civilian control of the military) would allow the (civilian) decisions makers such a gap in their resume. A proper frame of reference would greatly assist the civilian command to understand the scope and depth of our existing military capabilities, and have a much better grasp of our **true strategic and tactical needs.**

Elected officials are briefed in a jumble of jargon emanating from the MIISSC's organizational processes that employ acronyms and jargon that have no real meaning for civilians. The officials' opinions are therefore almost entirely abstract, based on fleeting impressions made during whirlwind tours of weaponry, and machines with flashing lights and displays in command and control centers in big ships and aircraft.

A Congressperson is usually a lawyer, or business man, who has never served in the Military, or in the defense structure, or **taken a course in logic.** Consequently, there is not much that they could possibly understand except in an unfounded abstract fashion. They obtain their 'experience' sitting on committees while being briefed by impressive looking military brass behind closed doors. They feel important, part of a secret club.

Naturally, they want the latest and greatest technology built in their Congressional District or State because, of course, they already have an eye on re-election. Nothing sounds more impressive while electioneering than *"look at the jobs that I brought into this town."* They have no real desire or motivation to exercise regular independent judgment. They are ultimately in control of all the buttons on the shiny new weaponry and equipment since they also control the purse-strings. It is far too seductive a power trip for any clear-headed decision-making. And so, one unnecessary weapon and complex system after another is rubber-stamped, or forced into production for purely political reasons, along with its accompanying bloated budget. Once started, such programs are nearly impossible to stop.

A Few Other Points

As with the chamber-of-horrors that is our foreign and militaristic (certainly not defensive) policy, it is much the same problem with our welfare state. At the same time that the MIISSC, and the Chickenhawks, bleed us dry at one end of the now nearly exsanguinated Body Politic, the Welfare statists are doing the same at the other end.

We simply cannot continue to spend $1.3 trillion a year on the social-welfare portion of the budget. It is not only because those dysfunctional programs are actually acting as disincentives in developing independent and productive citizens, who carry their share of the load. It is also because they are bankrupting us.

The negative cultural effects of welfare hand-outs are patently obvious throughout the Country. It is no coincidence that, after spending trillions of dollars on social welfare during the past four decades, the actual welfare of the population has significantly declined, both culturally and economically. There is more poverty, broken families, lack of true education and increasing cultural disintegration. It is a direct, and perhaps intended, consequence that keeps the present elite in power.

How is it that practical, self-reliant common sense, so readily understood by the average person a century ago, can be so uncommon today? I am persuaded that it is due to the ascendancy of the iron triad of welfare, dumbed-down education in the schools, and the kept media. Sure, there is the allure of getting something for nothing. But now large segments of the population actually believe that it is their implicit right to receive welfare checks and subsidies, even when they are able-bodied and capable, or do not really need them. The Welfare State mindset also spreads the War State mentality into every facet of the Amerikan mindset. They are two sides of the same coin.

Even using this system's own calculations, it is obvious that there is proportionately more poverty in America today, than what existed at the beginning of the *"War on Poverty."* Another 'War' promoted and foisted on us by yet another pandering-to-special-interests President, the same Lyndon Johnson who dragged us far deeper into the bloody and hugely expensive mess in Viet Nam, than President Kennedy wanted, and probably ever dreamed possible.

We have an incredibly costly, and nearly completely dysfunctional, educational system all the way through the college level.

We certainly have no less, and possibly even more, illicit drug abuse than before the beginning of yet another war, this one the "*War on Drugs*," instituted by President Nixon at the close of the Viet Nam War.

'The War on Drugs' has increased, not decreased, the potency and availability of illicit drugs of all types. Even a person with a superficial knowledge of economics understands why that is so. The very same thing happened during The Prohibition. Surprise! We never seem to gain any common sense from prior experience of what manifestly did not work. Such 'prohibitions' inevitably create a huge underclass of criminals whose sole goal is to expand, and to squeeze more profit, from a black market that the Government itself has created! But wait, that necessitates yet another war. This one is called the "*War on Crime.*"

Even worse, it that is possible, is the plain fact that the use, and abuse, of legal prescription drugs is completely out of control, in a 'legal market' that is supposedly 'regulated.' Prescription anti-depressants are the #1 prescribed medications **and** the #1 abused drug. By every possible objective standard, it is much more devastating in its social and health repercussions than any illicit recreational drugs. Any rational person should cringe at the number and variety of anti-depressant, pain-killer and mood-altering drugs constantly advertised on TV, and routinely prescribed **to both adults and children alike,** by our so-called 'health professionals.' Who profits and at whose expense? Obviously, the huge pharmaceutical companies make colossal profits in this trade. Whose ear do they have in Congress and government?

The average semi-comatose American citizen, and their elected officials, must either wake up and "*smell the coffee*" or in very short order we will be toast as a functioning Republic. Coming up fast is a date that is certain and inevitable. It is when the U.S. Treasury will not be able to sell a T-Bill to fund the following month's MIISSC procurements, or make welfare and subsidy payments.

When that happens, all the T-bills and bonds will have to be purchased directly by the Federal Reserve, which in turn will immediately monetize (create the money to pay for) the expenditure. That will prop up the failed system for a short time longer, but will result in either runaway inflation or eventual defaults.

What happens then, folks? The price of the morning Starbucks latte may rise to $20 and more.

And so, let us follow the money trail…

5

Money: It Is All About Dead Presidents!

*Centralization of credit in the hands of the state, by means of
a national bank with State capital and an exclusive monopoly.*
–5th Plank of the Communist Manifesto by Karl Marx

*I believe that banking institutions are more dangerous to our liberties than
standing armies. The issuing power (of money) should be taken away from
the banks and restored to the people to whom it properly belongs.*
–Thomas Jefferson

We have a stark and obvious choice before us. It is something very clearly expressed in the two quotes above. The Federal Reserve Corporation, the European Central Bank (ECB) and the entangled global central-banking system cartel, have already failed. The entire system is insolvent and has been so for some time. The actual (as opposed to imaginary) reserves held in the global system comprise only a tiny fraction of the existing and pending losses. The losses are largely held "off-books" thanks to various account manipulations, along with outright fraud by the central bankers.

The latter fully deserve to be called "banksters" (a word derived from combining banker and gangster).

The only way for the central banking scam to remain in operation is by continuing to fool the People (known as "marks" by con men). The final implosion is being delayed as long as possible with ploys such as Quantitative Easing (QE), Stimulus, Liquidity, Loans, TARPs, ESF, ESLFs and whatever other gobbledygook they dream up next. All that is done to confuse and misdirect the marks in the con-game—who are us, the citizens. The banksters and their accomplices, the professional politicians, have been doing this for 100 years. Prolonging the game for

95

so long is the sign of truly accomplished con men. They have a few short years left until their game runs out to its inevitable end.

The administered *"stress tests"* on banks in 2010 were a sham. They either did not include 'off books accounting,' or assumed 100% 'mark-to-market' valuations for worthless or near worthless 'assets.' Global business and economic news reports are only a surface view of the ongoing death throes of the entire monetary system. It is **not a matter of if it goes down,** it is a matter of **when** and **to what extent.** It already will be bad. It may be catastrophic.

The concept of a large, central-banking monopoly was already a failed model more than a century ago. A century later, it is manifestly a false and fraudulent operating system, with all its expenses levied on the population, having embedded itself into everything, like the mythical, gigantic Kraken of Greek legend. This Big Con has been run for an extremely long time.

Working in a Coal Mine, Goin' Down, Down, Down

Working in the banking and financial industry on Wall Street, beginning in the late 1980s and on through the 1990s, gave me an excellent vantage point to help me realize what was bound to happen. Gathering requirements and reviewing internal operations from top to bottom of many major financial and governmental institutions, allowed me to study how those places function while observing their internal operations at close hand.

One must understand the primary reality. A large modern bank or financial company is nothing more than a group of workers, and a series of buildings used to house, support and operate a vast electronic infrastructure. It is a bricks and mortar facade, staffed with people, all built around an illusion. These companies 'make' nothing. However, they do create the illusion of being a large and important part of a supposed 'economy.' Fake 'money' and fake 'economy' go hand-in-hand.

A bit more background might be helpful. During most of the 1990s, I had a nice view from the Marriott World Trade Center, about 18 floors up, overlooking the World Financial Center, Battery Park and across the Hudson River to New Jersey. I did not spend much time admiring that view because I was rarely in my room or office. I worked as long and hard as I could to move projects along, so I that could spend more time back home in Colorado and less time in NYC.

I did enjoy and appreciate most New Yorkers that I met, and those in the surrounding megalopolis. During my sojourns in 'The Big Apple,' I made several friends and worked alongside some great colleagues. I just do not find New York, or most of the East Coast, an attractive place to live. Nevertheless, New York City is an incredibly vibrant place. It requires tremendous logistical, management and operational skills to keep it all running. For example, 28,000 trucks drive on and off Manhattan Island every day.

However, for someone raised in the rural West, it is not what I would describe as a *"human-friendly place."* Reams of restrictive regulations and 'laws' impinge on everyday life far more than in other parts of the Country, especially west of the Mississippi. I *will* say that it is easier to find one's way around NYC than Tokyo and its prefectures, or Seoul, Manila, Taipei, Hong Kong and other similarly densely populated, and closely packed, Asian cities, even accounting for the language and cultural differences.

In New York, and in most of the Boston to Washington, D.C. corridor, known as "BosWash," there seems to be a significant number of people convinced of their own innate superiority over other Americans. That plays well in Amerika but is totally misplaced in America. Many of those people look down their nose in a condescending manner at anything, or anybody, west of the Hudson or Potomac Rivers. They call that area, between the east and west coasts, the *"fly-over country."* This attitude is especially prevalent among those at the top of the so-called *"socio-economic heap."* Donald Trump is hardly a 'rare' personality type amongst them. Arrogance and ignorance seem to travel hand-in-hand in such circles. All they understand is the insular world in which they protect themselves behind high walls.

Most New Yorkers are not even aware how their inflated opinion of themselves naturally manifests itself in, for example, everyday conversation. Many Easterners and New Yorkers think that the East Coast power structure should run America. Some of those people actually harbor the delusion that they are smart enough! (Are you listening Mayor Bloomberg?) It is an important aspect in the story of how things have gone so badly awry in NYC's financial district, and all the way to Pennsylvania Avenue and *"Foggy Bottom"* in Washington, D.C.

Working on a project for the Federal Deposit Insurance Corporation (FDIC), and other commercial and defense contracts during the savings and loan (S&L) bailouts of the late 1980s and early 1990s, provided me a ring-side seat at the center of political power in Washington, D.C. I observed more of the political and economic scene than just the condition of the S&L and banking industry. When in Washington, I usually stayed in one of the hotels right across from, or close by, the White House or Capitol Hill.

I have several friends who have, through the years, worked in various administrations at the White House, Treasury and the Old Executive Office Building (OEOB) next door. I took several 'inside' tours through the various buildings. One particularly memorable experience was to sit in the small office at the exact same spot where the Secretary of State, Cordell Hull, was handed the Declaration of War by the Japanese Ambassador, Kichisaburo Nomura, on December 8, 1941. While those places are, of course, the site of many such events, I particularly savored that experience. My friends and former colleagues considered those places part of *"going to work."*

On the FDIC project, I commuted on the Metro from the District to Arlington, Virginia and the L. William Seidman Center, FDIC headquarters. Until then, I had never realized that official buildings could be named after people who were not even dead yet! In fact, when the FDIC Headquarters building was completed, Bill Seidman was the Chairman. It seemed overly puffed-up to me, but then what do I know?

In the 1980s, there were also defense and government contracts regularly bringing me to DC for meetings at Arlington's Crystal City with contractors, or military folks from the Pentagon, and various DoD subdivisions.

Another project had me commuting to Landover, Maryland, to Giant Foods headquarters. Thankfully, Giant Foods was a retail store network.

Working with "Giant" was a lot of fun as it was inhabited by what I refer to as "*real people.*" It was a great family-owned company that provided a service in the DC area that everyone needed. That was a refreshing change and contrast from 'official' Washington.

The contract work also included spending off-hours time with colleagues, co-workers and clients in the eateries, watering holes and hang-outs around D.C. Most were places where Congressional and Administration staffers go to 'drown' and play. I participated in many discussions, during which I heard many points of view expressed.

Those discussions, along with my years of study and work in systems design, engineering and economics, and dabbling in political science and law classes, helped put into proper perspective the viewpoints that I heard expressed. What was understood by the public at-large beyond the Beltway, was very different to what I directly encountered inside various corporations and government institutions.

Experts vs. Analysts and Engineers

I am emphatically not what anyone should describe as a financial '*expert.*' So-called financial *experts* of today are mostly mainstream Keynesian economists and adherents of the "*Chicago*" and "*Monetarist*" schools. They have repeatedly shown themselves inadequate to the task of understanding, defining or predicting the economy during this last decade, and actually even longer. It is simply impossible to argue otherwise, once the record is examined.

So my comments here are those of a 'self-educated analyst.' I have no letters behind my name in the finance field. What I am calling an *educated analyst* is simply someone who does research, uses objective facts, then applies logic and reason to reach a conclusion. Next, he tests those conclusions in the real world.

The reader is free to agree or disagree with my analysis. But I urge you to wait before making any judgment calls, until we complete a review of what I have witnessed and learned.

A mainstream financial *expert* usually has letters behind his (or her) name. For many of them, possessing such credentials has become a substitute for truth and knowledge. The *experts* may go through a similar process as do *educated analysts* to reach their conclusions. Or, they may give an unsubstantiated opinion devoid of objective analysis or tests. The pronouncements of these *experts* are viewed as the final word on the subject, no matter how wrong they were (or are).

Do not assume that I do not respect the educated. I know many fine folks with advanced degrees in many fields. However, the ones I respect never substitute their credentials for the truth, which is always arrived at by reasoned analysis based on the evidence. Truth is where it is found, not where it is desired or directed to be.

In our mad hatter, topsy-turvy world, it does not matter if a well-read and informed outside observer agrees or disagrees. The conclusions, or actually the opinions, of so-called *experts* become part of accepted doctrine and must be acted upon by central authority. *"The experts have spoken"* (cue in some stirring organ music or a fanfare of trumpets). Dissenting voices are silenced or, more commonly, ignored. That is particularly true if the *experts* are members of the authority structure that is directly responsible for 'managing' the economic system. They are the self-anointed, know-it-all, officially sanctioned *"wizards behind the curtain."*

Expert conclusions or opinions thus become the final authority on any subject. Informed observers are expected to suspend independent reasoning, and the sheep-like citizens to relinquish any responsibility for outcomes. *"Just be a good little citizen,"* and do what they tell you. Unfortunately, most of the population has acquiesced and abdicated their own responsibility in the decision-making process, allowing it to be conveniently turned over to such *experts*. Early on in life, they apparently decided it is so much easier, and so much more convenient, to let the *experts* do the supposed 'thinking,' even if they are flat wrong.

That process has occurred in most of the existing political-economic system. The debate over human-caused climate change is an obvious example. The *"majority opinion"* of the *experts* is now the final word on the matter. That wholly artificial construct must now be unquestionably supported. It is considered final despite the provable fact that it is perhaps the most unscientific proposition ever made.

The 'science' involved is based upon majority opinion, rather than actual, accurate and complete evidence, resulting from impartial observations, and the repeatable validation of test results, that true science requires. Of course, now there is a whole industry of people built around this construct. It is referred to as the *"Green Industry."* It has taken on a life of its own. Those who profit monetarily from the construct, will fight tooth and nail to preserve their meal tickets.

Their science data points are too few. The accuracy and calibrations are, at best, questionable. The samples being used are far too narrow in scope. The climate models are grossly flawed. Lacking sufficient hard data, the conclusions reached do not actually trace back to the evidence. The list of the unanswered questions would fill volumes. We are supposed to buy this construct of anthropogenic (human-caused) climate change, and then blindly act to pass "laws" to supposedly remedy the situation. It does not matter what it will cost, or if any of the "solutions" will work as intended. We are not allowed to either consider or conjecture that there might be (or, perhaps, actually is) an entirely different and natural explanation for what is happening, or that there might be other solutions.

Dr. John R. Christy, at the University of Alabama, Huntsville, has been one of the highest profile scientists to object to the hysteria, and the extremist conclusions, of the Inter-governmental Panel on Climate Change (IPCC). His research has shown, time and again, that *majority vote science* does not deliver the same conclusions as real science, since it does not objectively assess the data. He has repeatedly called the ideas for altering human behavior, and the development of supposed "solutions" to combat climate change, to be ineffective and actually damaging to the economy. His report may be viewed at http://thecitizenslaststand.com/christy.

Not since the beginning of the European Renaissance half a millennium ago, has such a centralized, 'theocratic,' majority rule view of science been imposed on the population in so many areas where it does not apply. A self-reinforcing "group-think" puts High Priests of Science, with useful idiots and enablers in the media close behind them, at the head of an absurd parade. The rest of us are considered to be mental serfs, who must bow down to the high and mighty lords, and follow their anointed path. We are required to pay the taxes to fund every cockamamie alternative energy "green" scheme, no matter how non-economical and destructive they turn out to be. (Adding ethanol to gasoline is a good example).

When Einstein stood alone with his theories, he was not shut out of the ongoing discourse on Physics, even when he could not prove that Relativity was an operating process of the Universe. It took nearly two more decades to eventually prove, through direct and indirect experimentation and observation, that even the central portion of his theories was correct. However, the other scientists did not vote "yay or nay" as to whether General or Special Relativity was legitimate or not. They waited for experimentation and observation to prove if it was true or false. They did not demand that Einstein "shut-up" as he explored other methods to prove out his theory.

Such thinking seems absent in the scientific community with regards to *"global warming."* That term has since conveniently (for its protagonists) morphed into the obviously pointless description *"climate change,"* now being applied to this tiny fraction of time in Earth's history. There is little question that climate change does occur on a geologic time scale. There have been Ice Ages and also periods when the entire planet was warm from the equator to the poles, as for example during the Eocene Optimum. It is obviously absurd to equate what may, or may not be happening today, and compare it to such situations. Who benefits from such scare tactics? That is the only relevant question to ask!

Economic and Monetary Experts and Group-think

A very similar theocratic majority rule group-think process is happening in the management of the monetary and financial system. One is expected to kowtow to the *experts.* Far too many of our decisions have been turned over to them for the simple reason that so many people have abdicated their role as individually responsible citizens. As a result, we are continually suffering destructive outcomes from the implementation of the decisions handed down by the so-called *experts.* The documented history of centrally mandated financial and monetary decisions in the

20th Century, from WWI and the Great Depression forward, is nothing less than a series of escalating failures.

It is the *consensus opinion* of so-called *experts* that has caused, and will continue to create, more pain and economic destruction than any free market ever did (or could). On its very worst days, prior to the creation of the Federal Reserve Bank in 1913, and the adoption of the concept of "*regulatory democracy*," a truly free market never did the sort of damage wrought by the Great Depression. It certainly never created the distorting economic behavior witnessed since the 1971 abandonment of the Gold Standard.

Without the Federal Reserve Bank, the huge government deficit spending spree facilitated by fiat currency, simply could not have occurred. Why is that? Because sound money and competitiveness, rather than the monopolistic issue of paper money at will, would be the standard of financial discipline. Markets for money would set interest rates. Booms and busts could not be exaggerated by artificially setting ("managed") credit rates.

During the 1970s and 1980s, did excess credit and money expansion cycles feel great during the "*Carter inflation*" or through the pain of having to take it down with the "*Volcker disinflation*" of the early to mid-1980s? Did it fix anything? Then more trouble began to be experienced in the 1990s. Since 2005, coming to the end of the 'supercycle,' it is already far worse.

If a truly free market had been allowed to continue to exist throughout the 20th Century, it is my contention that our economy would have actually grown more stable and steadily during the past 99 years, just as it did during the previous 123 years from 1790 to 1913. *Experts* and the average citizen do not seem to understand the ancient lesson and moral in the Aesop's Fables that we read as children. The Federal Reserve creates the economy of the Grasshopper, while a free market creates the economy of the Ant. Or, as in another fable, think of the Federal Reserve as the Hare with fast starts and stops, and a true free market as the Tortoise with a slower and steadier pace that wins the race.

Without the existence of the Federal Reserve, and the economics and finance bureaucracy, our economy would be much larger, more robust and resilient. With them, it is a warped and distorted parody of a properly functioning market economy.

With a truly free market economy, we would never have experienced the widespread adoption of the kleptoparasitic business model of making money-on-money, instead of focusing on productive wealth creation. We would be a country of savers and investors instead of spenders and borrowers. Who in their right mind saves dollars at 0.25% interest with inflation many multiples of that? Only the very foolish or the brain-washed do so. However, anybody would save at 0.25% when there is little to no sustained inflation, especially if the currency is also appreciating!

As we follow the money trail, recent history paints an ugly picture. A good read is "*The Creature From Jekyll Island*" (1994) by G. Edward Griffin. It is one of damage done to many, and how a few benefited enormously. It is clear, from examination of the record, that the central decision makers, in the monetary and financial system, very seldom suffer any of the real pain that the rest of us do at their hands. It is helpful to understand the history behind what is now unfolding. Using the control handed to this small cabal, and their accomplices, also allows them to privatize their profits but socialize their losses. That is totally reprehensible.

That fact alone should automatically condemn the existing system.

The *experts,* their employers and enablers now have the system rigged almost completely in their favor. The envisioned system of "meritocracy" intended by the Founders has been stealthily supplanted by a warped system of central planners and *experts.* It is a system where "*some animals are more equal than the others,*" as satirized in "*Animal Farm*" by George Orwell.

Even though they may use standard mathematical-analytical methods, it is the external framework of statistical and econometric collection and analysis, by Keynesians and Monetarists, that impairs their ability to arrive at the right conclusions. They are essentially engaged in "earth-centric" theories of cosmic analysis, applying them to the fields of economic and monetary policy. Their derived abstract econometric models are merely assumptions disguised as conclusions. It is as though they are convinced that they are Masters of the Universe, yet are unable to comprehend basic celestial mechanics!

The conventional wisdom of the *experts* and pundits is that free markets with sound, asset-based, competitive currencies cannot possibly work in today's world. Yet, the record plainly shows that they worked well during the first 123 years of our Country's existence. I listened to the 'educated' critics in the watering holes of Washington and New York.

Oh, that's so passé, we're so much smarter in the 20th Century than those primitives back in the 18th and 19th centuries.

The new technologies are vastly more sophisticated than those ancient relics and out-of-date concepts and ideas.

Imagine such comments being made by self-satisfied graduates of the "top" schools; the elite from Georgetown Law, Harvard or Princeton School of Economics, or the Tuck School at Dartmouth. All made while sipping Johnny Walker Blue Label or Glenfiddich in the company of equally smug and like-minded friends and colleagues.

Yet, those same *experts* never admit that 'fiat' (by decree) currencies, those not backed up by hard assets (such as gold and silver), have always failed dramatically, **every time they have been tried**, folks! The *experts* neglect to mention that a hard-asset system has inherent checks and balances that do not require external regulation. They have checks and balances that quickly punish failure and do not build **moral hazards** into the system.

Our current *"mixed economy"* is claimed by mainstream *experts* and media pundits to be *"free market capitalism."* Uh, right! When seeing such terms being bandied about, it is wise to remember that deliberately twisting the meaning of words is one of the first tools of propagandists who aim to turn reality on its head.

The current system is actually dominated by ever increasing governmental intervention that has enabled *mercantilism* which rewards certain industries, such as those in the defense cartel, at the expense of others, and *cronyism* which also favors some at the expense of others.

How could anyone pretend that is *free market capitalism?* There is no such thing in our Country today!

Fake money, business planning and organization by spreadsheet, sixty million words in the absurdly convoluted Internal Revenue Code, hundreds of thousands of pages of regulations, and broad governmental intervention in virtually every industry, how can that be called "free?" Calling it "free" when it is actually not free, introduces confusion in public and private discourse. It is a mockery of true free markets. It is hard to escape the conclusion that it is a deliberate ploy to muddy the waters.

Conventional *expert* wisdom believes that the economic dislocations caused by central planning create less pain than those allegedly inflicted by a true free market. In point of historical fact, it was during those times when debts could only be settled with sound money, backed by real assets, that the economy grew efficiently and steadily with short-lived natural setbacks. Without *"sound money,"* the system devolves to worthless promises to pay sometime in the future, without ultimate recourse.

The True Free Market Side

The books by both Thomas DiLorenzo ("How Capitalism Saved America: The Untold Story of Our Country's History, from the Pilgrims to the Present," published in 2004) and Dr. Thomas Woods ("Meltdown: A Free-market Look at Why the Stock Market Collapsed, the Economy tanked, and the government Bailouts Will Make Things Worse," published in 2009) are good places for the reader to begin any deeper investigation of the issues.

In a sound-money, free market economy, business cycles are shorter and shallower. Any booms due to excessive debt creation by private banks are quickly extinguished when the banks are allowed to fail. Market clearing occurs. The booms soon contract once investors realize that such expansions are false and demand the return of their hard asset deposits. That forces banks to call in debts, thus shrinking the money supply. Prices fall, which once again stimulates buying. It is the natural **self-regulating** recovery cycle at work.

Mismanaged private banks and companies go bankrupt instead of being "bailed-out" by the government to prevent them from failing. The continued subsidization of private banking and business failures with public money is actually an unethical and immoral practice encouraging imprudent, even criminal, behavior by banks and the financial services sector, as well as Big Business. As a consequence, the tacit acceptance of **moral hazards** is now embedded into their standard operational frame of reference.

A monopolist central bank operates under no natural checks and balances. It has no externally applied pressure against inflation. Check the historical record of this Country's money before and after the creation of the Federal Reserve with its heavy-handed manipulations of our currency. As an example, look at the period between 1789 to 1912. The dollar appreciated approximately 47%. Since 1913, it has depreciated approximately 97%. Another revealing example would be the recession of 1920.

The Non-Depression of 1920-22

From 1920 to 1922, America suffered a recession that followed soon after the end of the First World War. It might have developed into a full-blown depression if modern *expert* conventions had been followed. Instead, it was allowed to run its course by the Harding and Coolidge administrations. Both refused to succumb to the temptation to actively intervene.

However, *experts* espousing "modern" theories of economics later advised both President Herbert Hoover and Franklin Roosevelt. They combined to mismanage the 1929-1931 recession into the Great Depression that extended for a decade until the mid-1940s. The methods the *experts* used acted like a bellows fanning a fire. It was the longest, most widespread, and deepest depression of the 18th, 19th or 20th Century.

Why are so many people unaware of the true facts? The answer lies in managed public education and propaganda. The phrase "*Great Depression*" was coined to describe the unprecedented extent of the damage and dislocation to the world-wide economy. There is no escaping the fact that the Federal Government's interventions worsened the problems. (Read Lawrence Reed's "*Great Myths of the Great Depression,*" published in 1998, and updated in 2010). No previous recession through the 19th Century to the late 1920s and 1930s, when the Federal Reserve's interventionist powers were first applied on a broad scale, holds a candle to the Great Depression—and the "*Grand Correction*" that looms just ahead.

In 1920-21, the market and economic indices crashed just as hard and, in some cases, harder than they did in 1929-31. Price deflation was greater than at any other point in 140 years of record keeping. In only one year, unemployment rose from 5.2% to 11.7%! At that point, the Federal Reserve System was only 7 years old. The Fed could not pump huge amounts of fake money into the economy, as it does today. The Country was still on the gold standard. The dollar was not devalued as it was in 1933, when FDR issued Executive Order 6201 making it a criminal offense to possess monetary gold. In that instance, the citizens were forced to turn in any gold that they owned above a nominal amount or held in coin collections. It was then artificially re-priced to $35 from $21 an ounce. That led to an immediate loss by all those who had been forced into surrendering their gold and reimbursed at the $21 an ounce rate.

With no fake money being injected into the banks as reserves, no corporations being bailed out, and "toxic assets" that could not be bought up, the Fed had to let the banks and companies suffer their losses in 1920-21. Proper capital ratios began to re-establish within months of the beginning of that recession. The Federal Reserve and the Federal Government did next to nothing. They stayed out of the way. It was the very best policy to take.

In fact, the Harding Administration further assisted the recovery by vastly lowering tax rates on gains, down to 4% from 73%! That tripled the tax revenues coming from the wealthiest Americans (remember the Laffer Curve?). Because of the lower rates, many more of them stopped trying to hide their wealth. The additional money was used to pay down the National Debt from WWI by 25% in five years. Government spending was reduced by more than a third. It was truly the polar opposite of today's typical policies. During the Coolidge administration top personal income tax rates were dropped from 75% to 25%.

By 1923, the recession was over. The employment rate was back to where it was before 1919. President Calvin *"Silent Cal"* Coolidge continued and accelerated his predecessor's policies. By 1925, total Federal spending fell below 1916 levels, from $170 to $70 per capita. It stayed below $100 until the later Hoover and Roosevelt Administrations. There is good reason why the remainder of that decade was called the *"Roaring Twenties."* Calvin Coolidge is likely one of our most unappreciated Presidents. See the new book *"Coolidge"* (2013) by Amity Shlaes.

But during the next economic downturn, beginning in 1929, instead of letting the economy reset on its own, the Federal Reserve and the Federal Government played a decidedly aggressive protectionist role in the markets and banking system. Then matters really worsened. As a result of using the 'new and better' financial policies of active intervention, what should have been another short recession followed by a quick recovery, instead turned into the decade long *Great Depression*" that eventually affected the whole world. Just wait until we see how the *experts'* gigantic interventions turn out this time!

When there is no central control of money supply, and no governmental economic interventionism of any significance, along with a "sound" currency (i.e. hard asset-based), then economic downturns will be shallower and/or shorter. They can be nothing else! That was the case during the first 120 years of the Republic, during the greatest and most prolonged financial and industrial expansion ever seen in human history. Downturns were relatively short and shallow. Recoveries were rapid. Corrections were called "Panics" instead of "Depressions."

The Keynesian-Progressive Tail Wags the Dog

Think about this for a moment. Everything is backwards. The tail is wagging the dog. The greatest uncertainties are no longer generated from within by the dynamic interplay of competitive forces in a functioning economy. Instead, the uncertainties are artificially created from without by government officials and regulators, and Congress and the Federal Reserve.

Businesses must constantly ask themselves: Will there be new or changed regulations? Will there be new or changed taxes and tax breaks? Will some industries gain subsidies and others lose them? What resources may or may not be exploited? Will there be another military intervention overseas? What measures may or may not be applied to inflation? Where will the Prime Rate be reset? Will there be more tinkering with the money supply? These external uncertainties exaggerate the ups and downs in the business cycle. None of them are **normal** business or market factors!

So do '**We the People,**' actually benefit from the interventionist policies of the government and the Federal Reserve? No, we do not, except in a placebo fashion! Any benefits seen are either short-lived or nonexistent. The meddling is counter-productive and actually detrimental. Harming the economy harms the People. Interference makes matters worse because it creates artificial imbalances and harms this Country's economic interests, destroys the value of money, and distorts personal and institutional behavior.

Mainstream Keynesian economic historians grossly exaggerate the severity of "panics" during the 19th Century. Comparing them to the Great Depression is truly absurd. The use of the term "depression" for an economic downturn began to be employed during the late 1800s to indicate an order of magnitude greater severity than a recession or a panic. But the use of the term "Great Depression" was only employed after the more than a decade long economic depression that the Federal Government itself created with its policies from 1929 until the early 1940s. It was governmental and Federal Reserve Corporation (FRC) actions that exacerbated the 1929 recession, increasing it to a "depression" and then, as matters worsened and it spread to other parts of the World, it became *"The Great Depression."* To disregard the government's role in deepening and lengthening the Great Depression is either intellectual laziness or dishonesty.

The objective evidence is uncovered, explained and discussed in Professor Murray Rothbard's highly regarded *"America's Great Depression,"* (1963).

Unfortunately, because of the severity of what is coming, a new descriptive term is required. I have settled on calling the coming economic events *"The Grand Correction."* Its opening stages are now being experienced. It figures to be an even worse economic calamity than The Great Depression. It could well be a global catastrophe. Financial manipulations have been perpetrated by central planners in ways, and to an extent, absolutely unimaginable during the 1930s.

Beginning in the 1920s, economists of the *"Austrian School"* have accurately predicted the now obvious failures of Marxist, Socialist and Fascist political-economic systems, as well as the "softer" application of "Progressive" Keynesian and even "Conservative" Monetarist economic theory. So why have the vast majority of those interested in economics not joined the Austrian School? Because it only teaches a true free market view of economics. Since such a market place is inherently self-regulating, control mechanisms are unnecessary along with most the economists and lawyers infesting our current system. That conclusion is unwelcome to those drawn to power.

The recommendations and predictions of the Austrian School are not time-based or data driven but based on human behavior. Unlike the other schools of economic thought, the Austrian School does not advocate 'managing the economy' or controlling the money supply. Therefore, it provides virtually no central positions of power to decide and decree economic policy. All the current temptations for *experts* and politicians to meddle, manipulate and intervene, would simply not exist.

In sharp contrast, Keynesians and Monetarists are entrenched throughout the power structure of the world's economic, monetary and policy-making institutions. In those environments, the *apparatchiks* easily succumb to the corrupt influences of wielding power and the self-preening vanity of being considered *experts*. Their closed loop of group-think orthodoxy is threatened by anything that challenges their cherished beliefs, cozy assumptions and, yes, their lucrative careers.

Austrian School advocates objective research and analysis, making fact based conclusions instead of generating positions favorable to those who have bought and paid for *expert* counsel. With the vigorous application of Austrian School methodology, there is simply little to no possibility of fudging results to please those wanting favorable conclusions to validate their own narrow and inimical economic interests. The same sort of behavior is manifest in the current vogue of 'climate science.'

The principal difference, with other schools of economic thought, is that the Austrians are emphatic about the impossibility of managing an entire economy, especially with deeply flawed econometric (statistical) models such as those embodied in Keynesian and Monetarist theory. Fredrick A. Hayek, a leading light of the Austrian School, called such thinking "scientistical" buffoonery. "Scientistic" was Hayek's word to describe the marriage of the fake economic 'science' of the Keynesian and Monetarist schools with gross 'statistical' analysis.

The modern economy is in a constant state of flux. That is due to hundreds of millions of individual players making billions of separate economic decisions, each and every day. These decisions are amplified by computers making 'real time' adjustments without human oversight. The staggeringly diverse and numerous interactions that result are not reducible to simplified econometric statistics that are meaningful to "*manage an economy.*"

Considering the questionable validity of the limited, past-dated data gathered by mainstream economists, and the very mixed (usually incorrect) nature of their predictions, the sheer number of present day variables actually enlarges the gap rather than closing it. That makes a mockery of the assumption that a few *experts* can understand the sum of all the processes at work. The whole idea of general, econometric 'management' of a free economy is patently ridiculous.

A free market economy is not always pretty to watch but it will never be as ugly as a centralized, managed and hyper-regulated economy.

I earlier made the point that predicting long-term climate change is far too complex to be reduced to certainties at this point. We do not understand, or even know, all of the variables, or how they interrelate.

Although the market economy is a human invention, it is also far too complex to be conveniently reduced to statistics, explained by charts and externally managed *"by the numbers."* Anyone with even a cursory knowledge of Heisenberg's Uncertainty Principle in Physics, should understand the point that I am making here. The more precisely one property is measured, the less precisely others can be determined and known, or controlled.

Mark Twain popularized the saying: *"There are three kinds of lies: lies, damned lies, and statistics."* Nothing has changed to alter that insight. Statistics can be twisted, intentionally or not, to fit almost any premise. Throughout history, it has been obvious that individuals can convince themselves to believe just about anything, even if patently untrue. People so often see only what they expect to see, and hear whatever they want to hear. *"Conventional wisdom"* has been shown, time and time again, to be incorrect. That is the case with the beliefs of the mainstream economic system. It is fundamentally flawed and it has repeatedly failed.

A Free Market Education

So how does one go about learning, understanding and appreciating that the best economy is not managed but allowed to operate freely? I recommend reading the short volume: *"Economics in One Lesson"* by Henry Hazlitt (1946) along with a famous short story *"I, Pencil"* by Leonard Reed (1958). Further exploration will inevitably take a reader to the Mises Institute, one of the central repositories of Austrian School thinking (http://thecitizenslaststand.com/mises).

There is an underlying reason why the centralized command or 'managed' Communist, Socialist, Fascist, Keynesian, and Monetarist economic models fail. Each of them is imposed from above and controlled by an elitist group, usually self-appointed, or elected by an ignorant electorate. Depending on the degree of coercion and manipulation imposed by the elitist leaders, they fail at different rates, but they all inevitably collapse.

Those that feature the highest degree of command and control fail soonest. They are the most out of touch with the reality of how economies naturally function.

Any system of econometric management attempting to oversee complex human interactions, whether indirectly via reliance on flawed statistics, or by direct command and control, will fail. Tossing a coin would be a more successful way to make decisions!

The development of the *"social sciences"* is the root cause for the erroneous thinking that centralized, large-scale planning by government and corporations is feasible. In practice, it is far more efficient when individuals, voluntarily associating and working together, use non-coercive and co-operative methods.

Worst of all, for America and Europe, was the creation during the 20th Century of central banking cartels such as the Federal Reserve Bank Corporation and the European Central Bank.

There is no actual free market economy when the issuance of money is a monopoly and interest rates are set by a central authority. How could it be otherwise? New money creation should only be a function of net wealth (true capital—also known as "savings") and risk-assessment of future market production of wealth by the market players themselves.

Jefferson, Madison, Franklin and most of the other Founders knew that lesson two centuries ago, so why do we not? Has the convenience of cheap, fake money made it so easy to forget the lessons of history and economics? Even Alexander Hamilton, in spite of his desire for a National Bank, understood the need for a hard, asset-anchored, reserve system. He knew it would never succeed in the long-term if based on a monopolist issuance of fiat currency.

What is Money?

Let us step back for a moment.

What exactly is money? People think they know until they are asked to define it. Amazingly, most bankers and financial *experts* do not know either. The next time you meet one, ask them: "What are the three qualities that determine what is to be used as money?"

Money has three characteristics. It is simultaneously a:

- Store of wealth
- Unit of account

114

- Medium of exchange

Along with nearly all our citizens, the average banker or financial *expert* does not have a clue about the true meaning of money. The Federal Reserve has successfully transformed it into a meaningless abstraction. The Fed does not issue real money but instead a *"Federal Reserve Note."* It is not the dollar defined by Congress in 1792 as being equivalent to, and redeemable as, 24 grams of pure silver. It is make-believe, a financial sleight-of-hand. This charade only succeeds because it has enforced exchange value via legal tender laws and a believing public. It is a mass delusion that will eventually evaporate as inflation proceeds.

Sound money systems contain a key guarantee that is totally absent with fiat money. Sound money eliminates *"counter-party risk."* Counter-party risk is defined in Investopedia as:

The risk to each party of a contract that the counterparty will not live up to its contractual obligations.

Remember the first characteristic of money? It was initially invented to act as a store of wealth. Without the ability to end any transaction with a hard asset, instead of receiving only more promises to pay (in the form of fiat money), there is no true payment to close (or extinguish) the transaction cycle by the issuer. That is the critical element in all honest monetary systems, conspicuously absent with fiat money.

Our economy therefore exists in a limbo of mal-investment because there is no constant true measure of valuation. A "note" is a debt instrument (a promissory). It is not a stable store of wealth because additional notes may be arbitrarily issued, thereby diluting the value of the earlier notes. That is called inflation. There was a time when such activity was called **counterfeiting,** but that term is now only applied to private citizens, not to the government. Is that any wonder?

Money creation without the ultimate anchor of hard assets only creates the illusion of wealth.

The math is at a kindergarten or first grade level. Ask a young child: *"Is 2 the same as 3?"* He or she will laugh at you. *"Of course it isn't!"* Yet that is exactly what the *experts*, the PhDs and even Nobel Laureates in Economics, and the politicians and bureaucrats, all believers in Keynesian theory, are foisting on the American People. Despite *"legal tender"* laws forcing acceptance of fiat currency as a medium of exchange, and a unit of account, they are emphatically ***not*** a store of wealth. Therefore, they do not satisfy that characteristic in the three-part definition of money.

The 'dollar bills' used every day, in every kind of transaction, large or small, are not real money. I would suspect that less than 1 in a 1000 people has any real idea of the fakery, actually outright fraud, that is being perpetrated in plain sight, right under their noses.

John Maynard Keynes, his-right-honorable-self, the father of Keynesian economics, believed that the number who actually understood the truth to be far fewer. Or, perhaps he was exaggerating for effect. When alluding to Lenin's idea of controlling a country by debasing the currency, Keynes wrote:

There is no subtler, no surer means of overturning the existing basis of society than to debauch the currency. The process engages all the hidden forces of economic law on the side of destruction, and does it in a manner which not one man in a million is able to diagnose.

So ask yourself: "Why did our government do it?" Why did they apparently adopt the 2nd and 5th Planks of the Communist Manifesto? The answer is simple. It guarantees power and control. Do we actually have domestic enemies to go along with the foreign ones, or are we just plagued by idiots and dupes? The answer is both.

On the Internet, one can find two short and simple tutorials called *"Money As Debt I & II."* Inside of 90 minutes of watching them both, a viewer will gain a mastery of money not taught in any but a tiny handful of universities in this Country. Your view of the Federal Reserve, its fiat money and its position as this Country's central bank, will never be the same.

Have We Not Seen This Circus Act Before?

It should be immediately obvious that the whole reason behind the central banking cartel is to control monetary policy for the benefit and enrichment of a small group of central bankers. Naturally, this comes at the expense of the rest of us who have been forced to participate in that system, no matter how unwittingly, or how unwillingly.

This is an opportune moment to quote from President Abraham Lincoln again, who said:

You can fool all the people some of the time, and some of the people all the time, but you cannot fool all the people all the time.

It is time to wake up the rest of the folks out there!

A founder of the Austrian School, Ludwig von Mises, pointed out the unnatural and extremely harmful end results from the adoption of the Keynesian worldview, namely the central control of economies:

The wavelike movement affecting the economic system, the recurrence of periods of boom which are followed by periods of depression, is the unavoidable outcome of the attempts, repeated again and again, to lower the gross market rate of interest by means of credit expansion. There is no means of avoiding the final collapse of a boom brought about by credit expansion. The alternative is only whether the crisis should come sooner as a result of voluntary abandonment of further credit expansion, or later as a final and total catastrophe of the currency system involved.

His prominent student, Friedrich August Hayek, explained the fallacy even more tersely:

The curious task of economics is to demonstrate to men how little they really know about what they imagine they can design.

Indeed, how could a small group individuals, well-intentioned or not, using grossly flawed statistical data, possibly promulgate correct interest rate policy decisions in a dynamic free market? One that consists of millions of players and computers that together are making billions of decisions every day? Obviously, central control cannot possibly react quickly enough, or predict all the possible eventualities. The genius of the free market is that decisions, right or wrong, flow through the system quickly, with successes adopted and rewarded, and failures just as rapidly punished and eliminated. Nowadays, they are even more efficiently and rapidly processed by virtue of the Internet's existence.

A recent example of wrong-headed central control is the Dodd-Frank legislation. Did that stop the MF-Global collapse? It did not. Will it stop others? No, it will not. No regulator can ever see the next type of failure coming and never will. No amount of past legislation has ever stopped such things from happening or continuing. It is yet another instance of legislative insanity, actually expecting different results by repeating what did not work before. Attempts at regulation thoroughly confuse matters, throw everything further off-track and waste yet more resources and time, adversely affecting the lives of millions of American citizens, and people around the World.

Government-granted monopolies, selective regulation and tax policies, special subsidies and punitive selective enforcement, are also obviously counter-productive. It is keenly interesting how personal computers, and the Internet, exploded into being across the world in such short order without governmental interference. Did unregulated freedom of action have anything to do with the phenomenon, enabling this paradigm shift that has so profoundly altered the course of human history?

On one occasion, the government went after Microsoft for supposed "anti-trust violations." However, before the enforcement orders were issued by the Court, the rapidly evolving market had completely transformed the situation, rendering any possible infractions moot. It is only because government regulatory bureaucrats are way out of their league technically, and their control attempts so preposterous, that the IT and Internet worlds remain, for now, largely unregulated.

The small-minded and venal attitude of *"If it moves, tax it. If it keeps moving, regulate it. And if it stops moving, subsidize it,"* that Ronald Reagan warned against, is still very much alive in Washington, D.C.

Watch out, the recent Stop Online Piracy Act (SOPA) and the Preventing Real Online Threats to Economic Creativity and the Theft of Intellectual Property Act (PIPA) legislation, are just more of a continuing series (like the Cyber Intelligence and Sharing Protection Act—CISPA) that are certain to keep coming. Unless, of course, citizens awaken from their lethargy, and vote out of office the professional politicians who are prostituting themselves to special interests.

How the Federal Reserve Operates vs. Open Exchange Monetarism

Be aware that "*Interest is the price of money.*" Therefore, interest rates for borrowed money set by a free market would necessarily have to be competitive (and changed in real time)—just like the price of everything else!

The Federal Reserve does not even bother to deny that its choices of interest rates are usually counter-cyclical, a technical term meaning that artificially set interest rates are actually higher when they should have been lower, or vice-versa. Of course, the Fed does not acknowledge the harm that is done, since that would invalidate one of the central premises for its own existence. After the fact, the Fed attempts to counteract booms and busts exacerbated by its own faulty prior decisions, thus creating ever more extreme booms and busts.

Having "*painted itself into a corner,*" thus benefiting some few who will want things left alone, and to the detriment of the many others who vociferously want immediate remedy, there is greater pressure to "*get it right this time.*" The resulting delays, while new policy is being debated behind closed doors by the *experts,* only results in yet another imbalance to the previous imbalances created by this entire counter-productive process. In the end, the natural cyclical waves of boom and bust are vastly exaggerated, exactly as Mises and Hayek described.

Think of a drunken driver at the wheel of a car on a road at night. Barely able to discern the dividing line, sometimes wandering into the opposite traffic lane, sometimes running dangerously close to the side of the road, the driver makes sudden erratic course corrections, as well as abruptly slowing down or speeding up. Does that seem familiar? Welcome to the world of the Fed driven economy in Amerika today.

The free market is like a sober driver at the wheel of a car, alert and aware of his or her surroundings, adjusting to constantly changing conditions. Of course, there are bumps in the road, unforeseen difficulties, alterations in the flow of traffic, and the actions of other drivers that need to be considered. Yet despite the challenges, a safe, sober driver is not a constant threat to the welfare of others on the road, unlike a dangerous drunken driver.

It does not matter how many *"big brains"* are crammed into a conference room to make economic policy decisions, they will never be smart enough to replace the inherent self-correcting processes of the free market. The Fed does not work and never will. It needs to be phased out and terminated soon, if this Country is to survive in the long-term.

Profoundly worsening the ill effects of the monopolist central-banking cartel is that it now operates in a fiat currency environment. There is no established stable monetary value backed by hard assets. Welcome to *"just trust me"* economics.

Allowing a cartel to operate a fiat-currency system, without any hard-asset exchange to ultimately complete (or "extinguish") all market transactions, is a certain recipe for world-wide economic disaster.

As we all know, a chronic drunkard at the wheel of a car inevitably causes great harm. Continuing such a system means that the U.S. economy, as well the entire global economic system as presently constituted, will trigger a chain reaction freeway pile-up when the Federal Reserve drunkenly swerves into oncoming traffic.

Sovereign debt, fiscal and trade deficits, Welfare/Warfare statism, outsourcing, mal-investment, currency manipulation, stock and housing bubbles, all such distortions would be impossible without being propped up by the flow of fake money emanating from the Federal Reserve and the European Central Bank (ECB). Gresham's Law, that bad money chases out the good, is at the full flood stage.

Bad money is at the root of our problems. Sound money automatically corrals the effects of bad economic decisions made at all levels of private and public life.

So am I advocating pure *"laissez faire"* economics? Yes, as close to that as we can possibly achieve. We have never had a true free market in the modern era! No one ever seems to ask, after all the command/control and hyper-regulatory attempts have failed, why we cannot finally try the actual free market?

Yes, there must still be a sober alert driver at the wheel of a moving vehicle. Laissez faire markets punish criminal behavior in the market place. Theft, fraud and other chicanery, need to be severely and promptly punished. At present, some of the greatest "white-collar" criminals on Wall Street, and in the banking and financial sector, remain *"above the law."*

What we cannot afford are drunkards at the wheel who have been intoxicated by the heady brew of self-importance, academic distinctions, the wielding of great power, and the intellectual trap of believing in their own infallibility. In other words, the drunks in the central banks and all their enablers in government and Big Business who are also inebriated with power and only have their skewed interests at heart.

In stark contrast to the existing unsavory mess, the Austrian School free market economists do not use "scientistic" econometrics. Instead, Austrians study the economic behavior of individuals and market places to understand how a particular market operates at various transaction points. Then, using objective analysis, they make recommendations on how to change poor behaviors and encourage good ones.

The sober drivers in the market then choose among the recommendations. They either adopt or discard them, based on their own practical experience, gained while operating within a free market. The close monitoring of consequences provide a continuous feedback loop to refine those chosen recommendations. In such ways, the Austrian School serves the market rather than ruling it.

The Impact of Human Behavior on Markets

Underlying the Austrian approach in studying economic behavior and events is Praxeology, an important concept that is defined in Wikipedia as:

(T)he study of human action. Praxeology rejects the empirical methods of the natural sciences for the study of human action, because the observation of how humans act in simple situations cannot predict how they will act in complex situations.

Of course! Another instance when a piece of the puzzle falls into place. Aha! A myriad of purely individual human actions drive the market. Accordingly, the workings of the market cannot be abstracted into gross statistical models, graphs and projections that are supposedly scientific certainty. No matter how hard the Keynesians and Monetarists may try, they cannot successfully approximate the techniques used in the natural sciences to arrive at proper conclusions. Human behaviors on the individual level may be relatively consistent but those cannot be lumped together in a constant, measurable way to make predictions about mass behavior.

Yes, what the Keynesians and Monetarists generate looks nice and shiny. It has that *"scientific look"* to it. Nevertheless, it is *"garbage-in-garbage-out"* (GIGO). As any metals prospector learns early in their training: *"All that glitters is not gold."* The Austrians study, analyze and draw conclusions on all levels from the key indicator, which is human behavior. In so doing they avoid fabricating the statistical *"fool's gold"* of the Keynesians (followers of British economist John M. Keynes) and Monetarists (followers of the Monetary theory and money supply espoused by Milton Friedman and Anna Schwartz).

Once one has realized that it is subtle human behavior, not some *"scientistical"* nonsense that drives the market, it is easy enough to come up with real life scenarios. For example, let us say that there are two companies with similar strengths and prospects pursuing the same business plan. You are an investor trying to decide between the two of them. To all outward appearances, they both have the resources and personnel to succeed.

What you do not know is that the CEO of one of the companies is in trouble with the IRS. He succumbs to the temptation of embezzling investor money in a vain attempt to fix his problems. The investor money is therefore not utilized in product development. Any competitive advantage or parity with the competition is squandered. Eventually, the sordid truth comes out and the company goes out of business. The investors lose their money. The other company goes on to dominate its field.

Now just think of all the perturbations caused by human behavior, good and bad, multiplied by the millions. Based on that realization, it becomes crystal clear that centralized econometrics management, based on gross and frequently near meaningless data, is minimally useful in making long-term economic projections. The greatest problems with such flawed data occur when making enforced economic and monetary policy decisions regarding the price and supply of money in the economy. It is therefore easy to understand why virtually none of the established market and monetary controllers could see the real estate and financial crises coming.

Attempt to give one example of any correct economic projections by the Congressional Budget Office, Office of Management and Budget, Federal Reserve or any Monetarist or Keynesians forecasters. Now contrast that with the repeatedly accurate predictions made by Austrian forecasters of market behavior during the same period.

The "*wisest fools*" in the current economic power structure; Bernanke, Geithner, Krugman, Paulson, LeGarde, et al, wedded to econometric modeling, are using a fundamentally flawed decision-making paradigm to create a series of time-based conclusions. Those conclusions then become the basis of official policy that has little to no chance of actually succeeding in the long-term. There may be short-term and false "positive" results but they are actually ticking time bombs. Remember that their policy decisions are being implemented in an unsound monetary infrastructure, that is in direct contradiction to free market principles and common sense.

Firstly, their policies are negatively compounded by the propensity of central control groups to make serious errors and mistakes due to having limited information, assuring the introduction of added problems in the future economy.

Secondly, after making decisions which are typically counter-cyclical, they are implemented slowly because they emanate from a central management point. Bureaucratic inefficiency slows implementation of policy, thus further guaranteeing that the policy is out of sync with real-time market conditions.

On Wall Street, when traders and financiers attempt to create 'money' without creating wealth, that reinforces the tendency towards short-term thinking that is focused only on the next quarter. Long range business planning becomes extremely difficult. That is due to the uncertainties of what the central authority will do next.

Inevitably, there is an escalation in the severity in the fluctuations in the economy due to successive bad decisions, or even potentially good decisions made at the wrong time. Over time, the amplitude of highs and lows increase. It is similar to the difference between the jagged peaks and deep valleys of the Northern Rocky Mountains and the gentler gradations in a Basin-and-Range geologic formation.

More and more people are noting that the explanations and strategies publicly announced by the Fed, and the ECB, for 'fixing' the problems that they created, are making less and less sense. In the past, Alan Greenspan, former Fed Chairman, was an unquestioned master of obfuscation. He held the markets spellbound with his gobbledygook pronouncements. Fed Chairman Bernanke has lost that advantage.

It is now just a matter of time until the whole sham is exposed by its failures, followed by enough people calling for the Fed's phase-out and termination. More independent observers will accept that a return to truly free markets is the only practical solution. That will cause the Fed's supporters and insiders to virulently attack the only school of economic thought that has been vindicated and proven correct in its reasoning, namely the Austrian School. Do not expect the Keynesians and Monetarists to be graceful losers!

When will their failed theories be summarily rejected in favor of actual analysis and understanding of human economic behavior? At this point, your guess is as good as mine.

A Few Austrian-type Economic Predictions

Given that the predictions of the Austrian School are not time-based, or data driven, but behavior-based, an Austrian economist or analyst will

not predict economic events by forecasting **when** something will happen. Making predictions in terms of time, rather than behavior, is nothing short of bizarre. Instead, any economic analysis should explain **what** will happen, and **why** it will happen, if certain behaviors in the market persist, or if they are eliminated. That is why any Austrian analyst can make the following predictions with a high degree of certainty:

1. If the Fed does not submit to a transparent and comprehensive audit of its operational procedures and balance sheets, then The Federal Reserve Note will cease to exist as a viable currency. The U.S. Congress must order that audit now! The present opaque policies cannot be permitted to continue.

2. Government debt bills and bonds of the United States, Japan and the European Union will either hard-default, or soft-default due to continued inflationary policies. Either way, it is a default and not a value-for-value, actual repayment that will occur. Typically, governments attempt to inflate their way out of such situations.

3. Due to the size of the existing debt, and the virtually incomprehensible nature of the convoluted fiscal and agency entanglements between state governments and federal programs, at least half the States, and approximately a third or more of the Counties and Municipalities, will default as the Grand Correction cycle completes. Significant budget shortfalls for most of the remaining entities will persist until a bottom-to-top debt restructuring is accomplished by using sound money.

4. There will be no true near-term recovery from the current Great Recession. Nor is any real recovery likely for the foreseeable future. Short-term 'improvements' will prove to be transitory, illusory or statistical flukes.

5. Overall sector price depreciation will continue in residential housing and commercial real estate for the foreseeable future.* Any short-term upward statistical fluctuations will prove to be temporary or inflation-based. The overall trend is still down with 4 to 6+ million foreclosures yet to be processed through the banking system. It is estimated that 11-12 million house and

property holders are "underwater" with their mortgages. Market clearing must occur before any possible improvements occur in that sector.

6. There will continue to be overall sector price appreciation, in hard money terms, for basic commodities such as food, energy and certain luxury goods into the foreseeable future.* Short-term downward statistical fluctuations will again prove to be transitory. The real price of such things as firearms, ammunition, and farm and ranch land will continue to increase as economic disruptions and civil unrest increase.

7. Most major global stock indexes will oscillate with ever larger positive to negative swings until finally surging in an inflationary spike and then crashing in a deflationary spiral unless 1-3 (above) are dealt with immediately. Japan may already be close to a death spiral with the NIKKEI priced at ~15% of its 1989 peak (inflation adjusted), a 2:1 debt-to-GDP ratio, and so many negative demographics at work.

8. Certain market sector companies will increase in real value in contrast to the overall crash. They will be those engaged in exploiting primary resources and producing essential goods, technology and services, along with anything else that falls into the category of true wealth creation.

9. The primary precious metals (gold and silver) will likely continue their 10-year bull run for the rest of this decade, with intermediate corrections along the way in conjunction with index gyrations noted in 7 (above). The current bull-run in those metals is a direct response to the destructive ongoing fiscal, financial and monetary policies. Correct those and the bull-run will end. The remaining platinum group metals (PGM) will oscillate wildly based on their varying degrees of industrial and investment potential in the context of a lurching economy.

10. A large portion (at least two-thirds) of the current banking and financial services sector will disappear. *"Making easy money on fake money,"* rather than by true productive wealth creation, is no longer a viable business model. It never was. The current

manipulations of the existing system, here and abroad, can only continue until the implosion is completed.

Hyperinflation is an unlikely scenario in the modern central banking based system. Hyperinflation is the *death of money*. It would mean the end of central banks as they currently exist and operate. As much as an Austrian School economist might view the death of monopolist central banking as desirable, most central bankers will move heaven and earth to avoid that fate.

Do they have any weapons to prevent hyperinflation?

Other than bankruptcy, such weapons may be minimal in their effect. Behavior-based analysis of central bankers assumes that they will attempt to protect themselves from a hyperinflationary outcome. The hope is they are smart enough to prevent that scenario, even if it means losing most of their present powers. However, it is hard to be overly optimistic that they will be able to stave off massive inflation.**

In order to survive, the central bankers might agree to a competitive currency system in an effort to compete with emergent private currencies. Those will become increasingly popular as the old order crumbles. Or, the central bankers may re-adopt a hard asset-based currency reserve system. Or, they could transfer the primary monetary authority back to individual governments and only supply an exchange-based clearinghouse function.

The latter two possibilities seem unlikely. Firstly, it is improbable that they can accept the institutional discipline required. Secondly, their power would be so reduced that it would effectively end their cartel altogether. The central banking cartel may initiate massive-inflation as a way to survive, hoping that it will not become hyperinflation. The latter eventuality would result in a significant restructuring—with no guarantee as to their continued existence.

The European Central Bank (ECB) is entering into the run-up phase for massive-inflation that will be precipitated by the planned European Union (EU) bailouts of certain member countries. It is beginning to engage in the behaviors noted above.

The Bank of Japan (BOJ) is surviving on the interest carry trade, and because nearly all their sovereign debt was purchased domestically, thanks to that population's high savings rate. That ended in 2011. It is likely they will join a regional currency exchange system anchored by the Chinese Yuan with other Asian countries, or also try to further inflate their economy into prosperity again for a time. With a 200% debt-to-GDP ratio, their options are rapidly narrowing.

The Federal Reserve has almost certainly ensured that massive inflation will occur in the U.S.. That is due to continuing policies of stimulus, buying toxic assets and quantitative easing, vast expansion (350%) of the monetary base since 2008 and back-door participation (that they have been unable to conceal) in the various ECB bail-out scenarios for certain EU countries. If attempts to control inflation do not work, and massive inflation looks to become hyperinflation, then the central bankers may attempt other stopgap measures.

Let Us Try the NEW! and IMPROVED Fake Money!

Another scenario that has been bandied about is for the central banks to create, with the participation of the IMF and the World Bank, a new global currency, possibly calling it "Globo." However, there does not appear to be any effective way that central bankers can replace one failing fiat currency regime with another one. With the current one a massive failure, there is simply no logic or credibility in building another. And what exactly would it be based on? That should be apparent to even the stupidest politicians! It also could not happen via a Special Drawing Rights (SDRs) scheme, if they tried to anchor it that way, since that would be a deflationary monster. Such a scheme would fail more quickly, and on a larger scale, than even the current system. Why is that? Because where does the IMF go to get hard money for Special Drawing Rights, or to try another fiat scheme? It would have to come from all the economically failing countries, of course!

Nor could it happen through the reestablishment of an international central banking precious metal exchange system. The world's central banks no longer have enough precious metals, in their own reserves, to set-up such a system. Efforts to confiscate privately held caches would probably not sequester (i.e. seize) enough to start one.

Make no mistake, there are plenty of real assets, metals or other hard goods, to build a functional exchange-based series of systems with one hundred percent reserves. It is only a matter of having the desire while recognizing that it would need to be accomplished privately. It would not, and should never again, be enabled by means of any government monopolized, centrally-controlled exchange systems.

In 1950, the world's central banking system controlled approximately 47% of the world's above ground inventory of gold. Today, it controls about 17 to 18%. As in 1950, the world's richest people own approximately 8 to 10%. The sale of much of the gold once held by central banks, and new gold production, has mostly ended up in the possession of individual small holders around the World. The latter now hold between 70 to 75% of the inventory. In 1950, small, individual holders held less than 35%. The central bankers apparently bought into their own lie that fiat currencies were invulnerable! Interestingly, the central banks have again become net buyers of gold (even while they insist it is not money!). However, it cannot possibly be enough to restart a central bank managed gold standard. To purchase enough to do that would send the gold price through the roof and soaring into the stratosphere.

Continuing the existing Federal Reserve and government economic policies in our Country, will further increase the likelihood of massive-inflation occurring. There is no certainty that it might not also, unexpectedly and uncontrollably, morph into hyperinflation.

The EU, Japan and U.S. sovereign debt bubbles are set up to burst. Their fiscal issues will not be solved. The political will, even the understanding and skills to solve them, is conspicuously absent. So, where does that leave us? We need to examine how we operate as a population consisting of *"the 99% and the 1%."*

* Note: Sector Price Appreciation/Depreciation is not the same as Inflation/Deflation. The latter is a purely monetary supply increase/decrease phenomena. Sector Price Appreciation/Depreciation

occurs in certain sectors via market pricing factors as opposed to inflationary/deflationary pressures of the overall money supply. Eventually massive-inflation, or possibly hyperinflation, will overwhelm Sector Price Appreciation/Depreciation in all sectors of the economy until the final destructive spiral of a currency begins.

** Note: The definition of massive vs. hyperinflation is varied but the following is a reasonable explanation. Massive inflation is more than 25% but less than 100% annually. Hyperinflation is therefore more than 100% annually. Where hyperinflation ends has no definition. Zimbabwe holds the current record with monthly inflation which ran at 79,600,000,000%! Yes, you read that right—per month!

6

The Grand Correction?

*We seem to have entered the last days of the euro as we currently know it
... some extraordinary things will almost certainly need to happen to
prevent the progressive closure of all the euro zone sovereign bond markets,
potentially accompanied by escalating runs on even the strongest banks.*
–Report from Credit Suisse Fixed Income Research Unit, 11/2011

An appropriate name should be found to encompass the totality of the
unfolding events.

Financial writers Peter Schiff, Anthony Wile, Gary North, Doug
Casey, David Boaz, Tom Woods and others, all of whom are using the
Austrian School of economic thought as their guide, have for years given
the impending economic disaster descriptive titles. They use titles such as
Great Recession, Greater Depression, Great Unraveling, Great Reckoning
or Great Liquidation. In my opinion, none of those particular terms
sufficiently describe the magnitude of the event. Writer John Mauldin
uses the interesting term *"Monetary Endgame."* However, some of these
terms are useful to identify and examine phases during the entire process
of decay and collapse.

Please note that only one of those terms matches anything being said,
or written, by mainstream economists.

When the Great Depression of the 20th Century ran its course, the
institutions and mechanisms instrumental in exacerbating its severity
and duration, masked by WWII, remained in place. Foolishly, their
powers were actually increased, not decreased or terminated. Previously
flawed policies were amplified into clueless and destructive decisions that
over decades have steadily pushed us to the financial brink.

What has transpired, ever since the end of The Great Depression, has been a devolutionary process of bad policy growing like dry-rot through the world's economic system. Unfortunately, having thrown fiscal/financial discipline and caution to the wind, the U.S. shares the largest portion of the blame along with Europe, thanks to the latter's development of the Eurozone, and the exploding debt of member countries in the European Union (EU).

Those entrusted with political and economic power, have failed far too many of the moral, ethical and intellectual challenges arising since the end of World War II and, in particular, since the collapse of the Soviet Union. The enormity of their failures will soon be obvious to one and all.

Why the Grand Correction?

As events unfold they will be recognized as revolutionary in human history. In socio-economic terms, it is "...*the big one, Elizabeth*," like a massive earthquake and tsunami with many victims. Lives are changed forever. It is civilization changing in its scope and effect. Its repercussions will eclipse what happened during and after the Great Depression, World War Two and the Cold War.

Therefore, I have taken to calling it "*The Grand Correction.*" Life in most developed parts of the world will transition into a very different reality than the present illusion. Will it only be a massive "correction" or a descent into a new "*Dark Age?*" Our future actions as individuals will make a profound difference in influencing its eventual outcome.

It has causes decades in the making here, and abroad. The process was accelerated by President Nixon's decision to abandon the Gold Standard in 1971. It became unmistakably obvious in 2000 with the bursting of the tech bubble. That precipitated the first recession of the 21st Century. Subsequent efforts to pump up the economy by the Fed, between 2001 and 2005, set the stage for the housing bubble which burst in 2006. We have not recovered from the housing and financial crisis and are still feeling the effects today. The "*Great Unraveling*" aptly describes this phase of the Grand Correction.

The completion of this unraveling process has been artificially delayed. That was only made possible by huge increases in government deficits, and the expansion of credit and manipulation of the currency, on a truly massive scale, by the Federal Reserve. Among the government's misguided interventions were the Troubled Asset Relief Program (TARP), the American Recovery and Reinvestment Act (ARRA), and corporate bail-outs. Fed manipulations of the money supply included successive Quantitative Easing (QE1, 2 and 3) and credit expansions. All these measures only put off the day of reckoning. Some appeared to have artificially worked for a short time, but they were, and are, only short-term props for a very shaky economic house of cards.

This phase of the financial crisis is continuing far longer than today's mainstream economists would have us believe. We have not yet exited it because the necessary large scale liquidation (de-leveraging) of debt and malinvestment has not yet occurred in any meaningful way. So, the next phase would appear to be the *"Great Reckoning."* Only then will the main sequence of *"The Grand Correction"* take place. It will affect our entire cultural and economic structure. Because of the unprecedented size of the interventions, it will take a decade or more to conclude. There is no easy or fast way out.

Panic and the 5-minute Design Increment

We are now witnessing what History will likely record as the last desperate ploys of government policy makers and the establishment political parties. They are already exhibiting what the tech consulting business calls *"5-minute design increment"* behavior. In layman's terms, that means a totally reactive and "knee-jerk" panic mode.

When building a large scale system, a serious design flaw that is discovered too late in implementation, is typically patched with quick fixes mandated by management. That is despite the fact that the flaws can be serious enough to bring down the entire system. The correct procedure is to accept the short-term "hit" to the schedule, come to a stop and repair it. Once that is done, system building resumes.

Short-term fixes—*"5-minute design increment"* behavior—merely postpone the inevitable. When the system does collapse, failures may be vastly larger, perhaps even catastrophic. It could have been completely avoided if the design flaw had been resolved immediately. It is a clear example that prevention is always the best cure.

In the present case, market clearing and loss liquidation should have occurred immediately. Budget deficits and debt should have been reduced. The Federal Budget and the fake 'deficit-reduction' deals made since the summer of 2011 are typical 5-minute design increment fixes. The back-door Federal Reserve Loans and liquidity programs are the same.

Similar quick fixes are seemingly proposed every week in Europe by the EU and ECB. However, such delay tactics, such attempts to postpone the inevitable, have about run their course. The manipulators have exhausted nearly all such options. We can see, in the stalled employment and economic indicators, how such quick fixes have been virtually useless, both here and in Europe. Trillions have been wasted for minor blips and glimmers of momentary relief and false hope.

The Next Two Issues To Be Faced

1. Main ledger accounts for failing and bailed-out banks and business must be reconciled sooner or later
2. Bad debts accrued must be written off as unrecoverable and all those losses shown on balance sheets to understand their full impact in order to deal with them

In the short-term, creditors may allow themselves to be persuaded to accept other forms of additional debt or currency instruments (swaps). That realization is already causing U.S. and Eurozone creditors and credit managers many sleepless nights. The future "haircuts" on sovereign and other debt will make the Greek, Ireland and Iceland write-downs seem modest by comparison. "Haircut" is a euphemism for the unmentionable word—default. Using the term "default" would literally implode the enormous Credit Default Swap (CDS) and Collateralized Debt Obligation (CDO) markets in short order. Yes, they are that fragile!

As the failure of the quick fixes becomes increasingly obvious, the volatility of global equity and debt markets will increase. It is already so precarious that it is similar to *"jumping from moss hummock to moss hummock"* in a swamp. In the various global market exchanges, daily swings of 3 to 5 percent, or higher, will occur more and more frequently.

High Frequency Trading (HFT) will go into overdrive. The "flashcrash" phenomenon has already created thousands of **sub-second** market events that are not seen or recognized until long after they have already occurred. Global trade timing is *modeled in millionths of a second* to gain an advantage. Soon these will be greatly magnified in scale, creating very large events that cannot possibly be masked or overlooked. At your leisure sometime, watch the graphic at http://thecitizenslaststand.com/HFT and be properly mortified.

The relative valuation of the Dollar and the Euro, previously shifting by only a few basis points per trading session, is now being tracked and traded in tenths. More speculators are jumping in daily, or weekly, between the two currencies, seeking profits by "scalping" the top of the curve between the swings in face values. Those cycles will accelerate. Each one will be of shorter duration, affecting a broader portion of each index, and more violent than the last.

As each equity or bond market soars and slides, the Federal Reserve and European Central Bank will vainly pump out more dollars and euros to "stabilize" the system. These actions will have but one predictable outcome. They will finally provoke runaway inflation. According to Austrian School monetary theory, relatively benign inflation numbers below 2 percent will inevitably soar into the double digits, perhaps beyond.

The "blossoming" of inflation will be vastly amplified *"on the wings of electrons."* One frightening portent is the magnitude of bets made on the changing values of financial contracts. The notional amount of these "derivatives" placed in 2000 was a *"mere $200 billion."* Today, with vastly more powerful computing capabilities, and reckless individuals blinded by the "easy buck" syndrome at the helm of financial institutions around the World, this number exceeds $1 quadrillion, and it is accelerating. (As a point of reference, a quadrillion is generally recognized by numbering convention to be 1,000,000,000,000,000, a thousand million million). The top 25 U.S. bank holding companies have about one-third of those derivatives (~$330 trillion) on their books! Only the banks know what is actually "off-books."

For perspective, the total global GDP is currently $62 trillion annually (2012 dollars). The recent revelations about the magnitude of off-books derivatives "gray market" between JP Morgan, and others, holding EU sovereign debt, is truly frightening ($24 trillion on-books, estimates as high as $7 trillion off-books). The continued debasement of dollars and euros is rapidly stripping them of any semblance of being a *store of wealth.*" At a certain point, they will no longer be accepted as having any worthwhile value. Then the Grand Correction will get underway in earnest.

National and Global Bankruptcy

The global bankruptcy will initially proceed like that of any large corporation but with one major difference. National sovereignty is involved. In the eventual write-down, each country will have to come to terms with every other country, the banks and individuals, who hold their debt. Greece, Ireland and Iceland have already kicked off this inevitable process. Those were the first of the "PIIGS" (Portugal, Ireland, Italy, Greece and Spain) to give way. However, in Iceland, voters forced the banks to eat their losses, rather than keep the citizens on the hook for them.

Will the write down be 70 cents on the dollar for Greece but 60 cents for France? Will it be 80 cents for Spain and Italy? The write-downs will likely conform to the established pecking order of economic performance and military power. Initially, the United States is likely to come out in better shape. However, in the long run, the devastating consequences of global insolvency will result in a global "recession" beyond the wildest imaginings of its Keynesian perpetrators.

A safe bet is that the U.S. will keep its military footing at current levels, as long as possible, in order to secure the best deal from creditors during the write-down. After all, we are not spending more on militarism and "defense" than the next 25 or 30 countries combined for nothing, folks!

The Monetary, Credit and Debt Endgame

The endgame of the Grand Correction will not please creditors who financed failed attempts to keep the system going with "*5-minute design increment*" quick fixes. It will be especially unsettling and devastating for American citizens. They will finally be forced to confront the reality that overspending, debt and the continued erosion of the currency will virtually erase their entitlements, savings and pensions.

Of course, politics being politics, and stupidity being stupidity, a succession of futile quick fixes will continue to the bitter end. Finally, investors seeking safety will reach the last remaining "*mossy hummock*" in the middle of the global debt swamp. That hummock will be U.S. Treasuries denominated in Federal Reserve Notes and backed by illusory "reserves." As that last supposed refuge submerges under the combined weight of frantic and desperate investors, the World will finally realize that it is out of options. Unfortunately, there is no "*Inter-galactic Reserve Bank of Settlements*" to provide hard money to lend from extra-terrestrial sources! We will have to make it on our own, somehow or other.

Austrian School investors long ago made their move to high ground in anticipation of the coming financial tsunami. They have taken refuge in hard assets, including real property, precious metals and real goods.

Once those who have relied on mainstream economic wisdom realize that the currencies and 'paper' financial instruments hoarded are being reduced to their intrinsic value, which is **zero** (i.e. 0.00), a desperate stampede will ensue. They will seek financial safety in the only things that have been dependable depositories of wealth throughout the centuries: gold, silver, and commodities and goods. The demand for safety by the Keynesian Johnny-come-latelies will likely send nominal prices for such physical assets and goods soaring beyond anything currently imaginable.

The Grand Correction, so long postponed, will then continue in earnest, comprehensively destroying the old economic illusion.

In the next two chapters, we will examine how humans typically behave in such situations, and consider what strategies might be implemented to improve the outcome. We can still mitigate the worst effects before the full fury of the storm hits us. It is now time to batten down the hatches, and take some common sense precautions to reduce our personal danger.

7

The WARBI Paradox

Everyone thinks of changing the world but no one thinks of changing himself.
–Leo Tolstoy

We have met the enemy and he is us.
–Walt Kelly

To make positive and constructive changes in this Country, the very first step is recognizing and acknowledging the truth.

The citizens of the States have voluntarily embraced stupidity in their behavior and leadership. There is no other objective way to put it.

The next two chapters will explore and expose why individual, and large-scale human interactions, have predictable outcomes. There is no magic or mystery to it.

Embracing and Allowing Stupidity

"The Shining City On The Hill," envisioned by the Founders of this country, has gradually been perverted into '**Amerika,**' a bully, a cheat, an unaccountable and irresponsible global empire. Our founding principles and ideals have been corrupted in a pervasive atmosphere of institutionalized stupidity. Virtually no one escapes some personal responsibility for enabling this sad state of affairs.

A minority of people are indeed born mentally impaired. Existence can be cruel and capricious when rolling the genetic dice. It can also bestow the gifts of high intelligence and talent.

About half the population are born mentally capable but they choose to exercise very few of their gifts and so **act stupidly**. Even the most casual examination of our social, political, and economic landscape makes that abundantly clear. The mentally capable could **choose to be smart.** If a critical mass of citizens changed their individual behavior from stupid to smart, every aspect of this Country's life would be transformed for the better.

A low, medium or high intelligence quotient (IQ) has little to do with being smart. There is more than a germ of truth in the old joke that:

The A students become teachers. The B students end up working for the C students.

What is conspicuously absent, in personal behavior reflected everywhere in mass behavior, is the application of **practical common sense**, something all too uncommon.

Stupidity is extremely democratic. It affects the poor and the rich, the powerless and the powerful, and the young and the old. It has now infected **every level** of our population.

The WARBI Paradox

During 20 years in business together, I closely observed how my friend and business partner, the late Larry Notvest, successfully applied a specific set of behavioral and managerial principles. His premature death, in 1996 at age 52, meant that our association never matured to its fullest potential. However, he had already imbued in me most of those principles, and their applications.

Larry was a strong advocate of the ideas of Ayn Rand. When I was a teenager, I had read her novels, but Larry's influence led to a fuller appreciation of her departure from conventional wisdom, and her intellectual fervor to separate objective truth from subjective opinions.

Please note that I am not an Ayn Rand acolyte. I find her analyses and ideas compelling in some areas, but objectively deficient in others. I have found it helpful throughout my life *"to keep the best and leave the rest."*

Larry and I spent thousands of hours together exploring many technical, behavioral and management concepts. We then employed them in military and civilian life. Over and over again, we proved the practicality of certain ideas in successfully building and managing organizations. We came to realize that Rand's focus on the behavior of individuals was her greatest insight.

One of the most successful concepts that we developed, has an admittedly awkward name. We called it WARBI (WARBI = "We-Are-Run-By-Idiots").

When people are first exposed to this concept, most of them immediately assume that the only idiots are the leaders of an organization. In fact, that is only half the truth.

If WARBI thinking is present, it is because **everyone** in a particular organization is **enabling** it to one degree or another. The workers may be absolutely correct in stating that their bosses are acting like idiots. However, they are also idiots for permitting that sort of behavior. Thus the proper terminology for our concept is the **WARBI Paradox,** because the behavior of the bosses and the workers are two sides of the same coin—thus the paradox.

The avoidance of personal accountability and responsibility is typical of a **herd mentality.** Where individuals take personal ownership of organizational success, those organizations are using the **individual-cooperative** approach to achieve, and sustain, successful outcomes.

Federal Express was one of the best corporate examples of that behavior with their *"Absolutely! Positively!"* corporate mantra. It applied to each and every employee. Apple Computer was another example, although that company was significantly different in its approach than FedEx.

I found it present in certain military intelligence units as well. Those that operated in an atmosphere of mutual respect of all the members throughout the whole chain of command, invariably functioned far more effectively than those that had to rely just on the chain of command authority itself. If I worked in a unit where the troops were constantly reminded to *"respect the uniform if not the officer,"* I found that they were usually dysfunctional and performed poorly.

The most dysfunctional organizations that we encountered, were usually riddled with WARBI. The staff blamed the organization's poor performance, and their own unsatisfying positions and conditions, on *"the idiots in charge."* When we looked more closely, it was apparent that employees had aided and abetted the idiotic behavior of their leaders. Acting on that important insight, Larry and I concentrated our efforts on lower-level staff. That resulted in the greatest benefits to the whole organization.

We promoted methods that empowered workers in the lower echelons to enable group success, regardless of the behavior of management. Of course, improved behavior by managers created proportionately greater success. However, subsequent idiotic behavior by management did not preclude at least some success—if the lower echelons continued to function effectively.

Very clearly, the widely held belief that leadership must be "top-down" was at fault. It is actually the greatest single impediment to any business enterprise's **long-term ability** to function successfully and be profitable.

We found that no group of individuals was ever truly subservient to any leader unless they *accepted it.*

In those teams that fail, the **herd mentality** is the major problem. Team members mill around like dumb cattle in the stockyards, entirely subservient, and unaware of their impending doom. No initiative is shown by the team members, and none is expected of them. It is the classic employee attitude, reinforced through the years by the wrong-headed notion of tyrannical bosses that *"you're not here to think, you're here to do what you're told."*

In many cases, we had to fight the patently ridiculous mantra that *"there is no 'I' in team."* It is a cute little saying but a thoroughly wrong-headed concept. Teams succeed because most, if not all, individuals in the team take personal responsibility for the outcome. We found that technical problem resolution was comparatively easy if bad behaviors were corrected.

When previously dysfunctional organizations transformed into effective ones, we observed how the lower echelon's new attitude of empowerment spread *up* the management chain. Managers usually **readjusted their behavior**. First level supervisors learned to manage middle-level managers, who then managed upper-level managers. Those managers who failed to adjust to the new paradigm of personal accountability for outcomes, were then recognized as part of the problem and rapidly weeded out by their own superiors.

Were we always successful? No, there were organizations so riddled with WARBI that too few people were receptive to making the necessary behavioral changes. In some other cases, our position as outside contractors or consultants precluded us from introducing our methods. Predicting that a particular WARBI infected enterprise or organization was doomed to fail was easy. Inevitably, they were either liquidated via bankruptcy, or fell victim to merger or purchase by a successful rival.

WARBI Gone Wild

Across the land, WARBI thinking is rampant. The vast majority of people believe that all our problems are due to the idiotic behavior of our leaders in Congress and in The White House. Citizens infected by WARBI thinking believe that *"throw the bums out and replace them"* will solve the Country's problems, even though that method has failed for decades. They never take into account their own failure to be responsible citizens. There is widespread reluctance to accept that **we get the government we vote for.**

In the not so distant past, most people understood that no leader, or group of leaders, could ever be the actual cause of our Country's failures or successes. Until the 1950's, it was clearly understood that, if our leaders were a problem, it was due to the behavior of the citizens. The People had to fix the situation themselves. They knew, beyond a shadow of doubt, no matter if their *"station in life"* was high or low, that they actually held the real power by virtue of controlling their own lives, and by the value of their votes.

America worked then because most citizens were very familiar with the foundational ideals and principles of this Country. They cherished them. They understood the need to individually nurture and protect American values. Many more took personal responsibility to fix problems. It was an era when the gap between elected officials and the "man-on-the-street" and the "man-on-the-farm" did not loom so large. Professional politicians were much less the norm.

143

The lesson of the WARBI Paradox is that every capable American citizen must hold themselves personally accountable and responsible for the social, economic and political outcomes that we are now experiencing. Only then will there be a secondary effect on politicians who will **readjust their behavior.** The election of true citizen-legislators, and a President who is only temporarily *"first-among-equals,"* will follow. They will know that responsible and accountable voters will expect honorable and prudent stewardship from them **as public servants,** confined to the powers accorded to them in the Constitution.

If we hold our present course, there will only be more of the worst behavior—everywhere in **Amerika.** The increasing incidence of corrupt behavior, and attendant scandals, evident in governmental, political, legal, corporate and even religious institutions today, is clear evidence of that trend.

Look inside yourself and ask:

Am I part of the problem, or part of the solution?

Do I expect the leaders to solve my problems for me?

Do I have as much responsibility as they do in solving problems that are larger than all of us?

Have I fulfilled my responsibility as an independent citizen just by casting my vote or is more required of me?

What is the real cost to me, and to my family, neighbors and co-workers, if we fail to get involved and abdicate the decision-making process to others?

Honest answers will indicate whether or not each individual citizen believes in their own sovereign power to decide the destiny of our Republic. Shall we return to our roots to thrive and prosper, or shall we continue along the path to collapse and ruin?

8

Conspiracy, Power Elites, Personal Behavior and Individual Action

All rational action is in the first place individual action. Only the individual thinks. Only the individual reasons. Only the individual acts.
–Ludwig von Mises

He who sees the light shall know the darkness.
–Anonymous

Conspiracy

There are many active conspiracies. Thousands are hatched, every day of the year, to further specific agendas and group-think interests. Only a few survive their infancy.

There are also conspiracies that do not actually exist. The rumors of their existence are intended to benefit their instigators. Most of them never achieve any traction, even amongst the credulous.

It is wisest to observe who actually profits and how they do.

By definition, no conspiracy is noble or unselfish, even if the originators, and their willing accomplices, delude themselves into thinking otherwise.

Conspiracy is defined as:

1. A plan to commit an illegal act together: a secret plan or agreement between two or more people to commit an illegal or subversive act.
2. The making of an agreement by conspirators: the making of a secret plan or agreement to commit an illegal or subversive act.

3. A group of conspirators: a group of people planning or agreeing in secret to commit an illegal or subversive act.

Most conspiracies fail because they are imposed on others against their will. They fail because they are in opposition to natural law. They fail because they are abnormal or artificial constructs, inherently limited and flawed.

Most conspiracies are far less effective than their creators, or their often acquiescent victims, admit. That is not to deny that some conspiracies have caused widespread death and destruction. Some spiraled out of control, as the worst aspects of human nature were expressed, and **The Law Of Unintended Consequences** took hold. In the 20th Century, Communism and Fascism are prime examples of unnatural and flawed conspiracies that did gain great power, for a relatively short period of time, usually just a few decades. When compared to many great civilizations, that is a mere blink in time.

Fortunately, it has now become much harder to keep anything secret. That is due to the Internet, and the social media that it spawned and enables. Institutional secrecy is becoming harder and harder to sustain and maintain.

The Internet has the great virtue of being the medium of near instant exposure. Conspirators have *"Nowhere to run, nowhere to hide."*

For proof, type the words *"central banking conspiracy"* into any search engine. Over 600,000 links will be displayed that focus on the central banking conspiracy, hatched way back in the late 1800's.

Another failing, but more recent, conspiracy is Anthropogenic Global Warming (AGW). There are more than 750,000 sites on that subject.

Recent socio-political events in the Middle East, and elsewhere, reveal that human nature remains unchanged. A simple set of rules is governing the behavior of the people involved. Instead of wasting time in exposing the many fallacies about what is really happening, we will take a different route. Anyone would come to similar conclusions after a serious study of many texts on psychology, sociology and conspiracy theory. I propose to save you some trouble.

Power Elites

As a starting point, there is the so-called Power Elite. Some prefer the term Powers-That-Be. Once one has dug deeper into the understanding of how the World really works, there is not much supporting evidence that they have much control over anything for very long. The "Thousand Year Reich" lasted only twelve years. The Soviet Union crumbled after 69 years, despite being on the winning side in World War II.

Nevertheless, many conspiracy theorists are undeterred. They produce all sorts of "evidence" for events where the "only possible explanation" is the existence of diabolical plots. They point the finger at the Mossad, the CIA, "The 300," The Bilderberg Group, The Council on Foreign Relations (CFR), The Tri-lateral Commission, The Illuminati, the international banking cartel or others. They are reported as the tentacles of an everlasting mastermind, the power elite. In fact, plots and conspiracies are typically far too narrowly focused to be in sympathy with others.

For example, look at the purges that take place within political power elites as factions contend with each other. How could that create a co-operative atmosphere with other elites with very different goals? Conspiracies are criminal by definition. Think of the apt description of North Korea's leadership as *"a criminal gang masquerading as a Country."*

Based upon many years of observing the inside workings of top-level military, public and private organizations, especially in the intelligence gathering and financial services sectors, the facile explanation that conspiracies are behind everything appears to me to be **extremely unlikely.** These imagined conspiracies only lead down intellectual blind alleys into emotional dead ends, fueled by self-delusion.

In his seminal work, *"An Inquiry into the Nature and Causes of The Wealth of Nations,"* published in 1776, Adam Smith re-introduced (from an earlier work) his metaphor that an *"invisible hand"* automatically self-regulates the free market.

Stepping back far enough from the trees to see the whole forest, could there actually be an Invisible Hand self-regulating social and political affairs over the long-term? Some readers, and many of the "sound-bite" afflicted, will misinterpret that last sentence to validate the existence of a Grand Unifying Conspiracy. There "must be" a second layer of deeply hidden control of the Controllers. "*Ah-ha*" they will shout, "*You see!*"

Let me be very clear. Something inherently self-regulating is always thrown out of balance by external control seeking to regulate it. Piling multiple layers of regulations on top of regulations, eventually creates a state of **hyper-regulation.** When that occurs, **civilization-changing** alterations are the inevitable consequence. Pressure built up over time must be released. To use an analogy from geology, it is similar to continental plates piling up against each other. When a great deal of pent up pressure is suddenly released, as it must be, there is a correspondingly large earthquake. That is simple physics.

Our societal, political and financial woes correspond directly to the degree of oppressive and abnormal control applied in all spheres of human activity. At some point or other, the unnatural pressures must be released.

From that viewpoint, it is obvious that events in Egypt and elsewhere in the Middle East, "*The Arab Spring,*" are almost entirely inimical to the self-interest of the resident power elites. Nevertheless, many commentators allege that there are hidden "directed" conspiracies at work behind the scenes. There is usually plenty of hyperbole and polemic thrown in to further misdirect listeners and readers. In actuality, it takes very little probing to poke huge holes in such explanations.

Personal Behavior and Individual Action

How does a customer command the attention of entrepreneurs, the employment of workers around the World, along with resources and the transportation systems required, to produce and deliver a pencil, or an iPod or a car? It seems almost too simple to be true. The entrepreneur determines what consumers are buying, or want to buy, and then supplies a new or improved product.

If one buys what they are selling, it is produced. If one stops buying, it will no longer be produced.

Few who read Leonard Reed's "*I, Pencil*" will disagree that the "*invisible hand*" of individuals, seeking to further only their own interests, provides us with pencils. When the conversation turns to things political, few seem capable of seeing a corollary.

A similar process is at work in political and governmental systems. More and more people just want an honest government that does what it is supposed to do, and no more. They have begun to sense the truth of the old adage that the best governments are those that govern the least.

"Occam's Razor" should be invoked here. When selecting between various competing hypotheses, the one that makes the fewest assumptions, leading to the simplest explanation, is usually best. We are, after all, investigating what is happening, not indulging in fantasy.

Every single individual makes decisions every day that enable economic and political systems to operate. When those systems are truly free, uninhibited by the **hyper-regulatory psychosis,** then it can be presumed, and inferred, that there will be far fewer imbalances that cause societal pressures to increase to the breaking point. Citizens will be getting what they really need and want.

The late, insightful science-fiction author, Isaac Asimov, created the word "psychohistory," something that he artfully used in his novels. It is a useful term to keep in mind when developing a reality based view of mass human behavior. Asimov, a professor of biochemistry at Boston University, was also well known for his non-fiction books that sought to bring scientific understanding to a wider audience. He viewed his invented term 'psychohistory' as operating very similarly to the behavior of an atmospheric gas.

A better understanding of how a single molecule behaves in various environments, allows for a better understanding of how a mass of molecules will behave in the future.

No molecule **moves** as it does because it is part of the mass. However, the mass acts as it does due to the interaction of all the individual molecules.

Much the same applies to **acts** of human behavior. Many individual interactive behaviors influence and culminate in **mass human action.**

For example, when a single person enters a crowded stadium looking for his seat, he does not attempt to understand how all the other people are moving. That would be impossible. All he cares about is his current position and his final destination. He then moves as efficiently as possible to reach his seat. He does encounter and interact with all the other individuals with similar intentions on his way, but the whole time he is a free agent. He does not need to know what everyone else in the crowd is thinking, or doing.

Nor does it matter what the stadium's designer thought would be the most efficient path to a particular seat. Each person determines that for themselves, with varying degrees of effectiveness, based on their entry point into the stadium. If one studied each individual's path to the correct seat, it would naturally allow for a much better understanding of a crowd's movements within the stadium. If one looked only at the crowd's mass movement, it would be virtually impossible to accurately determine an individual's efficiency at finding his designated seat.

Most mainstream political and economic analysts believe that they can predict the future behavior of a population by amassing enough gross data, on past behavior by populations, and then extrapolating that into meaningful statistics. Little or no effort is made to actually understand the behavior of **individuals within the population** (meaning contextually). Their conclusions are, therefore, largely meaningless and often dangerously incorrect.

They have gone about it exactly backwards. They believe that mass behavior dictates what individuals will do. Worse yet, they believe that past mass behavior can predict mass behavior in the future. These so-called *experts* cannot therefore understand how spontaneous mass movements, such as 'The Arab Spring,' come into being. Nor could they see the *"Financial Crises of 2008"* coming, nor the larger one that is underway now. They will always be caught off-guard. They have virtually no chance of anticipating what will happen next, even if they are aware that conditions are ripe for a conflagration. The reason is that they live and think in a centralized-control paradigm.

We now have two premises to work with:

1. Outcomes in a large population are the result of millions of individual voluntary interactions. Each outcome starts with

different preset conditions. Understanding how individuals behave, helps understand the larger population's behavior.

2. Individuals are directed by others only if they acquiesce voluntarily. When individual behavior is coerced by threat of physical harm, incarceration, torture, or even death, the group's overall efficiency seriously declines. A slave is far less motivated than a free-man.

Even though individual human beings may appear to voluntarily behave and act in a collective way, it is only to the point that their individual needs and wants are satisfied, and no more.

Some 'social engineers' believe that 'social cooperation' can be induced. That belief is false. The higher the degree of enforced centralization, the lower the rate of truly voluntary behavior. A minimal level of laws and restrictions is necessary for maximum effectiveness. A population's efficiency is proportionately reduced by a corresponding increase in coercion. The standard of living in the "Workers' Paradise" of the former Soviet Union, compared to the USA in the same period, is a good example.

There is a common fallacy that socialism is "*cooperative management.*" It definitely is not **individually-cooperative** behavior because it is imposed on the individual. In its ultimate form, socialism always ends up being a highly centralized and coercive system of socio-political management by an elite. We previously referred to George Orwell's famous satire in "*Animal Farm*" where the pigs, who had seized control, had a higher status. "*All animals are equal, but some animals are more equal than others.*" In the Soviet Bloc, the Communist power elite "*pigs*" were known as the *nomenklatura* (meaning "elite bureaucrats").

Whether its adherents admit it or not, any form of socialism is implemented only through coercion. History has proven, time and time again, that coercive regimes invariably fail. So-called "*Social Cooperation*" only results when those caught up in such situations comply with petty regulations to mitigate further nuisance and interference, or to avoid actual pain and suffering threatened by those "*in charge.*"

Coercive systems are defeated with varying forms of resistance, culminating in success as soon as a critical mass of individuals refuse to buy-in anymore. The Soviet Bloc's collapse is an example. The fall of many Middle Eastern regimes in the recent past is another.

The Myths of Collectivism and Socialism

Let us explode some common myths about 'social' behavior. Think of organisms such as bees and ants. They have been described as "*social insects*" but are they really? Yes, they do live in communal hives and colonies. But is their behavior social-collectivist? Recent studies suggest that individual behavior by each insect causes a hive or colony to act as a "superorganism." This superorganism is a population of individuals cooperating on a large scale. It is not some form of "*insect socialism.*" Where is the coercion coming from?

Does the Queen bee or ant decide on hive or colony policy? Or, is she just an egg-laying machine? Does she telepathically broadcast commands and directives to drones, and workers? Or is every bee and ant just going about its own business? How are activities, important to the common survival of hive or anthill, accomplished if there is no centralized command structure? Are workers and drones in a constant state of apprehension, even fear, that they will so greatly displease the Queen that she will command, "*Off with their heads!*" Kind of silly when you think about it, is it not?

Fear comes from the abstract concepts of 'self' and 'future.' Bees or ants have no such awareness. They do have touch, sight, their internal instruction sets and pheromones to **individually** guide each one of them. They may sense external danger, or environmental threats, but those do not emanate from fellow hive or nest mates. There is no "*command and control*" structure. Each individual has a simple set of very basic instructions, genetically encoded. It tells them how to respond to various outside stimuli, and how to interact with their own kind. Queens, drones and workers have slightly different instruction sets encoded in them. Those create the conditions for efficient and harmonious behavior within the 'superorganism,' where each of them is a self-regulating functional part of the whole.

The instruction sets are programmed standard reactions. It is a very basic type of purely instinctual intelligence. On a mass scale, the insects appear to operate in highly sophisticated ways. However, they are merely repeating very simple actions enough times, with a few simple variations, to create the apparently complex beehive or ant nest.

For example, there are instructions on how to respond to stimuli such as *Food—Obstacle—Danger—Attack* as well additional code that instructs them to *Forage—Feed—Clean—Excavate—Build—Assist—Procreate—Protect—Defend.*

Hives or colonies, where individual bees or ants have a sufficiently diverse set of instructions, tend to survive and prosper. There is simply no evidence that anything more than simple **individual-cooperative** actions are at work. See PBS Nova Science Now video segment on "hive mind at http://thecitizenslaststand.com/hivemind.

Chaos Theory and Human Behavior

Chaos theory is a field of mathematics that studies dynamical systems where outcomes vary greatly despite very small initial differences. That, and the science commonly referred to as "artificial intelligence" (AI) and robotics, demonstrate very clearly how complex behavior can be instigated and maintained with simple sets of instructions. Go to any movie theater to understand how many different "artificial realities" this branch of mathematics can create.

In truly individual-cooperative human activity, there is absolutely no need for a centralized command structure such as Socialists, Communists, NeoCons or Progressive NeoLibs expect and demand. An all-encompassing statist *"social mind"* is demonstrably a myth of monstrous proportions. In stark contrast, the natural process is a series of individual behaviors and acts that cumulatively benefit the larger number of any population. Anything else is not based on how things really work. They are the invented justifications of megalomaniacs and control-freaks who wish for a population that acts in an 'insect-like' manner of their design based only on their flawed concepts of natural behavior.

Think of the game of *"Chinese Whispers"* or *"The Telephone Game."* When a message is quickly passed from one individual to another, it is possible, even likely, that the message received by the last individual has been garbled in transmission. Success only comes when the message received is identical to the one sent. It is voluntary cooperation, operating under a simple set of rules or 'laws,' not compulsion, that achieves the highest success rate.

Of course, humans exhibit orders of magnitude greater variation in their behavior than do bees and ants. Humans have far more complex brains and instruction sets. While some primitive parts of an individual human's instruction set are instinctual, the remainder is developed. The human brain consists of 80 to 120 billion neurons (nerve cells) and has a cerebral cortex absent in bees and ants. Mix in all the developed instruction sets, of which endless multitudes of variations exist, and then contemplate the fact that there are now 7 billion humans alive on the planet. Obviously, a mind-boggling number of possible human interactions therefore can, do, and will take place every day.

The idea of true collective (read: collectivist) behavior is perpetrated by those who believe, and insist that we believe, that there is a *"Social Mind."* It is the expression of a mono-centric, misguided view of human behavior akin to the pre-Copernican notion that the Universe revolves around the Earth. It is similar to the early futurists and science-fiction writers who postulated that one day there would be a single large computer that was all-knowing and all-wise.

Instead, we have billions of micro-processors that are proliferating as rapidly as their capabilities are expanding, and their dimensions shrinking. Quantum computing, here we come! The notion of a "Social Mind" is farcical, absurd and a total myth. Yet many social theorists and economists still espouse it, either subtly or overtly.

Everyone thinks their own thoughts. No two people think exactly alike on any subject, even those where they seemingly fully agree. Two people may have ideas in common that result in apparently similar expression or behavior. But no study has disclosed any evidence of identical minds. Even identical twins think differently, demonstrating significant variations in behavior. Each individual human's reactions to his or her environment will be entirely unique. Just observe people's behavior!

The simple question, *"Is it raining outside"* will usually elicit more than a simple "yes" or "no." There will be comments on how hard it is raining, how long it has been raining, if it is expected to last, and so on.

What gives the lie to the collectivist social model as being voluntary is that it must be centrally driven, organized and directed by a *"Dear Leader"* or *"Big Brother,"* along with *"special committees"* of control-freaks, and legions of enforcers. Knowing what we know about fundamental human behavior, how could anyone believe that a committee of others could run your life better when 98+% of us peacefully go about our business?

The hyper-regulatory process demands control of everyone in everything that they do.

Since self-evident, natural law is an *"inconvenient truth,"* the regulatory committees invent false laws and create arbitrary rules. Natural law is the full expression of voluntary actions and effective behaviors. Excessive laws and coercive regulations construct artificial systems that only last until reality overtakes and destroys them.

There is an obvious reason why *some* people want to promote collectivist thinking. Whether they are neo-conservative or neo-liberal, reactionary or Progressive, it puts them in positions of power to control and manipulate others. Megalomaniac, tyrannical and narcissistic 'leaders' use the supposed social or collective mind to justify their own behavior and actions.

Do not confuse organizational ranking with an arbitrary, centralized-hierarchy. When and where the individual-cooperative approach is given freedom to flourish, it consistently proves that those organizations quickly and efficiently accomplish much more than coercive ones. Think of the difference between obtaining a service at any retail enterprise, or waiting in line at the Division of Motor Vehicles in any State. Or, recall your friendly bookkeeper, or accountant, as compared to your last encounter with an IRS agent. The difference in the experience is explained by the degree of coercion involved.

155

Fundamental Behavior in Humans

Two **Fundamental Behaviors** always apply. They are:

1. Monkey see, monkey do.
2. Submission and obedience to authority.

There is a strong correlation between how humans and other primates learn and behave. This has been repeatedly confirmed in many studies and through direct observation. The two behaviors are intimately related, work together and have obvious survival value. They are the basis for individual behavior, both interactive and cooperative.

However, those two behaviors also have a downside.

The innovative researcher, Stanley Milgram, thoroughly investigated the powerful influence of the *"obedience response"* in seeking to explain how **The Holocaust** could have ever happened. His work firmly established the obedience response is embedded in each person, to a frightening degree, making monstrous behavior from anyone a possibility. Individual monstrous acts are bad enough. When megalomaniacs find ways to manipulate many individuals, the results can be horrific.

There are four **Modalities of Inaction** that operate in concert with the two fundamental behaviors. These explain why an individual (or a group) usually remain in their 'comfort zone' even when change is obviously necessary.

1. The security of the status quo and resistance to change
2. If forced to change, take the path of least resistance
3. If that path proves too difficult, deny that change is actually necessary*
4. Prolonged denial is overcome by events (reality). The individual then either gives up completely and surrenders, or dies, or is forced to make changes that take him out of his comfort zone

(*3. brings the individual back to 1. The loop repeats until 4 overcomes the looping behavior)

Some common examples:

- Over-eating and remaining sedentary until one suffers a heart attack
- Eating only processed food and contracting diabetes
- Pretending to be in a happy marriage until faced with the demand for a divorce by one's spouse
- Maintaining an outwardly friendly relationship with a neighbor until forced to file a lawsuit
- Publishing false financial reports for a company until it is obligated to file for bankruptcy
- Continuing to believe that the present Federal Government is solvent (or legitimate) until Social Security is destroyed by inflation.

These *behaviors* and *modalities*, while applicable to everyone, are not collective behaviors. Each person still chooses his reaction in each and every situation. Their subsequent decisions and actions are unique, usually shaped by previous life experiences.

Those who seek to 'collectivize' group behavior through coercion, absolutely refuse to look at individual behavior. They are convinced that group behavior—with data allegedly supporting such contentions—can be manipulated to exert control over a group, even over entire populations, to further their own ends and aggrandizement. **Statists** (of the Left or Right) pretend to believe that such coercion is necessary because *"the ends justify the means."*

It actually occurs only because you buy-in and allow it.

Every one of us is unique. Benoit Mandelbrot, the father of fractal geometry and Chaos Theory, demonstrated how a small change in the behavior of one element (or individual in a social context) in a group can create complex, far-reaching and large-scale changes in the behavior of the entire group, *one bifurcation (interaction) at a time.* Although the preset conditions embedded in systems may still be the greatest influence on the outcome, large-scale changes can result from the thoughts, ideas and subsequent actions of individuals, not from the false concept of *"collective action."*

When a flock of birds suddenly veer in apparent unison, it was actually initiated by a minute change of direction by an individual bird at a certain point and time. When a landslide occurs, it began when a single pebble, or even just one grain of sand, shifts position (for a myriad of reasons).

No observer can know ahead of time which individual, or what element, will instigate a new and different outcome. Any preemptive action by a central group of conspirators has a vanishingly low probability of achieving an outcome that is precisely as they want. They will never know which individual pebble to push to create their desired outcome. *"Round up the usual suspects"* will not work for the authorities this time! In mathematical terms, the number of variables in play is so staggeringly large, that no one can know how, when, and where a cascading chain of events will be initiated.

Chaos and The Butterfly Effect

Such phenomena were first called the *"butterfly effect"* by science fiction author Ray Bradbury, in his 1952 novel *"A Sound of Thunder."* That premise was later confirmed by mathematicians such as Edward Lorenz. The premise is that a random single butterfly can have a far-reaching ripple effect, altering subsequent history. Makes a mockery of academics who think that they have a handle on manipulated economics, or climate change, with their puny statistics, does it not?

A single recent example demonstrates this concept.

On December 17th, 2010, a street vendor, Mohamed Bouazizi, **set in motion** *"The Arab Spring"* by immolating himself to protest government permit regulations in Tunisia. The ripple effect of that one event continues to this day.

Perhaps such causations have only recently been accepted because so little **actual human history** has ever been recorded and properly analyzed. All history is the outcome of unseen individual events that cannot be planned or foreseen.

However, the effect of something seemingly inconsequential, with major sequential consequences, was recognized long ago, as in the old rhyme, *"For Want of a Nail:"*

For want of a nail the shoe was lost. For want of a shoe the horse was lost. For want of a horse the rider was lost. For want of a rider the message was lost. For want of a message the battle was lost. For want of a battle the kingdom was lost. And all for the want of a horseshoe nail.

Long before any thoughts of Chaos Theory, it was already understood that early histories (upon which later historians relied) were skewed, inevitably written from the victors' point of view. Imagine the odds that any present day historian can indulge in anything more than vague surmise and guesses as to what actually precipitated historical events. We think we understand History but do we really? With the much better informational record that the Internet provides, we can now perceive the skew between the controlled media "official" version of recent events and the unfiltered information provided by the open media.

In lieu of actual, or unbiased accurate records, historians naturally attribute much of history to the actions of kings, queens, princes, generals, premiers or presidents rather than to the unknown, and actually unknowable, actions of one or a few individuals. At best, it is an "educated guesses" history because of the multitude of potential hidden causes that exist at all times.

Preset conditions are often recognized as 'ripe for change' even before anything precipitates a change in the status quo. At other times, all seems quiescent. However, after the event, the inherent instability of the previous conditions is obvious.

Referring once again to natural phenomena, put any number of earth scientists in a room together. The vast majority will agree that the tectonic pressures building up make massive earthquakes **inevitable** in the Cascadia (Northwest) and San Andreas (California) Subduction Zones along the West Coast. It is not a question of if, but when and exactly where. Meanwhile people in those areas are proceeding with their lives as though the ground underneath them is inherently stable.

There are a few places where we have much better records to review our thesis. Look at three historical events, The American Civil War and WWI, and the recent one that is still playing out in 2012, the Arab Spring. In these three examples, it is very clear that change was inevitable. In these examples, we have the rare opportunity to view how an individual's act set the eventual outcome into motion. The only unknowns were **what** would suddenly break under the pressure, **where** that would happen, and **how** and **when**. The **fundamental issue** was large-scale coercion that finally became intolerable. It was a pile of kindling only awaiting for a spark to burst into flame.

The American Civil War was an event that became ever more likely when repeated compromises by politicians failed to address and deal with the central issues. One of them was the existence of that *"Peculiar Institution"* of human slavery throughout the U.S.. The latter existed in a Country whose own Declaration of Independence stated that:

> ... *all men are created equal,* ... *endowed by their Creator with certain unalienable Rights,* ... *among these are Life, Liberty, and the Pursuit of Happiness.*

As the Civil War ended with Union victory, John Wilkes Booth's unexpected action changed the ensuing events when he assassinated Abraham Lincoln. How might have Reconstruction played out if Lincoln had remained President? Would he have achieved his near-mythical reputation if he had died years later in his bed?

The assassination of Franz Ferdinand, Archduke of Austria, which precipitated WWI, illustrates how outcomes cannot be predicted, despite some of the major presets being recognized at the time. The social and political conditions were intolerable for many in Europe. There was simmering unrest. The Austro-Hungarian Empire was an unnatural construct based on coercion. In seeking to maintain the status quo, the Great Powers of Europe had interlocking treaties to prop things up that ultimately led to catastrophe.

The Serbian Prime Minister had an informant within the Black Hand conspiracy. He gave orders to apprehend the three young men (and four accomplices) being sent to carry out the assassination of Franz Ferdinand. He did not want Austro-Hungary to have a pretext to declare war. However, his orders were not relayed down the chain of command.

Later, in Sarajevo, an initial assassination attempt failed. The Archduke decided to continue the visit as planned. Instructions were given to change the motorcade's route on the return journey. However, the driver was not informed. Realizing belatedly that he had made a wrong turn, the driver backed the car into a side street to change direction. In the process, he stalled the car. That gave an assassin, 19 year old Gavrilo Princip, the opportunity to assassinate the Archduke and his wife.

If critical orders and communications had not miscarried, what would have ensued? Might cooler heads have prevailed over time? Would something unforeseen and unexpected, such as the emergence of a Nelson Mandela type figure, eased the course of inevitable change into a more moderate process? It is impossible to know.

All we can say is that Princip's action, one that he lived long enough to regret, profoundly affected the course of the 20th Century. The Bolshevik seizure of power in Russia (facilitated by the German High Command), and the rise and fall of Nazism (a direct sequential consequence of WWI), would not have occurred.

The large and small changes of direction caused by *"The Great War"* changed the course of countless lives. If the war had not taken place, the author of this book, his collaborators and countless readers, would probably never have been born. The random workings of chance in another reality, one where WWI did not take place, would have spun a very different set of circumstantial meetings, associations, friendships, relationships, marriages and offspring.

If a single butterfly can alter the course of history, then any one individual's action **may** have civilization-changing consequences. Closely examining The Arab Spring reveals absolutely **no evidence** that anyone was, or is, in overall **sustained control of anything,** on either the side of the uprisings. There is little doubt that it was inspired by one person's individual action on a street in Tunis. It can therefore be reliably inferred that when more individuals can indeed *act freely*, there will be a geometric increase in the probability of different outcomes.

Conspiracies—Do They Exist?

The mistaken view that omniscient Controllers are hidden behind the scenes, exerting their iron will to manage the 'Fate of the World,' is a simple-minded delusion. There are far too many variables in the human matrix. It is literally impossible to *"think of everything."* Until after the fact, there is no way to identify the exceptionally rare key individual actions from all the other human interactions constantly taking place.

Throughout a person's life, individual acts range from a multitude of small ones to a few large ones. Extreme actions are very rare. Virtually none of those have the far reaching consequences of those made by Boothe, Princip or Bouazizi. Nearly all individual actions have extremely subtle consequences, even in a single person's own life.

In the case of monarchies and entitled nobility, or other systems of hereditary power, or any long-term conspiracies, there are no guarantees that intelligence, ability or talent will be expressed in succeeding generations. History is full of examples where the rich and powerful are followed by offspring, or successors, who are weak, shallow and sometimes complete imbeciles. Some individuals are irrational and unpredictable even by the standards of the prevailing status quo.

There are always competing factions inside centralized power structures, with shifting alliances as individuals vie for influence, even employing **agent provocateurs** against rivals.

Politics makes for strange bedfellows.

Conspiracies can also be constantly undermined from the inside even by their own adherents. There will be the typical limitations endemic in any large organization, including careerism, corruption, ignorance, insubordination, misdirection, mismanagement and, of course, the WARBI Paradox at work.

How *could* multi-generational conspiracies be maintained with such obstructions?

If one could go *"beyond the grave"* and interrogate them, I suspect that the originators of virtually all the 'great conspiracies' of the past two thousand years, would admit that their plots mostly failed, or went completely awry.

Everything that happened in the 19th and 20th Centuries demonstrated that power structures attempting to exert central control were neither practical nor beneficial.

In this day and age, there is a broad spectrum of governance ranging from overt through covert coercion, from the tyrannical to the **hyper-regulatory.** Believing that any power elite has the ability to compel only certain results, confers on it a surface veneer of legitimacy, and gives it unfounded confidence that it is actually in control of events. An interdependency is at work between the coerced and the oppressors, akin to the one that is often formed between prisoner and guard, or hostage and kidnapper, that perpetuates a vicious cycle of negative reinforcement.

Erase the *belief* in the inevitability and invincibility of centralized power, and it is starkly revealed as a mass delusion that is only enabled by the **Two Fundamental Behaviors.** It is an illusion masquerading as reality. The child's tale of *"The Emperor's New Clothes"* is an apt metaphor. Yes, the "Emperor" is indeed prancing around in his thong!

If one buys into what they are selling, it is produced for them. If one stops buying, it will no longer be produced.

Let us look at current events in the Arab World. Without consciously acknowledging it, the people there finally realized that they were fed-up with their existing masters, those who interfered in the fulfillment of their own individual destinies. They were pushed and prodded by agitators from all sides. They rose up against the corrupt and—what proved to be—fragile entrenched power structures. The innate desire of humanity for freedom and liberty is unquenchable. Even those countries where the Arab Spring has Islamic Extremist undertones, many participants are expressing the desire for freedom and liberty. Many are not spewing out messages imbued with religious hatred. Most people, everywhere around the globe, just want to be left alone, with as little government interference as possible, so that they can pursue their own lives, in their own way.

Many more such events will inevitably happen around the World. All those who accumulate power hate this, no matter their political stripe or ideological slant.

Notice how the Tea Party, Occupy Wall Street and the European street movements are already frightening every authoritarian or hyper-regulatory government? The Occupiers, largely ignorant of economics and true freedom, are easily manipulated by the Left. However, even a broken clock tells the time correctly twice a day. The protestors know that the banks and financial companies are broken. They just have trouble articulating why due to decades of propaganda and inadequate schooling. The same is true of many Tea Party adherents. Question them in-depth and many have trouble articulating their ideas below a superficial level. However, they know that 'something' is profoundly wrong with the current set-up.

Why does the Internet scare the Controllers so much? It is **decentralized** to such an extent that it is **effectively uncontrollable, presenting yet another confounding element to central control.** The private sector 'tech weenies' are typically smarter and far more numerous than their government counterparts. Underground hackers have demonstrated, time and time again, that *"resistance is futile."*

Efforts to regulate the Internet, such as SOPA, PIPA and the Anti-Counterfeiting Trade Agreement (ACTA), Cyber Intelligence Sharing And Protection Act (CISPA), etc., will all fail as individuals develop "workarounds" faster than governments can slam the doors. The Internet represents more of a challenge to them than the Gutenberg press ever did to the medieval authorities of Europe.

Fortunately, any interference with the workings of the Internet will largely destroy its usefulness to the power elite. Ironically, because it is now ubiquitous everywhere, they need and use it, too. They cannot beat it. They must join it—even though it is an instrument of their eventual doom.

Personal behavior and independent action are the greatest determining factors in the course and direction of our Country—indeed of all Humanity.

On both a personal level, and on a cultural population scale, habitual patterns of thought are very resistant to change. Yet human beings are very adaptable where technology is concerned. For the near term, there will be jarring juxtapositions of archaic patterns of thought adapting to the latest forms of data retrieval and instantaneous communications.

For example, we will continue to see Muslim extremists, in tribal areas of Afghanistan and Pakistan, using cell phones, and the Internet, while still thinking and behaving in ways that hark back to the 8th Century. In more developed parts of the World, the would-be Controllers of the government, the judiciary and the economy, will continue believing in outmoded models of central power while increasingly relying on the Internet—an unstoppable force for decentralization.

For the many around the World, and in this Country, who have already shed, or are shedding, old ways of thought, how can you individually assist in accelerating the replacement of archaic centralized control systems? Share what you have learned by modifying your behavior! For most people, convinced against their will, or remaining unconvinced, any active proselytizing only works to a limited degree, if at all. Action has always spoken louder than words.

What Do We Do?

The would-be powers of the World cannot stand if enough people lead by example, the single most effective teaching technique. It is absolutely aligned with the first of the two Fundamental Behaviors. As a natural consequence, the second Behavior will kick in, and take effect, when a critical mass of people realize that they are their own masters.

In the case of the United States, the Founders provided the framework. It was and is to **educate every possible individual to understand, and then act, according to the principles of natural law and natural rights that allows 'emergent systems' to flourish and thereby ensure freedom.** (See Chapters 12 and 13)

165

Therefore, thoroughly educate yourself in the foundational principles and ideals that gave birth to this Country. Go about your daily business as an honest, responsible and effective citizen. People can learn again the central premise of the **American Experiment which is being their "own kings and queens."** **Amerika's** power elite will then crumble into nothingness. It bears repeating that *U.S. citizens are presently giving tacit permission for widespread misgovernance.*

The true tenets of Freedom and liberty exercised at every level of human behavior in **an individual-cooperative** fashion, is the only **sane course of action.**

Events happening in *"real time"* are rarely as they initially appear, and are in a constant state of flux. This gives an enormous advantage to the individual as compared to large, complex, centralized, slow-moving, error-prone, decision-making entities such as governments. The latter are inherently incapable of rapidly dealing with any changes.

Consequently, governments remain static and unresponsive at first. If they fail to eventually co-opt or control events, they inevitably fall. In desperation, some resort to violence to enforce their will and protect the self-interests of the "insiders." The present day events in Syria are a good example of such forceful reaction.

This inability of governments, or the power elite, to respond to crises is aptly illustrated by this rule of Field Marshall von Moltke's:

No battle plan ever survives first contact with the enemy.

In *"the fog of war,"* it is impossible for governments to gauge what is actually happening while simultaneously predicting the future course of events. Successful outcomes of government activities rely much more on chance than on foresight, or the formulation of appropriate responses. That explains why true governmental success is so rare. It underlines the importance of strictly limiting governmental powers.

Time after time, in virtually every situation, government planning and actions result in long-term outcomes that are detrimental to all but a tiny fraction of the population. A great deal of effort is then expended by the government, and its beneficiaries and stooges, to explain away the failures. Usually, the next step is to repeat and increase the scope of already failed policies. It is all extremely wasteful and expensive.

There is no infallible and invincible power elite truly *"in charge"* of the present or the future. That fallacy is used by them to maintain their increasingly precarious positions. The slight psychological advantage that they enjoy quickly evaporates when a relatively small number of individuals are no longer fooled by the pretense, and consistently refuse to accept their assumed mandate.

The core power elites number fewer than 6,000 individuals, in a worldwide population of 7 billion. The elites are experiencing increased difficulty in maintaining their grip on power. The power elite of each generation began losing their perceived power with the advent of the printing press and the mass circulation of the written word. The Internet is exponentially accelerating that process, in part because it now includes audio and video created by individuals at-the-scene that are not filtered by Big Business/Big Government media. Big Sister may be watching, but she can seldom act in time to "maintain (her desired) order."

Schemes such as the *"human-caused climate change"* scare, the central banking conspiracy and most governmental policies, are being correctly perceived by more and more citizens as means to centralize power. The Internet is inexorably speeding up the process, between the time they are proposed and promoted, and their exposure as frauds and failures. For that very reason, some people refer to the Internet as a "disinfectant." Access to the truth is swelling the numbers of those resisting the latest elitist nonsense.

The free market operates on information. The better the information, the better a market performs. It has been possible to grossly distort it for over a century because much could once be hidden. That is no longer true. A higher degree of accurate information, and the existence of sound money, will cause it to snap back into shape. The control and manipulation by those, whom Ayn Rand correctly identified as the "looters," will be overcome.

In its final convulsions, the concentration of wealth and power will severely contract. Many of the last vestiges of centralized control will collapse. That is a certainty. As Herbert Stein said:

167

If something cannot go on forever, it will stop.

It cannot be stated often enough that centralized and coercive control structures **never have** and **never will work** in the long-term. The Founders of this Country purposely designed a political system with a small government of strictly limited powers. They knew what so many today apparently have never learned. The Founders understood the **timeless and universal principles of natural law.** Why do so many in the country not know this? There is a simple answer. It is the first **Modality of Inaction: The security of the status quo and resistance to change.**

From 1750 to 1913, this Country was on an unparalleled trajectory of growth in virtually every sphere of human activity, eclipsing anything else ever seen in all of Human History. Despite the Civil War and Reconstruction, this was mostly due to staying faithful and true to the founding ideals and principles, bequeathed by the foresight and efforts of the Founders. Big Government policies of **over-regulation** began on a large scale in the 1930s - resulting in the Great Depression.

After 1971, with fiscal policies unconstrained by a hard, asset-backed currency, as a consequence of the centrally-controlled flow of fiat money, we entered into the period of **hyper-regulation** with no effective check on the growth of Big Government.

On our present course, the near future will be increasingly government dominated. The two wings of the same bird of prey, the Republicans dedicated to warfare, and the Democrats dedicated to welfare, wish to force the Republic's once-sovereign citizens to slave in a "new world order." That can and will only last until that artificial construct fails catastrophically.

Where To Now?

This book is intended to provide a plan of action whereby citizens can restore the Republic's former greatness while, hopefully, avoiding a violent revolution when the current infrastructure crumbles. The restoration must be accomplished by individual action via peaceful means. Our goal here is to take advantage of this transitional period to educate and prepare the People.

Citizens need to understand the true nature of what we are confronting so that they are not overcome, and immobilized, when the going gets rough. Efforts by the looters will inevitably fail. It is our job to hasten their departure (stage left and right), and ensure that this current situation does not happen again, at least for many, many more generations.

During the American Revolution, it has been estimated that 10% or fewer of the colonists actively supported the rebellion. At most, perhaps a third of the population was sympathetic to the cause. Only fifteen to twenty percent remained loyal to the British Crown. The rest were neutral.

This should give us all hope. The truly important leaders may never be known to History. One of them may be staring back at you from the mirror each morning when you brush your teeth.

It is the responsibility of everyone who understands the message of this book to start doing his or her part. Understanding our present situation, and its dangers, only increases the urgency to act in an individual-cooperative fashion. If enough people "*get it,*" and then act along the lines that I will propose in the following chapters, we can indeed "snatch victory from the jaws of defeat" and restore **Our Country** to greatness.

9

Propaganda and the Media

… it was under Wilson that the first great propaganda slogan was coined and emblazoned everywhere, to make Americans start thinking favorably of democracies and forget that we had a republic.
–Robert Welch

Social theorists (now called "Progressives" in political terms) gained traction in the early years of the 20th Century with the success of Woodrow Wilson's propaganda (now called "*public relations*") phrase "*making the world safe for democracy.*" Amazed at how quickly the American people accepted the idea, Edward Bernays, who worked in the Wilson administration during the First World War, began to study how public relations could create other changes in the population's understanding of crucial geo-political issues of the day. Ominously, his work caught the attention of Joseph Goebbels and Joseph Stalin. *Life* magazine named Bernays as one of the "100 Most Influential" people of the 20th Century.

In addition to developing the slogan noted above, he also created another one almost equally effective in changing the public's perception of America's proper role in world events, with "*bringing Democracy to Europe.*" For his efforts Bernays was invited to attend and participate in the Paris Peace Conference in 1919, which yielded, among other things, the charter for the League of Nations, the precursor to the present United Nations.

In his first major work on these ideas, "*Propaganda,*" (1928) he wrote:

*The conscious and **intelligent manipulation** of the organized habits and opinions of the masses is an important element in **democratic*** *society. Those who manipulate this unseen mechanism of society constitute an **invisible government which is the true ruling power** of our country ...*

*We are governed, our minds are molded, our tastes formed, our ideas suggested, largely by men we have never heard of. This is a logical result of the way in which our **democratic society** is organized.*

*In almost every act of our daily lives, whether in the sphere of politics or business, in our social conduct or our ethical thinking, we are **dominated by the relatively small number of persons ... who** understand the mental processes and social patterns of the masses. **It is they who pull the wires which control the public mind.** (**emphasis** added)*

After the war Bernays was instrumental in creating **slogans** (i.e. manipulations via propagandizing) that are remembered even today:

- *"Pancake breakfast"* to support politicians in their election campaigns
- *"Bacon and eggs"* as the true all-American breakfast on behalf of the poultry and pork industries
- *"Ivory Soap: It Floats"* and *"99 and 44/100ths Percent Pure"* for Proctor and Gamble
- *"Crest with Fluoristan"* and *"Nature Thought of It First"* one for Proctor and Gamble's fluoridated toothpaste, and the second for the allied American Dental Association's media campaign in favor of the fluoridation of water
- *"Dixie Cup"* a campaign to replace public drinking glasses by claiming that they were unsanitary

The successes of such manipulations of public opinion supported the belief that the *"social mind"* can be modified scientifically. As seen in Chapters 7 and 8 such manipulations require accepting falsehoods as fact, resulting in the public *"buying in."* However, once understood as deliberate manipulation, the propaganda theme fails as demonstrated nowadays by the emergence of *"social media"* vs. *"mass media."*

Mass media may be defined as the one-way (or "simplex") transmission of information (or misinformation) from the top down, from the center to the radius, from the one to the many. Those with an agenda send endless streams of one-way messages to a captive audience, seeking and expecting to influence its behavior to their advantage.

On the other hand, social media may be defined as a two-way (or "duplex") communication system with non-captive participants and without any manipulative agenda.

As a result, the credibility of social media is increasing while that of the mass media is decreasing. The social media model is actually an improved method of distributed, individual communication.

That is reflected not only in the decline of viewership of the major mainstream media, but also in the declining effectiveness of its various propaganda themes. Successfully challenging the big three (ABC, NBC and CBS), which essentially controlled the flow of information in this Country for 50 years, is the explosion of alternatives, including cable and satellite TV programming, which now cater to every conceivable choice, and any possible niche market. In addition, the invention of *TiVo-type* technology, a digital video recorder with the capability of skipping over advertising messages, and the proliferation of web-only sources, can effectively neutralize attempts to manipulate public opinion.

Internet social media is all about the interaction between individuals, with two-way discussion and critical analysis of mass-media memes and messaging. It is not surprising that younger adults are increasingly rejecting the mass media in favor of the Internet with its multiple interactive sources of 'unedited' information.

More and more young adults no longer receive *any* of their news and information from a mass media source. Instead, they rely completely on the Internet to stay informed with their personal digital devices.

Many older people criticize such behavior without understanding the significance of the change. Granted, much of the information available via the Internet is mindless drivel. It is accurately perceived by the older generation as a complete waste of time. However, the Internet sources still provide a vastly better, more accurate and dependable source of unbiased information than does the mass media, which also churns out massive amounts of drivel. Accordingly, via the operation of the free market, Internet sources are increasingly selected by young people as the favored source for all information.

Few doubt the effect that the social media, perhaps *"interactive media"* is a better term, is having around the World, especially as the influence of the centralized, controlled-media structure wanes. The only question that remains is: When will it fully take hold here in the U.S. to facilitate political change as it has elsewhere?

H. Marshall McLuhan, the originator of *"the medium is the message,"* and *"the global village,"* anticipated some of these shifts. He foresaw the rise of the World-wide Web in 1962 when he wrote:

The next medium, whatever it is ... will transform television ...

A computer as a research and communication instrument could enhance retrieval, [make obsolete] mass library organizations [and enhance] the individual's encyclopedic [search] function.

Recognition of this sea-change, in accessing relevant and accurate information, is important in our discussion. We now know that it gives an individual an alternative to the kept media's often disingenuous reporting. This means that one can opt-out by simply deciding not to "buy-in." By so doing, an individual no longer gives tacit support to the kept media for his or her understanding of world events.

Once again, here is the rule:

If one buys into what they are selling, it is produced for them. If one stops buying, it will no longer be produced!

Following this rule thwarts and neutralizes the mass media which has long expected its audience to unquestioningly accept its slanted point of view, thus remaining passive as events unfold according to its agenda. People who stop buying in represent a very real threat to both its agendas and its continued existence.

In the late 1990s, the increasing power and accuracy of search engines, and online references, had improved to the point where they began challenging the veracity of traditional mass media sources. As a collector, checker and cross-checker of facts, I found it easy to use these tools to test the mainstream media's truthfulness. When watching, or listening to, the mass media's pundits, writers, commentators and experts, I developed a sort of internal buzzer. It went off whenever I saw or heard something that was demonstrably incorrect.

What I observed in the mass media was an endless number of misstatements, factual errors, misconceptions, misrepresentations and invalid conclusions. The error-rate is so high that there seems to me simply no reason to watch the "mass" or "mainstream" media for anything other than entertainment value! Perhaps to get a weather report but even in that case, Weather Underground on the Internet is more accurate and useful!

Traditional mass media is rapidly becoming obsolete as a means to control or direct public opinion.

Here is a tip. If you really want to know something, look it up and then cross-check what you find using the tools available on the Internet. That vastly increases your chance of getting the facts straight.

Only watch the mainstream media for entertainment with its "... *bubble headed bleach blonde who comes on at five.*" (Thanks and a hat-tip for that to song writer Don Henley).

Build your own Internal buzzer and **do not buy-in.**

10

A Short Examination of Ponzi Schemes and Confidence Games

Of all tyrannies, a tyranny exercised for the good of its victims may be the most oppressive. It may be better to live under robber barons than under omnipotent moral busybodies. The robber baron's cruelty may sometimes sleep, his cupidity may at some point be satiated; but those who torment us for our own good will torment us without end, for they do so with the approval of their consciences.
–C. S. Lewis

Ponzi Schemes as Public Policy and Social Welfare

The U.S. Social Security System is the very definition of a Ponzi scheme.

"Investors" who enter later into a Ponzi scheme keep the money flowing to those who entered it earlier.

With regard to Social Security, there are two additional factors:

1. Everyone must participate by force of law
2. When the money runs out, and there are more beneficiaries than taxpayers, the administration sells additional government debt to the Fed to bring in even more fake money to continue sending out the checks

Therefore, Social Security is a huge government sponsored Ponzi scheme—on steroids! Have no doubt about it. Bernie Madoff could only have dreamed about having his own Treasury Department, ready and willing to print up more T-bills to sell to the Federal Reserve backed by *"the full faith and credit"* of the United States. He would have enjoyed such a **power to deceive** that neither he, or Charles Ponzi, could ever have possibly conceived. He might have kept his scam going for years and years longer than he did. Instead, Uncle Bernie wound up in prison because he did not have the United States Treasury, the Federal Reserve or the imprimatur of the United States government to back him up. Dang the luck!

Question: Are you going to accept a Social Security check when it arrives? Are you going to let Medicare and Medicaid, or the Part D Prescription Drug Benefit, pay off your medical bills? Sure you will, because it is "*owed to you,*" right? You paid in! Besides, past the age of 65-67, one has no other choice, correct?

Question: Do you think any of Bernie Madoff's "investors," even if they suspected that it was a Ponzi scheme, really cared a whit as long as their checks arrived on time? It is impossible to believe that none of them had any idea of what was really going on.

Social Security, Medicare, Medicaid, the Prescription Drug Benefit, and now the new Patient Protection and Affordable Care Act, derisively referred to as *ObamaCare,* are all Ponzi schemes, built on and enabled by fraud, force and gullibility. This explains why so few, even the most "respectable" Republicans, dare to speak the truth. They know that the supporters of those programs, aided and abetted by mainstream media, will label any honest assessments as being "mean-spirited." At least Madoff's scam forced no one to participate. That is not the case for U.S. taxpayers enmeshed in these government frauds.

Outside of the government world of make-believe, is it not reasonable to expect a return-on-investment after one has paid-in? If an investment is advertised as returning a certain pay out, then there is a reasonable expectation of what the percentage rate of the return will be. But what if the pay-out exceeds the promise! Do you return the 'excess?' Or, do you do nothing? Who would complain about such a favorable outcome? Many of those in the government benefit system, almost half the citizenry, today receive far more in pay-outs than they ever paid-in, even when calculating in a decent return-on-investment.

So, how many of the "investors" in these government-sponsored Ponzi schemes will send their checks back when their payout exceeds, or even far exceeds, their pay-in plus a good return? Participants in all such schemes only care when one implodes. That is when they discover to their astonishment that *"my checks don't come any more!"* Or when they realize that the checks that do come in are effectively worthless due to inflation. Until then, most folks would consider it foolish to send the checks back. The real question is: How can we end these vast pyramid schemes?

I recently saw a letter to the editor, about the Social Security and Medicare Ponzi Pyramids, which claimed that: *"even a moron could understand this."* Really? Does the average person understand what constitutes an actual Ponzi scheme? Or how that relates to Social Security, and similar government frauds? And if they do, do they really care as long as the checks, or direct-deposits, continue to come in?

Take a look at recent polls about altering Social Security. Almost everyone is in on the scheme, so why should they care? Any suggestions to apply sound economic principles resulting in lower payouts, or a complete phase out, are met with loud protestations: *"Don't you dare touch MY check!"* Instead, insincere promises are made by politicians to *"fix it."*

When a government spends money that it does not have, in order to make payments, what do people think that means? It is all fake money! It is the same as taking a $10 bill from one pocket, putting it in another, and then claiming that you just made $10. And then following that bit of tomfoolery by pulling out the very same $10 bill from the second pocket, and then stating that you just made an additional $10. Terrific! What a great Country!

Con Games the Government and 'Banksters' Play

Let us take a look at con games. They are attempts to defraud someone by misplaced 'confidence' in the con man. A recent, well-known and highly popular con game is real estate mortgages. When someone takes out a mortgage on a home, one is most likely required to make a substantial down payment. (For the moment, we will ignore the low and zero down-payment mortgage scams that fueled the real estate bubble). A down payment represents a serious promise, enforced by law, to make consecutive payments for up to 30 years. As a result, the mortgagee has "skin" in the game. Consequently, they have a serious incentive to keep payments current to avoid defaulting. Otherwise, they lose their home and all their investment.

The entire process depends upon the creditability of the bank. In fact, the process depends on the **creditability of the entire banking system**. But what "skin" does a bank have in the game with Fannie Mae, Freddie Mac or VA loan guarantees?

The answer is nothing! From the very beginning, it was a scam. Not even one thin (real) dime of a bank's money was in play! Normally, in a properly functioning fiscal environment, when a bank makes a bad loan, then their capital and reserves are at risk. However, in the case of real estate mortgages, when a mortgagee defaults on a house, the bank has a tangible asset (the building) to sell. They put no actual money into the transaction. They did not pay the expense of erecting the house. That risk was assumed by the builder. The bank gets to keep the down-payment along with any mortgage payments that the defaulting mortgagee already made. What a great deal that is for banks!

How many people in the United States understand the concept of fiat-fractional, reserve banking? I would estimate that number is far less than 1%.

The moment that the loan documents were signed, the money for the loan was created **by that signature.** The money amount of the check, made out to the sellers by the bank, was "created" in the act of printing the check. The bank used none of its own money.

Here is how the fiat-fractional, reserve banking scheme works.

If a bank has $100,000 in reserves on its balance sheet, it might be comprised of (let us say) $10,000 in cash. This could be the bank's own investor capital, customers' deposits, plus whatever the bank might be holding as a loan from the Federal Reserve, or another bank in the system. With the 10% fractional reserve system, the bank would be free to 'loan' up to 90% of its balance sheet, or $90,000, to the home buyer with the property as collateral.

Please note that the bank **did not disperse any** of the $90,000 from its reserves balance sheet. When the mortgagee signed the papers, the loan created $90,000 of *"loan authority"* for the **house.** The bank (mortgagor) still has $100,000 but that is considered to be *"committed reserves"* that are fully loaned against. Now there is $190,000 in the banking system.

In this example, please note that the $90,000 did not belong to the bank in the first place. It belonged either to the bank's depositors (checking and savings accounts), its investors or to the Fed. The net effect, when the homeowner secured a $90,000 loan, was to increase the supply of money in the monetary system by $90,000.

If the bank wanted more *"lending authority,"* it only needed to find more depositors, or borrow more money from the Federal Reserve System, to add to their "reserves." Then it could 'lend out' (create from thin air) another $9 for every $1 received into the 'reserves.'

Question: Where did the Fed get the money to 'lend' to the bank?

Answer: The Fed created it electronically with a keyboard entry out of thin air!

When that newly created money was given to the mortgagee to buy the home, the original owner (seller) either used that money to pay off their old loan to their own bank or, if they owned the property outright, simply deposited it in their bank. Either way, that payoff created $90,000 in new 'reserves' for their own bank. The augmented 'reserves' now meant that particular bank could loan out up to 90%, or $81,000, to someone else.

By the time this layer upon layer, fractional 'money multiplier' effect is complete, that original $90,000 loan becomes almost $1 million in 'new money,' as it wends its way through the banking and economic system. If the home sells again in the future for $110,000, and that amount is deposited in any bank, then that next bank is free to create another $99,000 (90% of $110,000) in new cash 'reserves.' That is used for yet another set of loans totaling more than $1 million in new loans (again, assuming a 10% fractional reserve system). And so it goes, onwards and upwards, in the 'house of cards' financial and economic system.

The con actually gets even better for the perpetrators. The banks involved in the central bank scam also enjoy the benefit of interest paid on money that they created out of nothing. That comes from the interest that the mortgage holder has to pay back over the life of the mortgage loan. That had to be earned in the **real** economy. (Unless, of course, the mortgagee is participating in one or another state or federal welfare programs). This is the second process by which the Fed is able to expand the money supply outside of our control.

Over time, just like taxes, interest is supposed to "sterilize" a significant portion of the new money creation by drawing excess money out of the economy. However, that can only occur when higher interest rates are charged as compared to the rate of new money creation. Since only a small fraction of the loan principal is being paid back in any given year, the constant inflation of the money supply goes unnoticed. It ends inevitably with the destruction of the purchasing power of the currency. That is when, as with all fiat (fake, without real backing) currencies, it is reduced to its intrinsic value which is **zero.**

It is an elegant con game which is based, so far, on the credibility of the con man, namely the banking system itself. Every $1,000 created out of thin air by the Fed, can become $10,000, or more, depending on what reserve ratio is used. At a 3% fractional reserve ratio, the money multiplier (money created) becomes approximately 30 times the banks' reserves.

This confidence game is known as *"fractional reserve banking."* The bank loans out money created electronically, collects interest on that money for the life of the loan, and takes over the house if the homeowner defaults. Risk to the homeowner is 100%. Risk to the bank is near zero. The scheme persists until the bank has too many homes and no buyers. Banks have to loan to survive and prosper.

Multiply this simple example by the huge number of operations required to fund the Federal Government's deficits, those that pay for wars and entitlement programs. Deficit spending is a method to directly inject inflation into the mix when selling government debt to the Federal Reserve.

The role of the Fed in the scam is not just enabling the expansion of the money supply. It also has the purpose of allowing the government to spend money for programs that the taxpayers would not allow, if they were given the chance to say no. The Fed is essentially the funding mechanism for the expansion of government. The Fed is the ultimate con game.

Now let us talk about Quantitative Easing. This entry in Wikipedia explains the Fed's strategy of Quantitative Easing in a remarkably candid way:

A central bank implements quantitative easing by purchasing financial assets from banks ... with new electronically created money ... risks include ... higher inflation ...

The second round of such purchasing of financial assets from banks (QE2) ended in June of 2011. It succeeded in expanding bank reserves by nearly 50%. This required that the Fed purchase nearly 61% of all term Treasury debt as few in the private market, in their right mind, would buy soon-to-be-toilet paper paying out essentially zero interest.

With the implementation of QE3, the Fed will literally purchase all of the government's debt, in some manner or other. It will likely start by implementing more bad mortgage purchase programs and continue the bailing-out of Freddie Mac, Fannie Mae, Ginnie Mae and Sallie Mae. Then they can return to directly purchasing T-bills in large quantities. To see how this will work out for the United States, please direct your attention to the European Union and its current difficulties with Greece and the other PIIGS (Portugal, Ireland, Italy and Spain). Bear in mind, what is visibly going on is just the tip of the iceberg.

Sadly none of this is myth or speculation. It is the way that the banking and the Social Security systems works. Our great-grandparents, all the way on down to those citizens now entering the workforce, have been, or are being, conned. Our children, their children and grandchildren, will be stuck with the bill. That will be paid by defaulting, either a soft default through inflation, or a hard default with the abolition of present day mortgages and all entitlements. It can never actually be paid for outright because it is too enormous.

Despite having nothing truly at stake in a mortgage, other than as a bookkeeping entry, the major banks were pushed to the edge of default when the housing market bubble burst. Their books had became so fraudulent, through the loan-reselling of securities, also known as 'derivatives,' that those books had to be reconciled. But the major banks were then—only temporarily—propped up by the Federal Government with the claim that they were "too big to fail."

The banks were supported by the morally hazardous practice of using taxpayer bailouts, along with the support of the effectively insolvent Federal Deposit Insurance Corporation (FDIC). In the long run, there is no way to keep the books balanced. All that cheap money creation resulted in too many bad (malinvestment) decisions by the private market, which began imploding in 2007.

Five years into the so-called Great Recession, we still have a long ways to go. The current estimate, in early 2012, is that approximately 4-6 million foreclosures have still not been processed. It could well be a much higher figure. That is because 11 million mortgage holders (~1 in 4) are underwater. With home prices continuing to decline overall, many more mortgagees will also be forced into foreclosure.

Since 1992, the Social Security Fund's $2.5 trillion in surpluses have been gutted. They were loaned out to buy-down the published deficits. Now those IOUs ("warrants") have to be paid back as they come due, which adds right back to the published deficit. The Federal Reserve and the Federal Government have nothing at stake because it is the American taxpayers who are on the hook for all that debt. For the Fed, it is all just electronic book-keeping entries. The winners, as per usual, are the first-in-line banks (at the "discount window") and Wall Street's financial institutions, along with elected officials, government bureaucrats and their cronies.

Exposing the Fraud and 'Fraudsters'

What exactly did anyone expect to happen, once we moved to a 100% fiat (not backed by gold, or another hard asset) currency, when President Richard Nixon took the United States off the Gold Standard in 1971?

Ever since, the entire system has been based on a fraud. It is taken just a little over 40 years to destroy the "full faith and credit" that America built up over the previous 200 years.

It is hard to understand how the American taxpayer cannot see the frauds, the cons and the schemes being perpetrated in the Social Security and banking systems. There are nearly endless ill effects such as Social Security insolvency, deficit spending, a national debt that is greater than the Country's total economic output, the mortgage crisis, Wall Street fraud, government contracting scandals, and the like. When a currency is devalued, not only does good money go into hiding (in the form of gold and silver coins) but so does public and private morality.

Eventually, reality will overtake the wishful thinking of the present financial status quo. The true nature of Social Security, and the other entitlement programs, will become crystal clear when they fail completely. All of us on the receiving end of such programs will suffer, just as Madoff's "investors" did when his scheme came crashing down.

Once the victims accept the reality of these frauds, will they then demand the prosecution and jailing of all the criminals involved? At present, it is hard for them to act while the con is still being maintained. All those who will suffer greatly when everything collapses, are currently reluctant to make any reformist demands. After all, the checks are still arriving on time. As we have already discussed, the status quo is a comfortable place for most people. Denial of reality is part of that process.

All these fraudulent schemes will be maintained until the very last possible moment. Then the duped, the conned and the defrauded will fall off the edge of the cliff, just like Wile E. Coyote chasing the Roadrunner in the Looney Tunes and Merrie Melodies cartoons. When they finally look down, and the illusion of being on firm ground vanishes, they will find that the truth hurts. Politicians know and fear this eventuality. Most of them continue to support the frauds. When the con games end, what will happen to them is too terrible for them to contemplate.

At this point, there is no way to "fix it." Any opportunity to do so probably passed by several years ago. The "USS Fed Fraud" first glanced off the debt 'iceberg' in 2007. Instead of letting the market liquidate to clear bad debts, known as "market clearing," the Fed and the Federal Government just circled the ship around and dreamed up ways to worsen the problem. They then chose to take dead aim on the iceberg at "full steam ahead" by emergency lending, additional stimulus, TARP, bailouts of everyone except Lehman Brothers, quantitative easing, cash for clunkers, etc., etc.

Charles Ponzi was a piker compared to Bernie Madoff, who is a piker compared to the Social Security System, which is a piker compared to the Federal Reserve's support of endless spending by the Federal Government, and the lending practices of the banking system.

Few want to know the truth now, whether on the subject of the budget, the deficit, the dollar, the economy or anything else. And so, a giant tsunami of increasingly unserviceable debt will soon wash over us.

Most want to believe that the recovery from the Great Recession is real. After all, the President and all those smart people say so! Early in 2012, 1.2 million people fell off the long-term unemployment rolls but the mass media blared out that Obama put a net 250,000 people back to work! The government would not lie, would they?

Many are now shouting out that idiots are truly in charge. But the WARBI Paradox is two-sided. Nobody escapes without at least some blame.

Firstly, we need to ignore the rantings of those who put our Country in such peril. Secondly, we must concentrate on how to secure our own lifeboats. Thirdly, we must figure out how to patch up the "USS Fed Fraud" before it sinks us completely.

This warning, about 'national' banks, by Thomas Jefferson is a tribute to his foresight, in a letter to John Taylor in 1816:

I sincerely believe, with you, that banking establishments are more dangerous than standing armies; and that the principle of spending money to be paid by posterity in the name of funding, is but swindling futurity on a large scale.

11

A Short Examination of Philanthropy and Dependency

*Philanthropy is commendable but it must not cause the philanthropist
to overlook the circumstances of economic injustice
which make philanthropy necessary.*
–Martin Luther King, Jr.

One popular tool of the power elite is the purposeful distortion of the meanings of words. An excellent example is the word "philanthropy."

Merriam-Webster defines it as "*an act or gift done or made for humanitarian purposes,*" implying a charitable, voluntary act that is performed without any outside compulsion required. However, nowadays philanthropy is celebrated by the mass media when wealthier folks in our population 'give back' their wealth to those less well off. "*Give back?*"

The Fallacy of Giving Back

We hear the phrase "*giving back*" as if it is something noble and wonderful, but it is instead another shameful example of how something once noble has been degraded by the Progressive worldview. It has been degraded into meaning something that is required or "owed" by those who are "*better off than the rest of us.*" It also implies that it was originally "taken" away from those less well off.

How does that mindset work when a person with the least amount of money engages in philanthropy by giving his or her time, something much more precious than money? Such small scale philanthropy is—by far—the most common and successful. Yet, the mainstream media now applies the same *"giving back"* mentality to those folks when it profiles their causes. **That is ludicrous, another subtle variation of the same propaganda mindset.** Those folks 'owe' their time to no one.

Today, the term *"giving back"* clearly implies an obligation on the one doing the giving. But a true gift is not an obligation. It is an altruistic action that expects nothing in return. Someone who gives a gift expecting something in return is not truly giving but is making a transaction with the expectation of getting something in return. That is what makes true philanthropy so exceptional.

Conversely, in today's upside-down world, so many who now receive such gifts expect, or even demand them, rather than being grateful for the gift of time, goods or money. This inversion of reality is another example of the *"misanthropic impulse"* (hatred of or contempt for mankind) which does not celebrate the gift but questions, or even attacks, the real motives of the giver.

If one is going to give (in the original meaning of the word), it should be a hand-up and not a hand-out. To have the recipient, or worse, the politically-correct elite, question or dictate the motive behind the gift, while also demanding it, mocks and perverts the entire concept of giving and receiving. However, this viewpoint serves the purposes of those redefining the terms.

Such determined degradation of the concept of philanthropy and charity contradicts human nature. That is aptly illustrated by the old Chinese proverb:

Give a man a fish and you feed him for a day. Teach a man to fish and you feed him for a lifetime.

Here, in one succinct statement, the difference between enslaved dependency ("I am entitled to the gift") and prosperous independence ("I am glad to be able to make the gift") is made crystal clear.

Individual moral enrichment and the advancement of civilization are achieved not in dependency (especially if it is expected) but in prosperous self-reliant independence.

One should respect Bill Gates' great success as an entrepreneur. However, with regard to his mindset as a philanthropist, or respect for his political views, he merits only faint praise. His fuzzy minded, feel-good 'philanthropy' obviously and directly contradicts the focused entrepreneurial acuity that made him so successful.

When he and his wife, Melinda, set up the Bill and Melinda Gates Foundation, it became the world's 2nd largest philanthropic organization, with an endowment of $33.5 billion. Many in the media were giddy in their contemplation of this event, and lavish in their praise that such a vast sum was to be *"given back"* or *"given away."* Such praise is sickening and completely misguided.

Of course, the Gates Foundation is free to *"give away"* their money in any way that it wishes. However, if the Gates' had used their wealth to capitalize private micro-lending banks, a research institute for the application of broadly based and small-scale capitalism, or the like, it would have focused the Foundation on truly productive philanthropy. Enabling those micro-banks, in conjunction with private educational institutions, whether Gates Foundation owned or not, to invest in appropriate economic projects, attuned to the local culture while teaching the essentials of **true capitalistic** enterprise, would have been the ideal approach. If any of the assisted endeavors could not be run to make a profit (i.e. be self-sustaining), that would be the cue to try something better. However, the mainstream media would have likely excoriated such an approach for being *"selfishly capitalistic."*

Such approaches give individuals around the World the opportunity to learn how to fend for themselves, rather than become dependent upon handouts. Using that approach, the $33.5 billion in the Gates Foundation would automatically multiply many times over. It would eventually have allowed untold tens of millions to escape poverty and *ideological servitude* simultaneously.

Politically-correct philanthropy positively affects a much smaller number of people, provides far fewer ancillary benefits and creates very little additional wealth among those who receive it. Sure, it will help some people for a time but, once consumed, any benefits will disappear. It is like the fish that only feeds a person for a day. Giveaways, and non-profitable ventures, are not a sustainable model for those receiving such skewed so-called philanthropy.

Even the Foundation's proclaimed goals of *"expanding educational opportunities"* will be limited. Providing computers to schools and libraries is a nice gesture, and appreciated in the short run, but who will maintain the computers, and upgrade or replace them when appropriate or obsolete, since hardware and software co-evolve so rapidly? Will the Gates Foundation come back, year after year, to maintain and upgrade the equipment at every facility? Perhaps this should be called the *"consumptive giving"* approach? The gift of those computers is only reinforcing a consumptive dependency model. It is not teaching a principled model of pure entrepreneurial initiative on how to creatively achieve financial independence and liberty!

A Better Model

An "entrepreneurial" model of investment and capital-creation makes the benefits permanent by seeding education, basic technology and capital. It is adapted to fit the realities of a local community's day-to-day activity and customs. It teaches the principles of how to achieve sustainability. It should fit their level of development, address the *"circumstances of economic injustice"* and build on that, as made clear in the Martin Luther King quote at the beginning of this chapter. That model develops self-sustaining individuals, communities and economies that provide a return-on-investment, both for the 'seeders' and the resident 'owners.'

It has been proven, over and over again, that the cure for poverty is a condition in which political freedom prevails, more so than any other circumstance. To the extent that existing philanthropic models ignore such approaches, the money might as well be thrown into a hole, next to the various communities where it is provided, for the local people to dig out and spend until it is all gone.

The World is littered with hi-tech developments and aid projects brought into "Third World" countries by agencies and philanthropic groups. Most provide money and aid that winds up in the hands of the rich and powerful, with little benefit accruing to the general populace.

Those projects usually crumble away shortly after everything was installed because the country, or region, had not achieved the level required to maintain a modern economy. Or because so much "aid" was siphoned off that the projects were never completed.

In stark contrast, by utilizing the micro-development model, small-scale profits are re-invested into expanding existing enterprises, or into developing new enterprises in the community, which then continues the enrichment process without end. The individual "aid" amounts are so small that the local, corrupt political system does not even bother with getting its hands on them. On objective examination, all examples of successful sustainable development will be found to be due to a bottom-up and not a top-down approach.

For proof that "*consumptive giving*" fails miserably in its stated goals, one only has to look at what happens to most of our foreign and lending "aid," transferred from the U.S. taxpayers to the "needy" in other countries. The International Monetary Fund (IMF), World Bank, USAID and others, do not help countries through their lending practices. They wind up destroying them. This has been happening for decades. Just look at the record in South and Central America, Africa, Eastern Europe and now Central Asia—anywhere that the perverse hand of Progressive "philanthropy" has intervened and intruded.

In addition, these programs were used for years as part of our intelligence apparatus. See "*Confessions of an Economic Hit Man,*" by John Perkins (2004).

The Progressive philanthropy of government enforced Foreign Aid, as Congressman Ron Paul has repeatedly pointed out, is not only fallacious, but a complete failure. He said:

To me, foreign aid is taking money from poor people in a rich country and giving it to rich people in poor countries.

That is the dirty little secret of U.S. Foreign Aid, masquerading as "philanthropy" for political cover.

Similarly, the Gates Foundation would likely better serve mankind if it would follow the example of Bill Gates' former business partner, Paul

Allen. He has invested in numerous forward-looking ventures that will serve Mankind in the future, such as Scaled Composites (Spaceship One), Virgin Galactic (sub-orbital space flights for paying travelers), Stratolaunch Systems (to provide launching capabilities into orbit around the Earth) and many more. Progressives can be heard to complain that Allen is using his wealth only to increase it. *"He's just a greedy capitalist pig!"* Meanwhile, they ignorantly sing the praises of his former business partner who has turned his back on the entrepreneurial approach that made him (and many others) so wealthy during his business career.

With a net worth of $13 billion and counting, Allen obviously has no need to increase his wealth. He is expressing the natural desire to invest in improving the lives, and the opportunities, for generations that he will never see. If he succeeds, his wealth will increase, along with those of other individuals around the world. If he fails, he alone bears the loss. That is probably the most profoundly equitable form of philanthropy of them all.

Let us look at another example of someone who was criticized for not making politically-correct philanthropic decisions during his lifetime. Steve Jobs was much more straightforward, and thus even more vilified, than Allen when it came to *"giving back"* his wealth. Jobs declared that his "philanthropy" was based on bringing to market the most *"insanely great"* (Jobs' own words) products to benefit people. Even after his death, his company continues to bring to market products that improve peoples' lives.

Although counter-intuitive for some, the wealthiest people in the world became philosophically and materially wealthy by creating ventures that honestly and successfully serve the broadest, least fortunate and poorest portions of the population. Through those products, the poorest became, and become, less poor. It is a perfect example of the natural law philanthropy of the marketplace since *"the tide raises all ships."*

Another great example of real business-based philanthropy is found in the Howard Hughes Medical Institute (HHMI). Originally created as a tax shelter to keep money out the hands of the IRS (by itself, a good thing!), HHMI has grown into one of the world's largest private medical research foundations.

Keeping his money out of the government's hands was one of the best decisions that Howard Hughes ever made. Who could argue with the results? Today, the Institute annually funds more than 800 individual medical research projects, with grants of more than $1 million each. It has an endowment of more than $16 billion. It takes little imagination to consider what the Federal Government would have done with that money in, for example, Iraq or Afghanistan!

Inventing and bringing to market products and services that truly benefit people, and are affordable for the largest segment of the population, is one of the best effects of true capitalism at work. Those products help populations improve their standard of living and quality of life. Some products may start out being extremely expensive, initially used only by the richest folks. Soon the price comes down to an affordable range for millions more. It is part of a natural "trickle down process." The change in the expense of airline travel, from the start to the end of 20th Century, comes to mind. The price of desktop computers, cell phones and Internet service are among the countless examples of that process.

Capitalism's creativity becomes a wealth multiplier. It is unfortunate that so few people understand how this creative aspect of human nature works. That lack of understanding is a sad testament to both our public educational system, and to the anti-capitalist (or just plain ignorant) mentality of the mainstream media. It is the result of the shallow and uncritical thinking that emanates from the Progressive mindset that currently controls them both.

The Problem With NGOs and Other Government Efforts

Although somewhat more effective than government-sponsored and run aid programs, non-governmental organizations (NGO) have weakened their impact by accepting so much of their aid from government sources. True aid and charity should be of very short duration, with the goal always being to exit the situation that prompted the aid as quickly as possible. Instead, NGOs have become embedded in countries and, in many cases, succeed in building dependency, instead of eliminating it.

Any government model or agency, no matter how minimal it appears to be in the beginning, immediately metastasizes, firstly into bureaucracy and then into dependency. That is how the government 'aid' model sustains itself. The problem is also one of political involvement where none is needed. There are literally hundreds of examples we could cite here. The Department of Health and Human Services budget is $900 billion annually. That is in an area where nothing was spent prior to 1964. What do we get for our $900 billion? It would astound one and make for a chapter all by itself.

One of our family's several volunteer efforts was spending many weeks working in Louisiana and Mississippi after Hurricane Katrina in 2005. It was an all-volunteer private effort started in El Paso County, Colorado. We saw the results of the disaster firsthand. We witnessed the effectiveness of such private efforts in alleviating the suffering, and in helping affected individuals regain their footing. We also saw the huge waste and misanthropic application of the government efforts.

There were many private efforts vastly more successful and effective than anything the Federal Emergency Management Agency (FEMA) cobbled together—at many times the price tag. Did you see the private efforts on the evening news? It was all about promoting the government efforts. While FEMA concentrated along the visible areas of the coasts, most of the devastated inland areas went unserved, except by volunteer efforts. The money that was wasted but never did anyone any good was simply mind-boggling. It happens every time FEMA is called into action.

The failed (and failing) efforts of the FEMA model amount to "*a disaster after the disaster.*" Given the propaganda spiel about how it is so essential, it should therefore seem incredible that Americans were previously able to build, and rebuild this Country, through every kind of natural and man-made disaster imaginable! It must be astonishing both to Progressives, and many "conservatives," to learn that we were able to do anything for ourselves in the days before Jimmy Carter and FEMA. Given the money and resources wasted on FEMA, just imagine if those tens of billions had been left to multiply many times over in the private economy, to be in turn available to donate in private and vastly more effective relief efforts.

Back to the Future Philanthropy

During the first two hundred years of this Country's existence, it was real charity, and truly productive philanthropy, that added so much to the well-being of the citizens. It was all done without government coercion or tax breaks. Citizens have been sold the bogus idea, thanks to our educational system and the mainstream media, that the government is the greatest philanthropist of all, even while it confiscates our money to enable its (at best) mediocre results. Worse yet, its deficit spending is effectively spending our grandkids' money before they even acquire it. That turns once independent citizens into dependents waiting, unprepared, for the next disaster.

12

A Quick Tutorial on "Rights"

If a majority is capable of preferring their own private interests, or that of their families, counties, and party, to that of the nation collectively, some provision must be made in the constitution, in favor of justice, to compel all to respect the common right, the public good, the universal law, in preference to all private and partial considerations.
–John Adams

Watching the media, and listening to the average politician or fellow citizen, makes it obvious that there is mass confusion in most people's minds regarding the subject of 'rights, delegated powers and privileges.'

It extends from average citizens clear on through to the Justices of the U.S. Supreme Court. The recent *Citizens United v. Federal Election Commission* ruling that the government could not restrict political expenditures by corporations and unions, because they violate "the right to free speech" is but one egregious example. Justice Ruth Bader Ginsberg's recent comment, "*I would not look to the U.S. Constitution if I were drafting a constitution in the year 2012,*" is another proof of incomprehensible confusion (or ideological intent) at the core of the federal judiciary.

Traveling around the Country over the past couple of decades, I have found that the typical immigrant taxi driver is vastly more knowledgeable about rights, and our Constitution, than virtually all native-born citizens. Most people born here seem to take it for granted that freedom is free, requiring little or no exercise of personal effort or responsibility, and believe without question that war is required to secure and maintain freedom.

It Always Starts With Natural Law

On the contrary, maintaining freedom involves the continual application of universal principles, constantly demonstrated in the self-evident nature of reality, called "natural law."

Safeguarding freedom emphatically requires continuous exercise and vigilance. **It is a task that is an intrinsic and implicit part of being a citizen of this Constitutional Republic.**

There are two competing theories on the origin of natural law.

The first one is theological, arising from the belief that our Universe was created by an external pre-existing, super-natural being. God (or a variety of other names) therefore devised and set into motion the laws that govern this Universe.

The second one resulted from the application of the scientific method that seeks to objectively verify that the Universe is regulated by consistent physical laws and processes that may operate independently of intelligent activation. Explanatory theories are developed and then proven through observation and experimentation.

The ideas are not mutually exclusive. In actuality, to operate a government, it makes little real difference which idea is accepted as the origin of our World and the Universe. The observed operation of natural law is the same regardless of which is origin idea is correct. It is "self-evident."

The Declaration of Independence, and the eventual Constitutional Republic which followed, exhibit a very clear understanding and application of natural law to usefully enable the best form of governance. That is why, regardless of theological belief or scientific understanding, we can all live together under the same set of governing principles. The Declaration merges both the theological and scientific ideas into a single concept of governance by and for the People:

We hold these truths to be self-evident ...

The Constitution codifies those ideas into a charter for governance with "*... the consent of the governed ...*" in a Union of sovereign nation-states.

One of the best modern expositions of natural law is W. Cleon Skousen's book, "*The 5000 Year Leap: A Miracle that Changed the World,*" published in 1981. Mr. Skousen, a devout Mormon, emphasized a mostly theological viewpoint. However, he also included references to common law and the writings of the famous Roman scholar and politician, M. Tullius Cicero. His book includes both biblical and secular concepts to describe natural law.

As yet another indication of the genius of the Founders, both natural law explanations are valid and reconcilable within our political system. We must end the "*culture war*" raging over the theological or scientific underpinnings of our government. It is a futile and fruitless argument that is being prolonged by certain groups with less than noble motives. Some wish to manipulate particular constituencies. Others wish to establish their moral superiority. More to the point, those in positions of power are using this non-issue to divert attention away from real problems. Solving those problems would likely terminate their stranglehold on the Republic. Keeping people polarized and distracted makes it far easier to rule them, as in the old Roman dictum, "*divide and conquer.*"

Even after more than 250 years of debate, there is still widespread confusion. Firstly, as just described, there has been a conscious and deliberate attempt to mislead citizens. Secondly, most of the population is unwilling to think for themselves. With the enormous gains in material wealth over the past two centuries, and all the distractions of modern life, most citizens are exercising what I call "the blissful convenience of ignorance."

There are two classes of rights: unalienable and alienable. Neither is granted by government. They are endowed to every person simply because they are alive and breathing. Both classes of rights apply solely to human beings and to absolutely **nothing else.**

Unalienable rights cannot be given up, or contracted away. Alienable rights can be given up, or contracted away.

For example, an individual cannot give up, or contract away, the right to life, or the pursuit of happiness. On the other hand, an individual can give up the right to a trial by jury, or contract away interest in, let us say, a piece of property.

The right to *possess* property is unalienable, the right to *dispose* of it is alienable. One's beliefs or opinions do not change that equation in the least.

Morality

Morality begins when people respect the rights of others. If for example, one does not respect another's life, or their pursuit of happiness, one cannot expect anything but the same attitude in return. It is **The Golden Rule.**

Objective morality applies to all individuals throughout the World, regardless of government or culture. Governments and culture can either infringe on morality and rights, or stay out of the way. Their proper role is to protect rights and liberties while imposing no subjective morality. That includes any peaceful and lawful endeavors encompassing lifestyle choices and the desire for material rewards. Transgression of objective morality, such as unlawful force, murder and theft, properly fall under the jurisdiction of courts and governance.

Subjective morality is exclusive to different groups and individuals. It cannot be effectively governed. Thus the truism that "one cannot legislate morality." Or as Thomas Jefferson put it so well:

> But it does me no injury for my neighbour to say there are twenty gods, or no god. It neither picks my pocket nor breaks my leg.

It is helpful to remember that moral principles are universal and timeless. Thinking that they apply only to Americans is another unfortunate example of contemporary delusion.

The Myth of Special Rights

What about the "*special rights*" increasingly being codified into laws and regulations? Remember the point made at the beginning of Chapter 11 concerning the subtle modification and outright inversion of word meanings? There are no "special" rights. It is akin to saying that some

200

people are *"more equal"* than others. Adding such qualifiers to "right" or "equal" is a logical absurdity to hide the real truth of the matter.

So-called *"special rights"* are a disguise for organized governmental theft. There is no right to another's food, clothing, jobs, housing, medical care and education, any more than there is a "right" to own cars or iPods. No one can be denied their right to pursue obtaining those things but there is no right to take them through misappropriation or force. The promotion of "special rights" is just another tool for looters and manipulators to centralize yet more power into the hands of the government, which is then required to satisfy those supposed "special" rights by taking (i.e. stealing) from others.

As Ayn Rand once pointed out, whenever someone proposes a "special" right, such as medical care or education, it is helpful to ask, *"At whose expense?"* That simple question immediately reveals both the deception, and the fraud itself, aptly summed up as *"robbing Peter to pay Paul."*

It should not escape any rational citizen's notice that the promulgation of "special" rights is a reliable indicator that legislatures, and the courts, are out-of-control and violating their constitutional mandate and public duty. A government enforcing "special rights" is doing so at the expense of actual rights.

The phrase *"special rights"* actually means *"special privileges."* Very obviously, there can be no true equality of rights when some individuals are made *"more equal"* than others by extending them special privileges. Anyone giving it a moment's thought, realizes that special privileges extended to one person, or to a constituency, are at the expense of another person, or constituency.

Creating new inequalities to redress past inequalities, is ethically and intellectually indefensible in our system of governance. Applying either theological or scientific definitions, natural law is **inherently self-regulating**. Just as with free market economics, applying artificial regulation in the socio-political sphere is a recipe for chaos and failure. We are sinking ever deeper into a morass where even the supposedly wisest of us, installed in positions of great authority, are blurring the distinctions between subjective and objective morality, between what is private and what is public, and between what is individual versus organizational.

In the recent landmark *Citizens United v. Federal Election Commission* ruling, the Supreme Court majority opinion was fundamentally wrong. Why is that? It is very simple. **Rights apply only to individual human beings.**

That ruling was a glaring example of the failure to apply elementary logic. Frankly, the average first grader could grasp the point that **only a thinking individual can know that he or she has rights.** That obviously does not apply to non-thinking, artificial entities such as governments or corporations. The latter are strictly limited to the **powers delegated** to them by the people who organized such entities. This Supreme Court decision was just as absurd as granting rights to potted plants or animals. To re-iterate, how can anything that **does not know it has rights be "endowed" with them?**

Thanks to the Internet, and non-traditional social media, there has been a growing awareness by citizens of corrupt acts in the political and economic life of this Country. Among them have been outright theft and abuses of power. However, there is very little thought apparently being given to the corruption of more abstract, but nevertheless fundamental and vital, ideas such as the rights of the individual. The distortion of the true meaning of individual rights is creating confusion in the courts resulting in severe limitations on our personal and societal freedoms.

The confusion is so pervasive that almost no one is considering the implications of the probable long-term detrimental effects. The justice system has been degraded into a blind free-for-all scramble to "get mine." It is creating the classic political conundrum where, by seeking to satisfy everyone, no one is ultimately satisfied. There is no sense of proportion, no sense of long-term consequences and no rigorous application of logic and good, old common sense.

The courts have gone far beyond their constitutional mandate by condoning "*special rights.*" They have applied flawed definitions of civil rights and anti-discrimination laws that are actually imperiling the Country. The course of justice is not served by fresh injustices. Almost every child is familiar with the old saying that "*two wrongs do not make a right.*"

Although this subject of individual rights is a whole book in itself, let us take a quick look at some situations that citizens confront every day.

- It is illegal for a citizen to be denied a job opening, or an educational opportunity, in the public sector due to any type of "discrimination." On the other hand, in the private sector, they can be so denied due to all sorts of factors *considered* discriminatory.

- If an individual property owner refuses to convey a portion of their property to another, they are completely within their right to do so.

- If a sole proprietor wishes to "discriminate," then it is his or her right to enjoy the freedom to choose with whom they do business. The owner of a private business cannot be forced to serve anyone. A property owner cannot be compelled to rent or sell to anyone.

- There is usually a price to be paid in the free market for discrimination. However, in private property situations, that price is borne by the individual rather than society at large. It is just another aspect of natural law that every effect has a cause.

- If the proprietor of a business, or a property owner, decides to incorporate, then he or she has contracted away certain individual rights in order to enjoy the rewards of that public, commercial legal association.

- No individual property owner should be compelled to seek (and pay for) a government license merely to exercise his or her rights to do what they want on their own property that harms no other person's rights or property. Nor should they be coerced into abiding by arbitrary requirements.

- If a citizen is living in an incorporated area, township or city, or is part of a home owner's association, they have voluntarily agreed to contract away certain individual property rights in order to reap communal benefits.

Do I Own Myself?

The grotesquely complicated, ridiculously inefficient and clearly rapacious tax system is without question inimical to every possible interpretation of individual rights. By any standard of objective morality, it comprehensively trashes the rights of the individual. It might be helpful for all citizens to recall that the issue of unfair taxation was the spark that ignited the American Revolution.

When the Founders set up the government of this Republic, they made the carefully considered decision to base the political system on natural law. Therefore, our governance relies on timeless principles of practical and inherent self-regulation. The Founders realized that justifications such as *"the divine right of kings"* were excuses for absolutism and centralized power. However, there was, and is, a great risk in our system of governance. It was well understood by the Founders. They made constant references to it in their public and private statements.

Everything depends on the individual understanding 'self.' Our system relies implicitly on a pro-active citizenry that can think and act in an individual-cooperative manner. Most of our problems and issues are a result of an apathetic population that has abdicated responsibility, entrusting it to others. Unfortunately, those "others" are only looking out for themselves. Anyone who says differently is lying. If they insist they are not, ask them if they will give their life for yours, then work them back from there. Will they lend you $5000 to go to college? Will they pay your rent? Buy your food? You will learn about their devotion to "self" very quickly. The evidence is everywhere and mounting.

To help think about the importance of the 'self' in making anything work, let us use the example of cars on the road. Every one of us relies on other drivers to be in a state of individual 'self-regulation' to keep the traffic flowing. Although there are accidents when, for whatever reason, a driver lapses out of a state of self-regulation, for the most part the individual-cooperative actions of millions of drivers is successful. Therefore, one can state that road traffic is self-regulating. The only function of 'rules of the road' is to facilitate the successful accomplishment of billions upon billions of real-time decisions made by individuals to keep everything flowing. Road traffic usually proceeds with minimal difficulty and without outside coercion. Any problems are traceable back to individual human errors of judgment.

Just as every driver must be self-aware and make multiple active decisions when on the road, every citizen must appreciate their importance as individuals, the workings of natural law and their rights as sovereign individuals.

There is no "granting" of rights by other people or by constitutions. As already stated above, individual rights exist as the natural result of being alive. They existed innately long before any human beings were objectively aware of their existence. Awareness made them apparent. The only purpose of the U.S. Constitution, and the Bill of Rights, is to protect and defend those pre-existing rights, which are the basis for civilization itself.

If American citizens, and their elected officials, who have sworn to uphold and protect the Constitution, neglect their duty, then individual rights and liberties will inevitably be lost to authoritarianism, and then totalitarianism. As we have repeated many times already, any system based on coercion is bound to fail in the long run. That is why there is a *"clear and present danger"* of neglecting to actively exercise rights and principles incorporated into the U.S. Constitution, which can work equally well now, as they did 200 years ago.

A *"new interpretation"* of the U.S. Constitution, as Justice Ginsberg seemed to imply, is nonsensical. One would hope to see a greater degree of intellectual rigor, and simple common sense, expressed by an individual on the U.S. Supreme Court. Her comment makes as much sense as stating that we can re-interpret the Law of Gravity, or any other natural processes. There is no need to 'update' the correctly evinced principles of the U.S. Constitution. We simply need to actively follow it, and not ignore its obvious grasp of human behavior and interactions.

Calvin Coolidge, one those rare exceptions with the appropriate temperament, intellect and vision to properly act within limits of the constituted role of President, said in 1926:

It is often asserted that the world has made a great deal of progress since 1776, that we have had new thoughts and new experiences which have given us a great advance over the people of that day, and that we may therefore very well discard their conclusions for something more modern.

But that reasoning may not be applied to the great charter (The Declaration of Independence). If all men are created equal, that is final. If they are endowed with unalienable rights, that is final. If governments derive their just powers from the consent of the governed, that is final. No advance, no progress can be made beyond these propositions. If anyone wishes to deny their truth or their soundness, the only direction in which he can move historically is not forward, but backward, toward the time when there was no (law that defined) equality, no rights of the individual, no rule of law or by the people.

Those who wish to proceed in that direction cannot lay claim to progress. They are reactionary. Their ideas are not more modern, but more ancient, than those of the Revolutionary fathers.

To think that time changes such meanings would be similar to saying that the *"new math"* tells us that gravity works differently today than it did 3000 years ago. Proven fundamental truths do not change with time.

The purveyors of the *"living document"* concept (i.e. malleable, flexible) are attempting to encroach on rights by attempting to make citizens believe in the absurd. As with any charter, the Constitution is either enforceable or amendable. It is not "living" so it cannot be re-interpreted over time. If it was, it would be useless as a Constitution as would any contract. The document is instead **amendable in order to add to it, or to change it to reflect further extension of true principles.**

The reason that Constitutional amendments are so hard to pass is that, firstly, they must correctly extend the body of principles already contained in the document. Secondly, they must evince or extend a proper function and role for government. Lastly, there must be

206

overwhelming agreement on the part of the citizens and the States to make any changes. To have massive support, the principles involved must very obviously be considered 'held in common' by all concerned.

Even then mistakes are made, as with the 18th Amendment (Prohibition). As soon as that was passed, it became obvious that the points just made above were violated. Furthermore, it was not common to all. It was also impossible to enforce. Yet it took 14 years to repeal. The after-effects of Prohibition have been horrendous, leading directly into encroachments on individual rights and state powers, the wars on drugs, on poverty, on gun ownership, and all the other assaults perpetrated on the sovereign citizens.

The same will prove true with the 16th Amendment (the income tax), the 17th Amendment (direct election of senators) and the Federal Reserve Act. The same was true of Jim Crow laws, government organized discrimination or the granting of special rights, interference in intrastate commerce, etc. Experimenting (or perhaps "messing") with Liberty has caused a number of problems, but we can fix them if more people understand the process, which is accomplished by understanding natural law and rights.

The Constitution is only advanced by properly enforcing, or amending, its charter. That is true no matter how difficult that may be in practice. It is not advanced but degraded by attempts to find weasel words to get around, or ignore, the self-evident truths and timeless principles that it embodies. We eventually partially "fixed" the problem of slavery but then immediately set about creating new forms of it (in all but name).

The Constitution is corrupted, rather than improved, through the use of subterfuge and new 'interpretations.' Even a general understanding of the document still does not prevent mistakes from being made. Those mistakes may be repealed but there is only *one process to enforce and amend* the Constitution. Any other methods to 'interpret' are frauds and usurpation, nothing more.

As the proper understanding of the fundamental truths embodied in the foundational documents of the Republic is relearned, so will the pressure from the People and the States to reverse the backward slide into authoritarianism. That is being orchestrated by usurpers and manipulators, with the help of the courts and the kept media. If we stop buying-in to the frauds of those who would steal our liberties, then the Constitutional process itself will ensure the healing and repair of our great Republic.

13

The Self-Reliant Citizen: An Emergent System

The only freedom which deserves the name is that of pursuing our own good, in our own way, so long as we do not attempt to deprive others of theirs, or impede their efforts to obtain it.
–John Stuart Mill

Let us review and explain some practical approaches to regaining our freedoms and restoring the Republic. Anyone thinking that it will be easy, because there is a convenient quick fix or panacea, is deceiving themselves.

There is no avoiding the fact that we are due for a fall. The question is how hard will we crash? I believe that there is still time to avoid the worst, but the window of opportunity is swiftly closing.

We still have a choice between taking the high road or the low road. The high road will be shorter, faster and much smoother. It will take us right back to the foundational principles in a fairly straight line. The low road will be longer, twistier, slower and much bumpier. On the low road, we will painfully relearn that the foundational principles of this Country are the only ones that work in practice. Either way, we must return to the basics to ensure our future. Otherwise, there will be no great legacy to pass on to future generations. America, and indeed the World, may fall and fade into another Dark Age.

For more than a hundred years, looters and manipulators have furthered self-serving agendas that are utterly inimical to the best interests of both the citizens and our Union.

Fortunately, a century will not be required to repair the damage to our wellbeing, political equilibrium and economic stability, assuming that we take the high road.

The Self-Reliant Citizen

The restoration of the Republic is utterly dependent on individual citizens reasserting their power as **sovereign beings**. We must return to the foundational principles that **self-governing** individuals, and families, are the **essential building blocks** for a just and equitable society, where all are free to enjoy *"Life, Liberty and the pursuit of Happiness."*

For their own sake, and for the good of their fellow citizens, every capable adult citizen must embrace the absolute necessity of being **self-reliant**, a natural end result of understanding and practicing successful **individual-cooperative** behaviors in accordance with natural law. The necessity for self-reliance is not some romantic notion, as popularized in old movies and books celebrating the Old West, that are now ridiculed and derided by the central-controllers. It is the essential key ingredient of all successful civilization. After two centuries, we know for certain that informed, individually assertive and mobilized citizens are the *"last best hope"* for the salvation of this Country, and the ultimate progress of all Mankind.

The Two Main Issues to be Tackled.

Firstly, there are far too many "takers" and too few "producers." Nearly half of the citizenry is now receiving some sort of governmental assistance or paycheck. Obviously, far too many inherently capable people are not carrying their fair share of the load. Not only is this a moral and ethical problem, but it is economically unsound and unsustainable. It is artificially maintained by printing more and more fake money to "assist" the non-producers, a self-defeating process that also accelerates the destruction of the cohesive family unit. Half of the "assistance" goes to those completely dependent and the other half goes into less noticed, subsidized activities or corporations. Among them are the federal employees, local government and private sector corporations and their employees, who receive government payments for unauthorized functions.

Secondly, there is still blind trust being placed in false leaders. Accompanying each *"Great Leader"* is the wasteful and incompetent interference of centralized power with all of its innumerable committees, departments, agencies, enforcers and 'czars.'

The only solution is a citizens' movement promoting greater self-governance and self-reliance **from the ground up**. It will be built upon the pre-existing smaller government entities that are much closer to the People, not a central authority as practiced for the last century. Those entities are the local municipalities, townships and counties that are currently dominated by, and subservient to, the centralized power structure of the Federal Government. To effect such a solution, voters must stop voting into office the preening, narcissistic "professional-politicians" and instead elect true "citizen-legislators," who are respectful of individual rights and property.

There is a natural upwards progression in creating a just and equitable society. Just as with any edifice, it begins with the foundations. Every successive level of the structure is dependent on the integrity of the previous level. The first and most essential building block is the individual. Next comes the integral family, followed by the local community, town or city, county, state and, lastly, the Union. The ongoing denigration and destruction of the individual and the family, by encouraging every form of social dependency, along with authoritarian "father knows best" control, is destroying that foundation.

Each governmental level should be subservient to the previous one. Why is that? Because the previous level of governance empowered and authorizes it. To think otherwise, is to believe that a building is erected from the roof on down, with the foundation being the last part emplaced. Any child would laugh at that nonsensical notion. Yet, that is exactly what is now happening in social, economic and political terms. The Federal Government and the Presidency, along with the U.S. Congress, are being exalted as "*more equal*" than the originating governmental entities.

The aggrandizement of the Federal Government is now so top-heavy that it is like a structure where the building materials, from the basement on up, have been progressively removed to create an ever more elaborate roof. Any self-respecting structural engineer or inspector would condemn such a building as unsafe. Those living in the lower floors will be crushed when the sheer weight of the roof eventually crashes downward, much like a giant game of Jenga Blocks. For a while, it all remains standing, until the wrong block is removed. Then the whole structure gives way. Recall those images of collapsed buildings after an earthquake (or the WTC), where many floors fell one on top of each other like a squeezed accordion? When the integrity of the load bearing components is inadequate or is simply blown out, the destruction of the whole structure is inevitable, no matter how grand and secure the roof, or facade, may appear.

All citizens living under the current *"Roof of State"* are actually in great peril. We must urgently remove the overbearing weight of the supranational central government and restore the integrity of the foundational political structures. That must begin at the individual citizen and family level. Everyone must carry their portion of the load by involving themselves, as informed and rational citizens, in local government. By restoring their own sovereignty, citizens have the power to restore the integrity of the entire Republic. Without it, the Republic is done and gone.

Our political system was deliberately organized, and gelled into a Constitutional Republic, over a period of about 15 years. It began as a loose confederation of sovereign states, joining in the 1776 Declaration of Independence, and fighting together in the Revolutionary War that freed us from British rule. The Articles of Confederation formally ratified the arrangement into quasi-nation-states in 1781. That was a temporary step since the Articles neither clearly nor completely defined the common and separate powers held, or relinquished by, the member sovereign nation-states to a central government. The first and second Constitutional Conventions created the governmental structure for a closer union in 1787 and 1789. That structure retained many of the features of the much more limited confederation that preceded it.

Please note that throughout that entire process, when our Constitutional Republic was being formed, no legal entity known as the *"Nation of the United States"* came into existence. The words 'nation' and 'national' appear nowhere in either the Declaration of Independence or in the U.S. Constitution.

The preamble to the Constitution says:

*We the People of the United States, in Order to form a **more perfect Union** ...* (**emphasis** added).

Therefore, the United States is a union of sovereign nation-states. It is not a single nationalist-state.

The Union consists of 50 co-equal nation-states.

The President was to be elected and installed in office as a Chief Executive Officer (CEO) working for the shareholders who were, and are, the sovereign citizens residing in those nation-states. The President is a hired hand, a contract laborer for a strictly limited period of time, ***not a ruler***. The President is not the Commander-in-Chief of the People, or of the States that comprise the Union. He is commander-in-chief of a subservient agency, the government military force created and funded by the Congress, that was intended solely to defend and benefit the Union of sovereign nation-states.

Let us be very clear why authoritarian nationalist forces attempt to militarize and make *War on Everything* from Poverty to Drugs to Terror. It puts the President and the government 'in charge' of every aspect of daily life.

The Constitution only grants specific, defined, limited and enumerated powers to a federal government whose *sole purpose* is to serve those sovereign nation-states. The Constitution very deliberately *does not create a supranational government*. The separate sovereign nation-states have **temporarily and voluntarily** ceded certain limited powers to the Federal Government.

The problem is that the latter has assigned to itself non-constitutional powers. It started with Reconstruction, then extended wartime powers into peacetime through continual war-making. Next, it moved on to so-called "revenue sharing" that places the States in a position of dependency to it. That same classic form of pressure, "*the power of the purse,*" is also applied via "*federal grant money*" to other 'lesser' governmental institutions inside the States, including local municipalities, townships and counties.

These are not abstract or irrelevant distinctions. They are at the core of the difference between what is defined in the Constitution, and originally implemented, versus our present governmental situation. They are critical in understanding how to untangle ourselves from the current mess. They are the key to formulating a coherent plan to restore the Republic.

Efforts to change the citizenry's understanding of our original political system began after the Civil War. Prior to the 1860's, the Union was commonly referred to in the plural, as in *"the United States are ..."* After the Civil War, the common usage was changed to the singular, as in *"the United States is ..."* That was one effect of the success of the Northern states in preventing the Southern states from voluntarily leaving the Union, even though they had voluntarily created and joined it. From that point forward, the Union has continually devolved into today's **attempt to create a single nationalistic state.**

Although it may seem a very small thing to change just one word (i.e. **are** to **is**), actually that is an enormous fundamental change in political perception and perspective.

If the Founders' original intention had been to create a single national state, there would be no need for state constitutions. The States would have merely been identified as political subdivisions of a single "Nation," just as most counties and parishes are defined and chartered as subdivisions in a State. We would have a *national* rather than a *federal* form of government.

During the 19th and early 20th Century, a wave of nationalism swept the World. It is still manifesting itself, here and abroad. Whether calculated or not, nationalists have turned everything upside-down. Events now occurring in Europe are the clash between sovereign nation-states and a giant supranational, bureaucratic entity (the European Union).

In the U.S. Constitution, the sovereign nation-states delegated a few of their legitimate functions as powers, in a strictly limited charter, to the Federal Government, their designated agent. Those functions concerned the common defense, relations with foreign powers, and policy between the States. It also established a Judiciary to check and balance the powers of the Executive and Legislative branches, but **not** to check the powers of the People or the States. The Constitution further delegated a number of administrative tasks (post roads, coining money, certain tax collections, etc.). There was never any implication, or any desire, that the Federal Government should involve itself in the private lives of citizens, and the affairs of the States, to even a small fraction of the degree that it has usurped and assumed with its currently pervasive powers.

Understanding the times in which they lived and thought, makes it very clear that when the Founders spoke of the Republic as a "nation," it was not in the legal sense. To them it was a romantic allegory. They meant that we had become a "nation" of like-minded but individual citizens who shared "*self-evident*" principles, thus the use of phrases such as "*One Nation*" and "*E Pluribus Unum.*" Since then, the meaning of such phrases and words has been deliberately shifted and altered to serve nationalistic agendas.

The perversion of the original intent of the Founders has been proceeding for the past two centuries. "Progressive" authoritarianism began with the Hamiltonians almost immediately after the Constitutional Convention. However, even the original Hamiltonians would be appalled at what has occurred since then. Nationalism was aggressively promoted and instituted following the Civil War. At the beginning of the 20th Century, the onrush of nationalism and centralization was greatly accelerated by the policies of Presidents Theodore Roosevelt and Woodrow Wilson. In the 1930's, most of the now familiar institutions of nationalistic governance were emplaced during Franklin Roosevelt's administration. The adherents of centralized nationalism took deliberate advantage of the ignorance and apathy of citizens amid the stresses of the time. They employed all the tools of propaganda to misdirect the citizenry, greatly assisted by a compliant or ignorant mainstream media.

Why has there been such a long and focused effort to subvert the Constitution? Because some persons, unhappy with the original checks and balances inherent in the constitutional apportionment of responsibilities, have always desired more power for themselves. It is a historical fact that has been demonstrated time and time again. In the present day, similar minded forces ignore the Constitution's restraints altogether. The good news is that, by doing so, they are actually exposing their fundamental weakness. Their positions now rely on the continued ignorance, apathy and complacency of citizens. An informed and aroused citizenry is their greatest threat.

Throughout history, power elites have recognized that it all comes down to perception. It is a war to influence the mindset of the individual citizen, whether they are 'dumbed-down' or 'intellectuals.' Totalitarian regimes have the most effective propaganda and public relations machines. Progressives, nationalists and authoritarians are very well aware of this fact. They will use whatever tools are available to them. Some are the "*useful idiots*" whom they promote to assist them in achieving their self-aggrandizing goals. Such people are rife throughout the political parties as well as the mainstream media. So far, the power hungry have been able to concentrate their power, opposing the natural will of the People and dominating the sovereign nation-states. They have done so via exploiting the **Modalities of Inaction** (defined in Chapter 8) as well as effectively using the **WARBI Paradox** (outlined in Chapter 7).

However, while they may have won a significant part of the propaganda battle, they have have not yet won the war. The adoption of the Federal Reserve Act, the 16th Amendment (the Federal Income Tax), and the 17th Amendment (direct election of senators), were admittedly significant victories for them. They have also used clever 'interpretations' of the 14th Amendment to further their aims. The various "War on ..." policies that they have invented, and their budgetary entrapment of the States, have been the principal, and most successful, tactics that they have employed to pursue their strategy to subvert America.

To a certain degree, the other constituent parts of the Constitution are still fending off the worst efforts of the centralizers. That probably explains the recent strategy by Progressives to ignore the Constitution almost entirely, in order to circumvent its limitations on them, while hoping that the dumbed-down, mostly uninformed citizens will not notice. There has also been a campaign in certain quarters declaring that the Constitution is outmoded, and no longer relevant, in this "modern" age. That is a pure propaganda play. It is part of a continued 'across the board' effort to misdirect and confuse the population.

The awakening process for citizens must include discarding the notion that men and women in high positions are beyond all criticism, that they can do no wrong. It is a serious mistake to place "off-limits" any questioning of any leadership's ideas and motives, no matter how popular they may be. Push aside the myth-making machinery and one is guaranteed to find persons no less flawed than the rest of us. Presidents such as Lincoln, Roosevelt (Theodore or Franklin), John Kennedy, Richard Nixon and Bill Clinton may have been *great men* but, in each case, history reveals that they made mistakes and showed poor judgment. Presidential behaviors have ranged from poor to outright criminality in office. Power elites depend on the average citizen denigrating themselves by comparing them to the myths surrounding so-called VIPs. Citizens that actually believe in their own self-worth, considering themselves just as important as the *"Leaders,"* are a threat to those *"in charge."*

Truly enlightened people who become leaders understand the damaging effects of personality cults. During their lifetimes, they usually reject the homage of their admirers or followers. Only lesser men and women embrace and manipulate the *"Great Leader"* syndrome while gaining and holding power.

When their adherents, supporters and cronies attack someone for questioning a leader's ideas, or decisions, they are usually protecting their own positions. A true leader never feels insecure about being questioned. They do not feel threatened by free speech. They have no need to erect *"no free speech zones"* of silence around their administrations. Their responses to questioning allow them to restate their principles and educate others, rather than hiding or manipulating the truth.

Why the Original System Worked

As described in earlier chapters, I spent many years involved in high-level system engineering. That gave me considerable practical experience in recognizing effective design work. None of the systems on which I worked could function well based on a flawed design. When I embarked on an in-depth study of The Declaration of Independence, and The U.S. Constitution, I quickly recognized the elegant design principles embedded in those remarkable documents, as well as a very few obvious flaws.

The architecture of any successful political or economic system must be based on certain objective criteria that are common to all and independent of personal opinion and prejudice. Only when "self-evident" principles of natural law are employed, can the system function successfully as a self-organizing unit. To all citizens, the system must exist in an objective and independent form, utterly impartial, unable to be subjectively interpreted. Otherwise, there can no basis for fundamental agreement about its structure or intent. Subjective opinion being what it is, there would be no common understanding held by all informed citizens.

One can invent systems that degrade humans, such as communism, socialism, fascism, authoritarianism, Progressivism or Neo-conservatism, from ideas and theories that have little to do with the reality of fundamental human behavior and natural law. One can then dress them up with pretty descriptions to make such systems look grand and glorious so that gullible people will buy-in. However, if their designs violate the fundamental design principles of human behavior and natural law, they all will inevitably fail.

Two examples from disciplines outside of political philosophy will serve to make my point.

1. Gravity and planetary motion are a constant. That is an observable and predictable fact. No matter how many measurements are made, they are always the same from every point of view.
2. When an electronic circuit is designed, it must conform to Ohm's Law ($E=IR$—the relationship of voltage, current and resistance) or it will fail every time that it is energized.

Successful political philosophy has very similar qualities. No political structure will operate successfully in protecting the rights of individuals without employing "self-evident" fundamental truths and principles of natural law that cannot be redefined or re-interpreted. People may **want**

to believe otherwise but it does not matter. Their desire to believe otherwise, does not change the immutable nature of those operating truths and principles in the realm of political philosophy.

It is worth noting that many of the Founders were interested in both the natural sciences and the principles of engineering. The most obvious examples were Benjamin Franklin and Thomas Jefferson. Jefferson studied natural law as well as science, engineering and mathematics. He utilized what he had studied along with an abundance of common sense and literary talent, when he took the lead role in the Committee of Five, among whom was Franklin, that drafted the Declaration of Independence.

Was it also mere coincidence that the developer of the modern gold standard for currencies was Sir Isaac Newton? In 1717, as Master of the (British) Mint, having established the bimetallic relationship between gold and silver, he created a rational gold standard. That system worked very well for centuries before it was foolishly cast aside in favor of a fiat currency (i.e. paper money) without hard assets to back it up.

Emergent Systems

Austrian School economist Friedrich Hayek's magnum opus, *"Law, Legislation and Liberty,"* published in 1973, contrasted two conflicting views of society. One is 'ordered' (i.e. static and artificial) and the other is 'emergent' (i.e. dynamic and natural). Hayek noted that an emergent society is the best guarantor of human liberties.

Complex systems and patterns **emerge** out of many relatively simple interactions. **Emergent systems** are much more than the addition or collection of many parts. They are creative, not sterile. They can have the quality of being transcendent. Each of the parts is vital but it is the interplay between them that creates something wholly complete yet grander than expected. The result is something that could not have been predicted by examining and studying the individual parts in isolation.

A prime example is how consciousness and advanced intelligence **emerged in humans.** It is wholly natural in operation (regardless of whether or not it had its origin in divine or natural development) yet clearly transcends all the constituent biological parts of the human body.

Higher order animals have the same basic functional parts. None have the consciousness and intelligence of humans. Every one of us is an expression of how the whole can be greater than the sum of its parts.

Hayek's work has been expanded to include the concept of a *"system of systems"* (SoS), a new and more effective type of organizational understanding. It accomplishes far more than would be the case by merely adding together a series of simpler systems and subsystems. **That is the key to understanding the behavior of all systems.** Once understood, it becomes absolutely clear that centralized (i.e. communist, socialist, fascist, authoritarian, statist, etc.) political and economic control systems will **always** fail. There is no other possible outcome, at least not in this Universe.

Emergent systems evolve naturally out of the basic architectures found in nature, observed by science, and expressed in technology, along with the workings of the free market. An example was the original SoS comprised of all the parts that made life possible on Earth. Whether one believes in a theological or scientific origin, it is true that as soon as the constituent parts were present, they formed the fundamental building blocks for the **emergence** of life that spread across our planet.

The life forms varied widely in different epochs but shared the same basic characteristics. Life will remain viable and continue to expand in new emergent systems as long as those fundamental building blocks remain in place. It will end if they do not. The study of the ecologies found in nature has established this beyond all doubt. It does not matter whether those building blocks are found in the harshest of conditions, such as the bottom of deep ocean trenches or on the top of Mt. Everest. One day, similar building blocks may be found on a distant planet!

In all human affairs, similar processes are at work. When Johannes Gutenberg invented the movable type press in Europe, he had no idea of the enormous consequences. The interjection of his printing press **into the marketplace** kicked the Renaissance into high gear, followed by the Protestant Reformation and the Age of Enlightenment. The printing press comprehensively overthrew the previous system of (literally) **cloistered knowledge.** Transitioning from a few handwritten original and copied manuscripts, to millions of printed books with any number of copies, enabled the dissemination of information on a much larger scale—with incalculable effects. It facilitated a variety of emergent systems in virtually all areas of human activity and education. Emergent systems of the free market have given us virtually every man-made wonder that we have and enjoy today.

The United States is an emergent system established by informed individuals who had had the opportunity to study and consult a wide variety of texts on many subjects. That would have been impossible in the ages before Gutenberg's revolutionary innovation.

In the present day, the same process is at work with the Internet. Its potential as an enormously effective communication tool was obvious from the start. However, it was the emergent system of the World Wide Web that made Internet communication explode in a multitude of ways that its originators could never have imagined.

The personal *"digital life"* enabled by devices attached to the Internet is the most successful technologic SoS ever conceived. However, it is just another emergent system that evolved from the revolutionary explosion of knowledge created by the base technology of the printing press, the second wave of the *"Information Age."* The first wave was the invention of writing as a storehouse of knowledge for present and future generations. When there is a universally available store of knowledge, such as publicly accessed libraries of books, the individual initiators responsible for emergent systems are empowered to assimilate information from many different disciplines. That is expressed in a multitude of new and different combinations, sparking advancements of human creativity in every field of activity.

Some of the concepts for early *"packet-switched networks,"* and later the Internet, derived from the mathematical formulae previously used to enable safe and efficient railroad switching yards. Those developed from the need to switch boxcars between trains, and entire trains between different lines, all part of systems to precisely manage the timely movement of freight and passengers in railway networks. Efficiently switching 'packets' of digital data from end-to-end through the digital 'tracks' of an electronic network requires much of the same mathematics. There is no magic involved in boxcars or packets of data.

The World Wide Web itself is the base architecture for the emergence of new systems of social networking and the organization, retrieval and (most importantly) sharing of information, concepts and ideas. We are now well into the third wave of the Information Age. The possibilities appear to be virtually infinite. Even more than the failed reactionary attempts to prohibit *"subversive knowledge"* with book burnings, and other forms of censorship, those in power are unable to suppress the flow of ideas on the Internet. That is increasingly evident across the globe, no matter how backwards and repressive the regimes that are supposedly *"in control."*

It is extremely important to understand that our Constitutional Republic is not just an expression of an emergent system in the past tense, but also in the present and future tenses. The Declaration of Independence and the U.S. Constitution were, are, and will be the base architecture for a political system that guarantees freedom and liberty. It is through individual empowerment in such an environment that advancements in our material and philosophical civilization emerge. It is safe to say that what will occur in the next 150 years, will likely again far eclipse anything seen in the past 5,000 years—**if we take the high road** out of our current morass.

It was the codified system of political freedom and liberty in 'The American Experiment' that enabled the development of the emergent systems that propelled the United States to unparalleled levels of technical achievement and prosperity. It may still do so.

Centralized vs. Fully Distributed Emergent Systems

However, almost from the beginning of the Republic, looters made one attempt after another to put themselves at the head of the line and benefit unfairly. In the 20th Century, these kleptoparasites increased their disproportionate share of power and wealth. In the 21st Century, they have come close to strangling the political and economic systems envisioned and put in place by the Founders.

Nevertheless, it is important to realize that it took 200 years for them to nearly succeed in subverting the base architecture of our Constitutional Republic. Perverting natural law, or its principles, does not create anything new, it only corrupts them. This realization should encourage those involved in restoring The Republic.

Every attempt at artificial control and centralization generates new emergent systems to circumvent them. However, once the base architecture has been sufficiently corrupted by such attempts, resulting in a cancer in the Body Politic, the system begins to die. We have reached that point. It is time for the citizens of this Republic to exert their power by direct positive action in the way that they individually choose to conduct themselves. The temptation to succumb to the *"if you can't beat them then join them"* syndrome never works when you enter into the company of thieves and control-freaks. Too many citizens have taken that path of least resistance, or just thrown up their hands in despair and opted out in denial. That accelerates the on-going failure until Modality of Inaction #4 takes over.

When taxes and regulations are circumvented by their intended targets, another round of taxes and regulations are enacted in response. Attempts to circumvent or neutralize the new ones are then met with yet another round of taxes and regulations. It is an insidious process of escalation from an already unnatural state of **over-regulation** into the grotesquely counter-productive mode of **hyper-regulation**. Such activity continues until the whole system is crushed under its own unbalanced and excessive weight. That is but one of the blindly destructive behaviors of the corrupt and manipulative persons who have taken over the government.

President Reagan summed it up quite well when he said: *"If it moves, tax it. If it keeps moving, regulate it. If it stops moving, subsidize it."* Then it dies.

When subsidies, inherently unfair and counter-productive because they are at the expense of someone else, are continued long enough, the entire artificial construct utterly fails. However, the main reason that political and economic centralization is so fiercely defended is that:

The benefits of centralized systems always accrue to those closest to the center. The most harm accrues to those furthest from the center.

A successful political system must adhere to the principles that permit it to survive and prosper. What is true in any engineering discipline is equally true in any political order.

If the foundational principles, goals and objectives of a political system are flawed, it will decline and fail over time. The failure rate will increase, and the level will be moderate, disastrous or catastrophic, depending on the severity and number of embedded flaws. This explains the successive failures of communism, socialism and fascism. Today, policies from all three of those failed systems are being unnaturally grafted onto our political and economic "Liberty Tree" by Progressivism and Neo-conservatism. These infections must quickly be excised to save our Republic. Even a system designed correctly from the outset will begin to fail when enough parasitic growths infect it.

The entire political and economic system, and wealth creation itself, must be as "fully-distributed" as possible. The lesson is very clear from studying information systems. For example, desktop computing in the workforce quickly doomed the centralized control system of mainframe computing. Full distribution of desktop computers, and now laptops and tablets by the tens of millions, has so empowered individual workers that there have been enormous gains in effectiveness and productivity. The very same process works when individual citizens empower themselves in the political and economic spheres.

Studies in many different fields of technology have consistently demonstrated that vast centrally controlled system architectures fail so comprehensively, and so catastrophically, as to make them useless. That is equally true for political and economic systems that are centrally controlled. Think of the many 20th Century collapses of regimes that put hierarchic collectivist concepts into practice. Likewise, all of today's centrally controlled and dictatorial governments will eventually fall. Too-Big-To-Fail is not just a useless concept, it is an inherent threat to the entire cultural, social, monetary and economic system.

The authoritarian "progressive" system, a century in the making and currently being enforced in Washington, D.C., is obviously failing. It has never been a matter of if, only when. It is the predictable result of a corruption introduced into a healthy and finely-designed system. It is like a computer virus that has infected an operating system, or a disease that has taken hold in a previously healthy person's body.

The Dangers That We Face

Has the damage that has been done to the system also irrevocably damaged the Constitutional framework so carefully wrought by the Founders? You and I, members of the jury, are still deliberating that question.

Those who seek to control and manipulate, and those committed to the ideology of centralization, hate everything about the personal freedoms inherent in emergent systems. They hate spontaneous order and self-organization, they hate the inevitable de-centralization that it brings, and they hate the true free market because it is so much harder for a government to loot. They are reacting to threats to their power, and their capability to leech off the current system that benefits them at the expense of most citizens.

The United States' present-day dysfunctional political and economic system has limped along for decades for three simple reasons:

1. We are the world's largest debtor
2. We provide the world's reserve currency
3. The dollar has been artificially protected as the world's transactional currency for petroleum

The three work hand-in-hand. However, this triad system has almost run its course. It is unlikely to be sustained much beyond 2020. Those believing that it will last longer will be unpleasantly surprised by the suddenness of our financial collapse. The day of ultimate economic reckoning is a mathematical certainty. The numbers do not lie, only the timing is unknown.

What level of failure is going to occur? We are rapidly moving from moderate political and economic disruption into something analogous to what pilots sarcastically refer to as a *controlled crash* and that is **only if immediate corrective actions are taken.**

Otherwise, if the current course is maintained, without facing the realities of massive fake money creation, increasingly disruptive economic controls and re-interpretation or abrogation of the U.S. Constitution, the crash will surely be catastrophic. We will not be saying *"any landing you can walk away from is a good one."*

In such a crash, it may well be lights out for America.

14

Let Us Stop Killing the Republic

*The first step in saving our Liberty is to realize how much
we have already lost, and how we will continue to lose it
unless fundamental political changes occur.*
–James Bovard

Choking Commerce

It should be no secret that the life blood of any society is commerce. A very plausible case can be made that, once past the hunter-gatherer survivalist stage, all advances in the human standard of living, and in the material prosperity of society, are due to unrestricted, voluntary free trade. Even during the earliest hunter-gatherer period, humans were already bartering goods and services, and had invented the abstract concept of assigning value to scarce commodities, a method of exchange that eventually morphed into "money."

Novel concepts and ideas also traveled along with the traders. In pre-historic times, trading routes already covered vast distances, long before the words "international" and "network" were coined. The cross pollination of modes of thought, as well as practical technologies, and the relocation of raw materials and foodstuffs, shared between hitherto isolated groups of people, was the greatest impetus in the emergence and subsequent development of civilization.

America has been the single greatest beneficiary of unrestricted commerce in goods, services, ideas, inventions and technologies. Despite this obvious validation of the free market, nowadays **economic growth is**

being stifled by the hyper-regulatory psychosis gripping our judiciary, legislatures and government.

To draw an analogy, every person understands that it is manifestly stupid to drive a car while simultaneously pressing down hard on both the brake and the accelerator pedals. That will obviously damage the drivetrain components. Eventually, the engine will be destroyed and the car will be immobilized. Yet that is what is being done to our economy, the veritable engine of our prosperity and wellbeing.

The Federal Reserve's many manipulations of the money supply have made it virtually impossible for legitimate businesses to make long-range forecasts of future earnings and profits. Let there be no doubt about it. The Fed's policies are diluting and debasing the value of the currency. It is nothing less than counterfeiting and *"price fixing."*

Beyond the issue of the Fed's behavior, the economy cannot grow naturally when it is artificially limited by arbitrary and constantly changing governmental laws, regulations, and decrees. Where is the incentive when any monetary profits will firstly be debased, and secondly consumed, by a reckless and confiscatory government? Entrepreneurs will refuse to take risks.

Just as an aircraft loaded beyond its weight limit cannot get off the ground, our economy's carrying capacity is being grossly exceeded.

The Founders designed and put into motion a political system intended to maximize individual wealth creation, essentially by *"getting out of the way"* of the citizenry and their varied enterprises. Less interference with individuals is rewarded by greater growth of America's economy. It has been calculated that every dollar released in the private sector generates a three to five times return, or even more in certain high technology areas. By contrast, the optimum return in the governmental sector is close to one to one. The numbers do not lie.

That result was anticipated by the Founders. They had an acute understanding of the self-evident modes of human nature and behaviors. They knew how those would play out in the private sphere, and in the public arena.

Our Constitutional Republic's political, legal and economic system is unequivocally the best ever designed. In systems engineering terms, we call it *"maximum requirements traceability."* That is 'tech-talk' indicating that the end result inevitably corresponds to the original design. The fact that our system has survived to this point, despite so much parasitism, manipulation and misconduct, is a spectacular testimony to the excellence of the original design.

It is taken more than a hundred years of systematic looting, and incremental tampering, to drag the Republic down. Even so, despite its present damaged and weakened state, all is not yet lost. I am certain that the Republic can be repaired and rejuvenated. It will take hard work but it is wholly worthwhile. Besides, we have no other choice. The alternative is too frightful to contemplate.

It is true that the Constitution is only a parchment document or, as President George W. Bush is reported to have said, *"just a god-damned piece of paper."* But no charter, however carefully conceived, enacted and enabled, can succeed in the long run if it is being constantly compromised by looters and usurpers. The cancers of collectivism and nationalism have taken a long time to sicken the Republic. Restoring it to good health will require a considerable effort. Those individuals who have profited from its malaise, will fight like cornered rats to prolong their power, prestige and privileges.

Most citizens are unaware that the idea of a central bank of the United States is nothing new. It has been a pet project of all those seeking to collectivise and centralize power into the Federal Government. *The First Bank of the United States* was created by Congress in 1791 but, in 1811, its charter was allowed to expire during President James Madison's administration. Five years later, under the same President, it was revived as the *Second Bank of the United States.* President Andrew Jackson refused to renew its charter in 1836. The country proceeded just fine for the next seven decades without a central bank, through the Civil War and during the massive expansion of the Country from coast to coast. Finally, in 1913, the Federal Reserve was signed into being by President Woodrow Wilson.

As has happened with most central power mechanisms, the Fed's originally limited charter was incrementally re-interpreted to give it more control over currency and monetary policy. In the 1970's, Congress finally gave it the sweeping powers that it has today. That decade featured some of the worst financial decisions ever made by elected officials, such as President Richard Nixon's decision to take the United States off the Gold Standard, which ushered in the present era of fake money.

Inflaming Nationalism

The Civil War was a significant boost for the proponents of nationalism. It was the deadliest clash of ideologies in this Country's history. The provisions built into the Constitution for peaceful change, via the amendment process, were repeatedly overridden and ignored. Passion overcame due process. A century and a half later, that has not changed. Due process, an absolutely essential part of a just and equitable society, is more and more often being tacitly circumvented for expedience's sake by legislators and government officials alike.

How did this happen? It was by deliberate and calculated intent, as in the legal term *"with malice aforethought."* Many times it was enabled by co-opting and perverting the good intentions of crusaders for social justice, and reformers against political corruption and malfeasance. It is an ironic commentary on the human condition. Good can be manipulated into bad by the unscrupulous bent on enriching and aggrandizing themselves, no matter the cost to others.

Restoring the Republic requires the willingness by every citizen to unflinchingly confront some unpleasant truths, and to shatter some longstanding myths. Remember, History is written not only from the victor's viewpoint. It is also used to retrospectively justify their actions. Power elites, and their minions, are particularly adept at subverting the historical record to serve their ends. The American Civil War is a prime example.

Going where *"angels fear to tread,"* let us take an objective look at the highly emotional issue of slavery. Setting aside the fact that it is morally reprehensible, and an intolerable infringement on every precept of human dignity and individual self-worth, the plain truth is that the Civil War was not a crusade to rid America of that *"Peculiar Institution."* The Abolition of Slavery, as a political movement and force, was never an important factor in the attempted Secession by the Southern States. At least, not until it became politically expedient for Lincoln. Sorry, sometimes the truth hurts but, remember, *the truth will set you free.* The Civil War was largely due to the economic strangulation of the South, resulting from the tariffs and taxes imposed by the Northern States.

By the 1850s, the *economic system of slavery was a dying institution.* For obvious reasons, slaves are inevitably the least efficient and motivated workers. The agricultural South was fast falling behind the *"Free States"* of the rapidly industrializing North. Although slavery persisted in less developed parts of the World, particularly in Africa, where the slaves had been purchased from other Africans, the developed countries in Europe had already outlawed slavery, or were in the process of doing so. It was being accomplished peacefully.

Furthermore, moral outrage against slavery in America was steadily increasing on its own. Committed Abolitionists actively helped escaped slaves gain their freedom. Stories of the Underground Railway, enabled privately by individual citizens, are now largely forgotten. All the credit is given to Abraham Lincoln in his role as President, as if only he had taken action to terminate the infamous practice. In truth, it was largely due to the actions of many individuals, in both the North and South, who recognized its immorality and inefficiency, long before any action was taken by Lincoln to abolish it.

Although the numbers that escaped were relatively few by comparison to the enslaved population, it is reasonable to suppose that the trickle of successful escapees would have become a torrent. That would have hopelessly crippled the already failing institution. The slavery issue would have resolved itself naturally, as the economic justification for continuing it steadily deteriorated, as public opinion shifted and as more slaves took the initiative to escape.

In fact, the Civil War retarded the **true emancipation** of slaves, and their incorporation into the larger society. Since slavery did not die a natural death due to the War, and the Reconstruction policies forced on the South, it created a backlash of covert and overt resistance that caused a great deal of additional suffering. *"Jim Crow"* laws enacted and enforced between 1876 and 1965 essentially put real emancipation in stasis for almost a century.

The noble cause of ending slavery was subverted and co-opted by the forces of nationalism and centralization in the North. The South retaliated by mistreating the freed slaves and later their descendants. As we have already mentioned many times in this book, coercion always creates imbalances and upsets the natural processes by which problems are resolved over time. This is universally true, even if the original motivation for the application of force was well intentioned.

It took another one hundred years, when the Civil Rights Movement effectively used peaceful means, to accomplish what might have happened generations earlier. However, just as the inevitable workings of natural law were disrupted and thwarted by the Civil War and its aftermath, the powers-that-be then foolishly decreed that special privileges, such as so-called Affirmative Action, should be extended to the latter-day descendants of the freed slaves and others.

Such measures, masquerading as positive and noble, led to yet another cycle of counter-productive resentment and resistance. In fact, such policies have slowed down rather than sped up the assimilation process. Favoring some citizens in the present day, at the expense of others, to redress wrongs done long ago involving earlier generations, is not the solution. It is neither logical nor ethical. As the old saying goes:

Two wrongs don't make a right.

Again, we have to look at who ultimately benefited. Yes, you are correct, it was the centralizers. The color barrier has now been breached in many offices in the Country, including the Presidency, the Cabinet, the Armed Forces, the Supreme Court and in virtually all other areas of public and personal life. Is it not high time to end the last vestiges of Jim Crow laws, and terminate the special privileges that are fundamentally inimical to the concept of equality for all citizens?

Power elites have an unspoken contempt for the ability of the People to do the right thing. They justify their positions of power by meddling with the natural processes whereby social issues are ultimately resolved, usually at far less cost to both individuals and to society. Their meddling demonstrably worsens, rather than improves, each situation that is at issue.

Lincoln did not enter office with any intention of abolishing slavery. That was made very clear in his first inaugural address. He stated that he had:

> ... *no purpose, directly or indirectly, to interfere with the institution of slavery in the States where it exists. I believe I have no lawful right to do so, and I have no inclination to do so.*

His own words makes the myth-makers look silly.

It was only two years into the War, when it appeared that the North could lose, that Lincoln decided to issue, as a purely political expedient, the Emancipation Proclamation. Before doing so, he had explored possibilities such as shipping all the slaves back to Africa to entirely "*solve the problem.*"

Lincoln's overriding goal was to "*save the Union.*" He declared that the Union was indissoluble. Any voluntary withdrawal (secession) by any of the Sovereign States (despite the fact that they had voluntarily joined in forming the Union in 1789), was intolerable to him, even if it was perfectly legal and constitutional.

His determination to prevent the secession of the Southern States cost the Country 600,000 lives with another 1.5 million citizens permanently maimed. Three million citizens were impressed into military service between 1861 and 1865. As a proportion of today's population in 2012, the 600,000 killed in the Civil War would be about 7.5 million people!

Think about those numbers. Would anyone today accept the death of 7.5 million of their fellow citizens in order to keep the Union together? Even if a civil war had the noble intention of ending slavery? Would we not find a better way? Many believe that we would. Americans who go so blithely along with the Lincoln myth, and its horrendous century-long outcome, would never accept that today. But then, they never even think about it.

The carefully constructed *"Lincoln and the Civil War"* myth portrays him as a saint. Few people have any knowledge of the suppression of individual rights, suspension of habeas corpus, mass arrests, the censorship of the Press in the North, and other infringements of the Constitution that he authorized. They do not talk about Lincoln's plan to buy back the slaves and export them back to Africa. Nor do most people know that Lincoln personally approved the strategy of *"total war"* and *"scorched earth"* policy deliberately waged by General Sherman, and others, upon the defenseless civilian population of the South. The civilian deaths in the South have never been counted.

Yes, the truth hurts. For any skeptics reading these lines, I suggest that you check out these books:

1. *"The Real Lincoln: A New Look at Abraham Lincoln, His Agenda, and an Unnecessary War"* by economics professor Thomas DiLorenzo
2. *"Lincoln Unmasked: What You're Not Supposed to Know About Dishonest Abe"* also by Thomas DiLorenzo
3. *"Forced into Glory: Abraham Lincoln's White Dream"* (2000) by Lerone Bennett, Jr.
4. *"Lincoln Uncensored"* (2012) by Joseph Fallon and Jeffrey Tucker

Until recently, the "history" of Lincoln and the Civil War was only written by those seeking to portray the outcome as just and benevolent. That is due to their adherence to nationalistic and statist political agendas.

However, despite successfully preventing the Secession, which in fact increased public acceptance of nationalism, none of the next wave of amendments to the Constitution succeeded in transforming the Republic into a nationalist state. In 1863, as already noted above, nearly two years after the beginning of hostilities, and for purely political reasons, Lincoln issued his Emancipation Proclamation. The unintended result was that the impetus for increased nationalism was temporarily set back. The still divided and war-weary populace remained sufficiently aware of the foundational principles and ideals of the Republic. That thwarted and prevented any **immediate** usurpation by centralizers. They were therefore forced to wage a slow campaign of attrition to pursue their agenda, and achieve their goals, by way of the Courts, Congress and the Presidency, using every dirty trick of subterfuge, fraud and outright illegality at their disposal.

Enabling Centralization

Fifty years after the Emancipation Proclamation, usurpers finally achieved the breakthrough that they had long sought. In 1913, the Republic suffered three deep wounds with the establishment of the Federal Reserve, the enactment of the Federal Income Tax (the 16th Amendment) and the direct election of U.S. Senators (the 17th Amendment). One hundred years later, it is now not hard to see how those three measures greatly facilitated today's massive expansion of power by the Federal Government. They also had the effect of greatly expanding the opportunities for looters and manipulators to comprehensively sabotage the Republic, dragging us to the brink of economic destruction.

We now recognize the inherently genocidal and dehumanizing nature of Communism, with all its resulting horrors, as seen in Russia, China, Cambodia and elsewhere, where millions perished.

It is almost impossible to fathom how two of the three measures could ever have been approved. They were actually plucked straight out of the Communist Manifesto:

A heavy progressive or graduated income tax (Plank #2)

Centralization of credit in the hands of the State, by means of a national bank with State capital and an exclusive monopoly (Plank #5).

The third of the unholy trio, the 17th Amendment, was clearly inspired by the desire to transform the Republic into an outright democracy, in direct defiance of the carefully considered warnings against doing so by the Founders.

The historical record clearly shows that multiple frauds were perpetrated in order to enable putting into effect all three of these measures.

- The Constitution was directly violated by tossing aside Article 1, Section 8, Clause 4 to secure passage of the Federal Reserve Act, and its legal tender laws
- Regarding the 16th Amendment, I invite skeptics to read *"The Law That Never Was"* by Bill Benson
- Irrefutable evidence of the usurpation of the U.S. Constitution took place in the supposed passage and ratification of the 17th Amendment
- The Supreme Court has refused to rule on the issue, stating that it was *"a political question"*

We will now examine the third item, the 17th Amendment, in greater detail.

The **appointment of U.S. Senators by state legislatures** is a critical part of the checks and balances required for effective and just governance, as envisioned and designed by the Founders.

- The **appointed** Senators were intended to **represent the Sovereign States**
- The **elected** Representatives were intended to **represent the Sovereign Citizens**

That was by conscious and well-reasoned design. It enabled a bi-cameral legislature. This blends the **best aspects of a republic** with a counter balance provided by the **best attributes of a democracy.**

This is an exceptionally important point that must be understood by any citizen claiming to be concerned about the fate of this Country.

It explains a great deal about the polarization that currently afflicts us. A state of affairs that has rapidly destroyed the work of earlier generations of Americans, who sought to establish a just and equitable society with opportunity for all.

The Founders were avid students of History. They knew full well that **those who cannot learn from the past are condemned to repeat (even magnify) its mistakes.**

The two great historical examples in Western Civilization that they examined were the rise and fall of the Ancient Greek States, particularly Athens, and the Roman Republic. There, for the first time in recorded history, political systems had evolved beyond rule by hereditary monarchs, or a succession of tyrants and despots. The Athenian Democracy and the Roman Republic were experiments in enfranchising (at least some of) their citizens into the process of making social, economic and political policy.

The Ancient Greeks invented democracy. Their intellectual advances in philosophy, and their development of the scientific method, were undermined by the **worst attributes** of democracy, which led them into argumentative divisiveness and demagoguery, culminating in decline and absorption by Ancient Rome.

The Romans created the first great republic. Their organizational skills, and application of technology, were undermined by the **worst aspects** of republicanism, leading them into aggressive conquest and centralization, eventually retrogressing into Imperial Rome with one man rule.

With that in mind, the U.S. Senate was to be a republican body, and the House of Representatives a democratic one, so that this Country could avoid the fate of either the Ancient Athenians or Romans.

Democracy's greatest flaw is the **propensity to be overwhelmed by its innate populism.** In its worst form, a sort of mob rule ensues, with nearly mindless reflexive actions that are incapable of seeing beyond the present moment and perceived individual self-interest. It is easily whipped into a frenzy by demagoguery and propaganda. Yet that visceral and emotional quality is also its greatest strength.

Republicanism's greatest flaw is the **tendency to be excessively cerebral and calculating** with its accompanying elitism and urge to dominate. Yet its innate pragmatism, conservatism and ability to *"see the big picture in the long-term"* are its greatest strengths.

With the **de facto** enactment of the 17th Amendment, Senators and Representatives are now both elected by popular vote. In that case, why have two legislative bodies? What is the point? Would it not be more efficient to have just one? Taking that line of reasoning one step further, if the U.S. Constitution was indeed intended to be **national**, then why are there 50 **separate state constitutions?**

The 17th Amendment's fraudulent nature is revealed by looking at Article IV, Section 4 of the Constitution which declares that:

The United States shall guarantee to every State in this Union a Republican Form of Government ...

There is no mention in the language of the 17th Amendment of anything that repeals or supersedes that Section. If the Republican form of government is effectively ended by this amendment, then that guarantee was illegally abrogated. Thus the amendment is unconstitutional **on its face.**

Nothing prevents proposing, passing and ratifying an amendment as long **as it is done according to the procedures found in Article V of the Constitution:**

The Congress, whenever two thirds of both Houses shall deem it necessary, shall propose Amendments to this Constitution, or, on the Application of the Legislatures of two thirds of the several States, shall call a Convention for proposing Amendments, which, in either Case, shall be valid to all Intents and Purposes, as Part of this Constitution, when ratified by the Legislatures of three fourths of the several States or by Conventions in three fourths thereof, as the one or the other Mode of Ratification may be proposed by the Congress ...

Those requirements were not properly followed in the case of the 17th Amendment. There are actually **two ways to propose** amendments and two methods to ratify them.

238

1. An amendment may be **proposed** by a two-thirds majority vote in both houses of Congress. It must be followed by **ratification** by three-fourths of the States (or by three-fourths of state conventions convened to consider the amendment).

2. An amendment may be **proposed** at the request of two-thirds of the States. That must be followed by **ratification** by three-fourths of the states (or by three-fourths of the state conventions convened to consider the amendment).

Each state must ratify the **exact** language of the amendment, including punctuation. **No changes** may be made by the States when considering ratification. It is either yes or no.

Furthermore, an additional **proviso,** underlining the supreme importance that the Founders placed on ensuring that any amendments to the Constitution were very carefully considered, is contained in the last clause of Article V. It is a **safeguard** of the **sovereignty of the States:**

Provided ... that no State, without its Consent, shall be denied its equal Suffrage in the Senate.

This *"equal Suffrage"* meant that each state had its own voting power in the U.S. Senate, which directly represented the States, right up until the 17th Amendment went into effect. Each sovereign state's legislature therefore had its own representation in the Federal Government, the same as Sovereign Citizens had direct representation in the House. That was an integral and vital part in the design of the checks and balances, that the Founders realized were required in government, after carefully studying the failure of the Athenian Democracy and the Roman Republic.

The Founders knew that all legitimate government derives ultimately from the People, as in the famous phrase from the Declaration of Independence *"... with the consent of the governed."* Therefore, the Founders vested in the House, and not in the Senate, all the basic powers of a federal form of government, in particular the power of the purse and declarations of war. However, in order for the States to be governed within the federal system, they had to **also give their consent** through their representatives, the Senators in Congress, for any laws made by the Federal Government.

Thus "*equal Suffrage*" safeguarded the interests of the States from the natural democratism of the House of Representatives. The House, in its turn, checked the natural republicanism of the Senate. Why is this last clause of Article V so very important? Because any state that does not give its consent to an amendment by virtue of its guarantee of "*equal Suffrage*" cannot be denied that guarantee. Otherwise, it is an obvious contradiction in terms.

Therefore, a state which rejected, or never held a vote to ratify, the 17th Amendment is entitled to send its legislatively appointed senators to the Senate. That is because an amendment changing "*equal Suffrage*" **requires unanimous consent.** That never happened!

As a consequence, the 17th Amendment **failed to meet the constitutionally mandated requirements** under Article V of the Constitution. It is therefore **invalid** "*... as to its intents and Purposes.*" Ten States failed to ratify the 17th Amendment because they never even considered it. Utah actually rejected it. Simple arithmetic suffices to show that the amendment is not constitutional since there was no unanimous consent given by all the States..

The following is an excerpt from **Wikipedia:**

> *Ralph A. Rossum, writing in the San Diego Law Review, notes that the debate over the amendment's adoption lacked "any serious or systematic considerations of its potential impact on federalism." The popular press, the party platforms, the state memorials, the House and Senate debates and the state legislative debates during ratification focused almost exclusively on expanding democracy, eliminating political corruption, defeating elitism and freeing the states from what they had come to regard as an onerous and difficult responsibility.* (**emphasis** added)

To repeat, the debates not only "*lacked any serious or systematic consideration of its impact on federalism,*" but concentrated instead on *"freeing the states from what they had come to regard as an onerous and difficult responsibility."* The primary impact of the 17th Amendment was scarcely even discussed! This successful circumvention of the mandated responsibility of the States, further emboldened the centralizers into more procedural misbehavior. Tacit acceptance of irresponsibility always encourages yet more irresponsibility. Any parent of an errant child knows that!

What Does the 17th Amendment Fraud Mean Today?

The passage of time, even after nearly one century has elapsed, emphatically does not make the discussion and understanding of this unconstitutional amendment any less important, or any less relevant. In order to effect any remedy to cure our current precarious position, it is absolutely imperative to know what we have lost or, more accurately, what was stolen from us.

Since 1913, we have had an unbalanced Congress. Just look at the results! The U.S. Congress both legislates **and** authorizes expenditures. It must function as originally designed to properly discharge its mandate. How can it do so if it has been thrown so far out of balance?

During the past 99 years, America has morphed into Amerika, a duopolistic Warfare/Welfare State headed straight for ruin. The modern day Republican Party promotes a Warfare State. The modern day Democrat Party promotes a Welfare State. Because we have foolishly circumvented the wisdom of the Founders, we are saddled with the absurdist fantasy that both are possible, or even desirable, as in the infamous phrase of President Lyndon Johnson promising *"guns and butter "* during the **undeclared** Viet Nam War.

The fraudulent 17th Amendment is a constant reminder that the Federal Government has superseded the authority of the Sovereign States. They are constitutionally mandated to act as a check to block any unconstitutional usurpation of power by a central power base.

Beginning the process of correcting this situation is laughably simple. The Utah State Legislature, the very same body that had earlier rejected the 17th Amendment, could immediately dismiss its popularly elected Senators and appoint two new ones. Utah's Secretary of State would then issue each of them Certificates of Election enabling them to be seated in the U.S. Senate. In one bold move, one of the Sovereign States could initiate a reversal of the gradual *"slide into ignominy"* of state legislatures, whose sovereign powers have been usurped by the centralizers in Washington D.C.

Such a move would no doubt be challenged by the Department of Justice (DOJ). For the sake of argument, let us see if the U.S. Attorney General would actually have a case, assuming that we are still a Republic and following our own laws.

1. There would be the issue of jurisdiction. How could the Federal Government's executive branch establish its lawful interest in what is obviously a state matter? As part of the Executive Branch, the DOJ has no legal interest.
2. The U.S. Senate itself has no procedural or lawful interest unless it first alters that troublesome last paragraph of Article V. (Good luck with that!)

Thus directly blocked, could the DOJ take an indirect route and help a private citizen file a case in Utah? That would also encounter a roadblock. Such an approach would be impossible because it was never a citizen's issue in the first place. It is solely the responsibility of Utah's legislature. Under Article V, the appointed Senators would represent the State's interests. An individual cannot simultaneously be **both** a citizen and the State Legislature. That is an obvious contradiction in terms.

The U.S. Attorney General would be forced to realize that the Federal Government has no lawful or proprietary interest whatsoever, in deciding how the States pick their U.S. Senators, as stated in Article I, Section 4. Furthermore, it would be a direct and specific violation of Article IV, Section 4.

Following Utah's lead, the other States could introduce similar bills to nullify the 17th Amendment, returning us to the Founders' well measured reasons for the original constitutional checks and balances. Otherwise, the definitions and strictures enumerated explicitly in Article IV are useless and thus impotent. Our once great Republic will continue to slide into **unchecked democratism**. Long ago, in Ancient Athens, that was proven to be impractical, a prelude to despotism. That was followed with its conquest by Imperial Rome, which had itself been preceded by **unchecked republicanism**, when it was originally a republic.

This review of the *"triple play"* that is allowing our Country to slowly slide into totalitarianism would not be complete without mentioning Woodrow Wilson, inaugurated in the same year of 1913. Wilson is arguably America's most counter-productive president since the Civil War. As noted earlier, he was implacably determined to *"make the world safe for democracy,"* Wilson was soon followed by his progressive brother-in-arms, Franklin Roosevelt. He completed the process begun by Wilson to demolish any political structures and institutions that did not conform to **unchecked democratism.**

The Next Attack on the Republican Form of Government

One of the last vestiges of the original Republic is the Electoral College. Interestingly, there is organized pressure to eliminate it, too. In recent years, the National Popular Vote movement has ramped up its campaign to eliminate that constitutional check against unbridled democratic rule. If it succeeds in destroying our ability to elect a President in a purposely balanced procedure, it will be the final nail in the coffin of the Republic envisioned, and so carefully constructed, by the Founders.

Meanwhile, the *"Imperial Presidency"* grows ever more powerful, and the U.S. Congress thrashes about in deadlock, without any check and counterbalance by the (supposedly sovereign) States.

If the Republic is continually being compromised, why even bother calling it a republic? This Country is already widely, and **incorrectly,** being identified as a democracy.

The continuing successful attempt to dismantle the Constitution is similar to parting out an old truck in a salvage yard. No responsible citizen can continue to sit around and watch this without doing whatever he or she can do to stop and reverse it.

For those responsible citizens this book is primarily directed.

Candidate For Public Office or Sovereign Citizen?

Is running for public office the answer? As I increased my own political activism over the past two decades, I have often been asked why I did not run for office. My answer is always the same. I already hold the highest office in the land. I am a Sovereign Citizen!

All the solutions to our present difficulties, in every sphere of social, economic and political life, revolve around the principles embodied in the immortal words beginning with: "*We the People ...*"

To fix our Country's problems, more people must join in encouraging, motivating and activating everyone to exercise their rights, responsibilities and sovereignty as citizens. I am just dumb enough to think, after all these years, that that is exactly what our Founders figured out and intended us to do. Why reinvent the wheel? Understand how it works and repair it!

It makes no sense to run more of the same candidates. We first need a much better crop of candidates. To enable that requires better education of all citizens and the thorough vetting of the real qualifications of candidates. Until then, those currently in office must be severely disciplined to observe, and faithfully follow, the existing charters, mandates and laws.

Naturally, I hear from people that things have already gone too far. They say "*just give up and live with it.*" I am sorry, but I am the fool who heard, understood, believed and took to heart the concept and ideals of our Constitutional Republic, just as I was taught in 8th grade civics and history class, as well as what was taught at the family dinner table, and around campfires under the stars. What I learned since has proven that it was not bunk. I did not think so then. I definitely do not think so now.

A sovereign citizen's duty in a Constitutional Republic is the single most important civic function in all of human history. Only such a citizen can hold his or her elected officials accountable to that precious document, the U.S. Constitution. This Country was not formed to produce Kings and Queens to rule over us. In our system, **we are the Kings and Queens.** Unfortunately, today's citizens are uninformed and confused about this fundamental truth.

244

In a properly functioning republic, elected office is a great honor and responsibility. I greatly respect those few good citizens-legislators who willingly serve in such positions.

We must remember that an office holder **is always subordinate to the Sovereign Citizens** who elected him or her to that position. The Founders repeatedly emphasized that the primary building block of the Republic is the individual acting as a responsible, informed and self-reliant citizen. The Founders would be shocked and dismayed at the sloth and apathy of the average citizen in discharging their civic duties. The Founders labored hard and long to formulate an economic, judicial and political system that would not repeat the mistakes of the past. The Founders would be profoundly chagrined to observe that which they abhorred, and warned against, is now occurring solely because so many have abdicated their individual responsibility in wielding their sovereignty as American citizens.

An informed citizen's responsibility emphatically does not end with voting, once every two or four years. Voting is only one of many responsibilities he or she bears in our *"by the consent of the governed"* system.

Citizenship is not going to a public meeting only once every few months when the mood strikes us, or when an issue directly impacts our livelihood or wallet. Citizenship involves an entire range of individual responsibilities, beginning with learning and truly understanding our constitutional system and **then continually holding** our elected officials **accountable** to it. That is most effectively accomplished at the local or municipal level. Then, and only then, can we say:

We the People of the United States, in Order to form a more perfect Union ... (**emphasis** added)

We will explore how simple such a strategy can be in the next chapter.

15

Keeping It Simple

Everything should be made as simple as possible, but not simpler.
–Albert Einstein

Simplicity is the ultimate sophistication.
–Leonardo Da Vinci

KISS—Keep It Simple, Stupid.
–Old Engineering Principle

As a general rule, large and seemingly intractable problems are solved by sorting out their constituent parts. Then it is possible to recognize those that are causing the problem and deal with them. Problem solving is very similar to weeding a garden.

Every system has a *"tipping point"* beyond which it becomes unnecessarily complex and increasingly inefficient. Somewhere between *"too simple"* and *"too complex"* is the ideal balance point.

The growth of the present day government's powers depends on increasing the levels of unnecessary complexity. We are reaching the zenith of unnecessary complexity with **hyper-regulation** in every aspect of our governance, whether it be at the individual and local level, or at the public and 'national' level.

Stating that *"the best government is one that governs least"* does not imply that governance is unnecessary. It should be as unrestrictive as possible to the individual citizen, while simultaneously safeguarding every other citizen.

Therefore, it is easy to spot the self-serving agendas of those in power who promote the idea that problems can only be solved by even more complex systems, created and operated by them. Once that falsehood is revealed, so is their method of masking the fact that real solutions are actually relatively simple. Behind the smokescreen of complexity, they continue to manipulate the citizenry in order to profit just themselves. A "solution" that employs unnecessary complexity is no solution, it is the next problem.

Big and Small Government Complexity

The current disintegration of the European Union (EU) is a case in point. The now discredited assumption that all of Europe's trade, commerce and developmental problems could be solved by the imposition of a single monetary unit was false from the start. The nonsensical notion of strengthening the EU, by the creation of a more tightly integrated European super-state, is a "solution" that will only increase the severity of their problems.

Every time that the level of complexity is increased by imposing centralized control, and empowering unelected expert technocrats and bureaucrats, the problems are not actually solved, they are hugely magnified! Any problem can be solved once it is broken down to isolate causes from effects. At that point, the problem should be addressed by those actually seeking a solution, not by those using it as an excuse for self-aggrandizement and increased levels of control.

If you have ever been in a homeowners' association (HOA), or on a school board, you will recognize what usually happens. Problems are complicated rather than simplified. Expanding the scope of problems ensure that they will never be solved. If the "*committee model* "is adopted, virtually every problem becomes more complex, unless reined in and redirected by specific individual action within the group.

Otherwise, opportunists will ensure that complications increase while the committee's power expands. Often those who know better remain silent. If they had only acted at the appropriate moment, the opportunists, seeking to further personal, subjective goals, would have been stopped dead in their tracks. What usually ensues is the WARBI Paradox in all of its unsatisfactory and inefficient manifestations.

In an HOA, when homeowners ignore covenants, more of them are created. In the corporate world, when a process does not work, additional procedures are formulated. In the bureaucratic realm, when regulations fail, more rules are promulgated. In the political arena, when laws are not followed, more legislation is enacted.

That is almost invariably the response. Yet it is obvious that increased complexity is never a solution to an underlying problem.

The EU's loose fiat currency system is demonstrably not working. Instead of ending it, the policy maker's knee-jerk response is to call for more "integration." That will allow the bureaucrats in Brussels to promulgate thousands of new regulations.

Problem Solvers, Problem Makers

There are "*problem solvers*" and "*problem makers*." Those seeking only to solve a problem determine the root causes and then implement simple solutions. Those seeking power and self-aggrandizement, invariably make the problem larger and more intractable. That counter-productive approach permeates our current system—from top to bottom. Those familiar with Scott Adams' cartoon strip "*Dilbert*" know why it has been so popular for decades. It is a daily reminder of the destructive behavior of those with aggrandizing agendas.

Who has not observed that laws are selectively enforced because there are too many of them? Yet what continues to be the official response? It is almost always the same. We "*need more laws*" along with **more enforcers!** When regulations fail to modify people's behavior, the answer is always more regulations! Are these real solutions? Of course they are not! Instead, the added layers of complexity serve as camouflage for the looters to increase their power and perpetuate their existence.

Washington, D.C., is the ultimate paradise for looters. It has the fewest producers per capita because so few **produce anything** of value. Their principal goal is to enact more laws, regulations and complexity to provide themselves with greater job security. It is hardly surprising that most of them are lawyers, lobbyists and bureaucrats.

At the seat of power, no problem is reducible to simpler terms, and no program is ever eliminated. Every nickel in the departmental budget must be spent. Otherwise, next year's might be reduced! Legislation was once thought to be too complicated if it exceeded more than 50 pages. Now they are hundreds or thousands of pages long. The Internal Revenue Code (IRC) began with less than 50 pages. It set a maximum rate of just 3% on **dividend income**. The IRC now contains 60 million words encompassing 70,000 pages, taxing every possible form of income, at five to ten times the original rate. It even includes compensation that was never defined as "income" when the Federal Income Tax was first instituted, such as wages! Why is that? The government "needed" more money! The definition was then expanded into nearly every possible form of "revenue enhancement."

Then Comes the Hyper-Regulation

The Internal Revenue Code (IRC) is dwarfed by the Federal Register, a compilation of all of the rules and regulations issued by federal agencies. In 2010, it exceeded 81,400 pages. The government spends $55 billion just to administer, and **selectively enforce**, all its rules and regulations!

Little of this **hyper-regulation** could take place without superseding the limits, set by the Constitution, at both the Federal and State level. To understand the impact on our daily lives, read Harry A. Silverglate's book "*Three Felonies a Day*," (2009). Every citizen unwittingly commits an average of three or more crimes or infractions each and every day, merely by going about their daily business. This represents the criminalization of an entire population!

Compared to the attention directed at the trillion-dollar handouts to the big banks, and to Wall Street financial firms, remember how much media time was expended on Martha Stewart's utterly trivial by comparison "*insider trading*" conviction?

Quoting a former Senate investigator, Matt Taibbi of Rolling Stone magazine, wrote:

Everything's f----d-up and [yet] nobody goes to jail!

Those few who are prosecuted, and jailed, have committed "statutory" crimes. Seldom seen among them are those persons who have committed real felonies. Interesting how they have tight insider connections to the power elite, is it not?

A truly criminal travesty of a fair and equitable society is being daily perpetrated on millions of acquiescent citizens without even requiring enforcement at gunpoint!

Enacting "laws" against people that do not involve property damage or personal and financial injury to others has absolutely nothing to do with crime. Laws should only address actual criminal behavior. Increasing the complexity of the "law" facilitates the abuses of the power elite. Misappropriation through fraud and the destruction of property or personal injury are real crimes. However, the Government has fabricated vast multitudes of statutory non-crimes that, in effect, criminalize everything from personal substance use to the amount of water that a toilet flushes!

That is why we imprison more of our population than any other country on Earth, even the totalitarian states! This is happening in the supposedly *"freest nation on the planet!"* There are innumerable "criminals" in the penal system who have committed no real crimes. That has conveniently taken the focus away from real crime. Many criminals are escaping punishment. In fact, they are being rewarded, particularly in Big Business and Big Government!

So How Does One Simplify?

Over the years I have found that when a complex problem in system engineering, or in a business organization, cannot be explained in simple terms, it was always an indication that the actual problem was not understood. It invariably opened the way for someone to propose complicating the problem rather than solving it. If that person held power or authority, it was rare that anyone would speak up in an attempt to propose a simpler approach or solution.

On the few occasions when I was an employee, I was never a conformist. If a problem was being complicated, instead of being simplified, I found that highlighting that fact was the best way to resolve it. Of course, that did not endear me to some senior managers or executives. However, as a consultant, I did not care about internal politics. I called many a pet project "ugly" and saved lots of time, effort and money. Speaking up also influenced others who, despite knowing better, would likely have remained silent.

There are far too few contrarians speaking up against needless complication. Most people allow others to "grow the problem," rather than solve it. Speaking up is not easy until something goes wrong. By then it is too late and management will parcel out the blame to others, who are often blameless. Employees absolve themselves of responsibility by invoking the WARBI Paradox. Although speaking up saves everyone's time and effort, it does not always ingratiate one with other members of the 'team!'

As an aside, consider carefully where you select your friends. It is wiser to find friends outside of government or corporate employment, at least until more people learn to think for themselves and speak out independently. Only then will this Country get back on track.

Just as parents worry about the influence of their children's friends, adults are no less susceptible in their associations with others. That is especially true with friendships. It is best to avoid the usual personal intrigues and office politics that can exert far too much peer pressure on a person "*to get along, go along.*" Unfortunately, that often leads to acceptance of the improper behavior that is all too common in Government and Big Business.

During the 1990's, my consulting team and I discovered that every organization we encountered had many more personal behavior problems than technical, procedural or organizational ones. Time and again, we witnessed people adopting the second **Modality of Inaction:** "*If forced to change, take the path of least resistance.*" In fact, resisting the status quo is usually the simplest, easiest and most direct path to problem solving success.

President Kennedy provided one of the better visions of why America exists at all. In a speech at Rice University, on Sept. 12th, 1962, he said:

*We choose to go to the moon. We choose to go to the moon in this decade and do the other things, not because they are easy, but **because they are hard,** because that goal **will serve to organize and*** *measure the best of our energies and skills, because that challenge is one that we are **willing to accept**, one we are **unwilling to postpone**, and one which **we intend to win** ...* (**emphasis** added)

Kennedy made it very clear that taking the path of least resistance never had, and never would, get America anywhere. I highly recommend reading the entire speech. Just type "*Address at Rice University on the Nation's Space Effort, September 12, 1962,*" into your search engine. It is one of most intrinsically American speeches made during all of our history. It is just as applicable to the challenges that we face today.

In his time, Kennedy was referring not only to space exploration, but also the challenges presented by the Civil Rights Movement, and the threat of communism and nuclear war. In our time, most citizens have abdicated responsibility for preserving the Republic in favor of personal convenience. We have turned a deaf ear to another of Kennedy's famous statements:

Ask not what your country can do for you; ask rather what you can do for your country.

It seems that we are no longer willing to do the things that are harder yet simpler. Too many of us are taking the "... *path of least resistance.*"

There is a greater degree of conformity, as in being "politically correct," and far less celebration of individual freedom, than ever before in our Country. Precisely at a point in History when we need to recognize and strengthen the individual's spirit to think and act freely, most Americans are mindlessly shopping at the mall, watching sports or playing video games. In view of the constant attacks on the relatively few productive citizens who have achieved success by exercising their initiative in a non-conforming spirit of free enterprise, that is not altogether surprising.

The Failure of Japan, Inc.

As an example, I usually point to Japan. In the early 1980s, when I returned from overseas, there were constant discussions, and endless concern being expressed, about the inevitable rise of *"Japan, Inc."* At that time, there was a perception (supported by mainstream media and entertainment) that Japan had become an unstoppable business juggernaut that would soon take over the World. However, I was unconcerned in view of what I already knew about Japan. I had spent two and a half years in the Far East, often going in and out of that country. I was familiar with their economy, having worked with Japanese nationals on various projects. In addition, I spent considerable time traveling throughout Japan and interacting with its people. Living in that economy as I did, I found that individually we had much in common. However, their larger culture negatively limits the individual, adversely affecting their behavior as a people.

Then and now, that country suffers from serious systemic flaws inherent in its culture, and embedded in its governmental organization. What I observed was that much of Japan's apparent success, which Americans attributed to their individual work ethic, was due to highly collectivized behavior. The Japanese have an innate willingness to conform completely to the dictates of central authority, in order to complete a task. Such oppressive conformity is cultural, reinforced by centuries of allegiance to their *"Divine Emperor"* and a government that still has much in common with the feudal lord and vassal system of mutual patronage and obligation. The continuation of such behaviors, just one generation earlier, nearly destroyed Japan during WWII.

It remains a key weakness of the Japanese system. Very little is accomplished by individual initiative. Unilateral action is discouraged. Very few workers are willing to go against group consensus. An environment of enforced acceptance results in little opportunity for the creativity, and the willingness to change, that is necessary for long-term success. Maintaining the status quo, rather than taking risks, inevitably results in stagnation. This explains Japan's *"lost two decades"* of the 1990's and 2000's. It is Japan's fatal flaw, as they continue to slowly sink deeper into economic and cultural malaise.

I consider the Japanese culture to be misanthropic. It degrades the individual. There is massive alcoholism among workers. Depression and suicide is endemic. The Japanese birthrate is below replacement levels.

The population, currently at about 127 million, is declining by about one million persons every year. It is projected to fall below 100 million by 2050. Their culture is moribund. It will cease to exist in a few generations—unless some drastic changes are made.

Less than ten years after I left that country, the symptoms of Japan's malaise became obvious to even the most casual observers. Japan's economy went stagnant and stayed that way. In 1989, the NIKKEI stock market index peaked at 38,915. That index has not traded significantly above 10,000 since 2007. Currently it is stuck in a trading range around 9,000. In inflation adjusted terms, the NIKKEI has lost 85 percent of its 1989 value! Unfortunately, it is not too much of a stretch of imagination to see the similarities here, and project a similar outcome.

Because of their stultifying conformity, the Japanese have been incapable of moving outside of their *"comfort zone"* paradigm, despite the plain fact that their economy, banking system and culture are slowly withering away. Japan's citizens will soon be faced with the fourth **Modality of Inaction**: *"Prolonged denial is overcome by events (reality)."* They will have to completely surrender to the inevitable, or decide to make fundamental changes in their behavior to save their country.

Those cultural behaviors were recently and very publicly highlighted when an investigative report for Japan's Diet (Parliament) was released. It concerned the TEPCO Fukushima nuclear power station disaster in the aftermath of the great *Tsunami* in March of 2011. The report outlined certain cultural tendencies that explain virtually every one of the subsequent failures at the plant:

... fundamental causes are to be found in the ingrained conventions of Japanese culture: our reflexive obedience; our reluctance to question authority; our devotion to sticking with the program.

In such a culture, the leaders in Japan are often selected on a consensus basis. In other words, the leader is often the person who can best represent and voice the group's collective interests. Individualism and (the) decision-making process are often rejected, especially among traditional organizations like the government or

255

corporations. As a result, someone who has original or different ideas is more likely to be cast out of a group.

Are We Following Japan?

It was not until the 1990s that it became obvious that America was also in a serious state of decline. Look at us now! We are among the most medicated populations on the planet. A partial list of indicators is the rate of alcohol abuse, the vast number of prescription anti-depressants being consumed, and the proliferation of black market drugs that are the blowback from the escalation of the 'War on Drugs.'

The family is in decline, the marriage rate dropped by one-third in the last 30 years, and there is widespread sloth as evidenced by the obesity epidemic. There are 2 million super-morbidly obese persons weighing 500 pounds or more. There is another 15 million people who are morbidly obese. Two out of three people are overweight, including many young children. Diabetes from poor diet, in all age groups, is epidemic.

This should not be a mystery for any observant American. People trapped in the strait jacket of mindless conformity, political correctness and under the thumb of an oppressive government, will always find ways to rebel, even if they are self-destructive. It began as early as the 1960's culture of escapism, substance abuse, 'sexual freedom' without commitment, depression and suicide. Such behaviors represent an escape from lives dominated by the bleak and joyless world of collective conformity. However, on closer analysis, that so-called "counterculture" was just another form of conformity.

Look to the Baby Boomers today to see how their "ideals" turned out. Observe their dependency on Government hand-outs, loans and subsidies to the middle class, their conformity to the status quo, and their pointless votes for either Tweedle-Dee Republican or Tweedle-Dumber Democrat. Witness their desire for more and bigger government programs of all types. There has probably never been another generation in history that has been as comprehensively co-opted as the Baby Boomers!

The United States, Japan, and Europe are on the same deadly path of cultural and political conformity. Each of those national or supranational governments has generated an enormous hyper-regulatory culture that is layered over the top of the people's culture. It introduces enormous complexity into daily life, as it attempts to enforce conformity through coercion.

We are only cruising about 30 years behind the former Soviet Union and its satellites. Significantly, we are behind only because we adopted an outwardly benign form of societal coercion in the 20th Century, rather than the Soviet's outright psychotic tyranny. Do not be confused by the superficial nonconformity of today's Americans. True personal freedom and liberty is now almost non-existent.

True freedom is not guzzling a six-pack while watching weekend TV sports or a weekend spent in Las Vegas. It is not gorging on junk food while watching "reality shows." It is not that new off-road SUV or a sports car exceeding the speed limit on the freeway. It is not jogging on the beach or working out in the gym. It is not a body covered in tattoos and festooned with piercings. It is not listening to culturally subversive "*metal bands*" or "*gangsta rap*" music.

Those are superficial indulgences with little connection to the true expression of human freedom and liberty.

Many people idolize bizarre (need I mention Charlie Sheen?) or pathetic (Alex Baldwin?) "celebrities" as 'cool.' What a parody of cool! How could such ludicrous and absurd personalities possibly be considered cultural icons or national treasures? All that superficiality is just another variation on conformity.

There is nothing intrinsically wrong with such behaviors—to each his own. The issue is that the very same people who idolize such nonsense, make little to no attempt to take any real responsibility as citizens. They act as if the Republic runs on autopilot. They do not appear to understand the meaning of personal accountability. They do not participate in the true exercise of their rights and responsibilities in any ways that are more than superficial. They want the outward trappings of freedom and liberty without expending any time and effort, other than buying-in to some cause by sending in a donation, or perhaps voting once in a while, when they are upset about an issue. Vanishingly few regularly show up at their City Hall, County Commission or State

Legislature to effectively direct their elected representatives in proper behavior whenever those officials have strayed out of bounds.

In the realm of governance and politics, they are mindless sheep doing exactly what they are told, without enjoying any of the fruits of real freedom. They do not exercise the necessary degree of personal responsibility in outcomes. Most such citizens have no understanding of our history, political principles or the processes that are necessary to maintain a free republic. They are just out *"Jay-walking,"* nighttime fodder for Jay Leno. Will we continue down the path that is changing the Republic into a democracy and then its inexorable slide into a dictatorship? Or will we reverse course, recognizing what made America unique in all of human history, and restore and then faithfully adhere to our foundational principles once more?

We are now at the crossroads. It should be no secret that we are heading straight into disaster. The good news is that there is no secret about which turn at the crossroads will lead to ultimate success! We have simply forgotten that *"one nation ... with liberty and justice for all ..."* means holding and exercising universal and timeless principles in common. Understanding our foundational principles will help us to recognize, and then reduce, the needless complexity that allows manipulators and looters endless opportunities to enrich themselves at the expense of the rest of us.

Restoring the Republic begins in every American home with informed and self-reliant individuals. **It will only be accomplished by keeping it simple.**

Keep the beauty of simplicity in mind during every discussion, whenever concerned people gather together to discuss and resolve problems in the workplace, or in the political process. It is the foundation upon which all positive and practical changes for the better depend.

16

Back to the Future: The Renewal

If there are any flaws they are in ourselves, and our task therefore must not be one of redesign but of renewal and reaffirmation, especially of the standards in which all of us (should) believe.
–Elliot Richardson

Who Were We?

Think of the sacrifice, discipline, tenacity and enormous effort that it took by tens of millions people to build this amazing Country. Compare that to how easy we have it today, no matter what our individual circumstances may be in life. We should weep an ocean of tears when we consider how easily and quickly we have lost sight of, and abandoned, the guiding principles, ideals and values of all the many founders and pioneers of this Country.

As a boy, I read constantly about the explorations and exploits of the early settlers, both east and west of the Mississippi River. My dad collected everything that he could find on the subject. Magazines such as **Old West, True West** and **Real West** were stacked neatly around our home. I totally immersed myself in them, eventually realizing that they were only a partial description of what had taken place. Most of the personal stories of those brave men and women, who risked everything, went unrecorded.

For 300 years, beginning with the colonists and pioneers, people struggled to build the greatest Country that the World has ever known. They literally began with nothing but their dreams of freedom, liberty and self-sufficiency. The pictures, illustrations and stories in the books and magazines that I devoured as a child, were a mere fraction of the reality of the American Dream. The legacy left to us should cause every thinking American to refuse to let it disappear, in the space of a single generation, without standing up and fighting for what once was—and what can still be again.

There are millions of untold stories exemplifying the sheer force of will required to prevail against all the odds on the prairie, in the mountains, and through the forests and swamps, to build mining camps, villages, cattle ranches, farms, railroad towns and cities. Their *can do* spirit of grit, determination and fortitude, combined with creative ideas and intelligence, surmounted every obstacle in their path.

A great example of that continuing pioneering spirit is the Wright Brothers. Their goal, privately funded by themselves, was to be the first to fly a man in a heavier-than-air powered 'aircraft.' On December 14th, 1903, they made four successful flights. Samuel Langley, financed by the United States War Department, had spent one hundred times more money than the Wrights, but never successfully flew his design, the Langley 'Aerodrome,' in two attempts made on October 7th and December 8th, 1903.

A mere sixty-six years later, Americans landed on and explored the Moon! The way had been cleared by commercial and military developments, and facilitated by the recruitment of German scientists who had developed Hitler's V-2 short range ballistic missile in World War Two.

For millennia, the lives of most people were usually, in the words of the political philosopher, Thomas Hobbes, "*solitary, poor, nasty, brutish and short.*" Before the United States came into being, the vast majority barely eked out a living. They were usually hungry. They rarely rose above the previous generation's standard of living. Nor did they make any real, broad technical breakthroughs to improve their conditions.

Yet in the space of little over 200 years, the American Republic made a "*5,000 year leap.*" The Founders had designed a social, economic and political system that allowed individuals, for the first time in History, to exercise their natural rights to profit from their own efforts and to keep what they earned. The government's designated responsibility was to protect citizen rights with minimal intrusion in private affairs and free enterprise.

Admittedly, that system was not entirely perfect. No new design ever is. Its flaws need to be recognized and remedied. We were, and are, still learning. Because of ignorance, apathy, arrogance, or the lust for power by imperfect people, the essentially well designed system still failed to fully respect and protect every citizen's unalienable rights. However, any failures in measuring up to its embodied ideals and principles, are due much more to faulty or non-existent implementation, than to bad design. Our job is to restore the Republic, remedy any flaws that took us off course, and re-dedicate ourselves to the true American Dream. That is still as valid as it ever was in the past.

Who Are We?

As much of this book documents, most of our ills have been perpetrated by our government "... *in the name of the people.*" Our challenge today results from the abuse of governance by a group of men and women called lawyers, bureaucrats, thugs, looters, thieves, deceivers, aggrandizers, and manipulators. They have deliberately used the illegal expansion of government powers, far beyond the constitutionally mandated confines of the original system, for their own short-sighted benefit. They have now morphed into what can only be termed as autocrats, dictators, czars, tyrants, despots, and ultimately, cruel and capricious fools.

Part of the ignorance and apathy of most citizens results from our unparalleled material advantages. Those came about only as a result of this Country's implementation of its foundational ideals and principles. Until recently, we enjoyed such an unprecedented high standard of living that it was all too easy to take it for granted. Most people still consider this paradigm shift in living standards to be both normal and stable. It is all too easy to be distracted and seduced by the fruits of our *"5,000 year leap."* People put all their effort into material gain rather than into any principled maintenance of the Republic that has so blessed us. With little if any understanding of why we are so blessed, we are in mortal danger of quickly losing all the advantages bequeathed to us by our ancestors.

Drawing from yet earlier iterations of the same general statement, the great American Abolitionist and advocate for Native Americans, Wendell Phillips, said:

Eternal vigilance is the price of liberty.

Unfortunately, that is far too inconvenient a truism for most to understand and accept. Each and every generation is actually responsible, in its turn, to maintain our liberties.

One of the Founders, Thomas Paine, was absolutely correct when he wrote on September 12th, 1777, that:

Those who expect to reap the blessings of freedom must, like men, undergo the fatigue of supporting it.

Interestingly, that was the opening sentence of his topical essay entitled *"The American Crisis."*

Just imagine where the Republic is headed if it continues to degrade at the same pace as it has been during the past 30 to 40 years. Think about Congress continuing to ignore its Constitutional mandate and expanding its power by passage of bad law after bad law after bad law. Visualize the proliferation of additional regulations outside the reach of Congress by regulatory agencies exceeding their legal mandates. There are now 15,000 to 20,000 of those new regulations promulgated every year. Then consider that the courts are essentially ignoring the Constitution as they busily re-interpret, twist, add, and modify laws, giving us *policy guidance, opinions, rulings and interpretations never dreamed of by the Founders.*

Then, add in the hundreds of thousands of new regulators, inspectors, agents, officers, clerks, managers, compliance personnel, support staff and contractors required to even selectively enforce all the new laws, rulings, edicts, commands and mandates. Care to imagine what kind of world our children will inherit if we continue to allow this governmental madness?

We cannot realistically pay for the **hyper-regulatory** excess that is presently enacted. It is nothing short of lunacy to think that there is any chance of paying for the continued expansion of **hyper-regulation** for another 20 or 30 years and beyond!

Materially and scientifically, Americans have made amazing advances. By contrast, we are about as advanced as a first grader in terms of philosophical sophistication. The dumbing down process in government schools has made the latest graduates of high schools the least informed of any generation in our history. They know next to nothing about how our own system of governance and economics (known as "political-economy") should work. No matter our age, we are all far from having the depth of understanding that is required to defend our unalienable rights to "... *Life, Liberty and the pursuit of Happiness.*" Most are powerless against those who have subverted the government. That will persist unless citizens understand the beauty of the constitutional framework that the usurpers are so eager to destroy. Only armed with such knowledge, can we successfully fight back and prevail against them.

Those wishing to use government powers to exercise their will over the People, believe that citizens must to be managed and directed for "*their own good.*" Unfortunately, far too many citizens are willing to accept such control. They do not realize that they are relinquishing essential rights in the process. They are giving up their precious gift of life and liberty, as well as the opportunity to express their full human potential, to others to use for their narrow and short-sighted goals.

If you let someone else plan your life, you'll discover that they do not actually have much of a plan for you.

Although our vast financial and fiscal debt and continuing deficits are at the crisis point, the greatest danger is our mental deficit. Most citizens lack the understanding of the basic principles that undergird our rights, freedoms and liberties, and the economics of the free marketplace that those enable. They are the muscles and sinews of the Body Politic. Without being exercised, they atrophy and wither away. The fiscal deficits and debts are a direct consequence of citizens not exercising their civic responsibilities as the legitimate shareholders in this Country.

A large segment of the population is enjoying 21st Century conveniences and toys but is mired in 8th Century mental behavior. Most citizens act as if they are serfs, beholden to the ruling class, kowtowing to their masters, relying on them for continued favors and subsidies, even pleading for and depending on hand-out sustenance. They are failing to exercise the responsibilities that go along with being sovereign citizens. Their unalienable rights are being abrogated by the government and ruling class. These citizens are so out of touch with what they really need to think and do, that they will often parrot as gospel truth the "feel good" platitudes purposely programmed into them by the government, via the mass media and public schools, to justify its illegal controls and activities.

Worse yet, many citizens **believe** that the current policies of elected officials, and the Federal Government, are actually faithful to the vision of the Founders. There is unquestioning acceptance simply because the policies emanate from the government, a *"higher authority,"* despite being unlawful, illegal and unconstitutional. Such behavior also blindly denies the reality that our government's increasing deficits, and the massive growth of the Country's debt, are pushing us into inevitable insolvency, and eventual bankruptcy. They are confidently, and mindlessly, assuming that all government promises, in either its aspect as the welfare state or the warfare state, will be kept, or are even achievable and desirable.

They unknowingly, but ever so willingly, trade their rights and liberties for the false safety and security of Big Government. Half the working population willingly gives up the first 30% or more of their labor as taxes. Those are then transferred to the nearly 50% dependent upon the government in one form or another. Dependency is thus fostered on both the productive and the unproductive. Those dependent upon the state for handouts, now believe that they have an inherent right to them. Those paying for the handouts have adopted the distinctly uncharitable attitude of, *"I pay my taxes. Why should I do anything for myself or for others? The government should take care of it."* That is the compound interest of co-dependency!

Tax revenues now account for less than 60% of the government's spending. The rest is borrowed by selling U.S. Treasury Notes to often hostile foreign interests and countries such as China, or conjured out of thin air by the Federal Reserve. The latter is an unconstitutional entity creating fake money that is then used to buy government securities that will soon be worthless. This allows all sorts of mad-science schemes to be hatched and funded. Among them is a global empire that, in the name of security, is actually weakening and worsening our safety every passing day. Once upon a time, it was humorous to say: *"Just be glad you're not getting all the government that you're paying for..."* Today, we are getting much more than we are paying for, in the form of waste and a mindless obedience to government dictates!

The out-of-control government spending is absolutely unsustainable. Annual trillion-dollar-plus deficits will now routinely, for the foreseeable future, be added to the current (2012) $16 trillion debt. Unless something is done, this will continue until the whole house-of-cards comes crashing down as predicted in Economist Herbert Stein's aphorism *"If something cannot go on forever, it will stop."*

The current madness will begin to end when lenders demand "risk premiums" to cover the possible, but actually very probable, default of the U.S. Government debt. In the short run, that will increase the government's costs to borrow and thus automatically enlarge the annual deficits. The Country's debt burden will grow even more enormous. It is a "death spiral" which can only end badly. Suddenly, on one very 'bad hair day,' the welfare checks will either no longer be issued, or will have most of their purchasing power eroded away by inflation. Then the whole absurd fiscal/financial fantasy will truly be over.

This scenario is accelerating because taxes, and the monies raised by accumulating foreign and Federal Reserve debt, are being funneled into an endless parade of government bureaus, and to pay their workers. Most government schemes have an extremely high failure rate due to corruption, errors in judgment and institutionalized stupidity. **Every one of them continues on despite manifestly failing.** The government compounds the failures by doubling down on the worst programs.

265

The failures then generate calls for more subsidies as "remedies." How often do we hear that *the funding wasn't sufficient for our purposes* or that *half-hearted efforts always make things worse.* One economist, Paul Krugman, a Nobel Laureate no less, actually criticized the Obama Administration for doing too little despite its massive and unprecedented increase in deficit spending. He has called for literally trillions in additional spending. He will no doubt loudly declare, when everything comes crashing down, *"You see, I was right, they weren't bold enough."* Never let it be said that the minions of Big Government are not experts at creating alibis for themselves! Interesting how they always have back door exit strategies from the messes and failures that they themselves helped create, is it not?

To all intents and purposes, we are currently all living like indentured servants on a giant surreal plantation with the government playing the role of "Massa" looking down from a big white house on the hill.

On the surface, the modern day conservatives and liberals, who are very different in their thinking from the original meaning of those terms, each have about half of the fundamental problem diagnosed. Neo-Conservatives (including social conservatives) have some comprehension of the inherent self-regulating mechanism of a truly free market, although that is increasingly debatable. They have very little understanding of human nature and behavior. Neo-Liberals (Progressives) typically have better understanding of how people naturally think and behave. However, they have next to no understanding of the importance of property rights in maintaining a just and equitable society, and their grasp of even elementary economics is virtually non-existent.

The Neo-Conservatives and the Neo-Liberals are two sides of the same bad coin. Whether one chooses to call them "Republicrats" or "Demopublicans," they support Big Government, combining the worst aspects of their respective ideologies. Our job is to take the halves that they have abandoned and combine them, just as originally envisioned and intended by the Founders as part of what is termed *classic liberalism*. That is defined in Wikipedia as:

*Classical liberalism is a political ideology, a branch of liberalism which advocates **civil liberties** and **political freedom** with **representative government** under the **rule of law** and emphasizes **economic freedom**.* (**emphasis** added)

A good summation of traditional conservatism was expressed by Baron Hailsham when he wrote:

Conservatism is not so much a philosophy as an attitude, a constant force, performing a timeless function in the development of a free society, and corresponding to a deep and permanent requirement of human nature itself.

Who Could We Be?

Those aware of the importance of merging the best aspects of classic liberalism and traditional conservatism, are presently just a small fraction of the population. They are being attacked concurrently by both the Neo-Conservative and Neo-Liberal economic and political establishments as "libertarians" or "constitutionalists." (Is it not utterly amazing that some people in this Country would attack others for being "Constitutionalists?!") In this case, that is actually a good sign. It says something about the correctness of the positions espoused in this book. The proponents of Big Government correctly view them as a threat to their hegemony on power.

Classic liberalism, today's libertarianism, and true constitutional conservatism, are embedded in the design of the Republic. Once citizens truly understand those ideals and principles, then the enlightened and advanced thinking of the Founders becomes crystal clear.

Nowadays, critics call such thinking "*unrealistic*" or "*a wish to return to the 18th Century.*" What they are refusing to acknowledge is that those ideals and principles were derived from the **timeless** writings of some of the greatest thinkers in the History of Mankind. Such criticism only exposes an inability, or unwillingness, to learn the self-evident lessons of History. Such fundamental ignorance of the advanced ideas espoused by the Founders, actually confirms the critics' desire to retrogress back to an age of ignorance and despair, when monarchs and despots ruled at the expense of the population. That was the eventual fate of the Athenian Democracy, and the Roman Republic, when their original ideals and principles were corrupted and subverted.

By dismissing the Founders' very valid reasons for the original design of the Republic, contemporary critics are actually encouraging corrupt practices. Then, by claiming that it is not corruption but *"recognizing present day realities,"* they imply that transactional or situational ethics will solve problems far better than the 'ancient' ideals and principles of the 'distant' past postulated by 'dead white males'. In so doing, they confirm that they are nothing more than malevolent fools.

Many critics are purposeful deceivers seeking to disguise their real intentions. They declare that a militarized welfare state provides *"safety and security."* Citizens are distracted by popular entertainment, sporting events and escapist television that is nothing more than today's version of the *"bread and circuses"* of the Roman Empire of 2000 years ago.

After more than a century of intentional and unintentional sabotage, this Country is on the brink of a social, economic and political implosion. If any of the present day *expert* social engineering actually worked, then why are we now facing imminent disaster? **We the People** must demand an end to all the meddling, social experimentation, fake money printing, decrees, endless regulations, overseas interventionism and unconstitutional acts of professional politicians (politicos), government agencies and bureaucrats. If we do not, what is left of the fruits of over 200 years of freedom and progress will be squashed and squandered.

Neither side, in the polarized economic and political right and left ideological divide, is willing to abandon their counter-productive behavior. The pervasive ignorance and apathy of the majority of citizens appears to be irreversible. In the not so distant past, normal people would recognize their mistakes, and then take the corrective actions necessary to avoid repeating them. But in the strange world inhabited by the *"Ruling Class,"* so called by Angelo Codevilla, mistakes and failed policies are ignored or compounded by "doubling-down" on failure in ways never seen before. The power elite refuse to behave like rational individuals and implement strategies used successfully in the real world to fix or eliminate problems. That would take away their power!

It is especially discouraging to witness productive people, living and working successfully in a somewhat 'real' world, who put aside any critical thinking when making political decisions. They listen to the siren song of left or right wing politicos, particularly during election season, believing in a fantasy that rotating the incumbents in Washington D.C. will actually make a difference.

The only real answer is to resurrect, renew and strengthen **in every possible individual citizen's mind**, an understanding of the bedrock principles upon which the Republic was founded. The omnipresent factionalism and polarization in today's political process is a virulent cancer. The lure of temporary material success, artificial security and comfortable conveniences, have overridden common sense, and the ability to discern truth from fiction.

Ironically, it appears that the most dangerous threat to liberty is not a vast conspiracy being implemented by insiders. It is embedded in the warp and weave of the system designed by the Founders! What idiots they were! They assumed that free and independent individuals, the Sovereign Citizens of this Country, would actively seek to inform themselves and purposefully participate in the political process, taking appropriate action when rules were broken, and principles violated or ignored. Instead, material success enticed citizens into focusing on the temporal and ignoring the permanent. They allowed themselves to believe that the initially benign government would remain that way without requiring any further effort and oversight by them. Warning after warning by the Founders to be vigilant and pro-active citizens have thus far failed to leave an impression on them.

Today, the idea that a limited government would remain within the boundaries of a Constitution penned 223 years ago is considered passé, irrelevant and even extreme by the majority of Big Government Republicans and Democrats. They occasionally make reference to a few of the document's clauses to justify certain actions but completely ignore the remainder. One half of the political establishment promotes the Warfare State while the other half promotes the Welfare State. That is a blatant rejection of the Founders' warnings to avoid overseas entanglements and wars, and their intent that there be a very well informed and highly self-reliant citizenry.

The politicos and their enablers pick out the parts of the Constitutional that they deem favorable to their progressive and authoritarian purposes. That cloaks them in aura of respectability but they have no intention of following the carefully considered code of political conduct that limits the powers entrusted in them. The rest of that grand document is simply cast aside. They claim that the Constitution is a relic of the past, the *"ideas of a bunch of 18th Century dead white guys."* It is a complete inversion of history that belittles the Founders' selfless determination to benefit posterity. It also belittles every one of us in the American Remnant, who still recognize and honor the Founders' noble socio-political master plan to create equal opportunity for **all** Americans.

The only way that this tom-foolery can be reversed is by restoring the true meaning of the Constitution in the minds of the citizenry. That most likely must be accompanied by replacing the Big Government Republicrat/Demopublican Party altogether. It is a shameful and shameless duopoly exploiting the "Good Cop, Bad Cop" technique to confuse and befuddle their hapless adherents on either side of the so-called "left and right" divide.

The Big Government Party, that gigantic Cuckoo Bird overwhelming the nest of governance, has totally embraced the *"carrot and stick"* management of the citizenry who, if the truth be told, they see as nothing more than sheep to be fleeced. It was the notorious gangster Al Capone who said:

You can get much farther with a kind word and a gun than you can with a kind word alone.

It was China's genocidal mass murderer Mao Zedong who stated that:

Political power grows out of the barrel of a gun.

Looking at the growing level of coercion, police and "security" in present day Amerika, it seems that the political duopoly is following the well-worn path of murderous gangsters and tyrants of the past and present.

As part of the Big Government Party's smokescreen to hide its less than admirable activities, one side of the duopoly claims that it wishes to take the right of firearm ownership out of the hands of the citizenry. As evidenced, time and time again, one of the principal goals of any totalitarian government is the sequestration of firearms in the hands of only the government, which is under their firm control. Of course, they loudly trumpet the ridiculous notion it is for the sake of *public safety.*

The Founders had observed that citizens who could not defend themselves were easily subjugated. Perhaps some of the anti-gun lobby should pause and think how the establishment of our Republic itself was enabled by individual citizens who owned and used firearms? That was a significant factor in the successful revolt against the unrepresentative British rule of the original colonies. In actuality, as the professional politicians are fully aware, it is a forlorn hope that even the present-day befuddled citizens are unable to grasp that salient point. It is just another ploy to divert attention away from fundamental issues.

Our task is to resurrect, revitalize and restore the Constitution's limitations on governmental powers. Otherwise, the American Dream of fully representative liberty for every citizen will fail. As always, it ultimately depends on **We the People.**

It actually and inescapably depends on the person who gazes back at you from the mirror each morning.

Restoring the Republic will never be implemented by the Federal Government. Expecting it to be self-limiting is obviously not in the interest of those people profiting by its flow of funds supporting the continuity of the Warfare/Welfare State. Their incentive is actually the opposite. They want to further expand the government.

Recent polls prove the point. Those who are the suppliers, or the beneficiaries, of government largesse, have virtually no interest in decreasing or eliminating those unearned benefits. After all, it is a well-known human weakness to want something for nothing. If those polls are correct, expecting government to limit itself is a fantasy. Instead, sovereign and self-reliant citizens must work together to re-build the Union of the Sovereign States that are the only possible check on an unbridled Federal Government, just as originally conceived by the allocation of powers in the Constitution.

Let's Foreclose on This House

The Federal Government reminds me of Winchester House in San Jose, California. Sarah Winchester, an heir to the Winchester Repeating Arms Company fortune, spent $5.5 million ($71 million in 2010 dollars!) to continuously construct a home from 1881 until her death in 1922. It has 164 rooms, 10,000 window panes, 47 fireplaces, 17 chimneys, three basements and three elevators, all built without any discernible plan. The house is completely impractical. It was sold at auction to serve as a tourist attraction for $135,000 after Sarah Winchester died. Today, it is called The Winchester Mystery House.

Our government has **cost us tens of trillions of dollars** but it is worth far less. It is a complete Mystery House of its own. Much of it is dysfunctional. Some of it is non-functional. To repeat, it **cost tens of trillions of taxpayer dollars to engorge and maintain it over the last two decades!** What did generations of Americans get in exchange for their blood, sweat and tears, and all their expropriated wealth? All they have received in return is a false sense of security, disregard of their rights and liberties, a declining economy, a government on the verge of bankruptcy and paper money that is well along down the slippery slope to becoming completely worthless.

With agencies and offices spread all over the map, the Federal Government is just like The Winchester Mystery House. It has nearly 3 million employees, hundreds of millions of square feet of office space, another 1.6 million people active in the Armed Forces, hundreds of military installations in more than 130 countries, and 190 Embassies and subsidiary consulates around the world. The Federal Government is a veritable rabbit warren of offices, agencies, departments and units. It is an artificial construct based on a jumble of tens of millions of pages of laws, codes, regulations and policies that are supposedly being overseen and managed by numerous overlapping, and inherently incompetent, bureaucracies that were 'empowered' to implement them. This, folks, is an exercise in futility on a truly massive scale!

The costs for this monumental folly are ultimately borne by individual taxpayers. The government "pays" for nothing. It extracts and then redistributes the wealth of the People with a substantial portion absorbed by its huge and wasteful overhead expenses, and for paying interest on the colossal debt that it has accrued.

Such insanity cannot go on much longer. Soon, perhaps very soon, this monster that we cannot afford will begin its downward spiral and expire. That will occur on the day that the Treasury finds that it cannot sell a Treasury Bill to anyone except the Federal Reserve. At that point, the Fed will have to choose between two dreadful alternatives. As Austrian economist Robert Wenzel, founder of the Economic Policy Journal, said in a speech that he made at the New York Federal Reserve in April, 2012:

The noose is tightening on your organization. Vast amounts of money printing are now required to keep your manipulated economy afloat. It will ultimately result in huge price inflation, or, if you stop printing, another massive economic crash will occur. There is no other way out.

That day is closer than almost all dare to imagine.

Until then, so-called VIP politicians and government employees will fly (at the taxpayers' expense) in government jets around the Country, and the World, meddling where they have no business being. They will continue to partake of their free buffet of healthcare coverage and enjoy their endless goodies, benefits and perks.

Meanwhile, individual taxpayers footing the bill out of their hard earned incomes, still have to deal with the obtuse bureaucracies of the Social Security Administration, DHS, TSA, IRS and all the others.

The historical record is rife with examples of cultures experiencing long periods of calm and relative predictability until they suddenly crashed. That occurred when an unnatural government structure, and the accumulation of a long succession of manipulated events, reached a critical mass. The ensuing collapse of the entire system, and the end of the prevailing status quo, is both abrupt and painful. Evolutionary biologists call these events in the natural world *"punctuated equilibrium."* Social philosophers see such collapses as events that rapidly cause a *"paradigm shift"* in people's expectations. The Harvard historian, Niall Ferguson, compares it to Half Dome in Yosemite when a climber reaches the edge and faces a drop of 4,700 feet straight down to the valley floor.

We are about to learn, once again, that *"it is not smart to fool Mother Nature"* as in tampering with the natural self-regulating mechanisms of a truly free market, and manipulating a society that was originally formulated in accordance with natural law. Imbalances are always eventually corrected. In this case, it will cause great pain and be a very expensive lesson.

In most human activity, there are those who participate, those who watch and those who are totally unaware that anything is happening at all. My business partner, Larry, used to call that the "1-4-95 rule." One person acts to accomplish a goal, four people watch him act and the other 95 stand aside and ask: "What happened?"

Obviously, one of my principal goals in writing this book is to inform people of our great peril. Will enough citizens educate themselves soon enough? Can they override their tendency to act out the **WARBI Paradox** and continue their **Modalities of Inaction** (as explained in Chapters 7 and 8)? Will they come to their senses in time? Or will they simply let everything fall apart and then wonder "what happened?"

Without a significant proportion of the population rising above their self-imposed limits, our future is one of increasing degradation and war, leading straight to inevitable destruction before any sort of creative re-construction and renewal can occur.

However one characterizes those in charge, calling them the *"power elite, insiders, ruling class,"* or the *"Anglo-American establishment,"* it is a sure bet that they will attempt to marginalize the views, and demonize the character, of anyone expressing views such as these. Take a closer look and it is obvious that they have no actual defensible argument. As in Hegel's Dialectic, there will be distortions, quotes taken out of context, outright lies and ad hominem attacks with the intent to create a vicious cycle of false opinions and fraudulent actions leading to yet more conflict. It will be pure political theater, as in Shakespeare's Macbeth:

> ... *it is a tale, Told by an idiot, full of sound and fury, Signifying nothing.*

The power elite are on the wrong side of History. They are opposed to the ideals and principles embodied in the Declaration of Independence and the U.S. Constitution. Those great documents are in harmony with human nature, moral behavior and the workings of natural law that the power elite is willfully choosing to discount and ignore.

So, Let's Get the Ball Rolling, OK?

Since you have read this far, I will presume that you have decided to be involved in the fight. Or, at least you find the discussion interesting enough to pursue. Perhaps you already are involved and want additional tools and weapons to help in accomplishing the restoration of the Republic and our unalienable rights?

Please be aware that the basic steps proposed in the following chapters do not provide either quick or easy answers. Nor are they complete. What they do provide is a framework for action. You will need to be responsible for the vision, will and effort, just as the founders and pioneers of this Country did in their time. Never underestimate your importance. You hold the most important civic responsibility in the land. *You are a Sovereign Citizen.*

Rest assured, the framework for action is based on the original foundational principles and ideals of the Republic. Using and building on them, leaders in the freedom fight will emerge across the country. They will share ideas and implement strategies based on their understanding of the reasoning, and the choices made, when the Founders created the Republic.

The framework for action is derived from many concepts already discussed in previous chapters. The local level is the obvious place to begin involving a hitherto uninformed and uninvolved citizenry in the

275

political process. Because all politics begins at the local level, our primary task is to gain control of the government entities closest to the people.

In our system all citizens are designated as sovereigns. Be mindful that the designation has nothing to do with the Sovereign Citizen movement, which carries specific meaning within that movement. For our purpose, three of our leaders described it well what it means to be an individual sovereign when they said:

And this idea that government is beholden to the people, that it has no other source of power except the sovereign people, is still the newest and the most unique idea in all the long history of man's relation to man. This is the issue of this election: Whether we believe in our capacity for self-government or whether we abandon the American revolution and confess that a little intellectual elite in a far-distant capitol can plan our lives for us better than we can plan them ourselves.

–Ronald Reagan

It has hitherto been understood, that the supreme power, that is, the sovereignty of the people of the States, was in its nature divisible; and was in fact divided, according to the Constitution of the U. States, between the States in their United, and the States in their individual capacities that as the States in their highest sov. char. were competent to a surrender of yr whole sovereignty, and make themselves on consol. state so they surrender a part & retain as they have the other part, forming thus a mixed Govt. with a division of its attributes as marked out in the Constitution.

–James Madison

If ye love wealth greater than liberty, the tranquility of servitude greater than the animating contest for freedom, go home and leave us in peace. We seek not your council, nor your arms. Crouch down and lick the hand that feeds you, and may posterity forget that ye were our countrymen.

–Samuel Adams

So, allow me to speak plainly as sovereign citizen to sovereign citizen. Like me, you are obviously concerned about where we are headed, and you want to do something about it. Think of what I am about to say as a pep talk, a player-coach's half-time encouragement with suggestions and tips for his fellow teammates. I have done what I am asking you to do. I have been down and dirty. I have faced, and beaten, significant obstacles and threats. And I have had individual success. However, **what we need** is many more instances of **individual success—on a massive scale.**

- Only you can learn the essential principles and information necessary to take appropriate action.
- Only you can be responsible for your own education.
- Only you summon up the individual genius and initiative that gives you the power to take the action required in each situation.
- You are different from every other citizen but can be equally effective!
- You are a sovereign citizen of the greatest Country in the History of Mankind.
- You have a unique opportunity to participate in the greatest battle in our history, the restoration of this greatest of all countries.

But only if you decide to do so.

It takes no special hindsight or foresight to recognize what has happened, and what will happen, to our Country. Anyone willing to set aside ideological and emotionally driven positions for a moment, to take a dispassionate look at the reality of our situation, will soon understand exactly where we are headed. Look at historical precedents. Recognize how typical human behavior has played out for eons, apply a dose of common sense economics, and then the inevitable outcome of our present path is both obvious and frightening.

Because the power elite ignores every warning of imminent collapse, or runaway inflation, or massive defaults, the end of the *"American Century"* is certain. It will never be the *"American Millennium"* unless enough citizens are promptly galvanized into action. What is coming, is a horrendous implosion of the whole artificial structure that now exists, because of the pride and arrogance of the power elites—in both political parties. What is coming down will not be a *standard business cycle event.*

What is coming down is a once-every-several-hundred-years "reset" of the entire economic and political order. It is a transition of civilization of no less importance than The Dark Ages, The Renaissance and The Enlightenment.

In our favor, we have a tremendous reservoir of very talented and gifted citizens in our population, now working in the private sector. However, most of them are focused on their own individual challenges as entrepreneurs. They have the mercantile mentality of *"go along to get along."* They think that they can adapt to even the worst system and will not be destroyed by it. They are not thinking about their responsibilities as sovereign citizens. It is convenient for them to think that they can remain *"above the fray,"* leaving the enabling of positive political change to others. They must face the fact that many will have no business at all, unless they join in and become effective citizens, rather than currying favor with the government in order to survive.

If there are not enough positive political changes in the immediate future, the lack of real involvement by a sufficient number of talented and determined citizens will begin to be reflected in the 2012 through 2020 election cycles. Major mistakes will be made and great opportunities squandered.

Unfortunately, voters suffering from the *"Stockholm Syndrome,"* a condition when captives empathize with their abductors, are not ideally suited to pick the right leaders for Congress or the Presidency. In most cases, they have not yet picked good leaders for city or county office.

That explains a great deal why Barack Hussein Obama II was elected in 2008. America is currently a place of deeply buried secrets that no one wants to expose and fix. Obama's election was an expression of this situation. He is even worse than George W. Bush and the 'Karl Rovians' who preceded him, if that is possible. In Obama, the Country elected someone they really knew nothing about. The man had no record on anything of substance, providing essentially nothing for the public to judge. He is a vacuous emblem of the population's growing unwillingness to look deeper for fear of what they might find about themselves.

Candidate Obama spoke well, looked good. He fed on and assuaged their guilt. As President Obama, we now know that he is an empty vessel, representing not much more than the narcissism of power. Yet more than half of the voters believed (and may still believe) he was, at the very least, the *"lesser of the two evils"* candidate. President Obama is merely a direct, mirror image of where a large segment of the population has arrived, both mentally and philosophically.

If Obama is replaced by Mitt Romney, it only means that a sufficient number of the *'centrists and independents'* in the electorate tipped slightly from the welfare side of the present equation to the warfare side. If there is a "President Romney," his first term in office will only prove to be slightly less disastrous than the virtual certainty of a catastrophic Obama second term. Mitt Romney is a system finance person, trained in almost every failed economic rubric of the right, without any true understanding of natural law and long-term economic realities. He was one of the many successful manipulators of a failing system.

The Unsinkable, Too-Big-To-Fail Titanic

In the course of the movie *"Titanic,"* the scene shifts back to the present as the elderly survivor, Rose, describes events just before the ship collides with the iceberg. The crew responsible for finding the old wreck is sitting spellbound in the control room listening to her. Then one of the ship's crew, Lewis Bodine, says:

Incredible. There's (Captain) Smith and he's standing there and he's got the iceberg warning in his f---ing, excuse me, his hand and he's ordering more speed.

The expedition leader, Brock Lovett, replies:

Twenty-six years of experience is working against him. He figures anything big enough to sink the ship, they're gonna see in time to turn. The ship's too big with too small a rudder. It does not corner worth a damn. Everything he knows is wrong!

So will it prove to be with a "President Romney." Any mainstream Republican, who considers himself ready and able to fix this Country's dire predicament, will find out that *"everything he knows is wrong."*

The example of the Titanic seems very apt. I first read the story in the 1960s in the book by Walter Lord, *"A Night To Remember."* (1955). A tiny number of those on the ship knew the terrible truth of their situation as the forward compartments began to fill with seawater. The First Class passengers continued partying in the ballroom, enjoying their status as 'Masters of the Realm.' The Second Class passengers knew something was up but stayed in their cabins and ordered tea and dinner. They refused to put on their life jackets and go to the life boats. They believed the White Star Line's boast that the Titanic was "Unsinkable." Below decks, members of the crew, and Third Class passengers, were fleeing the rising water, or already drowning. Now visualize the likely behavior of today's fat cat Wall Streeters and Banksters, the Middle Class and the Working Poor in the midst of the economic crash that is all too likely to occur!

Two-thirds of the passengers on the Titanic perished because of the pride, arrogance and incompetence of a few. The remaining third who survived, did so by taking action, no matter how unpleasant, aided by the random gift of sheer good luck. The power, rank or social standing of most passengers had little correlation with who lived beyond that terrible night. Survival always requires taking action.

We will get virtually no useful information from the controlled mainstream media. They have failed just as comprehensively as the *experts* in foretelling any problems ahead. The phrase *"Too-Big-To-Fail"* may become as emblematic of our age as the appellation "Unsinkable" applied to the Titanic that sums up the hubris of the British Empire, just a few years before the cataclysm of WWI.

The world view of today's **Amerikan Elite** blinds them to possible outcomes that challenge their assumptions. Their ideology prevents them from recognizing that the immutable and inevitable workings of the market will correct itself dramatically because it has been so dreadfully distorted. The mass media itself is a *"part of the problem, not part of the solution"* along with the Federal Government, the Federal Reserve, the big banks and other revered financial institutions. None of them can see, or will admit that, *"a hard rain's A-Gonna fall."* They will almost all go to their graves making excuses, denying that anything of what ensues was their fault.

Strip away everything that the government is doing that has no Constitutional authority, or is simply wasteful, and the government would be about half its present size. Trillions of dollars taken from the citizens have already been lost as a capital asset that could have enabled a more productive economy. Instead, it has been wasted for decades in "stimulus," hand-outs, subsidy, loans, grants, injections (also creating "deficits"), militarization and MIISSC misspending, all justified to supposedly spur economic growth. Anyone who understands Bastiat's 'glazier's fallacy,' and the cost of *"that which is unseen,"* understands the staggering opportunity cost of all that useless government spending. That ill-advised parasitic drag on the productive sector, compounded over time, is the reason why our current GDP is only $15 trillion and not $30 to $40 trillion, or even more.

With the same population, but without the economic drag of our dysfunctional government, the vast majority of those on welfare and assistance today would instead have jobs with good incomes. The elderly and impaired could be helped, and supported privately, with little need for any government assistance. We could afford a reasonable and very strong defense. We cannot do so with the federal government diverting, and then squandering, more than 24% of our total output, year in and year out. Allowing this craziness to continue guarantees that the whole rotten structure will crash and collapse. The negative compounding of the opportunity cost has been proportionately much more costly to us than even the huge amount of the citizens' wealth that the government has squandered.

The government is steering the Ship of State straight into the iceberg of default and bankruptcy. The moment is close at hand when everything familiar is overwhelmed, and the "reset" occurs.

There is now no way of dodging the iceberg. If a sufficient number of informed and determined citizens begin to immediately take control of their own personal destinies, the very worst outcomes may be avoided. That will happen through involvement in local and state government, with the clear goal of making positive political changes with the guidance of our common enumerated principles that are already embodied in the foundational documents of this Country.

The alternative is that the citizenry might end up like two-thirds of the Titanic's passengers and go down with the ship.

For the moment, the choice of which scenario unfolds **may** still be ours to make.

17

The Restoration of Constitutional County Sheriffs

The more laws, the less justice.
–M. Tullius Cicero

*Nothing is more destructive of respect for the government
and the law of the land than passing laws which cannot be enforced.*
–Albert Einstein

I have got a touch of a hangover, bureaucrat. Don't push me!
–George Washington McLintock (as portrayed by John Wayne)

A key element in the restoration of the Republic is reconstituting the **proper role** of the County Sheriff. This is a top priority, the first step in the revival and restoration of our Country's foundational ideals and principles.

This must be enabled by knowledgeable citizens who thoroughly understand the proper relationship they have with all local government bodies, councils, commissions and legislatures.

It is vital that every County Sheriff understand his official duties, his reciprocal role in dealings with those who elected him, as well as the supreme importance of his position as the ultimate protector, under the law, of the rights of the citizens.

Nowadays, most County Sheriffs have little better understanding of the organizing principles of the Republic, or the State and U.S. constitutions, or their own County charters, than does the average citizen. This **must change** for there to be any hope of successfully accomplishing the great task of restoring the Republic.

The position of County Sheriff is one of the most important offices in the land. The proper function of that office ensures the protection and prosperity of the local citizens that he or she represents.

It is at the roots where the greenest grass grows.

Stated in another way, it is at the foundational level of the Republic where the strength of the entire governmental superstructure, on which it rests, is determined or undermined. Without a solid foundation in place, the whole structure will collapse.

A Short History of the Office of Sheriff

The office of County Sheriff is an institution of long standing. Wikipedia states:

> *The word "sheriff" is a contraction of the term "shire reeve," the King's protector. The term ... designated a royal official responsible for keeping the peace ... throughout a shire or county on behalf of the king, The term was preserved in England notwithstanding the Norman Conquest (in 1066). From the Anglo-Saxon kingdoms the term spread to several other regions, at an early point to Scotland, latterly to Ireland, and to the United States.*

Most Americans are familiar with the legend of Robin Hood and the Sheriff of Nottingham. In that case, an authoritarian king allowed a dishonorable sheriff to take advantage of his position, serving his own personal interests at the expense of the local population. In direct contrast, an honorable sheriff would have worked on behalf of the people in their enjoyment and use of the king's land.

In America, the concept of the sheriff, as established in English law, was altered as the result of the recognition that the People were sovereign, and not a king. The County Sheriff is still the protector of the People, but they are sovereign. The Sheriff is responsible for protecting the rights of the People in their use of the land. He is the primary "*peace officer*" of the County.

First we must understand the distinction and real difference between a *"peace officer"* and a *"law enforcement officer"* (LEO). The primary role of the peace officer is to uphold the Constitution and keep the peace, by ensuring that the laws involving property and persons are observed. If you are over 50 years old, you are undoubtedly familiar with that traditional role.

It is essential to understand the large difference between the concepts of a peace officer and a law enforcement officer. The peace officer is tasked firstly to uphold and defend the Constitution, and secondly to keep the peace and maintain order. His role is not to enforce any specific or particular law, unless he is so directed by a court of jurisdiction to execute a warrant or order. When it comes to an instance of observed 'law breaking,' in lieu of a specific warrant or court order, the Sheriff's assigned duty and role is as a peace officer, the judge and the jury in determining how the law will be applied in any given circumstances. That is the specific and unique task of the County Sheriff within our form of governance.

The County Sheriff's mandate is to protect the citizen's rights in his County. If a sheriff determines, on his own, that it is more important to keep the peace, and maintain order, rather than enforce a specific law, then that is his decision alone to make. This explains why, in our Country, the position is elected instead of being appointed, as was the case in England, Scotland and Ireland.

The Evolution of the Law Enforcement Officer (LEO) and the Meaning of The Law

In any review of most state constitutions, codes or statutes, one would find that almost all the original references were to sheriffs and police as *"peace officers."* I know of no original establishment of local police powers where the term *"law enforcement officer"* was ever applied. That term and concept did not exist until recently.

The role of a law enforcement officer is a bureaucratic position created to ensure the enforcement of statutory infractions along with criminal statutes. "Infractional" law enforcement leaves little room for independent thought or decision making by an officer. There is much less emphasis on keeping the peace and maintaining order. Consequently, there is much less reliance on, or concern about, constitutional rights. Law enforcement focuses on compliance, revenue enhancement, incarceration and punishment rather than pursuing justice and keeping to the spirit of the law, or safeguarding the rights of citizens.

The primary reason for such change is the virtual explosion of laws, issued not only by federal and state legislatures, but also by unconstitutional federal agencies. Most of these laws have been initiated through the creation of *"statutory and infractional offenses"* that are not actually crimes against persons or property. Skeptics are encouraged to read *"Three Felonies a Day"* by Harry Silverglate. According to Silverglate, the average citizen is likely to unknowingly commit three "crimes" every day as they conduct their personal business.

As a consequence, the United States now has the highest imprisonment rate of any country on the planet, with a ratio of 750 persons to every 100,000 in the population. That equates to more than 2.25 million persons incarcerated in local jails, and in state and federal prisons. There are another 5 million currently under state and federal parole supervision, or probationary control! The vast majority result from "victimless" crimes emanating from the explosion of statutory laws and regulations. Did you know that the U.S. has a far larger population, of convicts and ex-cons, than military active duty members and living veterans? How can this be in the *"freest country on the Earth?"* Do you think that this state of affairs is healthy or desirable for our Country?

These types of statutes, called *"prior restraint"* laws, concern infractions such as drunk driving and substance abuse. No actual crime against another person or property was committed. The expectation that a future crime may possibly be committed, as a consequence of an infraction, is the theory behind the "authority" to "interdict." Administrative and regulatory infractions result in many unintended consequences, including the actual and social costs of imprisonment, with little that is positive to recommend them.

These statutes do not deal with real crime, when identifiable harm, injury or property damage actually occurred. Instead, they are "statutory" infractions. Many are subjective, or emotionally based and are not *"objective harm"* laws.

In statutory infraction cases, another citizen is usually not the complainant. Instead, it is an entity of the government.

These are laws of "potential" harm when or where no actual harm (and thus no true criminal act) was committed. As a result, these statutes accelerate the criminalization of the entire population for minor, non-criminal infractions, where no harm has been committed on another or to their property. The War on Drugs is a perfect example, but is not the only case where this happens. Statutory infractions related to the **hyper-regulatory state** give rise to all kinds of false 'criminality.'

Federal regulatory agency regulations pouring out of Washington, D.C. fail to address any actual crime. They are only rules to supposedly prevent some unidentifiable potential harm that might occur—a vague description, to say the least. These *statutory infractions* are most obviously seen in the areas of the environment, food, health, occupation and safety. Another example is the federal agency called OSHA—the Occupational Safety and Health Administration—whose mission is allegedly to:

... assure safe and healthful working conditions for working men and women by setting and enforcing standards and by providing training, outreach, education and assistance.

As an important aside, I have relentlessly and consistently referred in my writing to these rogue government agencies as illegal and unconstitutional. In its mission statement, OSHA explains why that is so. It states that its job is both to "set" and then "enforce" standards. Under the Constitution, those two duties were wisely and deliberately **separated** so that no single branch of government could be the creator, arbiter and enforcer simultaneously. Under the Constitution, the legislative branch makes the laws, and the executive branch enforces them. In OSHA, those duties were unconstitutionally combined, with the very obvious "conflict of interest" that we observe today.

The many statutory infractions that grew out of the phony war on drugs, then exploded geometrically in number after September 11, 2001. The whole new set of statutory infractions was based on the *resolution* to conduct a global "War on Terror." However, it makes absolutely no sense whatsoever to make war on the *tactic* of terrorism. But doing so is easily explained if the real goal is total government control over the People. The PATRIOT Act, and the Intelligence Reform and Terrorism Prevention Act (IRTPA), breezed through the House and the Senate with nary a whisper of dissent.

Signed into law by President Bush in December, 2004, the new laws unleashed all manner of mischief, including setting up watch lists for terrorists on domestic and international flights, while ignoring basic human rights that are guaranteed by the (increasingly emasculated) Constitution. From there on, it has been a downhill slide for the average Joe or Jane Citizen's rights. That is thanks to the Department of Homeland Security and the Transport Security Administration (TSA), along with multiple and varied enhancements to the powers of the FBI, BATFE, IRS and numerous other governmental bureaus and agencies that promulgate an endless stream of new regulatory infractions.

Law enforcement officers (LEOs) is a category that did not exist until just a few years ago. It would likely be unnerving to many people to learn, for example, just how many of them are employed by federal agencies, such as the Department of the Interior. Also unnerving would be knowing the number of U.S. government bureaucrats who are now authorized to carry firearms, and to use deadly force in carrying out their "duties." How has this all happened, especially when there has been no change in Constitutional authority? The main reason is "Mission Creep."

As described in Wikipedia:

Mission creep is the expansion of a project or mission beyond its original goals ... it is usually considered undesirable due to the dangerous path of each success breeding more ambitious attempts, only stopping when a final, often catastrophic failure occurs. The term was originally applied exclusively to military operations, but has recently been applied to many different fields.

288

Thirty-five federal agencies now have LEOs, with approximately 50,000 employees authorized to carry firearms. The number increases year after year. The population of the U.S. has grown ~80 times (from 3.9 million) since the Constitution was signed and ratified. The number of federal crimes has grown thousands of times, and the number of enforcement officers 1000 times more. Do you believe the general population is exhibiting 12 times more criminal behavior, in proportion to the size of the population than in 1789? Neither do I.

With the further explosion of statutory law since 9/11, has come an accompanying and inevitable mushrooming in the number of LEOs, along with their expanded jurisdictions. Rivers of money, in the form of "federal aid" and grant funding, now flow into local police and sheriff's departments with the "official" purpose of supplementing their staffing, equipment and training budgets. Often the sums are significant. In some cases, they are up to a third of the total budget.

The unofficial, hidden purpose is to control such departments and tie them up with *"memorandums of agreement"* and *"understandings"* leading to overt demands, and restrictions on their freedom of action, that inevitably accompany the money. Of course, that "free" money is not free at all. The Feds make sure that strings are attached. This has been the primary reason why the traditional understanding of the duties of *"police officers"* has morphed into *"law enforcement officers."* This has occurred without most citizens even being aware it is happening.

Part of the funding is being directed into the "militarization" of those local departments to thwart imagined, or real, "terrorist" threats that they might face in the future. The more closely the Feds work with local police and sheriff's departments, the more the latter tend to adopt the same 'mindset.' An affinity develops between those providing the "free money" to buy equipment, to provide training, and so forth, and those on the receiving end. The sense of dependency develops further, as in the natural reaction of:

Don't bite the hand that feeds you.

In this environment, it is easy to see how the LEO mentality has migrated into local police forces, and sheriff's offices, eroding their sense of duty to primarily act as *"peace officers."* Such a change might have been barely tolerable, if it did not also involve a near complete disregard for the issues of jurisdictional responsibilities and citizens' rights. That makes such a change in attitude totally unacceptable.

One may remember how constitutional issues were depicted in movies such as *Tombstone, True Grit* and *McLintock!* There was always tension between the local sheriffs and federal marshals. The issue was always proper jurisdictional authority. That tension was not just a cinematic device. It reflected a reality of The Old West that should still exist today in the 'New West.' It is as valid as ever. A timeless principle is at stake.

How Did It Happen?

In the early years of the Republic, the role of the Federal Government in law enforcement was very limited. A careful reading of the Constitution will reveal very few instances of federal criminal jurisdiction. Expansion of that role is largely attributed, at least in the beginning, to the efforts of J. Edgar Hoover of the FBI, and Harry J. Anslinger of the Federal Bureau of Narcotics (FBN). Both of them were essentially out of work following the end of Prohibition. Looking to justify the continued existence of the bureaus that they headed, Hoover and Anslinger successfully found and created ways to do so. Ever since then, federal LEO positions have exploded in number. There were more than 50 specialized federal law-enforcement agencies created in the 20th Century. What is the lesson? 'Mission Creep' builds bureaus and provides further employment for more bureaucrats at the expense of the taxpayers.

In the beginning, whenever they came into a county, the jurisdictional role of U.S. Marshals or Agents was very limited. It was limited by the nature and structure of the Constitution, and the Republic it created. If a U.S. Marshal entered an *inhabited, established* county in order to serve a Federal Warrant, he was required to check in with the County Sheriff to get permission to execute that warrant.

Unless he was executing a constitutional, lawful and legal warrant, a U.S. Marshal *had no authority to execute any other law within that county*. Unless he was deputized by the Sheriff, he had no power to execute any other duty. Only if he was operating outside of inhabited established counties, did he have any enforcement powers or duties. Inside an organized county, the Sheriff was, and is, the supreme law enforcement authority.

The U.S. Marshal had enforcement jurisdiction inside Indian lands and reservations, and in territories before they became states. He also had enforcement duties in any area in a state that was not yet a designated county, provided that he had received permission from state officials, or was operating under orders from a federal court, in coordination with a state court with proper jurisdiction. U.S. Marshals were severely limited in their powers.

This led, as might be expected, to confrontations between federal agents and local sheriffs. Often the federal agents chafed under such requirements to submit to the local, but actually higher, authority. When a federal agent attempted to ignore or usurp a sheriff's jurisdiction, the Sheriff was forced to obtain a federal circuit judge to rein them in. The point we are making here is that informed citizens need to make the same distinction today, by supporting their local sheriff as the highest authority in the County.

The cause of this jurisdictional "tension" was the authority "chain" specifically and deliberately delineated in the U.S. Constitution, and in the State Constitutions. Here is why:

- The People are endowed with rights regardless of origin.
- The People created the entity of the State.
- The separate States then created a Federal Government at the Constitutional Convention to serve as the agent of the States, in a subservient role, to accomplish a small number of specifically enumerated tasks known as "delegated powers." (Government entities have no rights, only delegated powers derived, ultimately, from the People).

- Each state then created counties or parishes as political subdivisions which were chartered to allow for the election of officials for the various branches and offices in that county, including the office of County Sheriff.
- Those elected officials could then appoint officers to operate the various branches, in turn hiring employees to carry out specific enumerated functions and duties.
- Those officers and employees are subordinate to the County Sheriff when they are operating within the jurisdiction of the County on any issue with constitutional authority. (They are only authorized to execute orders and warrants when approved by the Sheriff to do so).

Thus authority flows *upwards* from the Sovereign Citizens through the Counties to the States to the Federal Government. It does **not** flow **downwards** to the citizens. Even when it is an issue of federal jurisdiction, whenever an employee or official of the Federal Government enters a county to perform their duties under the law, they must report to the County Sheriff. **In all cases**, the States and the Federal Government are ultimately subservient to the People.

It is therefore the responsibility of the County Sheriff to ensure that the rights and liberties of citizens are upheld, and to protect them from usurpation or abrogation by either the State or the Federal Government. In other words, it is the Sheriff's job to protect the land and the People from any potential "Kings and Queens" (supposedly "public servants") in the State Capitol and in Washington D.C.

One can thus understand how this ordering, by which authority flows upwards from the People, makes perfect sense. The Sheriff's position is the closest official entity in our system of governance to the citizens. This should result in the Sheriff being sensitive to their needs and rights, and to be reminded daily how tenuous his power is should he stray outside of his area of responsibility No other elected officials in a county are responsible for the direct enforcement of the law. County commissioners can create local ordinances. State legislators can create codes or statutes. But only the Sheriff is fully charged with the responsibility of enforcing them inside the County. That makes his position truly unique and its proper execution so fundamentally important in our government system.

It is worth repeating that the Sheriff is the **only elected law officer** in the County for a reason. The Governor of the State, or the President of the United States, is **not a law officer** but is an **executive officer**. The same holds true with the appointed U.S. Attorney General, or a state's Attorney General (elected in 43 of the States and appointed in 7). They are not directly charged with the enforcement of law but with their **proper procedural execution.**

The fundamental authority, with the greatest responsibility for 'law enforcement,' is entrusted to the elected officer charged with that duty—the County Sheriff.

The Sheriff is the only elected officer who swears to *support and defend* both the U.S. and the State Constitution as a peace officer. He is performing the first and primary duty of defending and protecting the individuals living on the land in his jurisdiction, the County.

It is very important to realize that the Attorney General of the United States, or a state patrol commander or municipal police chief is not elected, they are appointed. That includes employees of the FBI, the DEA, the IRS, the BATFE, NFS, BLM or any federal agency. Since they are not elected, they are therefore not directly accountable to the People. By definition, they must be subservient to the People's elected official wherever they reside or travel, namely to the County Sheriff.

The Sheriff is the highest elected law officer in the County, even when the President of the United States, or the State's Governor, are in a county. Accordingly, any other federal, state or local police officer or law enforcement office *must report* to the Sheriff for jurisdictional review and approval before they can execute their warrants or orders. The U.S. Supreme Court and other lower courts have confirmed this in their decisions, reflecting a reality that antedates the creation of the Constitution. This arrangement is not a fluke, a historical error or a misreading of the Constitution. It is a fundamental and deliberate design in our form of government to protect the rights of the People.

As noted earlier, the role of peace officer (PO) has unhealthily mutated into the term law enforcement officer (LEO) through the process known as "*mission creep.*"

When applied to the realm of rights and liberties, the Founders understood that tendency long ago. Thomas Jefferson, in a letter to Edward Carrington in 1788, wrote that:

> *...the natural progress of things is for liberty to yield, and government to gain ground.*

A Plan to Restore the Constitutional Sheriff to Each County

In order to successfully restore the Republic, it is extremely important to place the constitutional roles of the various offices in the proper order.

The following are the key elements needed for a comprehensive plan to insure the proper operation of a constitutional county sheriff's office:

1. Arrange a citizens' meeting with the County Sheriff and his key deputies to discuss and determine the degree of compliance and agreement to this plan. Affirm that all officers have properly filed their oaths of office.

2. Review all relevant agreements with federal agencies including the Drug Enforcement Agency (DEA), the U.S. Forest Service, the Bureau of Land Management and the FBI, as well as with other state and local law enforcement agencies. Using that review's findings, then determine the level of constitutional compliance between the Sheriff's office and those agencies.

3. Review the applicable law and jurisdictional issues in order to discover areas of unlawful jurisdictional intrusion, or over-reach, in practice and in enforcement. See "*A Treatise on the Law of Sheriffs, Coroners and Constables with Forms*," by Walter H. Anderson (below).

4. Develop and provide specific training and educational materials for the Sheriff's office personnel. Develop their understanding of materials as they apply to interacting with the County's citizens and external agencies.

5. If the Sheriff does not have an active Posse and a Sheriff's Auxiliary, establish them immediately.

6. Develop metrics to measure the completion of education, instruction and compliance by the Sheriff's office personnel.

7. Establish periodic reviews to insure that new staff members are trained and kept current on compliance to the Constitution according to their oaths of office.

8. Develop a simple scorecard, or dashboard commentary, regarding compliance that is regularly published in the journal of record for each county.

9. Provide website links to both SheriffMack.com and Oathkeepers.org

10. Provide contact information for the Sheriffs in Grant and Josephine counties in Oregon, and in San Miguel, Colorado, and other counties currently employing the principles of a Constitutional Sheriff. This will facilitate training and the exchange of information to promote the County Sheriff Project.

It is strongly recommended that this plan be coordinated with a 2 or 3 person, or larger, citizens' forum in each county to help implement the plan through the Sheriff's office. The forum should meet and report on a regular basis with his office.

It is also recommended that this plan be shared with other local elected officials such as county commissioners, city councils and mayors. Their understanding and support will be crucial to the successful implementation and maintenance of the project in each county.

The project should include the following three documents:

1. "*A Treatise on the Law of Sheriffs, Coroners and Constables with Forms*," by Walter H. Anderson, (1942, reprinted and published 1984 by James Von Schmidt). It can be accessed in .pdf format at http://thecitizenslaststand.com/anderson.

2. "*Unraveling Federal Jurisdiction within a State*" by Sheriff Gil Gilbertson of Josephine County, Oregon. It can be accessed at http://thecitizenslaststand.com/gilbertson.

3. *"Proposed Rule Changes by the U.S. Forest Service Law Enforcement,"* from the Western States Sheriff's Association, available in .pdf format at http://thecitizenslaststand.com/WSSA.

The first document is the most comprehensive review of the Law of the Sheriff ever developed. It was the standard that was once followed. For some reason (hmm … I wonder why?) it has fallen into disuse with the increasing federalization and militarization of law enforcement throughout the Country.

The other two documents review, and make reference to, areas where it is clear that the U.S. Forest Service and Bureau of Land Management (BLM) are attempting to overstep its lawful bounds within the States, and the jurisdiction of the County Sheriff, in land use and enforcement.

It is recommended that this plan be firstly implemented within mostly rural counties of the Western States, where there are large holdings of land under the control of the Federal Government. There the most intrusive, abusive and unlawful infringements on the sovereign rights and powers of the People, and the States, are routinely being perpetrated by an agency of the Federal Government.

The restoration of the Republic begins at the county level. The first step is reestablishing the fundamental role of the County Sheriff, as the primary elected protector and defender of the People and the land. As the understanding of the vital necessity of doing so, within those rural counties, grows ever more obvious to more and more citizens, then similar issues in metropolitan counties will become apparent, providing the motivation to adopt this plan there as well.

In the beginning, there may be resistance by some county sheriffs. That is to be expected. This plan represents a change in the status quo. Most people are resistant to change, even when necessary and positive.

In addition, this plan is certain to be resisted by federal "authorities" and LEOs. Every county and state should be prepared in advance for such resistance. That should be met with patience and firmness, backed by the necessary state acts and laws to punish illegal federal encroachments and violations of the powers in each of the States.

Any response by local and state authorities should always be defensive in nature. It should seek negotiation and avoid confrontation. If violence ensues, it must always originate from federal agencies, operating outside of their lawful jurisdiction. In the event of violence, **citizens should loudly question in public** why any federal agency would even attempt to respond with force.

It must be understood by everyone that these changes are absolutely necessary to restore all policing agencies to their historic, lawful and Constitutional roles. The current trajectory of overreach by many federal (or even some state) agencies is not acceptable, and is certainly not desirable, in our Republic.

This plan, and others developed to deal with similar issues, represents a reasonable due process approach to solve the issues. Agencies and LEOs refusing to honor such plans, as presented by the citizens and their sheriffs, despite the vast improvement they represent, will need to be disciplined through the political process to obtain their acceptance. The disciplining will be applied by a growing population of active, thoughtful, knowledgeable and involved law-abiding citizens, sheriffs and sheriffs' posses working together.

A Closing Admonishment

The following needs to be emphasized to avoid having anyone intentionally, or unintentionally, misconstrue or misinterpret the purposes behind the implementation of the County Sheriff Project:

- It is not an attempt to debilitate or degrade the proper enforcement of laws involving actual crime against persons or property.
- It is not an effort to hinder or impede the proper execution, or the due process, of the law.
- It is not an initiative to create a more powerful position of "super-sheriff."
- The Sheriff will still report to the People of the County.
- The Sheriff will submit to citizen review committees and be kept accountable by the votes of the citizens of the County.

- Misbehaving sheriffs will still be subject to recall elections, or be voted out of office at the next election, just as with any other elected official.
- It will still be the job of executive authorities, such as the Governor and the State Attorney General, to ensure the proper execution of the laws, and to ensure the proper conduct of those executing them.

The County Sheriff Project is designed to guarantee the proper functioning of a fully informed, constitutional sheriff's department in every county in the land.

The bottom line is that *We the People* actually empower, and thus control, the County Sheriff, just as we do all elected officials, along with their appointed subordinates and employees. The Sheriff is answerable to us. *We the People* also empower and control the state and federal governments.

The Sheriff determines how peace and order is kept in his or her county while simultaneously defending the rights of the citizens and protecting the land. Because the Federal Government is ignoring, or abrogating, those rights and failing to protect the land, it is more than fair and reasonable that *We the People* organize and mobilize for the defense of our counties, by ensuring that the vital and primary office of peace officer is held by a **Constitutional County Sheriff**.

18

State Powers and Nullification

The enumeration in the Constitution of certain rights shall not
be construed to deny or disparage others retained by the people.
–9th Article to the Bill of Rights

The powers not delegated to the United States by the Constitution,
nor prohibited by it to the States, are reserved
to the States respectively, or to the people.
–10th Article to the Bill of Rights

The next step in restoring the Republic is developing a healthy and robust understanding of the actual powers still held primarily by the Sovereign People, and secondarily by the Sovereign States.

As noted earlier, let us be absolutely clear on what constitutes "rights." There are no "*states' rights*" any more than there are "*government rights,*" "*corporate rights*" or even "*property rights.*" Those are long-standing myths. **All rights** are endowed in individual human beings and **nowhere else**.

Pay particular attention to the different wording in the two amendments above. People have endowed rights but no "special" rights. Our endowed rights cannot be taken away by other individuals or by governments. Governments and other entities have no rights except for whatever is delegated to them from the unalienable rights held by the Sovereign Citizens.

Thus, portions of certain individual rights, such as the right to self-defense, may be delegated as strictly **limited powers** to entities created by the People, to the States or to the Federal Government, and also to corporations. Those limited powers may only be exercised under the

299

terms of a lawful limited agreement such as a constitution. All and any positive law made subsequent to a Constitution **CANNOT** extend any power beyond those delegated powers, and **CANNOT** violate or exceed the originating right. Thus the principle is that:

No government can do that which, by right, no person can do.

As one example among many, then it follows that if counterfeiting money is a criminal offense for a person, then the same principle extends to counterfeiting by the government (as has been occurring since 1971).

The Power To Nullify

Traveling around various states, listening and talking with elected officials, and others, as well as reading about the principles involving state powers and nullification, I have found that there is a great deal of confusion in people's minds.

At this point, it may be helpful for the reader to take a short detour and obtain Dr. Thomas Woods' book "*Nullification: How to Resist Federal Tyranny in the 21st Century,*" published in 2010.

If you want to read even more, and completely immerse yourself in the subject, then read Dr. W. Kirk Wood's "*Nullification: A Constitutional History,*" published in 2009.

The following is a very condensed summary:

1. One state, several states or all the States **may nullify any federal law** that does not base its enacted power on at least one or more of the enumerated, limited powers in the U.S. Constitution.

2. Any one state may opt out of any federal law or program having no Constitutional authority.

3. If one or all the States allow the Federal Government to seize or create new powers for itself, without a corresponding amendment in the Constitution, they can do so by simply acquiescing.

No particular number of states has to agree on nullification. Nor do they have to work in concert for nullification to be invoked since each is a sovereign nation-state.

Nothing prohibits a state, or some or all the States, from acquiescing or "rolling over" in the face of unconstitutional federal pressure. Such acquiescence by one state does not prohibit, or preclude, any other state from opting out in the present, or in the future.

The following are some recent federal and state government interactions:

- The Federal Endangered Species Act was applied to the importation of Canadian Gray Wolves into five states. Those wolves were in no danger of extinction in those states because they had never lived there in the past. They supplanted the resident subspecies 'Rocky Mountain Timber Wolf' that were still present and not extinct. After the Canadian wolves were introduced, they were promptly declared to be under the protection of the Act, a typical example of the arbitrary exercise of federal government power without reference to local and pre-existing conditions. The affected states simply rolled over and acquiesced because the Wolf Program was accompanied with "federal aid" using taxpayer money and thus provided some additional local "employment."
- Arizona passed and signed into law a bill known as SB 1070, in April 2010. It required **stricter enforcement** of immigration laws than the feeble degree of enforcement that the Federal Government was implementing.
- California and other states passed "relaxed" drug laws concerning permissible "medical" and "recreational" marijuana use.
- The Montana Firearms Freedom Act was enacted to limit federal jurisdiction over firearms manufactured, owned and used within the State.
- Montana also has a 100 year old ban, the Corrupt Practices Act, on corporations spending money for political campaigns within the State.

Each of the above is an example of States choosing varied options and degrees of acquiescence or "nullification" of federal law. Of course, in all such cases, the dysfunctional federal district courts, and the equally dysfunctional U.S. Supreme Court, have issued, or will issue, convoluted and rambling so-called "decisions" based on *stare decisis* that only complicate the issues and the process of solving them.*

Every time that the Federal Government has exceeded its authority by usurping the rights, powers and privileges properly and constitutionally retained by the States, and primarily by the People, then that action is a legitimate target for nullification.

SB 1070 is an example where the State of Arizona had to step in to carry out the proper but **failed** duties of the Federal Government, namely controlling the Country's borders and preventing illegal immigration.

1. Article VI of the United States Constitution states: "This Constitution and the Laws of the United States **which shall be made in Pursuance thereof** ... shall be the Supreme Law of the Land..."(**emphasis** added). That article does not say "any law on any subject that the Congress, the President or the Courts wishes to make up and invent shall be the Supreme Law of the Land," but only those **"... in Pursuance ..."** of the specific enumerated powers in the Constitution.

2. If the Congress, or the Supreme Court, or any agency in the Executive Branch, creates a law, statute or regulation, or issues an opinion, in an area where there is no authority granted in the Constitution (under either Article I, II, III or VI), then none of those laws, statutes, regulations or opinions have any legal binding effect on any state, or on any person in that state. By definition, they cannot since they were not **"... made in Pursuance thereof ..."**

The first three numbered points in this chapter are critical in understanding the proper operation of our Republic. The next two numbered points (immediately above) describe, in part, why the Federal Government's powers are much more restricted than the People, or the elected officials within the States, and the mainstream media, currently understand.

The next point involves what the States can do next. That will be to restore themselves as truly *"free and independent states"* in keeping with the Constitutional Republic which they **voluntarily established** at the Constitutional Convention.

The True Nature of the Republic

The Founders never intended that any state conform to any other state. Only interstate commerce was 'regulated' by the Constitution. There were no drug, food, environmental, wildlife or other regulations as now promulgated and enforced by the Federal Government that reached into intrastate commerce or private business within a state, completely enveloping them.

The powers granted by the States to the Federal Government were severely restricted and carefully defined. If that was not intentional, then why bother with having *"free and independent"* states? Why would the States be required to ratify the Constitution and every amendment to it? If the Founders had intended that there be a single nation, then why did they not create states dependent on that single legal entity, but instead create a federation of sovereign states?

In actuality, the only general conformance was to be the common recognition by the States of the enumerated, limited powers delegated to the Federal Government. The Constitution required that the Federal Government conform to the States' interests as their designated agent, nothing more, and certainly not the other way around.

It is worth repeating that most of the restrictions and limitations noted in the Constitution, and its first ten amendments (the Bill of Rights), are applicable to the Federal Government and not to the States or to the People. Only in Article I, Section 10, do we see any specific restrictions on the States. With this in mind, where do citizens get the idea that this federation of sovereign states means that the States are *"all made out of ticky-tacky which all look just the same?"* (A tip of the hat to Pete Seeger.) Where did any legitimacy for the drive to **nationalize the States into a single entity** come from?

The federation that was established by the Constitution clearly intended that each state would be lawfully, culturally, politically and philosophically different, to the degree desired by the People of those states. The States would remain independent and free from the Federal Government's control except where they had specifically, and voluntarily, relinquished some of their powers, as specified and enumerated in the Constitution.

States were to be their own "laboratories." Supreme Court Justice Louis Brandeis came close to understanding what the Founders intended when he wrote in *New State Ice Co. v. Liebmann* in 1932:

> *It is one of the happy incidents of the federal system that a single courageous State may, if its citizens choose, serve as a laboratory; and try novel social and economic experiments without risk to the rest of the country.*

Brandeis was incorrect in one respect. It was not an instance of "*happy incidents.*" It was the Founders' deliberate intention to keep the States as free from federal intervention as possible to engage any "*novel social and economic experiments*" as were desired by the sovereign citizens of those sovereign states. Each state was allowed to be a 'petri dish' of self-government within the boundaries of its own state constitution, with minimal restrictions placed on that process by the U.S. Constitution.

The 9th and 10th Amendments to the Constitution only reiterated and reemphasized the point that the People and the States were supreme and sovereign, reserving to them all rights and powers not specifically enumerated and voluntarily relinquished in the Constitution to the Federal Government. The three branches of the Federal Government, the Legislative, the Executive and the Judicial, **were never intended to be, and are not, superior in authority to the States.**

The Founders clearly set forth in the Constitution that the Sovereign Citizens had created separate and independent states which together then ceded severely limited power to a *federal* government. The authority for governance flowed up from the People to the Federal Government via the States—not in the reverse direction.

Each state was supposed to be a different experiment in a 'free market of self-governance.' The entire Republic was set up as an open competition to see which states would create the best forms of government. As long as no state violated the law under the Constitution, as in Article I, Section 10, they were free to experiment with **self-governance in any manner that they wished**.

There was to be no centralized and concentrated economic control, or nationalist agendas, applied to *"free and independent states"* by the Federal Government. There was only to be a minimum of regulation governing interstate commerce, taxes and administrative functions.

How did the original intent get turned upside down?

No clearer example of the abrogation of the original limits on federal power exists than the notorious 1942 case argued before the Supreme Court in *Wickard v. Filburn.*

The **Wikipedia** entry says:

*The Supreme Court **interpreted** the United States Constitution's Commerce Clause under Article 1 Section 8, which permits the United States Congress "To regulate Commerce with foreign Nations, and among the several States, and with the Indian Tribes." The Court decided that Filburn's wheat growing activities reduced the amount of wheat he would buy for chicken feed on the open market, and because wheat was traded nationally, Filburn's production of more wheat than he was allotted was affecting interstate commerce. Thus, Filburn's production could be regulated by the federal government.* (**emphasis** added)

In this case, Supreme Court clearly **re-interpreted** instead of **enforcing** the Constitution. This opinion was the most convoluted, absurdly reasoned and outrageous usurpation of power taken by the Federal Government up to that time. Given its sweep, virtually any activity could then be claimed to lie within the jurisdiction of the interstate commerce clause. Worse yet, it automatically became a legal precedent used by government lawyers in later cases to justify additional federal abrogation of the rights of the People, and further control over the States.

Of course, then and now, a lifetime seat on the Supreme Court rarely means that the incumbent is either intelligent or wise, or possessing the not particularly rigorous mental power required to understand the constitutional ideals and principles so clearly expressed, and the checks and balances on governmental powers so carefully delineated, in the U.S. Constitution.

The Fallacy of Efficient Government

Apologists of such blatant usurpations excuse the Court by claiming that the Federal Government is supposedly more "efficient" in these matters, stating that "we need more efficient government." Even if that was possible, and it certainly is not, as evidenced by countless examples of governmental inefficiency, incompetence and waste, it is a completely spurious argument. The form of government in the founding charter was **designed to be limited, not to be efficient**. The Founders realized that the only way to guarantee wealth generation and general prosperity was to keep the government's hands out of the wallets and purses of the citizens, and out of the way of their exercise of free enterprise.

Efficiency is a desirable attribute in machinery, manufacturing and other technologies, private business, even to some extent in farming crops and raising animals, due to economies of scale, because of the uniformity of the constituent parts. It is an exercise in futility when applied to human beings in large groups, especially when based on collectivist and socialist political ideologies and agendas. In fact, as the number of individuals increases, the efficiency of any governmental organization lessens, as in *"too many cooks spoil the broth,"* and because its efficiency is not based on voluntary exchange of labor and the profit motive.

The most efficient human behavior is carried out by **self-reliant, sovereign individuals, and groups of them working co-operatively in voluntary exchanges of labor for mutual benefit and profit.**

Add another person to the equation and there is always the need for discussion and compromise. That invariably slows down any process or action. Ask any married couple! That inescapable factor in human behavior multiplies as a group grows. It loses more and more cohesiveness as the number of persons increase. At a certain point, at around one hundred persons, and unless the organization has a single function, the group efficiency, even in private endeavors, plummets even more steeply. The greater the number of functions added to a single group, the greater the inherent inefficiency.

Government bureaucracies are particularly noted for being inefficient. As I have already pointed out before in this book, centralizers and usurpers always resort to inverting the meaning of words to justify themselves. Thus, what they call "efficiency," is actually abysmal inefficiency on a massive scale.

Anyone with a spark of intelligence realizes that no person thinks or reacts exactly (or even moderately) like another. This has been conclusively proven, time and time again. Even genetically identical siblings think differently. I discuss the fallacies embedded in any social and philosophical theories of collectivism, socialism and communism, in Chapter 8. The repeated failures of political centralization are all the proof that any rational individual should require. The latest example is the unfolding collapse of the European monetary system and economic union.

Therefore, any consideration of so-called "efficiency" was intentionally left out of the organizational plan of our Republic and the Federal Government. The Republic was intended to foster maximum independence of thought and action by the individual citizens of the various states. Because a central government is inherently inefficient, the Federal Government's powers were strictly curtailed. Otherwise, the efficiency of the individual, the building block of any society, would be impeded. The Founders had observed and studied human behavior in every one of its aspects. Basic human nature has remained essentially unchanged throughout recorded history. Citizens can only thrive and prosper if they conduct their lives with an absolute minimum of governmental interference.

As Albert Einstein later stated so well:

All that is valuable in human society depends upon the opportunity for development accorded the individual.

So-called political and governmental 'efficiency' was considered extremely dangerous and counterproductive prior to the Civil War. Since then, often justified by the ideological pressure of nationalism and socialism, so-called "efficiency" in government has consistently demonstrated that it is inimical to justice, individual freedoms and liberties. The history of the 20th and early 21st centuries is inescapable proof. Average federal spending is now 2.5 times larger as a percentage of GDP than prior to 1930.

Italy and Japan each adopted "efficient" governmental systems in the 1920s, continuing to expand their centralized powers into the 1930s. Germany joined them in 1933, when the National Socialist (Nazi) regime took power. By the late 1930's, and through the middle 1940's, humanity was enmeshed in the convulsion of World War II, the effect of the illogical extension of those "efficient" totalitarian and militaristic regimes. After that war ended, the Soviet Union, another centralized power, seized the opportunity to absorb large areas of Eastern Europe into its "evil empire." In 1949, communists took over China and proceeded to drive that country further into the dirt.

The only 'efficient' characteristic of those governments was death, and the debasement of their surviving population into slaves of the State, except for a tiny minority deemed *"more equal,"* along with a *"Great Leader"* in supreme authority.

Many countries are still infected by socialism in one of its many disguises. They suffer the resulting economic malaise, along with the usual abrogation of the rights and the freedom of action of the individual. The United States is only a step or two behind them. China and India have to some degree learned half the lesson. They are quickly trying as much of the free market as they can possibly stand, mostly driven by the need to feed, house and clothe over a billion people each, so that they do not riot and kill the rulers.

At first, the centralization of political organization, money, credit and the economy gives the illusion of being efficient. But it inevitably fails. To

308

avoid just such a fate, the design of the Republic was neither "unitary" nor "efficient."

Why are there three co-equal branches in our constitutional government, along with a further bicameral division of the Legislature? That was done to prevent the Federal Government from combining the three separate functions of governance into a single tyrannical unit. The constitutional checks and balances were put in place in the design of the Republic precisely to avoid the false "efficiency" of centralization.

The U.S. Republic's conceptual framework thus avoided the creation of a monstrous "supreme authority," such as the General Secretariat of the Soviet Union. The centralized authority that the Soviets "efficiently" used to murder, or deliberately starve to death, millions of their own citizens.

So why are we allowing an Imperial Presidency of our own to develop, with its annual operating cost of nearly $2 billion?

An *"efficient national government"* is **directly opposed** to the best interests of a citizenry that is a *"free and independent people."* The Federal Government was purposefully restricted to prevent an involuntary and coercive system. Because the present Federal Government has been allowed to circumvent the system of *"checks and balances"* in the Constitution, our economy is in dire straits, and our individual rights and freedoms are under continuous assault.

State Constitutional Development

Just like the citizenry, each state was originally understood to be *"free and independent"* of the Federal Government in their internal affairs that fell outside of Constitutional jurisdiction. The States have their own separate constitutions because each state is its own country. Each one has its own government, culture, social mores, economy, philosophy and relations with other states based on their desire and understanding of **their own best interests**, restricted only by the limits voluntarily agreed to under Article I, Section 10 of the Constitution. In addition, each state was guaranteed a *"republican form of government"* (Article IV, Section 4) without any requirement to conform to any other state.

Many state constitutions are similar but they are never identical. New states joining the Union often picked clauses from the constitutions of pre-existing states. However, they always shared in common the clauses granting restricted delegated powers to the Federal Government. Otherwise, there were no requirements to conform to each other, or to the U.S. Constitution, in their chosen form, organization or structure of government.

There were four phases in the development of state constitutions. Those of the 13 founding states, those that joined after Independence but before the Civil War, those that joined after the Civil War into the early 20th Century, and lastly, Hawaii and Alaska.

While there are some variations in each of those phases, due to unique circumstances, there was a common pattern adopted and employed from the very beginning.

For example, as long as a state followed the common provisions delegated in Article I, Section 10, it is free to rewrite its own constitution, in part or completely. Many state constitutions contain clauses stating that it is the state's duty to do so. That is because, just as written in the Declaration of Independence, there may be a compelling necessity to do so:

> ... *whenever any Form of Government becomes destructive of these Ends, it is the Right of the People to alter or abolish it, and to institute new Government* ...

The original design of the Constitutional Republic allows every state to retain its power to resist any "overreach," any attempt to enforce a law on a state that is clearly outside the limited scope of power granted by the States to the Federal Government.

Regardless of how many times the Federal Government exercises its usurped powers outside of constitutional limitations, no matter if a state has previously acquiesced to such usurpations, or if such usurpations happened long ago, any sovereign state may recover any, or all, of the powers that it **voluntarily** delegated to the Federal Government.

310

Inherent Nullification and Interposition by the States

Decisions by Supreme Court justices, or declarations of executive power by government officials, whether they are elected or appointed, cannot abrogate the power of the Sovereign Citizens, or the States, over the Federal Government. The 9th and 10th Amendments make that crystal clear. The People are sovereign and through them, the States. The People hold the supreme power over both the States and the Federal Government. This is the constitutional foundation stone of the rule of law versus the rule of man. No matter how many times the People's rights and sovereign powers have been infringed or usurped, the People still retain them.

Nullification is the exercise of a process reestablishing the People's unalienable and alienable rights and the States' sovereign powers. Interposition places the power of the State between its citizens and the Federal Government, whenever and wherever the feds attempt to impose un-Constitutional Acts on any citizens in the State.

The Supreme Court's present role as arbiter in subjective morality disputes such as abortion, marriage, human sexuality, social welfare cases and the like, or on the issue of interstate commerce that is being abused as a consequence of its *Wickard v. Filburn* ruling, lies completely outside the scope of the powers assigned to it in the Constitution.

By its reliance on **stare decisis** (the abbreviation of *stare decisis et non quieta movere*, meaning "*to stand by decisions and not disturb the undisturbed*"), the Supreme Court compounds the problems created by its earlier errors of judgment. As noted earlier, the Supreme Court's 1942 blunder in the case of *Wickard v. Filburn.* served as the thin end of the wedge allowing the Federal Government to further intrude and interfere in the affairs of the Sovereign States.

The Supreme Court protects even its own flawed precedents through *stare decisis.* However, that has no force or effect on the People, or the States, if present day rulings are based on prior precedents that were clearly unconstitutional. Only lawyers trained in legalism in law schools, where the spirit of the law has been supplanted by situational ethics and subjective morality, would continue to insist on enshrining judicial errors

311

as immutable legal precedents, despite the ever-compounding mischief that ensues.

The engineering discipline expects exactly the opposite. Errors in design and implementation are corrected as soon as they are found in the review process.

The Supreme Court continues to operate outside of its Constitutional jurisdiction, as in the recent ruling that granted and affirmed political free speech "rights" to a non-person in *Citizens United v Federal Elections Commission*. That apparently compelled Republican presidential candidate Mitt Romney to make the obviously foolish statement that "… *corporations are people.*"

Despite the Court's nonsensical ruling, the plain fact remains that **governments and corporations have no rights**. Only people, sentient living beings, have rights. Imaginary "rights" created by courts are legal hocus-pocus. The courts apparently fail to realize that they are daily eroding their credibility with such nonsense.

Commercial speech is defined and limited by the nature of a particular commercial activity. Artificial entities such as governments and corporations may be delegated certain limited powers, as agreed to by the parties involved. However, any extensions of those powers must be confined within the context of those previously delegated powers. They are not inherent in an artificially created legal entity. Only Sovereign Citizens enjoy rights **protected** by the 1st Amendment. Corporations are legal fictions, nothing more or less than artificial constructs. People are sovereign individuals with unalienable rights automatically conferred on them by being alive. Governments and corporations are not alive, something obvious to the average first grade student, if not to the legal profession and the judiciary.

This definition by Ayn Rand may prove helpful:

A 'right' is a moral principle defining and sanctioning a man's freedom of action in a social context. There is only one fundamental right (all the others are its consequences or corollaries): a man's right to his own life. Life is a process of self-sustaining and self-generated action; the right to life means the right to engage in self-

sustaining and self-generated action—which means: the freedom to take all the actions required by the nature of a rational being for the support, the furtherance, the fulfillment and the enjoyment of his own life. (An excellent summation of the right to life, liberty and the pursuit of happiness.)

The *Citizens United* decision was inevitable because of all the prior contradictory mishmash of **stare decisis** precedents from which the Court made its bizarre and convoluted ruling. The only way to unravel that particular mess is to toss out all the nonsensical precedents leading up to that ruling. Then corporations would be properly limited to their commercial speech role. The State of Montana did so decades ago. Now cities and other states are jumping on board to stop corporations from reaching into areas beyond commercial speech. No U.S. Supreme Court decision can make it otherwise—unless the States acquiesce.

Emulating Montana's earlier action on commercial speech, is a present day opportunity for other states to exercise their power of nullification.

As already mentioned, neither the passage of time, or prior acquiescence by the States, grants more authority to the Federal Government than what was originally delegated to it. If the boundaries laid down in the U.S. Constitution, and its legitimate amendments, are crossed over, such additional assumptions of authority are usurpations of power and are therefore null and void.

The States have to "Grow a Pair"

This brings us to what may seem a surprising conclusion. If the Supreme Court issues an opinion outside of its jurisdiction, as spelled out in Articles III and VI, that opinion has no real legal standing. It does not matter how many prior precedents the Court has relied on in its ruling, or even how old those precedents may be. For example, *Wickard v. Filburn* dates back 70 years. The Court's opinion may be justifiably ignored by the States since the rulings are unconstitutional.

When the States realize that unconstitutional rulings are invalid, then perhaps the justices will revert to their assigned mandate per the provision of the Constitution. Until then, why should they? In order to exercise the 9th and 10th Amendments, the States have to *"grow a pair"* of *cojones.* As long as the States roll over and acquiesce, the federal bulldozer will keep moving ahead and flatten them.

The Supreme Court was not designed to self-regulate its own power. Nor were the Legislative and Executive branches of government. However, just as with the other two branches, the Court is constrained by the rights and powers of the People and the States. The Founders built in those constraints, along with the checks and balances between the branches, because they recognized that folly, guile, corruption and deceit are part of human nature. Honesty, integrity and principled behavior are not automatically guaranteed when obviously fallible human beings wear black robes and sit on the Court. What is seen in TV courtroom dramas every week, with judges portrayed as wise and all-knowing, is pure fantasy!

No state has to go to the Federal Government, or to federal courts, to ask for permission to act on any issue where the Federal Government has no jurisdiction. That is simply a waste of time and money. It confers no additional legitimacy when a state seeks relief from non-constitutional actions by filing lawsuits in federal courts. If it is already unconstitutional authority, what practical purpose does that serve?

There are already inherent dangers because of the fallibility of judges when courts are acting within their legitimate constitutional authority. Giving the courts and judges the opportunity to make rulings in subjective areas of subjective controversy on issues that have nothing to do with objective morality, such as committing murder and theft, is begging for trouble and getting it. Rationalizing that those we elect, or who are appointed, will automatically act in the citizens' best interest is being incredibly naive.

Would anyone seek court relief in a **private** matter knowing that the judge worked for the other party? That is essentially what happens when states seek relief on a public matter in the federal courts in areas where the Federal Government clearly has no authority. Is it any wonder that they almost never win such cases?

314

The concepts of "judicial independence" and "judicial restraint" are fictions. Is it not routinely assumed that a nominee to any of the federal courts, including the Supreme Court, is either "liberal" or "conservative," or in reality a Democrat or a Republican, and therefore not objective or independent? Since they are obviously appointed for political reasons, how could they ever be impartial in a conflict between the States and the Federal Government since they are members (and paid their salaries) by the latter? There is an obvious conflict of interest!

In the entire history of the Republic, rarely has there been a truly impartial judge. Those on the Supreme Court, and in the lower courts, are flawed human beings, just like the rest of us. Putting on a black robe confers no special dispensation from being a fallible human being. They have their own personal agendas and viewpoints. That is why the Founders carefully considered and wrote down the rules designed to limit their powers.

As Thomas Jefferson put it:

In questions of power, let no more be heard of confidence in man, but bind him down from mischief by the chains of the Constitution.

When a tough decision is required, each justice will nearly always favor the ideology of those who appointed him or her. They will not consider the citizen taxpayers, who ultimately are the source for their salaries, and from whom their power flows. They will not base their decisions on strictly objective **theoretical** constitutional principles that are in stark contrast to their ideological biases, or their subjective beliefs. They will chose to please those who appointed them, making decisions based on their ideology.

That is exactly why the Founders embedded a system of checks and balances in the Constitution. It seems that the Founders were far more astute about typical human behavior than most present day citizens.

Article III, Section 1 of the Constitution states that:

*... the judges, both of the supreme and inferior courts, shall hold their offices **during good behavior** ...* (**emphasis** added)

315

Their only role is to adjudicate cases falling within their jurisdiction, and to do so solely on constitutional grounds. Rulings that fall outside of their jurisdiction, must be addressed by either the Legislative or the Executive branches. There is no doubt about it. The Judicial branch has often failed to remain within its constitutional mandate. This is also an indictment of the Legislative and Executive branches who are likewise failing to fulfill their own responsibilities in the Constitution's system of checks and balances

Now it gets very interesting.

As I have already written in previous chapters, the Founders based the Republic's constitutional form of government on natural law and attendant rights. Those are described in Wikipedia as being:

> ... *rights not contingent upon the laws, customs, or beliefs of any particular culture or government, and therefore universal and unalienable.*

If natural rights are *"universal and unalienable"* then how could a split decision determine the constitutionality of a case? Surely it is a matter of either yes or no?

Having a majority opinion, as opposed to a unanimous one, in a constitutional case, is a logical absurdity.

For example, is the applicability or validity of the Law of Gravity subject to personal choice or majority vote? Gravity is an objective truth. Everyone who has jumped off a cliff to prove differently, quickly learned their error.

Furthermore, if all nine justices agree on the constitutionality of an issue, does that make it any more than just a legal opinion? Is it now "The Law of the Land?" Of course, it is not. It is the law of the case. Another case might give rise to a different conclusion. However, the constitutional principles remain the same. Otherwise, they are not principles.

A Supreme Court opinion, on a question of law that is outside of the Court's jurisdiction, cannot be binding on any person, or state, even if the opinion is 9 to 0. It is just an opinion, every bit as subjective as one you or I might have. It may be interesting, perhaps even persuasive, but it is certainly not constitutional. Since such an opinion is outside the Court's mandated jurisdiction, how could it be otherwise?

Article III, Section 2 of the United States Constitution is clear about the areas of jurisdiction assigned to it:

> *The judicial Power shall extend to all Cases, in Law and Equity,* ***arising under this Constitution***, *the Laws of the United States, and Treaties made, or which shall be made, under their Authority; to all Cases affecting Ambassadors, other public Ministers and Consuls; to all Cases of admiralty and maritime Jurisdiction; to Controversies to which the United States shall be a Party; to Controversies between two or more States; between a State and Citizens of another State; between Citizens of different States; between Citizens of the same State claiming Lands under Grants of different States, and between a State, or the Citizens thereof, and foreign States, Citizens or Subjects.* (**emphasis** added)

With this explicit language, it is clear that the Founders had no intention of creating a court that could override citizens' natural rights or redefine those rights. The Court's sole mandate is to enforce them.

The Supreme Court should only issue Unanimous Enforcement Orders and then only in cases where the need for enforcement falls within the Court's constitutional area of jurisdiction. That jurisdiction should be scrupulously and comprehensively explained at the outset of each enforcement order, referring to specific clauses of the Constitution. The fact that the Justices have never done so is most revealing.

Look at the procedure in criminal trials by jury. It is accepted that if a jury cannot reach a unanimous decision, then a mistrial is declared, or the defendant goes free. A judiciary using majority opinion to determine legal issues is deeply flawed. It is similar to having "majority science," where natural laws are decided by random opinion, not specific, proven and verifiable facts. An opinion is nothing more than the Court's subjective belief. Therefore, it does not have the force of law.

If the Court cannot arrive at a unanimous verdict, then the issue must be referred back to Congress. Only the Legislative branch of government has the constitutional mandate to enact laws. The issue may require a Constitutional Amendment separately initiated by the States or by the Congress.

We have allowed the Judiciary to stray so far from their mandate, and their responsibilities and enumerated duties, that they are now busily re-interpreting, and thus subverting, the foundational laws of this Country that were so carefully considered, after considerable research and lengthy debate, by the Founders.

Amendments are the Only Interpretive Process Allowed in the Constitution

Most legal scholars, lawyers, judges and legal experts will not appreciate the plain truth that the Supreme Court's sole responsibility is to enforce the law's constitutional principles. Its role is not to re-interpret the meaning of the Constitution in order to manufacture convenient excuses to meddle in issues that lie outside of its mandate. Judicial 'activism' or "*legislating from the bench*" has no constitutional legitimacy whatsoever, no matter how high-sounding, well-intentioned or cunningly disguised the "rulings" may be.

There is only one way that the enforcement of the charter creating the Republic may be changed. That is through the amendment process. The powers granted to any branch of government cannot be extended or broadened without being properly amended. Any other exercise of authority not specifically identified in the Constitution, and its **properly ratified** Amendments, are illegal usurpations of power that are automatically non-binding.

The difficulties inherent in the amendment process were deliberately embedded into the Constitution. It was intentional! Any possible amendments were to be very carefully considered, and then thoroughly debated, to prove that they truly served the best interests of the People. Amending the Constitution was not to be taken lightly. That is the essential point that most people want to ignore. If it was easy and convenient to ensure that we are always free and independent, then this Country would be called the "Utopian States of America."

The usurpers depend on the forgetfulness, and the apathy, of citizens who have lost the will and discipline required to prevent the encroachment of their natural rights by the Federal Government.

The Myth and Fallacy of the Living Constitution

Too many believe in the canard that the Constitution is a *"living document"* that must flex, bend, adjust and be contorted to 'suit the times.' Nothing could be further from the truth. Not understanding the timeless and universal principles incorporated into the Constitution, or not comprehending the reasons for its intentional limitations on government powers, and then failing to apply the discipline required to enforce and preserve it whole and intact, allows it to be systematically debased and increasingly ignored.

Only a tiny fraction of the elected officials at the state level understand their own powers in relation to the Federal Government. That is a huge contributing factor in the continuing abrogation and erosion of state powers. A few states have passed Sovereignty Resolutions but these are mostly feeble pleas to *"please leave us alone."* Almost none have passed any true Acts of Nullification.

In April, 2010, I testified on behalf of Colorado Republican State Senator Kevin Lundberg's State Sovereignty Resolution. This experience quickly confirmed my observation that most legislators are ignorant about the Republic's guiding principles. They have no real comprehension of how it was originally designed to work.

Immediately after I had completed my testimony, Democrat State Senator Bob Bacon said:

The whole idea of "state's rights" is dead. That horse left the barn a long time ago.

If he was correct, the U.S. Constitution has already been voided.

If he was correct, there is no Republic, and thus no federation of sovereign nation-states.

But he was dead wrong.

Despite what he and others may contend, the rights and powers of the People and the States never left the barn, **they are the barn**. All that Bacon and like-minded legislators can do is hope to somehow burn it down.

Senator Bacon's expressed point of view was shared by enough of the other Democrats seated on the review committee to ensure that Senator Lundberg's resolution was shelved. Unfortunately, the same attitude prevails in many other state legislatures.

We are not already living in a totalitarian state only because a few constitutional restraints on the government are still being applied by the Courts and Congress, almost in a spirit of nostalgia for the America that once was. We are now perilously close to losing even those token limitations on the growth of absolutist power centralized in Washington, D.C., something that will be the ruin of us all.

It is a total fiction that the Founders created a *"living document"* when they designed and implemented the Constitution. That is demonstrably false because the Constitution is based on **timeless and universal ideals and principles that protect natural rights that are self-evident.**

There is never a need to redesign a good design, only enhance it. Of course, the urge to tamper, manipulate, complicate, exploit, control and profit by self-serving "improvements" is irresistible to most career politicians. That is why the Founders made the amendment process so difficult. They were only too aware of human frailty. It was only by using outrageous deceit, and outright fraud, that the 16th and 17th Amendments were—supposedly—ratified.

In the satirical words of P.J. O'Rourke, some years ago:

Giving money and power to government is like giving whiskey and the car keys to teenage boys.

State Senator Bacon, and others like him, would greatly benefit from reading Michael Holler's excellent book, *"The Constitution Made Easy,"* published in 2012.

With so many people like Senator Bacon sitting in state legislatures across the Country, will those states ever actually pass Acts of Nullification to begin the process of restoring the Republic?

It had better happen very soon!

If the States do not regain control of the Republic that they formed, all three branches of the Federal Government will continue to impose their unconstitutional will on the citizens. When that coercive and centralized system eventually collapses, as it inevitably will, and the citizens learn the truth about how comprehensively they have been betrayed and swindled, a violent civil war could ensue. Will there be Democrat suicide bombers, and Republican death squads, roaming the streets? Read history, look at current events around the World, and remember that *"civilized man"* is just a veneer whenever manipulative, tyrannical governments are involved. Matters can, and do, get ugly very fast when pushed to the extreme.

It was our superb Constitution that shielded us from the multitude of horrors perpetrated on millions of our fellow human beings in other countries, both in the past and in the present.

The U.S. Constitution Cannot be so Casually Cast Aside!

During my testimony in September, 2009, to the panel of the State Powers Summit with the Republican Study Committee of Colorado, I made the statement that nullification is the only solution, and is the primary tool to reestablish state sovereignty. I noted that all other attempts, including lawsuits, resolutions and constitutional amendments, had or will fail for a variety of obvious reasons. Worse yet, those attempts usually direct attention away from the central issue of state sovereignty.

A *"respected Constitutional scholar,"* Professor Robert Natelson, responded that nullification **was not politically acceptable**. He expressed the view that the majority of citizens do not perceive any dysfunction in the current relationship between the States and the Federal Government. Furthermore, he stated that the Federal Government *"has all the nukes."*

I responded that even if many people are unaware of the problem, that still does not absolve a state legislature from its inherent responsibility to do its part in restoring the Republic. I then asked him if he did indeed believe that the Federal Government would launch a nuclear strike against a state that had passed an Act of Nullification. He merely shrugged.

Later on, in a private conversation between us, he indicated that he was "*just joking*." However, there is almost always an element of truth in any jest. Have the States already unconditionally surrendered to the supposed overwhelming might and majesty of the Federal Government? If not nukes, perhaps the Federal Government will send in the Army or its armed agents? If what Natelson implied proves to be true, then the Republic is already dead. We might as well accept that the States are subservient to the "national" government and that the citizens are no more than serfs. Then it is just a matter of time before the "national" government rounds up newly identified "dissidents," such as the author of this book, liquidates them as "subversives," or incarcerates them in concentration camps. What will **Amerika's version of Auschwitz** or **The Gulag** be called?

In a recent email that he sent me, the professor took the lawyerly path of obfuscation, insisting that nullification is "extra-Constitutional." How he can believe that a process mechanism, so clearly delineated in the organizational structure of the Republic, could be "extra-Constitutional" is beyond belief. To heck with the clearly expressed division of governmental powers in the Constitution, and the 9th and 10th Amendments! Prior to the writing of the Constitution, where Natelson is seemingly unable to spot any innate justification for nullification, a mere nobody named Thomas Jefferson, as part of a committee of five nonentities such as Benjamin Franklin and James Madison, wrote yet another defense of the right of nullification:

*We hold these truths to be **self-evident**, that all Men are created equal, that they are endowed by their Creator with certain **unalienable Rights**, that among these are Life, Liberty and the pursuit of Happiness —That to secure these Rights, Governments are instituted among Men, **deriving their just Powers from the Consent of the Governed, that whenever any Form of Government becomes destructive of these Ends, it is the Right of the People to*** *alter or to abolish it, and to institute new Government, laying its Foundation on such Principles and organizing its Powers in such Form, as to them shall seem most likely to effect their Safety and Happiness. Prudence, indeed, will dictate that Governments long established **should not be changed for light and transient Causes;** and accordingly all Experience hath shewn that Mankind are more disposed to suffer, while Evils are sufferable than to right themselves **by abolishing the Forms to which they are accustomed.** But when a long Train of Abuses and Usurpations, pursuing invariably the same Object evinces a Design to reduce them under absolute Despotism, **it is their Right, it is their Duty, to throw off such Government, and to provide new Guards for their future Security.*** (**emphasis** added)

Poor deluded Thomas Jefferson, and his equally befuddled fellow Founders, apparently did not know *"that the horse had already left the barn!"*

Are you one of the many who believe that those words are meaningless? That they do not direct a course of action to be taken when the dire circumstances of the People cry out for a change?

Our Last Due Process Mechanism

A multitude of justifications have been invented for the Federal Government's regulations, laws, agencies, programs and spending that cannot be found, either directly or implied, anywhere in the Constitution. These fabrications have been *"stitched together"* over time by either deliberate or unwitting usurpations.

Could it be that Professor Natelson cannot see the obvious in the Constitution, concerning nullification, simply because he does not want to see it? It is a well-known phenomenon that most people see what they want to see, and hear what they want to hear. With so many of the Federal Government's actions being, in reality, non-constitutional and therefore truly "extra-Constitutional," perhaps it is understandable that he has trouble with terminological exactitude?

In point of fact, the recourse of nullification and interposition is inextricably woven into the governmental structure of the Republic, as laid out in the Constitution. In the Preamble to the Constitution, the States determined *"to form a more perfect union"* not a more perfect "nation." We must understand, and be very clear, that this means that the States had no intention of being subsumed under a central (national) authority. They are sovereign entities in their own right, voluntarily federating together with an agency, the Federal Government, to serve them, not to be their master.

The Declaration of Independence, the construction of the organic Constitution and the 9th and 10th Amendments, fully support the case for nullification and interposition. There can be no doubt that it is the last, and the best, due process mechanism left to the People, and to the States. Otherwise, the sort of central government that we have seen in Nazi Germany, Soviet Russia, and Communist China has taken root. That form of authoritarianism will inevitably imprison or execute any individuals who dare to dissent.

The hour is late. We have no other choice. It is the only strategy that will work. The *"checks and balances"* of the three branches of the Federal Government have failed due to neglect, malice, negligence and acquiescence.

Bringing a suit before the Supreme Court is pointless since it has no legal jurisdiction in such matters. Furthermore, even if a state still brought such a suit before the Court, and actually won the case, it would only reinforce the notion that the Court has such jurisdictional powers, when it clearly does not. In fact, it is counterproductive to involve the Supreme Court. It is already meddling in matters far outside of its constitutionally mandated role. The Roberts' Court decision on the *"Patient Protection and Affordable Care"* Act ("ObamaCare") should have slammed the door on pursuing that course of action at any time in the future.

What about negotiating with the Federal Government's agencies to reduce their presence and undue influence on the States? That is completely backwards. The Federal Government, and thus all of its agencies, is subservient to the States in the governmental structure of the

Republic. Therefore, if the branches of the Federal Government are exceeding their authority, or are not performing satisfactorily, they should be effectively fired, just as the owner of a business fires an employee whose performance is inadequate or delinquent. Furthermore, if a state is dependent for funding from a federal agency, with money taken from the People in the first place, how could it possibly have any leverage in the process of negotiation, unless it first abandons its dependency?

What about substituting an Interstate Compact? It could work to a degree. However, that may also create an inversion of the proper relationship of a state to the Federal Government if it was not used very carefully. In any case, Congress would be required to vote on any such Compact. As virtually everyone is now aware, Congress is completely dysfunctional. Going by that route would likely be another exercise in futility, unless it was properly constructed to stave off any Congressional interference.

Do You Have the Courage of the Meeting Hall?

In this moment of our greatest peril, enough concerned citizens must firmly grasp and effectively employ the two tools of self-governance that are still available to them. Those tools are self-education and the meeting hall. It will take concentrated effort to re-learn the fundamentals of our constitutional form of government. Once so informed, then every citizen must consistently exercise their right, and their responsibility, to participate every day, and in every way, in local councils, commissions, caucuses, conventions, legislatures and elections, **culminating but not ending at the ballot box**.

If people do not have the *"courage of the meeting hall,"* they had better be prepared to have the *"courage of the revolution."* The latter eventuality will be the unavoidable consequence of failing to take action now in the grass roots restoration of our now faltering system of constitutionally safeguarded governance.

Our present government, accustomed to waging war all over the globe, will deploy its active military and militarized *"law enforcement officers"* against its political opponents. Remember all those German

325

Jews, and middle-class Russians and Chinese, who thought that barbarism was a thing of the past? How could that happen in civilizations where Goethe and Beethoven, Tolstoy and Tchaikovsky, and Lao Tzu and Confucius, had lived and breathed? Care to put yourself in the shoes of the Syrians of today in a country where a desperate regime is willing to do anything to preserve itself?

Here and now, in *"the land of the free,"* the Federal Government, engorged by years of accumulating powers through collectivism, centralism, nationalism and statism, is only benefiting the few at the expense of the many. Those who are presently in power will fight like cornered rats to preserve their power, prestige and perks. When the lies and false promises of the Welfare/Warfare State can no longer be sustained, and the whole artificial edifice crumbles with millions left destitute, those now running the Federal Government will turn to violence against the citizens to "save" the subverted Amerikan "nation" that they created. Opponents will be labeled as subversives and terrorists. The powers-that-be will then claim that they had no choice but to *"restore order"* for *"the common good."*

Realizing that such a scenario could happen, should not deter freedom-loving citizens from doing their duty. If anything, it should strengthen their **determination to keep it from occurring**.

It is time for the People and the States to stand up and demand: *"NO MORE!"*

For too long, we have been like the frog that will not jump out of a pot that is being gradually brought to a boil. That is because *"… it is not that bad!"* The welfare/warfare state, the nanny state, the dependency state, or whatever Big Government is called, must be dismantled so that we can rebuild and restore the Republic. We are now being slowly boiled to death by looters, manipulators and usurpers.

This is not wishful thinking, or a wistful longing to return to the 18th Century. Supporters of constitutionally-limited government do not want to turn the clock back. We want to set it right. The Republic, as originally designed and constructed, could have been improved and refined. By now it could have been extremely effective in the 21st Century, a marvelous example to the rest of the World. Instead, it has been subverted and converted into a gigantic, over-reaching and dysfunctional mess that looks like all (if not worse) the other failed experiments in governance of the past and present.

Politicians, and supporters of the Federal Government's expansion, are fond of saying that *"adults need to be at the table,"* in order to solve the Country's problems. By now, it should be clear that **they are the unwatched children playing with matches**. The real 'adults' are those who realize the immensity of our peril, who understand that the States must therefore reassert their powers over their servant, the Federal Government, through the constitutional process of nullification.

It is not the States, or the People, who actually created the mess. It is their designated agent, the constitutionally subservient Federal Government, that is the 'problem child.' The process of nullification required to reset the clock, has nothing to do with secession as critics do, and will, claim. Nullification is the final "fail-safe" mechanism that the Founders wisely provided as a remedy should the Federal Government overreach itself, thus upsetting the system of checks and balances in the allocation of powers incorporated in the Constitution.

A concerted and determined movement to implement state nullification and interposition must get under way soon. Lovers of liberty must educate their peers to understand that this strategy is our best and last hope of restoring the Republic. They must ensure that their local and state elected officials enact nullification ordinances to counteract the current, and ever increasing extra-legal and non-constitutional incursions by the Federal Government into local and state affairs.

As part of this growing movement, one good bumper sticker on every concerned citizen's vehicle(s) might be:

Support Your Local Constitutional Sheriff!

Anyone joining the Military takes the following Oath of Enlistment:

*I do solemnly swear (or affirm) that I will support and defend the Constitution of the United States against all enemies, foreign and domestic; that **I will bear true faith and allegiance** to the same;*

*and that I will obey the orders of the President of the United States and the orders of the officers appointed over me, according to regulations and the Uniform Code of Military Justice. (**emphasis added**)*

Thanks to my upbringing, the moral principles instilled in me and such knowledge as I had so far accumulated, I took that oath seriously. I still adhere to it today. Although I no longer have to follow the lawful orders of the President, or the *"officers appointed over me,"* I have found that there are many domestic enemies and adversaries. Indeed, throughout our history, even during the Revolutionary War, they have existed within our population.

The first group of enemies is the looters, profiteers, usurpers, manipulators and self-aggrandizers, whom Cicero so aptly characterized over 2000 years ago, actually embedded within the government itself. Their goal is a tyranny that they control. The second group of our adversaries is the incompetents, the ignorant, the uninformed, the complacent, the dependent, the lazy and the spineless. They only want to get something for nothing while doing nothing.

The first group controls the second group by ensuring their dependency on government largesse. Obviously, neither group has any interest, or motivation, in restoring the Republic, one that is emphatically not conducive to their misanthropic goals.

Because of the active resistance of the first group, and the dead weight of the second, it will be an enormous task to save the Republic and then pass it down in healthy condition to later generations of Americans.

Because of the 16th and 17th Amendments, along with Supreme Court rulings in cases such as *Dred Scott v Sanford, Wickard v. Filburn, Citizens United* and many others, it will not be easy to unravel the web of errors and deceits that have entangled the Country.

If the Federal Government and the duopoly of the two major political parties actively prevent the efforts of the sovereign citizens and the Sovereign States who seek to cure America's malaise via peaceful due process, such as nullification and interposition, then violent revolution is inevitable. To prevent great suffering and needless devastation, a much better solution is to understand that state nullification is the best tool to restore the Republic to viability, thus ending the Federal Government's, and the Federal Judiciary's, trespass and abrogation of citizen rights and state powers.

*Note: As this book was being prepared for publication, the Supreme Court did indeed issue rulings in the SB-1070 case, the Montana Corrupt Practices Act and the Patient Protection and Affordable Care Act. All rulings prove once again that all three branches of the Federal Government are dysfunctional. The minority, dissenting opinions in each case, clearly illuminate the extent of the deep-seated and counter-productive dysfunction.

19

An Agenda to Protect the People and the States

The Americans will always do the right thing ...
after they have exhausted all the alternatives.
–Winston Churchill

Those who make peaceful revolution impossible,
will make violent revolution inevitable.
–John F. Kennedy

For further guidance, let us look again at this passage in the Declaration of Independence:

*We hold these truths to be self-evident, that all Men are created equal, that they are endowed by their Creator with certain unalienable Rights, that among these are Life, Liberty and the pursuit of Happiness —That to secure these Rights, Governments are instituted among Men, deriving their just Powers from the Consent of the Governed, that whenever any Form of Government becomes destructive of these Ends, **it is the Right of the People to alter or to abolish it**, and to institute new Government, laying its Foundation on such Principles and organizing its Powers in such Form, as to them shall seem most likely to effect their Safety and Happiness. Prudence, indeed, will dictate that Governments long established **should not be changed for light and transient Causes**; and accordingly all Experience hath shewn that Mankind are more disposed to suffer, while Evils are sufferable than to right themselves by abolishing the Forms to which they are accustomed. But when a long Train of Abuses and Usurpations, pursuing invariably the* *same Object evinces a Design to reduce them under absolute Despotism,* **it is their Right, it is their Duty, to throw off such Government, and to provide new Guards for their future Security.** *— Such has been the patient Sufferance of these Colonies; and such is now the Necessity which constrains them to alter their former Systems of Government.* (**emphasis** added)

The Federal Government, with the connivance of the Federal Reserve, has so greatly transgressed the bounds set forth in the Constitution that, among other issues of paramount importance, it has put our monetary system, indeed our entire economy, in extreme danger of catastrophic collapse. If we do not act to reverse this situation, our government will have, in addition to wrecking our financial system, also destroyed our entire way of life.

Since such a government is obviously reckless and unaccountable, contemptuously disregarding and discounting the proper role of the States in restraining it, then such a government no longer represents the best interests of the citizens. Our duty as sovereign citizens is to restore the constitutional limitations on the Federal Government's powers, and then work to repair the damage already created by its abuses of power.

Obviously, we should have never arrived at this low point in the Country's existence. However, since there is no avoiding the problems, and this is **our government**, we have to cure the underlying causes of its misbehavior, and treat the effects of its misbehavior, just as we would deal with behavioral problems in our own family, community or town.

Even if catastrophic destruction is avoided, the restoration of the Republic must be accomplished in a way to guarantee the improbability of any future Federal Government misbehavior and abuse of power. The one and only way to ensure that is by the maximum ongoing participation by a 'critical mass' of citizens who actively and responsibly maintain their oversight of this Country's governance, just as originally conceived and set into motion at the Constitutional Convention in 1787. This means that any further reliance upon the "vote and walk away" method, of trust in those who hold office, must absolutely and irrevocably end.

If nothing is done, the fiscal excesses, and the counter-productive entanglement of state governments with the Federal Government, will cause immeasurable damage when the entire system unravels. When the misguided monetary policies, and fiscal budgetary excesses, cause the dollar to implode during the next few years, we will learn that having done nothing now to prevent it from happening, or at least mitigating its worst effects, will prove to be the worst of all possible inactions. (Refer to **Modality of Inaction #4**)

Delaying until the fiscal implosion is actually underway, before making any attempt to fix it, is akin to taking apart a Boeing 747 that is in-flight, but falling out of the sky, and trying to rebuild it into a 787 Dreamliner to prevent it from crashing!

As noted in the passage from Ludwig von Mises, quoted in Chapter 5, the coming fiscal correction is not a matter of **if** but **when** and **how**. If the States do nothing to prepare, there will be prolonged mass chaos. It would be a less disruptive event if the individual states enact various measures to protect themselves **now**. In my opinion, it is already too late to ensure a careful and systematic "*orderly retreat.*" Unfortunately, the restoration process should have begun years ago.

However, there is still a choice between two alternative scenarios. We could suffer a Soviet-style breakup with many nasty consequence, from which the Russians are still trying to recover, or we could do something more intelligent, reasonable and constitutional.

In information systems, we use the phrase "cutover" to describe the process of shifting from an obsolete system to a new or upgraded one. It often is not pretty. For example, when Virgin America shifted over to its new airline reservation system in the fall of 2011, the resulting temporary chaos created many flight delays and a great number of disgruntled passengers.

As state legislators and governors become increasingly aware of the coming fiscal implosion, and realize that it is now inevitable and unavoidable, they will have to determine what "cutover" options will work best in their states to mitigate the worst effects.

The ongoing disassembly of the Euro monetary system, possibly even the European Union (EU) itself, will be instructive. However, the coming changes in the EU, will be far less fundamental in their effects because the countries in the EU are more sovereign than the American states are (at present) in their relationship with the Federal Government. In addition, the Euro is neither the world's largest reserve currency, or pegged to the price of oil, as is the U.S. Dollar in the world market.

Obviously, making any systemic changes will meet resistance. That will come in the form of everything from *"That's crazy!"* to *"That's not the way we do things here"* and *"Not invented here."* Not only will those entrenched in the status quo need to be persuaded, or replaced, but there will be the even harder task of gaining cooperation between ideological opponents.

But there is no dodging this bullet! Either comprehensive changes are made to protect each state, and the process of restoring the Republic begins, or this last chance to preserve individual freedom will pass into history. The next centralized power structure that arises from the ruins of the present one, will be much more coercive and absolutist. It will be justified by saying *"you see, that nonsense of a Republic with a sovereign citizenry is total bunk."* If history has taught us anything, it is that the systemic failures of one form of oppression is followed by worse, as with Imperial Germany eventually morphing into Nazi Germany, Czarist Russia into the Soviet Union, and many other such examples.

As our fiscal and economic implosion proceeds, the States will have only two options. Either legislators will see the need to abandon political myths, biases and fallacies, and actually take concerted action to protect their state and its sovereign citizens, or they will do nothing. In the second case, their state, tethered to the Federal Government, will be pulled over the cliff and into the abyss. Each state needs to cut its umbilical cord to the Federal Government before it is too late.

In life and death situations, people (and legislators are people, too) have often achieved the seemingly impossible, figuratively snatching victory from the jaws of defeat. Motivated by the need to survive and prosper, negative situations have quickly been transformed into positive outcomes. This perilous moment in history calls out for unselfish effort, and great deeds, so that freedom and liberty will be experienced and enjoyed by all Americans in the future.

Every state's economy, and the degree to which it depends on the demand for its products and resources, is unique. Each state will have to put into place separate contingency plans for the imminent deterioration of global commerce. That breakdown will be the consequence of an artificially propped up global currency system along with the various failed and fraudulent attempts to revive it.

For some states, concentrating first on domestic internal economic recovery will be the best course of action. Later, the ways and means to strengthen external trading relationships with other states and foreign countries can be addressed. For states with large international trading relationships, their options on how to protect themselves will be more difficult and chancy.

Watching how the EU handles the economic situations in Greece, Ireland, Italy, Portugal and Spain will be instructive, although hardly a blueprint for the United (but separate) States to follow.

In early 2010, the author developed and introduced a series of ideas for the Colorado legislature to consider. It took the form of an agenda of resolutions that could be followed. To the best of my knowledge, there has been no other similar effort made elsewhere, except in a piecemeal fashion. The resolutions were intended to make the loss of financial ties to the Federal Government system less chaotic when the worst happens. This agenda of resolutions is far from complete but serves as a starting point. Other concerned individuals are invited to amend them as necessary, and also add additional ones.

Firstly and foremost, a state should retain any monies that would otherwise be forwarded to the Federal Government but which do not serve a constitutional purpose. Those funds would be retained by sequestration at the state level. Each state must reduce its dependence on so-called *"federal aid"* and take over those programs deemed necessary by both the citizens, and their representatives in the state government. The sequestered funds would allow the States to enact and to fund, at the state level, various programs now being provided by the Federal Government, unless they wish to terminate those programs.

335

Secondly, they must prepare to replace Federal Reserve Corporation Notes with their own private exchange-based systems along with the establishment of state-based banking.

There are certain concrete steps that each state must take, including:

- The passage and implementation of a Federal Mandates Act whereby each state would review every federal program that is currently enforced within any state. The review would determine each program's validity, impact and, most importantly, constitutionality. Following completion of the review process, the States would gradually phase out the federal programs found to be outside of federal jurisdiction per the U.S. Constitution.

- The protection of any **intrastate** manufacture, distribution, initial sale, ownership, possession and transportation of products from any federal **interstate** regulatory interference. This issue has already been addressed, in small steps, by states declaring that firearms, and other items manufactured or grown in their state, and owned by residents of that state, are free from federal regulation or other interference. Similar issues, such as the medical use of marijuana and drivers' licenses are already being identified as not being a part of **interstate** commerce, and therefore not in the Federal Government's constitutional authority to regulate. In effect, this neutralizes the Supreme Court's absurd decision in *Wickard v. Filburn*.

- The termination of all federal interference and taxation on prospecting, testing, exploring, drilling, extracting or distributing any mineral, oil or gas resources that do not fall under the Constitution's original meaning of "*interstate commerce.*"

- The protection from federal regulation, or other interference, of **intrastate** production, manufacture, distribution, initial sale, ownership, possession and transportation of any so-called "drug" or foods.

- The incremental divestment of funds held by local, county and state governments consisting of any and all U.S. Treasury bills, notes or bonds. That would continue until no such funds are held by the end of three years (starting in 2013) and/or until such time as the Federal Government returns to hard asset-backed money, and practices fiscally responsible debt assumption and issuance policies. Successfully resolving all these issues will likely require the passage of a constitutional amendment limiting deficits, as well as the issuance of governmental debt, to fixed (constitutionally mandated) percentages of this Country's GDP.

- The gradual reinvestment of those released funds into low to medium risk, highly liquid investments that are transparent and audited. That should include at least 25% invested in precious metals funds, or in actual physical holdings of such metals whenever practical. They would be held in protected and audited storage facilities. Reinvested funds may also be invested in state-issued securities, and high-quality private equity positions, whether in state or out-of-state, as fiduciary requirements may allow.

- Establishing a state-based private banking system that could perform some of the functions outlined above, along the lines of the State Bank of North Dakota, through which all state assets are deposited and administered. Those assets will become the initial reserve for that bank. The bank may be self-insured, or privately insured, but it may not be a member of the Federal Deposit Insurance Corporation (FDIC) or any other federal financial or banking insurance program.

- The passage of a bill such as Colorado's SB12-137 that recognizes and ensures the legality of payment of debts, public or private, in gold or silver coin as directed by Article I, Section 10 of the U.S. Constitution.

- Enacting laws that provide for the use of private electronic Digital Gold Currency exchanges. Such exchanges should be similar to those specified by HB09-1206 (introduced in the Colorado legislature in 2009) or HB10-1155 (introduced there in 2010). These exchanges are to be established and become operational within three years. They may be used by any political subdivision of the State for the payment of, or refund, of taxes electronically.

- The immediate repeal of all statutory authority granted to the Federal Government to deploy any National Guard troops to any duty outside the boundaries of a state, excepting those lawful calls to duty authorized under Article I, Section 8, Clause 15 of the Constitution, namely *"to execute the Laws of the Union, suppress insurrection and repel Invasions."*

- Ending any monetary or administrative involvement in any federal program or agency connected in any way with the spurious and insane *"War on Drugs,"* the Endangered Species Act, the Clean Water Act, and any extensions of the Environmental Protection Act.

- Ending all unconstitutional incursions in a state's **intrastate** commerce and wildlife management by negating the use of the Supreme Court's decision in *Wickard v Filburn* or in any federal wildlife laws. Wildlife and plant control are to be only within the State's jurisdiction whenever present within its borders, whether migratory or not. It should, at most, only be affected by compact between the States themselves, and should not involve the commerce clause of the U.S. Constitution. Any illegal extensions of that constitutional clause in a state's affairs should be instantly nullified by the Governor, with any necessary steps to nullify or interpose undertaken by both the State's Legislature and Attorney-General.

- Notifying the Federal Government that any attempt to pursue an investigation (of any kind), or to serve a warrant within the State, or any of its subdivisions, shall only be allowed with the knowledge, permission and participation of the appropriate peace officer agency within that state or subdivision. (See Chapter 17)

- Begin the transition of those portions of currently-held federal lands, especially in the Western States, to state control and ultimately to private ownership. Such lands include those held by the U.S. Departments of Agriculture and Interior which are not already designated as national parks, monuments or wilderness. During the process, the States will review federal lands designated under the American Antiquities Act of 1906, or by executive order, on a case-by-case basis for inclusion or exclusion from this transition. The purpose is to 'extinguish' title and dispose of all unappropriated land, within the next ten years, as directed under the Enabling Act for each state constitution. For more information, please see The American Lands Council at http://thecitizenslaststand.com/alc and the work of state Representative Ken Ivory of Utah and his HB-148.

What Happens When the Feds and Nationalists Resist?

When the States proceed as outlined above, agencies of the Federal Government will doubtless take active steps to protect their supposed "interests." Their responses may turn violent.

Nationalist interests will certainly seek to characterize such actions by the States as dangerous anarchism and subversion. They will most likely disregard any initiatives taken by the People to be free of the Federal Government's illegal interference and its abrogation of their unalienable rights. If there is even the suggestion of using force by the Federal Government to maintain its supposed "interests," such a suggestion should be an alarm call and rallying point for the People.

A number of federal agencies have for decades built lists, created plans and developed responses to grassroots movements for freedom and liberty. They have already classified patriots, certain conservative and libertarian groups, returning veterans, military retirees, Constitutionalists and others, as potential "*domestic terrorists.*" These plans will no doubt be ramped up in response to any actions undertaken by the States as suggested and outlined in this book.

When peaceful and lawful ideas, suggestions, agendas or actions, such as those proposed here, are viewed as "dangerous," then it is an obvious sign that tyranny is already in our midst. It should therefore be assumed that, no matter how peaceful or lawful such actions are, the Federal Government, and its agencies, will respond with violence. As history and current events demonstrate, if a coercive and centralized government perceives a real threat to its power, it will incrementally respond with increasing ferocity.

In such a confrontation, it is highly unlikely that an order to "*stand down*" will be issued to the agencies on the offensive. In fact, it is likely that they will plant agent provocateurs to incite any situation so that they can justify the use of force. They have done so before. They will do it again. They will also probably increase punitive enforcement measures to provoke a response from the States. That is a characteristic behavior of all authoritarians. They always expect to be obeyed without question, whether or not they have legitimate authority. The citizens of each state must be ready to respond with peaceful resistance. The tyranny of the Federal Government must be broken by exposing its moral depravity and coercive behaviors as, and when, it is put to the test by the lovers of liberty and freedom.

There will undoubtedly also be incidents engineered (false flag events) to purposely provoke some hotheads into violent resistance. There is a long history of that behavior by various federal agencies. The urge to fight force with force must be resisted at all costs, except when it involves actual self-defense of the People. The Federal Government's duplicity, and illegal actions, must be highlighted and exposed by clearly peaceful means. Violent resistance will direct attention away from the primary issues and, furthermore, be used to justify reprisals by the government. The use of the Internet, and other social media, will be invaluable to expose inappropriate behavior by the government, just as has recently been the case in other authoritarian countries around the globe.

This agenda to restore the Republic by the action of the States will be difficult both to enact and implement. It will take foresight, determination and flexibility. No one plan is sufficient to reverse our Country's slide into tyranny and guarantee the safe return to our foundational ideals and principles. Those who hijacked the Federal Government for their own purposes have been propagandizing, and implementing their nationalist agenda, outside of constitutional bounds, for over a hundred years. This cannot be resolved overnight. The most important thing is for enough citizens to wake up, educate themselves and stop their naive, or unconscious, support of the government's patently Un-American Agenda.

Naturally, it would have been much better if the citizens, and the States, had resisted federal encroachment more than 70 years ago when it began in earnest. It would have been easier if the public education system had not been hijacked by the progressive statists and authoritarians. It would have been easier if the fourth estate, the supposedly "free" press, had not been co-opted, purchased or intimidated. Let our hindsight be our foresight as we move ahead from our present situation.

The awful certainty of what will happen, if nothing is done to reverse course, should galvanize all of us into action to ensure that it can never happen again. Let us reaffirm the principles of natural law and unalienable rights, and the concept of the Sovereign Citizen, and the Sovereign State, so that we are once again a truly *free and independent people*," not the superficial, kept and dependent people that we most assuredly are now.

It is worth emphasizing, and repeating, that strictly limiting the Federal Government, by restoring its Constitutional bounds, is not an attempt to weaken the United States. That is what the nationalists would have everyone believe. On the contrary, the restoration will strengthen the Republic that has been compromised, and seriously weakened, by allowing nationalism, statism and creeping socialism to run rampant.

It is in our power to restore the Republic to a hitherto unimagined glory that will serve as inspiration for all of mankind. Let us do it!

20

So ... What Do We Do About the Feds?

If you do not change direction, you may end up where you are heading.
–Lao Tzu

In large part, the problem of the existing Federal Government will be resolved as a consequence of its own internal collapse. The devolution of the Federal Government, into its present monstrous shape and size, actually planted the seeds for its inevitable disassembly. Its own inertia guarantees that the disassembly will occur in a series of predictable milestone events. As discussed in previous chapters, the Federal Government's two greatest liabilities are its counter-productive, hyper-regulatory mechanisms and its unsustainable debt load. Prevention is no longer the cure. These issues required decisive action, no later than 10 years ago. The beast is muscle-bound due to excessive exercise of unconstitutional regulatory powers. Its insatiable thirst for funding has sucked the financial well dry.

The preceding chapters outlined a plan to minimize the damage, and clean up the wreckage, by taking pro-active steps at the State and local level. At the Federal level, there is very little that can be done now, except to watch it disassemble itself on the world stage.

Its political and administrative functions will essentially implode when it can no longer sell additional debt to anyone, not even the Federal Reserve. There will be no money to pay salaries of government personnel and contractors. There will be no checks or direct deposits for those receiving Social Security, and government assistance, unless the authorities go the route of massive inflation. Congress used accounting trickery to "buy-down" all the published deficits since 1992. It used

343

surplus Social Security and other funds, to the tune of $4.5 trillion in "warrants" (IOUs), and placed the monies into the general fund.

Would someone buy what remains? It will have no real market value because what is owed is vastly greater than any intrinsic value, and already can never be repaid. Perhaps all the buildings, and the land that the Feds control, could be turned over to the creditors for a nominal sum to recoup a fraction of a cent on the dollar? I say this largely in jest because, of course, the U.S. currency would have become essentially worthless.

Several basic functions of the Federal Government must necessarily be maintained throughout this period. One of them is the mutual defense of the United States. Our military forces will have to be reduced to a manageable and realistic size, without loss of its essential potency and effectiveness, in order maintain the defense of the Country against true external threats. The debt, and the accompanying fiscal and monetary issues, will follow their own course to resolution in a series of emergent systems.

The primary task we face in restoring the Republic will be fending off any attempts by totalitarians, Neo-Conservative statists, or Progressive Neo-Liberal authoritarians, to fill the vacuum with even worse forms of centralized control.

Doing absolutely nothing, while the existing government unravels, is inadmissible. However, it bears mentioning that a plan encompassing everything that **needs to be done** may well seem like an **impossible wish list.** Taking into account all the obstacles and inertia that must be overcome, to say nothing of the inevitable controversy and resistance, makes it so.

At a minimum, to avert the worst of what will otherwise occur in the next 10 to 20 years, the following 12 steps **should be taken** either immediately, or as soon as possible, in a methodical 'phase-down' of much of the Federal Government apparatus:

1. By whatever means possible, slash federal spending by $1 trillion in hard dollars in 2013. Continue cuts in spending until a true balanced budget is achieved no later than FY2016. Balanced budgets must be

mandatory every year thereafter via an amendment to the Constitution—exclusive of a war being **declared** to defend the United States from an imminent and **real** external threat.

2. Conduct a comprehensive audit of the Federal Reserve. Then initiate its phase-down and eventual termination, in order to enable the growth of emergent monetary and exchange systems which will evolve in a truly free market. Immediately abolish all "legal tender" laws currently propping up the supposed exchange 'value' of Federal Reserve notes. Amend the Federal Reserve Act to invoke operational transparency of the Bank for Congress, institute monetary competition, and limit any power to create fiscal damage, until the time when the Federal Reserve is dissolved.

3. Repeal the 16th Amendment and replace the federal income tax with a consumption-based tax. But only do so **after** accomplishing a balanced budget through spending cuts. The percentage rate of the consumption tax will be determined by the needs of a severely scaled-down Federal Government, and the creation of a debt pay-down plan, completed within 10-15 years, or following the repudiation of the accumulated federal debt.

4. In concert with the spending cuts, begin an immediate phase-down of U.S. military presence in foreign lands that are not **vital** to actual external American defense. Then reduce naval forces until a level of military preparedness is achieved that is sustainable and reflects this Country's actual strategic defense needs. Retrain, restructure and redeploy military personnel with revised and updated requirements that enable a potent and effective defense from actual external threats. The undeclared Global War on Terror will become redundant when the U.S. military reverts to its original mandate as a defensive force.

5. Reduce Embassy functions to the level necessary to support our citizens overseas, provide visa and immigration services, and coordinate peaceful commerce between our sovereign states and all others. Retain full Embassies only in those countries that recognize and support equal two-way reciprocal trade and security agreements. Any nations that do not will only warrant Diplomatic Accessibility

Missions. Phase-out all "foreign aid" and loan guarantees for arms purchases, along with overt and covert military assistance, to any foreign states not recognized by reciprocal treaties as our formal allies.

6. Begin the immediate phase-down of all but the most critical and essential "social safety net" programs until only those citizens in true need are being helped. All remaining federal programs will be turned over, and block-granted, to the States until a complete takeover, under state administration and using state revenues, is possible. Establish a deadline to either completely phase-out those programs within the States, or establish a timetable for the total transition of federal programs to individual state control.

7. As part of, and in concert with, points 4-6, Congress will abolish all departments and agencies of the Federal Government, including those originated or maintained under any "rational basis" court test rulings, that do not derive from direct Constitutional authority. Otherwise amend the Constitution to allow their continued existence and operation, but only with the correct constitutional principles allowed and employed.

8. Begin the transition to the States of all federal lands that are not part of National Parks, Monuments and certain designated Wilderness or Primitive Recreational Areas (determined on a case-by-case basis). Repeal the Endangered Species Act, the Clean Water Act and any other Acts or policies (in part or whole) that are found to usurp state authority. The one-size fits all approach, as presently conducted at the federal level, is impractical, arbitrary and wasteful.

9. As a follow on to item 8., the States should be the originators of any compacts, managed by adjoining states, intended to achieve goals for conservation, pollution and clean water, as common needs between affected states dictate. The States should also ensure that tort claims, at every level of each state's court and the federal system, are quickly and efficiently processed and adjudicated.

10. Repeal the 17th Amendment and return the U.S. Senate to its foundational role as each state's representation in the U.S. Congress, as originally intended.

11. End the War on Drugs to assist in securing our borders since complete decriminalization is THE ONLY remedy. This 'War' is encouraging the extreme profits made from trafficking illegal drugs by dealers, distributors, growers and manufacturers. It is 'law enforcement' that keeps it growing rather than cutting it back. Abolish the DEA, BATFE, TSA and the portions of HSA that are not directly involved with border security and monitoring. All other functions of external defense should be conducted by the DoD.

12. Discontinue all subsidy and welfare support for illegal immigrants to assist in securing our borders. Institute effective foreign worker visa programs to ensure that every guest worker has appropriate insurance, bonding, licensing and identification to work in the U.S.. Each guest worker will register and then pay, based on their income, an annual fee (along with all applicable taxes) to renew their visa, so that the foreign worker visa program is self-supporting.

Obviously, the 12-step program outlined above can only be implemented when there is complete and widespread recognition that the Federal Government, as presently constituted, is encumbered by a large number of systemic and institutionalized problems. Until such time as it is completely rehabilitated, and returned to its contracted constitutional mandates, so that it can be an effective institution once again, this Country will remain crippled, and the deterioration of our well-being will accelerate.

Much of this program can be accomplished by the States as set forth in chapters 17-20.

Of course, it would be better if it was accomplished by the actions of Congress and the President. Better yet, would be a scenario where the States and the Federal Government executed such a program by working in concert with each other.

Unfortunately, such enlightened actions are unlikely. The momentum of unfolding events suggests that it will continue to be a *slow train wreck*. Furthermore, there will be fierce resistance by the entrenched bureaucracies and beneficiaries.

Nevertheless, *"hope springs eternal,"* so I offer up this 12-step program as a way to proactively put the correct actions into motion.

21

The American Remnant

You can ignore reality, but you can't ignore
the consequences of ignoring reality.
–Ayn Rand

Just because you do not take an interest in politics
does not mean politics won't take an interest in you.
–Pericles

There is a principle which is a bar against all information, which is proof
against all arguments, and which cannot fail to keep a man in everlasting
ignorance. That principle is contempt prior to investigation.
–Herbert Spencer

One of the most famous passages in the Declaration of Independence
states that:

> *all men are ... endowed by their Creator with certain unalienable*
> *rights ... among these (is) ... the Pursuit of Happiness.*

Once upon a time, the citizens of the United States inhabited the
freest country in the world. Nowadays, they are no longer especially
happy. The Organization for Economic Cooperation and Development
(OECD) ranks Americans in 12th position on the 'happiness scale,'
behind people in such countries as Australia, New Zealand, Canada,
Sweden and Norway.

Could it be that it is difficult to pursue happiness when one's daily life
is so constrained by interference from all levels of government? Citizens

cannot engage in a single activity without the heavy hand of government, directly or indirectly, involved. The only way to re-establish ourselves at the top of the happiness scale is to greatly reduce governmental intrusions. Otherwise, we will never restore a contemporary version of the "*The American Dream*" or experience the true meaning of the phrase "*American Exceptionalism.*"

Eliminating unwarranted and unconstitutional governmental intrusion and interference in our daily lives, involves much more than voting in elections, or sitting around and complaining. Over the past 25 years, I have attended hundreds of public meetings of home owners' associations, school boards, fire districts, city councils, county commissions, state legislatures and also the U.S. Congress. I have volunteered for, and been appointed to, planning, budget, tax, community and ad-hoc committees. For decades, in every political cycle, I have participated in party caucuses, assemblies and conventions, as well as numerous political campaigns and city, county and statewide petition drives. I even worked as a paid field director for three states in a formal presidential campaign.

What did all that effort accomplish? Not much of immediate usefulness, I am afraid. That is because, in almost all those situations, I found that the level of fundamental and general understanding, and participation in our political system, by most of the population, is appallingly deficient. Those attending were usually people seeking something from the government, or wanting their representatives to provide something for them. Government can only give something away by first taking it from someone else. Government cannot produce. It can only consume. But those who understood this paradox were rarely in attendance. That is why it has been so easy for politicians to "*take care of business*" out of sight of most of the electorate.

Yet those years of activism did result, as also happened with the small percentage of other people similarly engaged, in creating the state of mindfulness required to tackle the greatest political task of our time, the restoration of the Republic.

There is a dawning awareness, by a growing segment of the population, that the present socio-political and economic systems are thoroughly corrupted, debased and ineffectual. That is evidenced by certain segments of the Tea Party and, to a much lesser degree, in the Occupy Wall Street movement.

On average only about half of those registered to vote do so in national elections. In local and state elections, the percentages are even lower. Worse yet, 30+% of the population who are eligible, never register to vote or participate in any fashion in the political process.

After an election, those who did take the time to cast a vote, usually cease participating any further. Career politicians, and the bureaucrats that they have enabled, are then left unmonitored to carry on with complicating our lives and feathering their own nests.

Elected and appointed officials busily enact more and more layers of government in response to the so-called "needs" of those seeking benefits, and desiring something for nothing. The result is government's insistence that we conform to endless rules and regulations, fill out numerous forms, and pay for licenses to start a business, to add on to our homes, to place our kids in schools, to see a doctor, to get a loan, to run a farm, to hire new employees, and so forth and so on, ad nauseam.

If *"taxes are the price we pay for civilization,"* as Oliver Wendell Holmes wrote, then the loss of happiness is the price that we are paying for a government that restricts our freedom and endlessly infringes on our liberties.

To illustrate, how many people have experienced the shock of discovering that obtaining all the consumer items that they desired did not translate into happiness? In fact, it harmed them. Why is that? Buying on credit, as most people do, creates an enormous burden of debt that is often nearly impossible to service, much less to pay off. The resulting financial drain, on their income and financial reserves, leaves them feeling trapped, creating great emotional turmoil and constant regret.

A very similar scenario is playing out with the government. In fact, it is now in the end game. Citizens buying into the false promises of the government to relieve them of the various burdens of Life, and shield them from its harsher realities, are rapidly realizing that the government cannot deliver on those promises. In fact, the government has brought us to the edge of ruin. Its reckless and unaccountable behavior now threatens not only our way of life, but our lives themselves.

This is the first generation in American history whose children will not "*have it better*" than they did. Our children will not have more freedom and liberty, or more material wealth. It is very likely that they will have far less. They will be the generations confronted with the lesson that "*there ain't no such thing as a free lunch.*" They will, in fact, be forced to pay for the free lunches already provided to, and consumed by, preceding generations. Talk about the sins of the parents being foisted on their children! Of course, it is completely unfair. It should impel any rational citizen to roll up his or her sleeves to resolve this mess as expeditiously as possible, even if doing so only partially mitigates the effects on succeeding generations of Americans.

More than 43 cents out of every dollar of the Gross Domestic Product (GDP) is spent by government. (For those of you who are skeptical, visit http://thecitizenslaststand.com/GDP.)

That wealth was essentially confiscated from individual citizens in the form of taxes, fees and licenses. Every dollar that goes into the government will invariably generate less than a dollar in return. That same dollar released into the private sector generates a 3 to 5 times return, and even more in certain high-tech fields. Simple math therefore tell us that our GDP could have been many times larger than it is today. And that loss of actual wealth generation, does not include the tens of millions of man-hours spent in complying with governmental regulations in every part of the economy. It does not include the cost of lost productivity when standing in lines, or waiting on the phone, in order to deal with government agents or clerks. With government consuming close to half of the country's economic output, it should be clear how counter-productive and destructive it has become. Not only is it destroying our prosperity, trampling on our freedoms and liberties, but it is robbing us of our rightful pursuit of happiness, too.

I have already quoted economist Herbert Stein's memorable and accurate statement that "*if something cannot go on forever, it will stop.*" The real question is how will it stop? Will it stop suddenly and catastrophically when the bond market finally recognizes that the government is insolvent, and then stops lending it any more money? Will it stop when the Federal Reserve refuses to create any more fake money to buy the government's worthless bonds, so as not to destroy itself in the ensuing inflation? Will it stop when the government takes total control of the entire economy, and begins assigning jobs to freshly graduated high school and college students in lieu of payment on their college debt? Or will it end through the actions of a determined and knowledgeable few who successfully begin to exercise their rights, and compel the States to exert their constitutionally mandated powers over the Federal Government?

If you are still reading these pages, you should by now have no confidence whatsoever that this situation can be resolved painlessly and completely peacefully. Believing that there is some magic potion that we can imbibe, or that a fairy godmother will wave her magic wand and make everything better, is the sort of wishful thinking that prevents people from undertaking any constructive actions to prevent their own destruction. Such has been the fate of so many people and countries in the 20th Century.

President Obama has repeatedly stated that his goal is to *"fundamentally transform America."* The question to ask is **into what?** He and his team have conclusively proven that they have never had an original thought in their lives, following another administration that had very, very few. They are compounding the mistakes of previous administrations by expanding on them. Doubling the government debt in three years is the same *"throw money at it"* problem solving *"quick fix, long-term pain"* technique that can never, ever, work in the long run.

Obama has proven, at least to his own satisfaction, that he was born in Hawaii. What he apparently discovered there, growing up, was how to surf. What he is doing now is riding the wave to complete the process, set into motion years before his administration, of subverting the Republic into a centralized, nationalist and socialist state. He is just riding that wave. He does not control it. He just looks good. (Well, maybe, he does not but he is trying to find the inside break.)

That misbegotten transformation has been going on for decades. Neither Obama nor his advisors know enough about simple economics, money management or human behavior and action (praxeology) to know that he has no chance of completing that distorted goal. There simply is not enough good money on two planets to pay for the implementation of his Marxist-tinged "*Dreams of My Father*" to turn this country into a total Welfare Hyper-Regulatory State.

Likewise, most Republicans do not comprehend that there is not enough good money on two planets for their alternative version of a total authoritarian Warfare State.

Because of the political duopoly's twinned hallucinations, the present day "Warfare-Welfare State" is unaffordable to even an economy that is twice the size of ours. No amount of fake money creation can change that fact.

In order to approach affordability, present day government spending must shrink **by at least 40%.** That can only happen if we begin the process of constraining the Federal Government to its proper limited functions, as mandated in the Constitution.

Once that has been accomplished, all the debt already accumulated must be paid down to zero. There is only one reason why the illogical revenue ruse of "spending more than we have" has continued so long. It has been enabled by the creation of fake money by the Federal Reserve, and by borrowing other people's money to make up the difference. The portion borrowed now exceeds 40 cents of every dollar being spent. One key part of the long-term plan to solve this catastrophic fiscal mismanagement is to terminate the Federal Reserve, so this unsustainable situation can never be repeated.

As I near the end of this book, I have to ask you, the reader, some tough questions:

> Are you one of those rare individuals willing to do something?

> Are you willing to step out of your comfort zone, resist the Modalities of Inaction and get into the fight?

> Are you willing to risk the convenience and ease of your current life, perhaps even risking your life?

This is not hyperbole. I am not trying to be dramatic. I have heard every excuse under the sun during the past twenty-plus years:

- "It is too hard." If you think this is hard, try federal bankruptcy or debt enslavement to foreign governments and rich investors.
- "I don't have the time." Make some.
- "I'm too busy at work (… or school, home, with kids …)" Who isn't?
- "I don't like politics." Neither do I.
- "Board meetings are boring." So liven them up!
- "I'm not good at this stuff." Neither was I.
- "I don't know how it works." Ditto.
- "I already voted and paid my taxes. What else do you want from me?" OMG!

The actual list of excuses is endless. It is nothing less than outright refusal to shoulder the responsibilities that go along with accepting the benefits of **being free**. You stand on the shoulders of those who sacrificed for over 300 years so that we could have what we have. If you wait for others to fix problems that are approaching and **will** affect you, you will die waiting.

The choice is down to one alternative. It is either summoning up the courage to face a meeting hall today, or summoning up the courage to face a violent revolution tomorrow. Unwillingness to engage yourself now, virtually guarantees that the second event will occur. Is it not obvious that the former will be a *"walk in the park"* as compared to the latter's *"ride through the valley of death?"*

Look around the world and at our own history. Do you really think that a bloody revolution, or another civil war cannot happen here, just because they already occurred once before? Are we so special that we are magically exempt? Are we excused from the consequences of **our** government's bad behavior and **our** apathetic behavior as citizens? Are we somehow immune from the fact that the worst aspects of human nature, that innate potential to perpetrate horrible acts of murder, mutilation and torture, are still the same as ever?

As our economic situation continues to deteriorate and government benefits end, mobs will form on our streets, just as they already have in Europe. The natural laws governing economics **cannot be violated for**

much longer without severe consequences. The currency, bond and other debt markets will ultimately respond to the reality of the profligate spending of our government, and its reckless promises to pay creditors with other people's money and/or fake currency created out of nothing.

Mobs in the streets will give the Federal Government the excuse it needs to resort with violence. That will be applied to anyone who questions or resists its claimed authority. We may witness atrocities beyond imagination. Revolutions such as the Arab Spring, the Velvet Revolution in Czechoslovakia, and others elsewhere, provide no sure template for what may be in store for us. During our own Civil War, that pitted brother against brother, son against father, friend against friend, there was no quarter given once the fighting began. Our Civil War killed more of our own people than any other we have ever engaged in, both in proportional terms, and in total numbers. To deny this possibility is to ignore our own history, and the typical human responses to extreme stress.

BUT THAT DOES NOT HAVE TO HAPPEN AGAIN!

The political calculus is amazingly simple. The number of activists, required at each level of government, scales up in a fairly constant ratio.

Only a comparatively small number of activist citizens is required to modify and change the thinking, and the behavior, of local politicians. For instance, in a small town of 50,000 people, a mere 10 to 20 *actively engaged* people showing up at a council meeting are enough to focus and guide the conversation. If 50 *actively engaged* people show up, and that is just 1 out of a 1000, to make it clear that the council had better think through its decisions and be able to defend them, that can be sufficiently persuasive to achieve a satisfactory conclusion. With a few more citizens than that in attendance, the issue will most likely be solved in their favor, especially if those people then work to remove recalcitrant officials through hardball politics.

If a couple hundred *actively engaged* people show up at the State Capitol, that is usually enough to favorably affect outcomes in Committee hearings. These relatively small numbers will get the ball rolling towards our goal of reviving local politics at the grassroots level, the essential step that will ultimately lead upwards through the levels of government to ensure the full restoration of the Republic.

In fact, the small but essential number of activists turning out for local politics equates to the effect of 300,000 or more people consistently converging on the Mall in Washington, DC. Double that number and the changes are very dramatic.

The real key to success is having people stay consistently engaged after rallies, not simply turning up *"to show the flag"* for critical, or hot button, issues and then vanishing. We also need, behind the most **actively engaged**, another significant proportion of the population that backs them up.

To repeat, all it takes is a few well-informed activists presenting principled positions on particular issues. Yes, that is literally all that it takes. Larger numbers turning up does not initially matter. **Actively engaged and consistent is what counts.** Offering a cogent and well-reasoned explanation is sufficient to direct outcomes. Mostly it involves saying "No!" to the latest cockamamie scheme that City Hall is advancing.

It begins with one individual who is determined and courageous enough to start the process in every neighborhood, town and city. The definition of a leader is the person who goes first. That is all that other like-minded folks are waiting to see. Then they will follow and the process of positive change expands and gains unstoppable momentum.

The Republic was carefully and deliberately designed to protect the rights of the individual citizen from the tyranny of the majority. That tyranny is an ever-present threat, no matter if one is in a union of 3 million, 300 million, 3 billion or more.

Most of us were taught by the 3rd grade that *"might does not make right."*

This Country is Not a Democracy - it is a Republic.

History repeatedly shows that democracies, by their very nature, are unstable and soon turn into the chaos of street mobs that are succeeded by tyrants. Remember that definition of a democracy? It is three wolves and one sheep voting to decide what is for dinner!

One of the challenges we face is that most individuals do not understand their roles as free and independent citizens in affecting political outcomes. Instead, they think and operate as part of a group, waiting to be told what to do. That is because they have been carefully trained in the public (government) schools in group-think. It is therefore uncomfortable for them to take a strong position and risk 'sticking out' from the crowd. That is especially true if that position does not conform to the norm. And so they are cowed into silence.

A cynic would say, after just a few hours of watching Senators and Representatives make speeches in Congress, that the system has become totally dysfunctional. A cynic would say that it does not matter who is elected anymore. A cynic would say that Republican or Democrat, the freak show of blame and counter-blame, and justification and counter-justification, will continue as always. A cynic would say that the government we have is the government that we deserve. A cynic would say that most people do not seem to care one way or the other.

Undue concern about the *"uninformed majority"* is misplaced. Decisions made by ignorant majorities are very rarely, if ever, superior to those made by informed minorities. The one-man, one-vote, knee-jerk approach is easy. Concentrated study, developing an understanding and then forming reasoned conclusions, is much harder. Few are willing to commit themselves. That is why a few knowledgeable and motivated citizens can be so effective because *"knowledge is power."*

The perils of ignorant majority rule is the reason why the word "democracy" never appears in the Declaration of Independence, or in the Constitution. A republic protects the rights and liberties of minorities. That is NOT the case with a democracy. It should be obvious in the different definitions of each one.

Let us once, and for all time, put to rest the canard that our society and civilization is maintained by the government. It is maintained by the willingness of 99 percent of the people to live peacefully together, and to voluntarily cooperate with neighbors and fellow citizens. It is government that is out of sync, keeping the population off-balance with its ruinous policies, laws and failure to deliver justice.

Ultimately, if most people understand, and are exercising their rights and responsibilities, it makes little practical difference if there is a constitution or not. It is merely a document that codifies and guarantees an objectively moral society by explicitly spelling out the **very limited role of government**. The ideal government gets out of the way of the citizens so that they are free to act in their individual best interests, and to conduct themselves as they choose, as long as they do not objectively harm others, who have exactly the same rights and opportunities.

It is reassuring to have the certainty that most people simply want to be left alone to proceed with their lives peaceably, while engaging in the voluntary and harmonious exchange of goods and services with their fellow citizens. Thanks to the guarantees in the Constitution, whether they realize it or not, they would indeed be pursuing their own happiness, enjoying the fruits of liberty and being secure on and in their property. Most people have no intention of hurting or taking advantage of their fellow citizens. After all, they might someday become a customer or be in business together!

It is therefore more than fair to ask, since the vast majority of citizens wish to enjoy peaceful and productive lives, why is the Federal Government passing so many laws, statutes and regulations? Why use the one percent of the population who are unable to co-exist peacefully with their fellows, as the excuse to dictate and regulate the lives of the other ninety-nine percent? The answer is inescapable. The present day government has attached to itself extra-judicial and unconstitutional powers **with the purposeful intent to control.** It is that control that now creates most of the increasing disruptions and unhappiness in the population. It is undeniable proof that the system of governance intended by the Founders has been comprehensively hijacked by usurpers, manipulators, looters, centralizers, control freaks and those that enjoy dominating others. **It could not be more obvious.**

In all of human history, the U.S. Constitution is the best way known to implement a system of governance that harnesses the inherently self-regulating qualities of natural law, and thus permit individuals to maximally benefit themselves, while living harmoniously in the midst of their fellow citizens.

The Preamble of our Constitution proves the point (**emphasis** added):

We the People of the United States, in Order to form a more perfect Union, ***establish Justice, insure domestic Tranquility, provide for the common defense, promote the general Welfare, and secure the Blessings of Liberty to ourselves and our Posterity,*** *do ordain and establish this Constitution for the United States of America.*

Now, take a good look around. Is that what the Federal Government, the Judiciary, and the Congress are actually accomplishing?

Let us take another look at the mindset of the Judiciary that is supposed to be an impartial safeguard, a check and balance, against the usurpation of powers by the other two branches of the Federal Government.

One of the Justices of the Supreme Court, Ruth Bader Ginsberg, someone **entrusted** with a constitutional mandate and role, actually says that she would not look to the Constitution for guidance! What a sad commentary on her individually, something that is likewise applicable to so many others in government, whether elected or appointed. It tellingly illustrates her obvious lack of discernment as to what is desirable in a government **serving** the interests of *"We the people."*

Not to single out and pillory someone whose selection and appointment to the Court was via the agency of an obviously tainted and highly politicized process, and therefore an ideological choice as opposed to an individual of genuine merit. However, by the evidence of her own words, it must be emphasized that the Constitution is based on objective and self-evident principles that she 'evidently' never did, or can no longer, grasp. There can be no impartiality and objectivity in the Judiciary with such persons emplaced in positions of great responsibility, whether "conservative" or "liberal." Chief Justice John Roberts has apparently joined the same club.

The Executive, the Judiciary, and the Legislative branches of government, now each demonstrably and obviously dysfunctional, act in direct opposition to everything that is spelled out so clearly and eloquently in the Preamble to the Constitution.

Carefully consider the following:

- Truly impartial and objective 'Justice' rarely emerges from our contorted and corrupted 'legal system.' It has become a warehouse system to store every cockamamie statute that Congress and legislators dream up to prosecute the People.
- The Judiciary now engages in extra-legal social policy making, as in "social engineering," as well as ruling on subjective morality in areas that are private matters.
- How is *"domestic Tranquility"* insured when overseas adventurism and interventionism has provoked foreign terrorists into revolving-door retaliations at home and abroad?
- The *"common defense"* has become an excuse to wage war, and militarize the world, to profit those controlling the Federal Government and the MIISSC cartel.
- The Federal Government does not *"promote the general Welfare."* It arbitrarily confiscates the citizens' wealth, redistributing it via Ponzi schemes, handouts, subsidies, "investments" and grants to the politically well connected. It then directly jeopardizes the *"general Welfare"* with its fiscally spendthrift ways and financial profligacy.
- Where are the *"blessings of liberty?"* Citizens are hemmed in by walls of laws, rules and regulations, then coerced into complying with them, greatly restricting their freedoms.
- How can our *"Posterity"* prosper when the Country is bankrupted as a result of reckless and unaccountable fiscal and monetary mismanagement?

Regarding the matter of the one percent of the population that are criminally inclined, including terrorists and psychopaths, there is no police state on Earth, even with policemen and policewomen posted everywhere, supposedly observing everything, that is capable of preventing criminal activity, terrorism or senseless acts of murder. It is always seemingly random. The time, place, and even the perpetrators, cannot be reliably predicted. The only certainty is that such will occur.

Fortunately, criminality, terrorism and psychopathic acts of murder are not normal behavior for ninety-nine percent of the population. They have no desire or reason to engage in such activities. Nevertheless, the near useless security and surveillance state continues to grow and grow ever larger.

Politicians, abetted by a kept media and press establishment whose governing principles are that *"only bad news sells,"* and *"if it bleeds, it leads,"* frighten the population into trading more of their freedoms for supposed security. Any promise to guarantee security cannot be fulfilled, even modestly. Such a promise is both illogical and patently unachievable. Benjamin Franklin was absolutely correct in stating that:

Any society that would give up a little liberty to gain a little security will deserve neither and lose both.

The only reason for having a government is to provide a shield of protection for the rights and liberties of the citizens against those who would take them away, whether domestically or externally. Such government is only legitimized when it is instituted *"with the consent of the governed."* The moment that a government fails to protect the rights and liberties of the citizens, who in the first place created and empowered it as their servant, it immediately forfeits its legitimacy. Like a bad servant who has failed to perform his, or her, assigned and agreed upon tasks, and is therefore dismissed by their employer, so it should be with this bad and unruly servant of *"We the People."* There is no denying that our government has failed to fulfill its strictly defined role. In fact, it has stepped far beyond the boundaries to which it was assigned and confined. It has, indeed, become an illegitimate entity.

Many elected and appointed officials, media pundits, columnists and commentators, constantly claim or imply that our rights are **granted** by the Constitution and therefore come from the government. That idea is completely and fundamentally wrong and is totally un-American. Such arrant nonsense should profoundly annoy and irritate every rational and informed citizen.

For the benefit of the aforementioned functional illiterates, who apparently have not read the text of the Constitution, let us make it crystal clear and beyond a shadow of a doubt that **the Constitution only guarantees our pre-existing rights will be protected and enforced.**

And for those who actually believe that governments grant rights, then think again. If that was correct, then a government could **easily take them away!** Fortunately, rights are unalienable and automatically granted to humans by virtue of being alive in this Universe.

I freely admit that there are times when I question the reasoning ability of the average American. Do they have any comprehension of their great good fortune of being sovereign citizens in the greatest republic ever conceived? Do they really appreciate and understand that they are truly unique individuals, in more than just a superficial way? Do they recognize that every person has been gifted with diverse and valuable abilities and talents at every level? Do they know that they once enjoyed unlimited opportunity to explore and express their creativity in this Republic, more so than in any other place on Earth, or at any other time in history?

Then why spoil their unequaled good fortune by depending on the government to confiscate from others to give them something for nothing? Do they have any idea that such dependency, or subsidy, is indefensible on moral or ethical grounds **if** they are able-bodied and mentally competent? Do they not understand the implication of the old saying: "*Robbing Peter to pay Paul?*" Do they have any inkling that they are willingly degrading their own status as sovereign beings into something akin to a family pet or farm animal?

Dumbed down in government schools, children are being trained to believe that they cannot control their own destinies. They are being discouraged from developing any personal initiative, or entrepreneurial spirit, but instead to take their places as dutiful employees of Big Government and Big Business. As part of their indoctrination, they are told that the government will always look after them, as long as they obey it implicitly.

Too many Americans have bought into the lie that every human activity must be controlled by authoritarians spouting social 'moralities' whose only real purpose is to justify the centralization of yet more power under their exclusive control. The majority of Americans are seemingly oblivious that such collectivist and socialist thinking, thwarts the natural self-reliance of sovereign human beings to pursue their own lives through peaceful means, while respecting the rights of others to do the same.

Time and time again, Americans have accepted, as gospel truth, absurd illogical statements from our supposed leaders. Former President George W. Bush said that:

We must abandon free market principles in order to save the free market system.

There is a word to describe such a complete contradiction in terms. That word is **nonsense.**

A majority of Americans have been brainwashed into accepting, the false claim of Malthusian theorists that the 7 billion people now alive on the planet are overloading its "carrying capacity." Therefore, the Earth must be "saved" from humans. In a great leap of illogic, that has been used to justify the sequestration of vast areas, especially in the American West, where the extraction of natural resources could be accomplished systematically and appropriately, under the management of the States and local communities. Such activities, most of which are sustainable, would create prosperity for millions, in turn stimulating the economy of the whole Country.

There is a prideful superiority complex and arrogance that has developed in the minds of elitist "environmentalists." They believe that they know better than the *"hicks and retards"* who will, they say, purposely despoil the areas where they have lived for generations, the very places that they intend to pass on to their descendants. Who in their right mind would intentionally bequeath a private 'wasteland' to their own flesh and blood? It needs to be pointed out that those areas that have suffered the most ecological degradation are those under the 'commons' guidance and control of the government, manipulated by absentee Big Business corporate interests. In ironic counterpoint to environmentalist propaganda, truly private and individually held property more often has a far better record of land and resource stewardship.

In reality, there is no such thing as "Environmentalism." It is a 20th Century ruse, cloaked in 'do-gooder' rhetoric, that is being continuously perpetrated on the population as part of an elitist agenda. On a finite planet with an expanding population, there is in reality only "conservation" and "conservatism." Unless one is ready to submit to forced sterilization and contraception, along with comprehensive population control and reduction (genocide), any belief in human "Overpopulation" is just another aspect of the misanthropic religion of "Environmentalism" that has no practical and achievable outcome.

Mankind is, and always will be, a part of Nature, no matter our apparent level of technological advancement. We are just another expression of Life. Ultimately, our survival will only be assured by finding ways to obtain, exploit and utilize more resources, both on and off the planet, by finding and using whatever is available throughout the Solar System, along with an efficient and economically sound system of conservation here on the Earth that benefits all humanity.

Putting all this into perspective, not a single planet with sentient beings has been found anywhere in our Galaxy, where there are perhaps as many as 400 billion potential solar systems. Furthermore, we inhabit just one galaxy in a universe of perhaps **400 billion galaxies, perhaps more!** Put another way, there might be as many galaxies as there are stars in the Milky Way.

Why are we so shortsightedly limiting our vast potential as possibly the only sentient species in our Galaxy, or possibly in the entire known (and unknown) Universe?

There has been an utterly astounding lack of imagination and vision by the political leadership of virtually all governments throughout history. Time after time, they have utterly failed to make anything but the most token efforts to encourage and stimulate advances in nearly every field of endeavor. The goal seems to be to tax and regulate the best into oblivion, and subsidize the rest into complete mediocrity and subservience. It is grand theft on an almost incomprehensible scale. It has thwarted generations of individuals from making a positive difference, succeeding in their own pursuits of happiness and leaving a legacy to their descendants. All of them have been shamefully robbed of the opportunity of expressing their mental and creative potential, to the vast detriment of Mankind.

Virtually all true 'progress' over the past two centuries has been made **in spite of the dead weight of government, and its often violent and destructive effects.** It both boggles and deadens the mind to imagine what was lost, and where we might otherwise be today. How different our lives would be if governments had consistently gotten out of the way of their citizens, protected the rights of their people, ensured stable monetary systems, and never been involved in the warfare and genocides that led to the premature death of countless millions of individuals. Ever since the time that authoritarian forms of government first enslaved their populations, ranging from genocidal tyranny to the subtle oppression of the social-democrats, humanity has been trapped in successive spirals of self-defeating behaviors. If we had instead continuously liberated our inborn potential, been free of oppression in all its guises, then humans might have already solved the central issue of our long-term survival as a species.

Instead, the single most 'important' endangered species on earth is now homo sapiens.

That statement most likely will shock a human-hating "Environmentalist." Why are we in such peril? Because we have consistently failed to learn from the mistakes of History. Nature can and will eliminate us from the face of the planet in the flash of a cosmic or terrestrial "extinction event," if we do not start focusing on our long-term survival. If we perish from the Earth, it is our own fault.

We should have learned those lessons long ago and moved far beyond our current state of constant warfare, genocide, poverty, depravity, corruption and darkness of the spirit.

As the prophet Isaiah wrote:

Therefore my people are gone into captivity, because they have no knowledge: and their honorable men are famished, and their multitudes [are] dried up with thirst.

Despite all of our unnecessary travails and failures, we nevertheless have compiled a huge store of knowledge that is now easily accessed by virtually anyone. It is a tool that has never existed before. We have a priceless depository of know-how and accumulated wisdom, literally at our fingertips, thanks to the distributed systems of the Internet and social media, a potentially unstoppable means for change that is practically immune to governmental censorship and control. We must take advantage of this once-in-a-millennia civilization changing opportunity. We must not squander this last and best hope of restoring the only governmental system ever designed in complete conformance with natural law and human nature.

We must act now and from now on. We must each fulfill our destiny as sovereign citizens. We do live in **potentially** the greatest country that man may ever know. But only if we make it happen. We must not allow the prison of tyranny to incarcerate us and extinguish the true manifestation of the American Dream. In fact, the future happiness and prosperity of all humanity depends on us. We were once a beacon of hope, enlightenment and boundless opportunity to the rest of the world. We can be so once again!

Recall these two lines (**emphasis** added) by Emma Lazarus and inscribed on the base of The Statue of Liberty in New York Harbor:

*Give me your tired, your poor, Your huddled masses **yearning to breathe free.***

The American Remnant

One of my stated purposes in writing this book is to serve as an inspiration and resource for the "American Remnant." (Look for the original use of the term "Remnant" in Isaiah, Chapters 10 and 11).

The American Remnant is the core group of citizens who still remember and understand the foundational ideals, principles and goals of the Republic. Many of them may not yet be engaged in its active restoration, but they have resisted the irrational ravings of either the Neo-Liberals or the Neo-Conservatives. They consciously realized that neither ideology was beneficial or desirable.

Those numbered in the American Remnant will discover this book by themselves. They are looking for answers and solutions, unlike the passive sheep in our population. If you are part of the American Remnant, this message is for you.

Over the years, I have discovered that it is easy to win debates with neo-liberal progressives defending welfare, and authoritarian neo-conservatives defending warfare. That is because neither group uses verifiable proofs that can actually be rationally debated. Both groups rely almost exclusively on parroting subjective opinions, simply repeating lines from mass mainstream media sources that cater to their ideological mindset. It would be humorous, if it was not so sad, how quickly they become emotional and resort to ad hominem attacks when they are confronted with reason and logic. That always happens, when they immediately run out of coherent answers to questions about where the authority exists in the Constitution, for either a Welfare or a Warfare State. Be prepared for such attacks when you support and espouse the ideas and principles presented in this book.

When a sufficient number of the American Remnant embraces this cause, and make their **individual** and **unique** contributions, then the restoration of the grand American Experiment will truly get underway. It is a process that has been slowly building momentum for decades, and has accelerated during the past 5 years. It will increasingly manifest itself throughout the remainder of this decade.

All power in our representational and constitutional form of government, flows upwards from the sovereign citizens, who empower all levels of governance. It is most *"fit and proper"* that the required changes to rescue the Country, in this time of great peril, will utilize that elemental force known as *"The Power of One."* The Power of One encompasses natural law and the best attributes of human nature. It derives from the action of **committed individuals**. When the cause is just, as it assuredly is in this case, where the restoration of the Republic is in everyone's long-term best interests, then it can be irresistible and unstoppable.

In 1835, John Anster made a very inventive 'free translation' into English of Goethe's masterpiece, *"Faust,"* completed in 1831. In 1906, in an essay entitled *"The Spirit of Work,"* another author expanded on one particular Goethe couplet that Anster had creatively paraphrased from *Faust.* The mountaineer, W.H. Murray, was inspired by that particular essay, and that particular couplet of Goethe's, when writing one particular paragraph in his book *"The Scottish Himalaya Expedition,"* published in 1951.

That sequence aptly illustrates how great ideas and thoughts can not only survive, but thrive as they are passed down through the generations. As they are studied and pondered, their essence becomes ever clearer. Faced with the challenges of creating a new country based on self-evident natural law, the Founders similarly expanded on a wide range of ideas and principles espoused by some of the greatest thinkers of all time. Those are embodied in the Declaration of Independence, the U.S. Constitution and the Bill of Rights.

Our task is to reverse the trend of corruption, perversion and neglect of the distilled thoughts of the Founders, and all of their rightful descendants. By restoring the Republic to its essential place in our lives, we can do our sequential part to ensure that its ideals and principles become **clearer than ever.**

The following excerpt (**emphasis** added) from Murray's book describes the essential attributes of *"The Power of One"* far better than I ever could. It should encourage all of us who, individually, comprise the American Remnant:

Until one is committed, there is hesitancy, the chance to draw back, always ineffectiveness. Concerning all acts of initiative (and creation), there is one elementary truth the ignorance of which kills countless ideas and splendid plans: that the moment that one definitely commits oneself, then providence moves too. A whole stream of events issues from the decision, raising in one's favor all manner of unforeseen incidents, meetings and material assistance, which no man could have dreamt would have come his way. I learned a deep respect for one of Goethe's couplets: **Whatever you can do or dream you can, begin it. Boldness has genius, power and magic in it!**

22

Are You Angry Like Me or Mad Like Them?

A time is coming when men will go mad, and when they see someone who is not mad, they will attack him, saying, "You are mad, you are not like us."
–Anthony the Great (251-356AD)

Never doubt that a small group of thoughtful, committed citizens can change the world; indeed it is the only thing that ever has.
–Margaret Mead

Over the years, I have discussed many of the ideas, principles and concepts presented in this book with some very smart people. Many of them encouraged me to get serious about setting it all down for the American Remnant, the people like you.

Now that I am writing this final chapter, I cannot adequately express my great personal satisfaction in accomplishing the task. It grew ever more insistent and timely as I observed the disintegration of everything that we hold dear about our way of life. My anger only increased at the unprincipled actions that have incrementally despoiled and subverted the greatness bequeathed by the Founders, the Pioneers and our ancestors.

After the terrible events at the World Trade Center on 9/11/2001, I felt compelled to largely abandon my technical career to pursue a life of intense political activism. My loyalty to our Constitution is second only to the love and loyalty I give to my wife and family. When I put my career aside, I thought that many more people shared my viewpoint. I presumed that a lot of those were ready and eager to engage them in restoring the Republic. Well, as it turned out, what they said, versus what they did, were two very different matters.

You Can Talk the Walk, But Do You Walk the Talk?

We have recently reached a critical nexus. The Supreme Court *majority opinion* in the ruling on so-called "ObamaCare," indicates that all three branches of government are nearly, if not already, completely dysfunctional. Instead of fulfilling their constitutional role as checks and balances on each other, they have inverted their original mandates. For many years now, they have been aiding and abetting each other's overreach of constitutional powers by executive fiat, legislative excess, and extra-judicial trespass.

In the opinion of Chief Justice John Roberts, this new mandatory health care system, with its punitive penalties for non-compliance that was created by the White House, and rubber stamped by the then Democrat controlled House and Senate, was justified by the power of the Federal Government to collect taxes.

However, the 'tax' imposed fits neither the definition of a direct or indirect tax that can be imposed under Article I, Section 8 of the Constitution. So Roberts fabricated one out of thin air. What he also failed to consider is that the permission to tax derives from *"the consent of the governed."* **It is not a governmental "right."**

Of course, the Court has previously decided that artificial constructs, such as corporations, also have "rights," another of the many indications that the Country's Judiciary has slipped into a Twilight Zone, where common sense and reason do not apparently apply.

Chief Justice Roberts, and the rest of the Justices who enjoy very generous salaries and benefits courtesy of the taxpayers, might do well to remember who actually pays for their lifetime meal ticket, whenever they stomp all over the rights and liberties of the citizens. His swing vote opinion has now added another burden on the taxpayers. He put protecting the institution of the Supreme Court, ahead of his duty and oath to the Constitution and the People. However, his decision will only hasten the day of financial reckoning when the government will not be able to send out salary checks, including his own!

I had noted the apathy and complacency of the citizenry long prior to 9/11. After that awful event, I was astonished at how it persisted. I am continually amazed that so many people continue to lead *"lives of quiet desperation*" unaware and totally unprepared for the economic and political calamity that obviously lies ahead. They are like deer caught in the headlights of an onrushing car.

Thomas Jefferson wrote:

... all experience hath shown, that Mankind are more disposed to suffer, while Evils are sufferable, than to right themselves by abolishing the Forms to which they are accustomed.

The Declaration of Independence has a particular ordering of rights that were deliberately and carefully crafted to emphasize that without life, there can be no liberty, and that without liberty, there can be no pursuit of happiness. Without happiness there is actually no purpose to life, liberty, or for that matter, the United States.

The Constitution was created "*... to secure the Blessings of Liberty to ourselves and our Posterity ...*" The designated purpose of the Congress, the Executive and the Judiciary, with their enumerated and purposely limited powers, was to ensure liberty. It was not to reduce, or extinguish, Liberty as those institutions are presently in the process of doing, day after day.

The dysfunctional Supreme Court legitimizes virtually every government enlargement brought before it. That results in perversely conferring the illusion of constitutionality on the unconstitutional. As a result of this witchcraft of illogical inversions of truth, the black-robed priesthood of Justices has permitted the Constitution itself to be used by the Federal Government as a weapon against the People and the States.

As noted by former Judge Andrew Napolitano, the U.S. Supreme Court, in the period between 1937 and 1995, failed to overturn **any** federal legislation on constitutional grounds! Therefore, the Federal Government was totally unchecked for nearly 60 years, given carte blanche to despoil the People and usurp the constitutional supremacy of the States.

To paraphrase the late President Ronald Reagan:

Are we better off and happier as a people than we were just a few short generations ago?

Is this Country projecting a shining example of liberty and happiness to the rest of the World? Is this government effectively protecting our liberties and thus enabling happiness?

Asking "*Why not?*" is simply a rhetorical question. Asking "*What can I do to change this?*" is its own answer.

This book is just one starting point for the **Restore The Republic!** movement. It is a project that will keep the American Remnant busy for a generation or more. Speaking for myself, I will likely be involved in it to the end of my days.

I owe no less to my ancestors, than I do to my descendants. All of us are indebted to those Americans who came before us. Just as they strove and struggled to leave a better place behind them for posterity, we must recognize that it is our natural and bound duty to do the same, in the remaining time that we are alive. Furthermore, we owe it to ourselves.

If you are unable to understand the value and worth in so believing, and acting on that belief, you are betraying yourself, your family and your fellow citizens. You are betraying the greatest hope, in all of human history, of enjoying all the blessings of life and liberty in a special place on Earth, where happiness is the norm, rather than the exception. Freedom is never free from its enemies and adversaries who must be resisted at all times.

Many have confused the very different meanings of the words pleasure and happiness. The former is fleeting and passing. The latter persists, positively influencing all aspects of an individual's life in both their personal conduct and their interactions with others.

The following quote is one of the best definitions of happiness that I have encountered. All those in the American Remnant, who join in the fight to restore the Republic, should be encouraged by these words of John Stuart Mill:

Those only are happy who have their minds fixed on some object other than their own happiness; on the happiness of others, on the improvement of mankind, even some art or pursuit, followed not as a means, but as itself an ideal end. Aiming thus at something else, they find happiness by the way.

Always keep in mind that accomplishing a *"more perfect Union"* was not, is not, and will not be the result of the efforts of a few 'great' men or women who were selected and anointed after the fact by 'captured' historians. The Union was, is and will always be the result of the accumulated work of millions of unsung and anonymous individuals. The Union is the manifestation of an idea. America embodies that idea. Some got it right. Some did it wrong.

The design of our governmental system was based on a close study of the mistakes and successes of History. We have mistakenly, intentionally by some and unconsciously by many, veered off the course that the Founders wisely placed us on.

Every generation must be taught, and continue learning, how to recognize the lessons of History as they apply to the present. Fortunately, we are not faced with creating the Constitution. We only have to restore its primacy in the conduct of our Country's affairs.

Raised as I was and observing what I have, makes my decision to involve myself in the restoration of the Republic both obvious and easy. Everyone who believes in the American Experiment of guaranteeing liberty, with the Constitution as the guide and reference, and who cares about our children and children's children's future, should make the same decision to add their unique talents and abilities to this great mission of restoring *"that which we hold dear."*

Just like robots, everyone stands, claps their hands over their hearts and recites the Pledge of Allegiance or sings the "National Anthem" at sports and other public events. Most do so reflexively and reverently. Yet those same people do little more in the way of exercising their civic duties than vote for candidates that they barely know, and for issues that they barely understand. Their engagement in the political process is almost non-existent beyond that point.

I am not attempting to force or shame anyone into joining this fight. I merely hope that what has been presented in this book is sufficiently persuasive that **you will voluntarily do your part as much for your own sake as for the 'common good.'**

Victor Hugo wrote:

> *All the forces in the world are not so powerful as an idea whose time has come.*

Will America remain a promise not kept? Without your invaluable help, the great vision of *"America the Beautiful"* may well fade into history as Mankind's last and best hope for freedom and happiness.

The Federal Government has decisively severed the bonds by which it was initially bound. The Constitution's chains have been broken by all three branches of government. The present warped and perverted result is like a fire that is out of control.

George Washington warned that an out of control government:

> *... is both a dangerous servant and a fearful master.*

If this present government remains unchecked, citizens will soon discover that the worst is yet to come. When the present system collapses as a consequence of abuses of power, and the subversion of the principles of natural law, that collapse itself could be used as a pretext by the unscrupulous and unprincipled, indeed the tyrannical and dictatorial, to impose an even more fearsome mastery over the People. Does any concerned citizen want something along the lines of a 'Soviet Union of Amerika?' Such a scenario is all too plausible.

The only rational response is for **enough of us** to take action by understanding and exercising our unalienable rights as sovereign citizens.

U.S. Representative and Presidential candidate Ron Paul listed ten principles for a free people in the Appendix of his book *"Liberty Defined."* They are reprinted below with his permission:

1. Rights belong to individuals, not groups; they derive from our nature and can be neither granted nor taken away by government.

2. All peaceful, voluntary economic and social associations are permitted; consent is the basis of the social and economic order.

3. Justly acquired property is privately owned by individuals and voluntary groups, and this ownership cannot be arbitrarily voided by governments.

4. Government may not redistribute private wealth or grant special privileges to any individual or group.

5. Individuals are responsible for their own actions; government cannot and should not protect us from ourselves.

6. Government may not claim the monopoly over a people's money and must never engage in official counterfeiting.

7. Aggressive wars, even when called preventative, and even when they pertain only to trade relations, are forbidden.

8. Jury nullification, that is, the right of jurors to judge the law as well as the facts, is a right of the people.

9. All forms of involuntary servitude are prohibited, including not only slavery but also conscription, forced association, and enforced welfare.

10. Government must obey the law that it expects people to obey and thereby must never use force to mold behavior, manipulate social outcomes, manage the economy or tell other countries how to behave.

The present government is ripe and ready to transition from the many subtle coercions that it practices today into outright tyranny. The Republic is currently being manipulated into becoming a social-democratic state, a curtain behind which oligarchs will control the Country's affairs for their own profit.

The rebuilding and restoration process begins in our own neighborhoods, towns and States. If the American Remnant does not repair and strengthen local government, there is no realistic hope of returning the Federal Government to its original role.

The time is now. Restoring our foundational principles begins with the first step taken by you and by me.

The longest journey starts with the first step.

Use this book as a starting point. We will all learn as we proceed. Freedom has indeed proved popular everywhere it has been tried. When initial successes are achieved, reinforcements will swell our numbers, creating yet more momentum, until we are an unstoppable political force and restore this *"land of the free."*

So, when you finish this book, will you put it down and return to the status quo? Will you complete the cycle of denial until your comfort paradigms collapse in front of you? Or will you refuse to anymore take the path of least resistance?

The great French playwright Moliere, nearly 400 years ago, made this very pertinent observation:

It is not only what we do, but also what we do not do, for which we are accountable.

Remember the task that William Wilberforce undertook? The British Slave Trade, in proportional terms, was as large and as powerful a political *"special interest group"* as is our present defense industry, the MIISSC or the Welfare and dependency system. With the help of a few friends, Wilberforce not only ended British slave trading in his own lifetime, he also ensured the eventual demise of any officially sanctioned slavery for all time.

Frederick Douglass, an emancipated slave, said in remembrance of Wilberforce:

Let no American, especially no colored American, withhold generous recognition of this stupendous achievement—a triumph of right over wrong, of good over evil, and a victory for the whole human race.

Today, the government warfare/welfare and poverty industries plantation has proportionately far more people enslaved to dependency, than were ever ensnared in the slave industry before the Civil War.

It is essentially the very same issue today. Are we free citizens, or are we slaves to our own government?

We actually have the advantage. We know what is really going on. We know the enemies and adversaries of freedom by their behavior and actions. We know the goals of the would-be controllers of our personal destinies. We know that we are fed lies every day in government statistics and the slanted manner in which the mass media reports them. We know their methods and their propaganda tools. We know what will happen if the Republic is not restored. We remember that history is filled with examples of the usurpation of the rights of the many by the few.

The old adage that "*the third time's the charm*," will prove out with the 3rd Republic. It will be the 3rd Republic that synthesizes and solidifies the best of the 1st Republic, while expunging the worst of the 2nd Republic. It will be the 3rd Republic that would have made the Founders, and all our own forefathers and foremothers, truly proud of us.

We know that right is on our side. Let us restore our constitutional guarantees, and our birthright as Americans, to enjoy **Peace, Freedom and Liberty—Forever!**

It is ours and it is there for the taking. Let us do it!

List of References

The following is a chapter by chapter summary of publications, books and various references throughout The Citizen's Last Stand. Only one source is given in each case. However, each usually has multiple sources and many publications can be obtained free or for very low cost online or in hardcopy.

Introduction

American Exceptionalism: Gordon Wood quote and definition, http://en.wikipedia.org/wiki/American_exceptionalism

Quote"Insanity is doing the same thing over and over again but expecting different results." Basic Text of Narcotics Anonymous (November, 1981), http://amonymifoundation.org/uploads/NA_Approval_Form_Scan.pdf

Chapter 2

"Puzzle Palace" by James Bamford (1982), Amazon:
http://www.amazon.com/Puzzle-Palace-National-Intelligence-Organization/dp/0140067485

"Body of Secrets," by James Bamford (2002), Amazon:
http://www.amazon.com/Body-Secrets-Ultra-Secret-National-Security/dp/0385499086/ref=sr_1_1?s=books&ie=UTF8&qid=135050011 8&sr=1-1&keywords=body+of+secrets

"The Shadow Factory" by James Bamford (2008), Amazon:
http://www.amazon.com/Shadow-Factory-NSA-Eavesdropping-America/dp/0307279391/ref=sr_1_1?s=books&ie=UTF8&qid=13505001 75&sr=1-1&keywords=the+shadow+factory

"War Is A Racket," by Smedley D. Butler (1935),
http://www.ratical.org/ratville/CAH/warisaracket.pdf

Slate Article: "Are Veterans More Suicidal Than Ever? Sept. 2011; IAVA Report: "Invisible Wounds," January, 2009:
http://iava.org/files/IAVA_invisible_wounds_0.pdf

Project for the New American Century (PNAC), (1997),
http://en.wikipedia.org/wiki/Project_for_the_New_American_Century

"The Pearl Harbor Myth: Rethinking the Unthinkable" by George Victor
(2008), Amazon:
http://www.amazon.com/Pearl-Harbor-Myth-Unthinkable-
Controversies/dp/1597971618

Chapter 3

"Petrodollar Warfare," by William Clark (2005), Amazon:
http://www.amazon.com/Petrodollar-Warfare-Iraq-Future-
Dollar/dp/0865715149

Chapter 4

"Imperial Hubris: Why the West is Losing the War on Terror," by
Michael Scheuer (2004), Amazon:
http://www.amazon.com/Imperial-Hubris-West-Losing-
Terror/dp/1574888498

"Imperial Life in the Emerald City," by Rajiv Chandrasekaran, (2007),
Amazon:
http://www.amazon.com/Imperial-Life-Emerald-City-
Hardcover/dp/B002MU0UME/

List of U.S. Military bases:
http://en.wikipedia.org/wiki/List_of_United_States_military_bases

"U.S. Defense Strategic Review 2012," an update to the 2010 QDR for
2012 can be found here: http://www.defense.gov/qdr/

"Act of Valor" (2012), Bandito Brothers Production company:
http://www.imdb.com/title/tt1591479/

"Update on the Latest Climate Change Science: The Natural Occurrence
of Extreme Weather," by Dr John R. Christy, University of Alabama:
http://scienceandpublicpolicy.org/images/stories/papers/reprint/update_
latest.pdf

"Animal Farm" by George Orwell, (1946), Amazon:
http://www.amazon.com/Animal-Farm-George-Orwell/dp/0451526341

"How Capitalism Saved America: The Untold Story of Our Country's History, from the Pilgrims to the Present," Thomas DiLorenzo (2004), Amazon:
http://www.amazon.com/How-Capitalism-Saved-America-Pilgrims/dp/0761525262

"Meltdown: A Free-market Look at Why the Stock Market Collapsed, the Economy tanked, and the government Bailouts Will Make Things Worse, " Dr. Thomas Woods (2009), Amazon:
http://www.amazon.com/Meltdown-Free-Market-Collapsed-Government-Bailouts/dp/1596985879

"Great Myths of the Great Depression," by Lawrence Reed, (1998, updated 2010),
http://econfaculty.gmu.edu/wew/articles/09/GreatMythsOfTheGreatDepression.pdf

"America's Great Depression," by Murray Rothbard, (1963), Amazon:
http://www.amazon.com/Americas-Great-Depression-Murray-Rothbard/dp/0945466056

"Economics in One Lesson" by Henry Hazlitt, (1946), Amazon:
http://www.amazon.com/Economics-One-Lesson-Shortest-Understand/dp/0517548232

"I, Pencil" by Leonard Reed, (1958), Amazon:
http://www.amazon.com/I-Pencil-ebook/dp/B003IWYFEO

"Money as Debt I & II," by Paul Grignon, (2009),
http://www.moneyasdebt.net/

High Frequency Trading (HFT) graphic file:
http://blogs.reuters.com/felix-salmon/2012/08/06/chart-of-the-day-hft-edition

"An Inquiry into the Nature and Causes of The Wealth of Nations," by Adam Smith, (1776), http://www.amazon.com/Inquiry-Nature-Causes-Wealth-Nations/dp/0199535922

Chapter 8

"Obedience to Authority: An Experimental View," Milgram, S. (1974). http://www.amazon.com/Obedience-Authority-Experimental-Perennial-Classics/dp/006176521X

"Social Forces in Obedience and Rebellion.Social Psychology: The Second Edition," Brown, R. (1986), Googlebooks: http://books.google.com/books/about/Social_Psychology_2nd_Edition.html?id=x-u5Mp2sJssC

"A Sound of Thunder." by Ray Bradbury, (1952), Amazon: http://www.amazon.com/A-Sound-Thunder-Other-Stories/dp/0060785691

Chapter 9

"Propaganda," (1928), by Edward Bernays, Amazon: http://www.amazon.com/Propaganda-Edward-Bernays/dp/0970312598

"Understanding Media: The Extensions of Man," by H. Marshall McLuhan (1962), Amazon: http://www.amazon.com/Understanding-Media-The-Extensions-Man/dp/0262631598

Chapter 11

"Confessions of an Economic Hit Man," by John Perkins (2004), Amazon: http://www.amazon.com/Confessions-Economic-Hit-John-Perkins/dp/0452287081

Chapter 12

"Citizen's United vs Federal Election Commission," Supreme Court of the United States, (2010) http://en.wikipedia.org/wiki/Citizens_United_v._Federal_Election_Commission

"The 5000 Year Leap: A Miracle that Changed the World," by W. Cleon Skousen (1981), Amazon: http://www.amazon.com/5000-Year-Leap-Original-Authorized/dp/0880801484

Chapter 13

"Law, Legislation and Liberty," by Friedrich Hayek (1973), Amazon: http://www.amazon.com/Law-Legislation-Liberty-Volume-Rules/dp/0226320863

Chapter 14

"The Real Lincoln: A New Look at Abraham Lincoln, His Agenda, and an Unnecessary War," by Thomas DiLorenzo (2002), Amazon: http://www.amazon.com/The-Real-Lincoln-Abraham-Unnecessary/dp/0761536418

"Lincoln Unmasked: What You're Not Supposed to Know About Dishonest Abe," by Thomas DiLorenzo (2007), Amazon: http://www.amazon.com/Lincoln-Unmasked-Youre-Supposed-Dishonest/dp/0307338428

Chapter 15

"Three Felonies a Day," by Harry A. Silverglate (2009), Amazon: http://www.amazon.com/Three-Felonies-Day-Target-Innocent/dp/1594035229

"Address at Rice University on the Nation's Space Effort," by John F. Kennedy (September, 1962), JFK Library: http://www.jfklibrary.org/Research/Ready-Reference/JFK-Speeches/Address-at-Rice-University-on-the-Nations-Space-Effort-September-12-1962.aspx

"Fukushima disaster could have been avoided, nuclear plant operator admits,"by Justin McCurry UK Guardian (July, 2012): http://www.guardian.co.uk/environment/2012/oct/15/fukushima-disaster-avoided-nuclear-plant?newsfeed=true

Chapter 16

"A Night To Remember." by Walter Lord (1955), Amazon: http://www.amazon.com/Night-Remember-Walter-Lord/dp/0805077642

Chapter 17

Website links:

Sheriff Mack.com, http://www.sheriffmack.com/
Oathkeepers, http://oathkeepers.org/oath/

"A Treatise on the Law of Sheriffs, Coroners and Constables with Forms," by Walter H. Anderson, (1942, reprinted and published 1984 by James Von Schmidt): Online: http://www.bcsbrigade.org/anderson-on-sheriffs.html

"Unraveling Federal Jurisdiction within a State" by Sheriff Gil Gilbertson of Josephine County, Oregon. Online:
http://www.defendruralamerica.com

"Proposed Rule Changes by the U.S. Forest Service Law Enforcement," Western States Sheriff's Association, available in .pdf format at: http://www.defendruralamerica.com/files/20110921WSSA.pdf

Chapter 18

"Nullification: How to Resist Federal Tyranny in the 21st Century," by Dr. Thomas Woods (2010), Amazon:
http://www.amazon.com/Nullification-Resist-Federal-Tyranny-Century/dp/B0057D8U2U

"Nullification: A Constitutional History," by Dr. W. Kirk Wood (2009), Amazon: http://www.amazon.com/Nullification-Constitutional-History-1776-1833-Constitution/dp/0761840117

Wickard v. Filburn (1942), Wikipedia:
http://en.wikipedia.org/wiki/Wickard_v._Filburn

Cornell Law references:
http://www.law.cornell.edu/supct/html/historics/USSC_CR_0317_0111_ZS.html

"The Constitution Made Easy," by Michael Holler (2009), Amazon:
http://www.amazon.com/Constitution-Made-Easy-Partiers-
Guide/dp/1402798326

Chapter 19

Colorado Senate Bill, SB12-137, Colorado Legislative Website:
http://www.leg.state.co.us/clics/clics2012a/csl.nsf/fsbillcont3/4EDF3AF7
50C8884D8725798800594C82?open&file=137_01.pdf

Colorado House Bill, HB09-1206,Colorado Legislative Website:
http://www.leg.state.co.us/clics/clics2009a/csl.nsf/fsbillcont3/107A082F6
E9A3E098725753E005BDC18?open&file=1206_01.pdf

Colorado House Bill, HB10-1155,Colorado Legislative Website:
http://www.leg.state.co.us/clics/clics2010a/csl.nsf/fsbillcont3/51B721949
D1B4E01872576A8002A2A82?open&file=1155_01.pdf

Chapter 21

U.S. Government Spending link:
http://www.usgovernmentspending.com/us_20th_century_chart.html

"How Many Galaxies in the Universe?" Online at Universe Today:
http://www.universetoday.com/30305/how-many-galaxies-in-the-
universe

"The Remnant" The Bible-King James version, Book of Isaiah,
Chapters11;11-12, Bible Gateway Online:
http://www.biblegateway.com/passage/?search=Isaiah+11%3A11-
12&version=KJV

Chapter 22

"Liberty Defined: 50 Essential Issues That Affect Our Freedom," by
Dr.Ron Paul (2012), Amazon:
http://www.amazon.com/Liberty-Defined-Essential-Issues-
Freedom/dp/1455501441

About the Author

Jeff and his wife, Colette, now reside in Fruitland, Idaho, and enjoy growing all kinds of things to eat in their two gardens. Along with the writing and speaking opportunities, Jeff regularly keeps in touch with his local, state and federal elected officials. He is currently working to move various aspects of the outline Plan in "A Citizen's Last Stand" forward at the local and state level.

His current professional/technical interest includes finding ways to continue the research and development of Model Driven Architectures (MDA), a software architecture that facilitates and automates the process of business model shakeout and application software development. He is also interested in advancing the global distributed-incorporation model of business formation.

In his spare time he appreciates any fishing opportunities that come along, the back-country and travel whenever possible. His next goal before he dies is to land a healthy Taimen fish specimen of more than 40 inches somewhere in Upper (or is it, "Outer?") Mongolia or the Kamchatka peninsula. Whenever possible he seeks out places to prospect for gold along the wild rivers of Idaho.

Author's Note

We are just at the emergence and rise of the 3rd Republic. It is the Author's purpose with The Citizen's Last Stand (TCLS) to facilitate and accelerate the growth of the 3rd Republic movement in concert with, and as part of, the 5-year old TEA Party, Freedom and Liberty Movement. Secondarily, to reset the Conservative movement itself into its historic principled framework and get it as far away as possible from the hands of NPD-disordered NeoCons who now attempt to control it. The first goal is for those of the Remnant joining-in to spread such publications, as this one, far and wide by helping them to go viral across the Internet, your neighborhood, community, cities and state. Both the ebook and the hardcopy have been reasonably priced in order to be affordable by almost everyone. As book sales proceed it is our goal to continue to lower the price as certain thresholds are attained to insure that they are.

It is not our intent to get rich but to grow the movement. You can help by encouraging as many others as possible to read and understand not just this book but all the other references used and pointed out herein. Monies raised will be plowed back into furthering and expanding this effort with the issuance of subsequent books, blogs, reference material, seminars and presentations anywhere and everywhere they would assist The People in advancing the freedom and liberty movement across North America.

The Author wishes to thank in advance all those that accept this task and move the ball forward. Those that wish to contact the Author directly, to share thoughts and ideas, please email him at jwright@timewarp.com. Look for http://thecitizenslaststand.com on the web, coming soon.

Made in the USA
Middletown, DE
25 September 2018